C. S. LEWIS

Writer, Dreamer, and Mentor

C. S. LEWIS

Writer, Dreamer, and Mentor

Lionel Adey

WILLIAM B. EERDMANS PUBLISHING COMPANY
GRAND RAPIDS, MICHIGAN / CAMBRIDGE, U.K.

© 1998 Wm. B. Eerdmans Publishing Co.
255 Jefferson Ave. S.E., Grand Rapids, Michigan 49503 /
P.O. Box 163, Cambridge CB3 9PU U.K.

Printed in the United States of America

03 02 01 00 99 98   7 6 5 4 3 2 1

Library of Congress Cataloging-in-Publication Data

Adey, Lionel
C. S. Lewis, writer, dreamer, and mentor / Lionel Adey
p.   cm.
Includes bibliographical references and index.
ISBN 0-8028-4203-8 (pbk.: alk. paper)
1. Lewis, C. S. (Clive Staples), 1898-1963.
2. Lewis, C. S. (Clive Staples), 1898-1963 — Books and reading.
3. Lewis, C. S. (Clive Staples), 1898-1963 — Psychology.
4. Authors, English — 20th century — Biography.
5. Mothers — Death — Psychological aspects.
6. Bereavement — Psychological aspects.
7. Authorship — Psychological aspects.
8. Loss (Psychology).
9. Mothers and sons.
I. Title.
PR6023.E926Z55 1998
823'.912 — dc21   97-46080
                                            CIP

The author and publisher gratefully acknowledge permission to include materials granted by
the following:

Extracts from unpublished material by C. S. Lewis copyright © C. S. Lewis Pte. Ltd. 1998,
and from *Rehabilitations and Other Essays* copyright © C. S. Lewis Pte. Ltd. 1939, *Selected
Literary Essays* copyright © C. S. Lewis Pte. Ltd. 1979, and *Boxen* copyright © C. S. Lewis Pte.
Ltd. 1985, reproduced by permission of Curtis Brown Ltd., London.

To Muriel

Contents

Preface

THOUGH PUBLISHED in the centenary year of Lewis's birth, this study of Lewis as writer has been long in the making. As far back as 1971, I noticed in his fifty-year correspondence with his oldest friend those fantasizing and moralizing or argumentative tendencies I dubbed "the Dreamer" and "the Mentor." Being for many years occupied with a monograph on his unpublished controversy with Owen Barfield and with works on other subjects, I could not pursue this theme until 1985-86, when a scholarship from the Clyde Kilby Foundation and a grant from the Social Sciences and Humanities Research Council of Canada enabled me to examine correspondence and other materials in the Wade Collection at Wheaton College, Illinois, in the Bodleian Library, Oxford, in the British Library, London, and in Cambridge University Library. Seeing other books through the press precluded starting on this one until 1987. By then I had decided to describe Lewis's early development and then devote a chapter to each kind of writing he attempted. These are arranged not chronologically but according to genre: literary history, practical and theoretical criticism, novels for adults and for children, poetry, apologetics, essays or addresses, and letters. Self-evidently, the "Dreamer" and "Mentor" aspects of his personality will be more evident in the introductory and later chapters than in those on his literary scholarship and criticism.

Inevitably, a critical survey of Lewis's work in different literary kinds is more of a description than a coherent argument. When considering his literary scholarship, especially on *Paradise Lost* and *The Faerie Queene,* it seemed appropriate to provide evidence of the continued importance and current standing of his work among Miltonists and Spenserians. This did not seem to be necessary with his fiction, poetry, apologetics, essays, and letters. Though some of my contentions, notably the lifelong effects of his mother's early death, have been anticipated in recently published biographical or critical works, I hope that readers can still find fresh insights here and be stimulated to reread this great literary scholar and master of English prose, and to examine with him some current assumptions about life and literature.

I cannot overstate my indebtedness to Lyle Dorsett, Marjorie Meade, Pat Hargis, Ruth Cording, and other librarians at Wheaton College; to staff at the British Library and the Bodleian, Cambridge University, and Leeds Public libraries; to my research assistants Kirsty Barclay-Fels, Debbie Bohay, and David Peterson; and to my colleague Diane Edwards, who read the manuscript. To Dr. Edwards I owe almost every comparison involving Charles Williams and many other valuable suggestions. Henry Summerfield and Burton Kurth offered other comments in countless lunch-table conversations, and Patrick Grant, Evelyn Cobley, and Terry Sherwood advised on matters within their fields. After more than once losing some or all of the text in my computer, I am indebted to Dave Shook, of Odyssey Computers, Victoria, and to David Mackenzie for its restoration, to Mr. Shook's colleague Che James and especially to Diana Rutherford of the English department staff for corrections and printout, and to computer staff at the University of Victoria for help in other crises. I must thank Curtis Brown, agents for the trustees of the Lewis estate, for permission to quote from Lewis's letters and texts. I am grateful also to the late Sir Isaiah Berlin for advice and permission to quote from an article of his, and to Kathryn Lindskoog for supplying journals at short notice. I have to thank Jennifer Hoffman, assistant managing editor at Eerdmans, without whose patient and skillful editing this book would have been a great deal less readable and reliable. Finally, I must thank Walter Hooper for advice and for devoted editorial work without which no informed comment on Lewis would be possible.

CHAPTER 1

Forming of the Dreamer and Mentor

THE QUESTION "Why another book on C. S. Lewis?" deserves a straight answer. We have biographies, explications galore of his apologetics and fantasies, even two excellent accounts of his literary achievement, but to my knowledge no book on Lewis as what from childhood he set out to be, a maker and reader of books.[1] Behind a compulsive writer usually sits a compulsive reader, not infrequently in a home riven by discord or bereavement. So it was with Lewis. He belongs to a line of authors from Wordsworth to Somerset Maugham who in childhood suffered the wound of losing one or both parents.[2] As Lewis records in his spiritual autobiography *Surprised by Joy*, when he was only

1. Biographies of Lewis include Green and Hooper, *C. S. Lewis: A Biography;* George Sayer, *Jack: C. S. Lewis and His Times;* A. N. Wilson, *C. S. Lewis: A Biography;* Paul Holmer, *C. S. Lewis: The Shape of His Faith and Thought;* and John Beversluis, *C. S. Lewis and the Search for Rational Religion.* Explications of Lewis's writings include Paul Ford, *A Companion to Narnia;* Hooper, *Past Watchful Dragons;* Richard Purtill, *Lord of the Elves and Eldils: Fantasy and Philosophy in C. S. Lewis and J. R. R. Tolkien;* Donald E. Glover, *C. S. Lewis: The Art of Enchantment;* Peter Schakel, ed., *The Longing for a Form: Essays on the Fiction of C. S. Lewis;* and Schakel, *Reason and Imagination in "Till We Have Faces."* The two accounts of Lewis's literary achievements are Chad Walsh, *The Literary Legacy of C. S. Lewis;* and C. N. Manlove, *C. S. Lewis: His Literary Achievement.*

2. Edmund Wilson, *The Wound and the Bow: Seven Studies in Literature,* 6-8, 107-11, 275ff.

nine he and his elder brother Warren lost their mother and in a sense their father, whose paroxysms of grief and rage embarrassed and alienated boys unused to seeing a Victorian *pater familias* lose his grip.[3]

Lewis wrote his juvenilia in tandem with Warren ("Warnie") and left very full records of his reading both in the fifty-year correspondence with his boyhood friend Arthur Greeves[4] and in what remains of the family library, now in the Marion E. Wade Collection at Wheaton College, Wheaton, Illinois. In these can be seen the emergence of an almost dual personality, the one a romantic, preoccupied with visionary moments when he both sees and longs for a beauty that is remote and austere, the other a rationalist, who exercises power and practices un-armed combat by means of counsel, instruction, the probing of assumptions, or destructive counterargument. The Dreamer, emanating from longing for his lost mother, finds expression in his fantasies and early poems. The Mentor, originating in unwilling identification with his father, a politically minded lawyer, impelled him to tutor and advise students and counsel the many who sought his advice in consequence of his religious broadcasts and apologetics.

The Bookish Dreamer

Lewis played the game of authorship as seriously as most boys played football, calling his filled exercise books "volumes" and marking their title pages "Leeborough Press" after the family home Little Lea. He never tried to interest a publisher either in those stories recently published as *Boxen* or in those still unpublished. Like most juvenilia, they appeal mainly to readers interested in their author's mature writing, so it seems legitimate to practice what Lewis condemned as the "personal heresy" of biographical interpretation by using them as guides to his mind, heart, and future interests. Though too often dismissed, the juvenilia can be most revealing.

3. Lewis, *Surprised by Joy,* 21.
4. Lewis, *Boxen;* Hooper, ed., *They Stand Together: The Letters of C. S. Lewis to Arthur Greeves (1914-63);* W. H. Lewis, comp., "The Lewis Family Papers," V, 180-83; VIII, 258-59.

"Jack," as he chose to be called, and Warnie dreamed of continents and islands: Jack of Animal Land, Boxen, and Piscia; Warnie of India. They remained partners for most of their lives: Jack as poet, allegorist, literary historian, critic, and fantasist; Warnie as his secretary and fellow Inkling, historian of seventeenth-century France, and compiler of a biography of his brother and of the Lewis family records back to 1850.[5] The brothers complemented each other in that Jack mentioned some member of the Inklings in almost every book but his family only in his autobiography, while Warnie was the family chronicler.[6]

Jack's so far unpublished "Life of Lord John Big of Bigham" purports to cover the period from 1856 to 1909, the year in which Lord Big dies and his former pupils, the twin kings of Animal Land, ascend the throne. The significance of that year in Jack's own life is clear, for it was in 1909 that Mrs. Flora Lewis, mother of Warnie and Jack, died of cancer after much suffering. Her letters, collected in the Lewis Family Papers, confirm Jack's account of her cheerfulness and warmth. One source of his intelligence, though not of his ineptitude in mathematics, can be inferred from her having taken first-class honors in that subject at Queen's University, Belfast, and tutored her sons in French and Latin. The trauma so movingly described in *Surprised by*

5. W. H. Lewis, "C. S. Lewis: A Biography," and "The Lewis Family Papers." As most readers know, at the meetings of that informal literary club known as the Inklings, held in Jack's rooms at Magdalen College or at two Oxford pubs, first the Lamb and Flag and later the Eagle and Child (nicknamed the "Bird and Baby"), not only the Lewis brothers but also J. R. R. Tolkien and Charles Williams read drafts of their works. Warnie's diaries, entitled *Brothers and Friends,* contain the best record we have of what the Inklings said to each other. Warnie, alas no Boswell, recorded topics rather than utterances.

In his letters, Tolkien deals mainly with how the group received his own stories; he also explains that the group's title was given by an undergraduate named Tangye-Lean to faculty-student meetings that soon petered out. Tolkien and Lewis applied the name to "an undetermined and unelected circle of friends who gathered about C.S.L." in his college rooms. Tolkien credits Lewis with a "passion for hearing things read aloud, a power of memory" and "facility in extempore criticism" far beyond those of his friends. See *Letters of J. R. R. Tolkien,* 162, 387-88.

6. "The Lewis Family Papers" has letters, etc., by family members from 1850. Entries by their father Albert and by "Jack" include speeches, stories, diaries, and poems. Diaries from 1922 to 1927 have now been published as *All My Road Before Me.*

Joy went on beyond her death, which took place on her husband's forty-fifth birthday, for within a month Jack had to leave his father's imposing new house, which looked over Belfast Lough toward the Holywood Hills, to join his brother at the unspeakable southern English preparatory school he called "Belsen," an educational slum mismanaged by a sadistic clergyman.[7]

Though his father had chosen the school, his mother had taken Warnie there in 1905, for Albert Lewis, apparently agoraphobic, refused to leave home even for family holidays.[8] In response to Jack's appeal for him to come and see Wynyard School for himself, an aunt came instead.[9] Ten years later, when Jack was wounded and homesick in a Cardiff military hospital, he again appealed in vain for a visit.[10] These failures of paternal duty worsened a relationship that was already tense in Jack's youth, as can be inferred from elements of the juvenilia. To Greeves after the war Lewis wrote of his father in terms that only the depth of his subsequent remorse can excuse. Among these was the sardonic name "Excellenz" or "Excellency," in the Boxen tales a polite salutation.[11] The trauma of losing, within a few months, his mother, his grandfather, and his home undoubtedly supplied some of the motivation for writing the "Life of Lord John Big."

Lewis insisted that the Boxen stories in no way anticipate the Chronicles of Narnia. They do, however, evince a number of lifelong interests. A minor instance is their author's early and sustained interest in *Hamlet.* In "Boxen, or Scenes from [Belfast] City Life," a scheming politician is named Polonius Green. Many years later Lewis drew extensive analogies from the play in his "Great War" controversies with Owen Barfield. In his first surviving notebook he called it Shakespeare's best play. He also chose the play as the subject of his British Academy

7. Wynyard School is described in "The Lewis Family Papers," II, 33-38. On the view from the house, see *Surprised by Joy,* 12.

8. *Brothers and Friends,* xi.

9. Their aunt's threat to have the boys withdrawn resulted in some improvement. W. H. Lewis, "Biography," 22.

10. W. H. Lewis, "Biography," 71.

11. "Excellency" in *Boxen,* 67, 126; "Excellenz" in Hooper, ed., *They Stand Together,* 259-60, 262 (Autumn 1919), 289 (June 1921); cf. Hooper's comments, 257-59.

lecture in 1942.[12] Perhaps the play especially appealed to him, as to many adolescents, because of his unresolved conflict with his father.

Lewis's ambivalent attitude toward women can also be seen in the Boxen tales. Like Somerset Maugham, who said that in eighty years he had never got over losing his mother,[13] Lewis was marked for life by his mother's death. Even as late as 1953 he told a correspondent that there was much of "mummy's little lost boy" about him.[14] In his Boxen stories he represented women either as prostitutes in theatrical guise or as predatory mothers bent on marrying off their daughters. Some years later, he complained to Greeves that he could never draw "female faces,"[15] and in 1922 he remarked to his father that the limited capacities of women students would make university teaching more difficult.[16] Such negative feelings toward women did not always prevail, however. In 1917 he enjoyed a friendship with a distant cousin from Ulster named Charlotte ("Cherry") Robbins, an army nurse then in training near Oxford, that seemed to be ripening into love when he was whisked away for pre-embarkation training. He told Greeves that she shared his interest in Norse and Wagnerian myths and was better looking than he had first thought. Forty years later, he looked forward to meeting her again when revisiting Ulster.[17]

His war service did nothing to promote normal, happy relations with young women and in fact, as he told Greeves, made him almost "monastic" about the sexual urges of young men.[18] Thus his incompletely expressed grief and vain longing for his mother combined with his separation from his cousin and his wartime experiences to inhibit him in youth from entering upon a lifelong partnership. Once back in Oxford he showed no interest in women of his own generation, but adopted his roommate "Paddy" Moore's mother as his own and for thirty years obeyed her every whim.

12. Quoted in *Boxen*, 9. The British Academy lecture was entitled "Hamlet: The Prince or the Poem?"

13. Richard A. Cordell, *Somerset Maugham: A Writer for All Seasons*, 18.

14. Letter to Mrs. Sandeman, 31 December 1953, in the Wade Collection.

15. *They Stand Together*, 79 (June 1915).

16. Letter of 26 July 1922, "The Lewis Family Papers," VII, 185.

17. *They Stand Together*, 192, 195 (1917), and 542 (1956).

18. *They Stand Together*, 214 (Liverpool military hospital, May 1918).

By hindsight, a couplet by Andrew Lang that Lewis misquoted to Greeves in 1917 to explain how spring made him lonely and dissatisfied — "The land where I shall never be,/The love that I shall never see" — reads like an epitaph for his mother.[19] His unacknowledged longing for her and uncomfortable dependence upon his father largely condition the subject matter of his imaginative writings, and also its treatment.

Those juvenilia that exemplify child-art rather than self-counseling were almost certainly written before his mother's illness. He grouped them under the heading "Animal Land." In one, "Manx against Manx," he ingeniously adapts the tailless cat in the story of Sir Peter Mouse, who sets a trap to avenge the severance of his own tail by a tailless mouse. The deadest of these early tales, a thinly disguised account of the fortification of the Pale in Dublin, was suggested by his father.[20] Needless to say, its vein is that of the Mentor.

The paternal influence that is merely visible in the court case that ends "Manx against Manx" hangs heavily over the stories Lewis wrote after his mother's death. What makes them odd reading is less the dressed-up animal characters than their incongruous mingling with human authority figures. In "The Sailor," probably completed in 1913, the hero Alexander Cottle is at once a cat and a newly trained officer of marines.[21] By describing him as wearing not a languorous expression proper to cats and to his compatriots but one of "intellectual briskness" tantamount to "ferocity" (*Boxen*, 153), Lewis holds up a mirror both to Ireland and to himself. On boarding his first ship, HMS *Greyhound*, Cottle meets his "mentor," a human gunnery officer whose "lazy, good-natured" countenance, described in much detail, seems modeled on that of the dandyish schoolmaster "Pogo," who regaled boys at Cherbourg School, Malvern, with gossip about actresses.[22] Cottle's fellow officer, the plump brown bear James Bar, is at once paymaster and victualler.

19. The lines should actually read: "The love whom I shall never meet,/The land where I shall never be." *They Stand Together*, 170-71 (February 1917).

20. In *Boxen* MSS at Wheaton.

21. My dating, based on the conjecture that the character Wilkins was modeled on "Pogo," a master at Cherbourg School, which Lewis attended from 1911 to 1913, is supported by the entry "1913" on the MS, by Warnie. But Hooper (*Boxen*, 18) adds that tales cannot be exactly dated.

22. Green and Hooper, *C. S. Lewis*, 30-31; Sayer, *Jack*, 31-32.

The first of the two "volumes" features a struggle between the idealistic Cottle, who seeks to improve the crew's gunnery by extra practices, and the vain but amiable Bar, whose name connotes both his rank and his chief pleasure. Having unwisely agreed to dine ashore with Bar, Cottle gets drunk with him, misses his ship, and has to make a dishonest excuse that the captain accepts to preserve harmony. Lewis concludes that Cottle and Bar have "become good friends if not good officers" by finding a "golden mean" between the one's "absurd idealism" and the other's "exploits" (*Boxen*, 194).

Lewis breaches his convention that developing characters are animal and mature authority figures human by introducing the First Lord of the Admiralty as a "tall, gaunt pig," along with a human field-marshal. The First Lord of the Admiralty, Oliver Vant, seems intended to resemble the author's father in his sad though "kind" face and in being a "pompous" yet "highly impractical philosopher, on whom the veriest simpleton could impose" (*Boxen*, 160). The resemblance is, naturally, more explicit in the frog Lord John Big, tutor to the sovereigns of Animal Land (Jack and Warnie).

After their mother's death, the boys had to spend whole evenings listening to political tirades when their father entertained fellow Ulster Unionists. The effects in the stories go beyond spymasters with German names, or campaigns by land and sea. Quasi-fact predominates over fantasy and form. Though only MacPhail, the ship's engineer, is borrowed directly from Kipling, there is an establishment of guardians of empire. More significant than the echoes of Albert Lewis's fear of bankruptcy and capacity for concealing anger beneath a mask of politeness is an authoritarian sadism to be found also in Kipling. In the unpublished play "Littera Scripta Manet," Bar is expertly thrashed by Lord Big for denouncing marriage as an obsolete custom akin to witch-burning or absolute monarchy. Violence is also substituted for argument in "The Sailor" when Cottle knocks Bar through a cabin door (*Boxen*, 179).

Both at home and at "Belsen" Lewis escaped actual physical violence, but he contended with it in sublimated forms until long after his religious conversion.[23] In *Perelandra* (1943), his hero Ransom fulfills an order to kill the Un-man, when unable to refute the latter's argu-

23. *Surprised by Joy*, 27.

ments, by smashing his skull. At times Lewis himself obeyed a compulsion to humiliate opponents by publicly demolishing their arguments, religious or secular. In 1933 he told Greeves that he feared becoming a "hardened bigot," losing friends by "shouting everyone down." Greeves, he continued, had "no idea . . . how much . . . time I spend just *hating* people whom I disagree with — tho' I know them only from their books — and inventing conversations in which I score off them."[24] He wrote this soon after publishing his *Pilgrim's Regress,* an allegorical refutation of modern heresies and errors that he later thought intolerant in tone. Guest speakers to the Socratic Club during the 1940s found themselves being scored off by Lewis, though more courteously than in the imaginary conversations.[25]

Even more revealing are the confidences to Greeves in 1917 about his own sadistic impulses. These range from defending the love of the whip by some Greek authors to an attempt while drunk to bribe fellow students into allowing him to whip them. In one daydream he used the lash upon a girl he admired.[26] There being no evidence that his fellow students shared this "passion," it surely had some more personal origin than resentment at the wartime sacrifice of young men, most probably a child's anger at being deserted by his mother for a better world.

This may explain why, save for an archbishop modeled on Laud, the Boxen narratives entirely avoid religion. Their child-author's dislike of church-going further suggests an unconscious rejection of his mother's deeply felt convictions. His more permanent dislike of Northern Irish puritanism was a result, as he explained while writing the *Pilgrim's Regress,* of its denial of pleasures to the undevout, its anti-intellectualism, its unpardonable intrusiveness, its indulgence of pleasures — gluttony or avarice — worse than those it forbade, and its failure to conduce to "peace, love, wisdom and humility." He regarded it, he told Greeves, as the form "the *memory* of Christianity takes" before dying out of a

---

24. *They Stand Together,* 466 (September 1933).

25. Hooper, "Oxford's Bonny Fighter"; A. L. Rowse says that Lewis, a "bullying figure," regarded "anything he disagreed with" as "heresy" (*The Poet Auden: A Personal Memoir,* 13).

26. *They Stand Together,* 171 (February 1917).

"commercial community," as indulgence in high church ritualism (in the church at Wynyard) was in a "fashionable community."[27]

Indications of early adolescence in the Boxen tales are Bar's man-about-town raffishness and the dandyism of Puddiphat the Owl, also caught from "Pogo." Lightly as he is let down in *Surprised by Joy,* "Pogo" probably encouraged Lewis to view women as either maternal angels or courtesans.[28] Despite some clichés taken from schoolboy fiction and the political conversations at home, the stories amply illustrate his adoption from childhood of bookish and mandarin attitudes, if not always mandarin language. In the four-act comedy "Littera Scripta Manet," Big rebukes another character for an unfortunate choice of imagery, a defect that boys not surrounded and conditioned by books are apt to overlook. Again, though most adolescents dislike self-righteousness in others, it takes a good ear to catch the flavor of priggery in Cottle's claim that his acquaintance with Bar cannot "justify my abusing the confidence which Lord Vant has reposed in me," or the mockery in Bar's threat that fellow officers "will feel justified in abusing your ears" (*Boxen,* 167). Considering how little the Lewis boys were permitted to see of downtown Belfast, a speech in "The Sailor" catches remarkably well the voice of the agitator:

> "Ah, have done with your talkin' an' pother! Come to something! Do you mean to strike or do yer nut?"
>
> "We do," cried a chorus of hoarse voices.
>
> "Aye, an' its right ye are! In the old days, the raily men did what work they liked, & none more. Were they any better than we?"
>
> "No!" came the chorus. . . .
>
> "Then strike! Let him know he cant do without us! Do we mind work? . . . No, but we mind tyranny!!" (*Boxen,* 192)

It is a pity that Lewis could not have used his ear for Irish speech in the proletarian dialogues of *That Hideous Strength* and *The Last Battle.*

The juxtaposition of animal with human figures that undermines the credibility of these tales betrays an abiding characteristic of Lewis: his unwillingness to let go of his past self. Just as he clung to the animal

27. *They Stand Together,* 432-33 (December 1931).
28. *Surprised by Joy,* 58-60.

characters so endearing to children while drawing adults in authority from the critical perspective of an adolescent, so when teaching at Oxford he often reread these tales and books by H. Rider Haggard and others that he had devoured in his boyhood. Far from being a weakness, incomplete metamorphosis was among his literary strengths, for it enabled him to treat the fairy story with critical seriousness and to compose tales that now rank among the classics of children's literature.

As an amusing fable on coming to terms with the world as it is, "The Sailor" reads best of the Boxen tales so far in print, but an even more interesting quest for self-knowledge is the unpublished "Life of Lord John Big." Lewis disguises the allusion to his father by making Big's birthdate 1856 instead of 1863. By dating his death as 1909, however, he hints that spiritually his father died with his mother. As Lewis points out himself in *Surprised by Joy*, Big uncannily resembles Winston Churchill in combining incomplete education with omnivorous reading, a multiplicity of talents, leadership by oratory, and a switch of party allegiance. While Big's lifelong friend Quickstepp seems like Warren in his practical and athletic superiority to Big and in his pleasure-loving temperament, Lord John himself shows aptitudes Lewis could observe in his father: powers of oratory and argument, wide reading, and interest in political and legal issues. More profoundly, he represents the boy-author's trying out of various roles and stances. Forbidden to explore dockland, but instructed to visit Parliament (i.e., Stormont) and art galleries, Lord John laments as did the Lewis brothers that so little of the city is open to him. Depressed by his ineptitude in games and unpopularity among boys humiliated by his intelligence and range of reading, the adolescent Lord John finds in "Mouse Valley" the inspiration to meditate and dream. Lord John's nervous collapse during university examinations, his fall into dissipation, and his consequent choice of a military career reflect the author's anxieties rather than his wishes. But the issue that, apart from Home Rule, preoccupies Lord John as grown-up politician and brings about his downfall reveals a profounder unease. Lord John campaigns for admission of the "Chess" to Parliament. As a nation without a homeland, they resemble the Jews, but as founders of educational institutions such as the "Royal Chessary" (probably Queen's University) they look like that elite of scholars, artists, and scientists for whom Ulster was, in Lewis's view, so unsympathetic an environment. Having discredited himself by changing sides on this issue, Lord John turns to his most successful role, that of tutor to the two crown princes, who ascend the thrones in 1909. A further explanation for this date may be that Lewis wished his father, rather than his mother, had died.

In this fictional autobiography Lewis tried out the roles of over-intense scholar in an unscholarly milieu, of man of action, politician, and tutor. Perceiving himself as too capable of seeing both sides to succeed in politics, and too dependent upon friendship to be happy as a scholarly recluse, Lewis settled for the role that in real life he was to play with distinction. Yet as a don he had to find or assemble a circle of friends and fellow scholars with whom to indulge his love of ale and good company. But the two roles he was to adopt in those portions of his vast output that lie outside the field of literary scholarship were the Dreamer, in his poems and prose fantasies, and the Mentor, in his tutorial work, religious apologetics, and essays. Not for nothing did *Everyman's Encyclopedia* list him in 1967 as "moralist and novelist."

The Compulsive Reader

Matthew Arnold's definition of the business of literature as "criticism of life" implies that readers compare their own lives with those of other places or times. In predicting that humankind would turn to poetry for the consolation and sustenance formerly sought from religion, Arnold implied a similarly vicarious experience of conflict, suffering, and fulfillment that would deepen and clarify the reader's own perceptions of life.[29] Lewis, who unlike Arnold lived to witness the idolizing of entertainers, sports figures, and political leaders, denounced Arnold's overvaluation of literature as vigorously as he denounced fascism and communism. Yet he unwittingly confirmed it, first by transmuting his early bereavement and conflicts into the Boxen fantasies, then by reexperiencing them in his favorite romances. His changing habits of reading mirrored the phases of his life.

Of romances by George MacDonald and William Morris first read in adolescence, Lewis, his biographers, and his critics have told us

29. "The Study of Poetry," in Arnold, *Essays in Criticism,* 2nd series, 2-3.

a great deal.[30] On romances by Edith Nesbit and H. Rider Haggard that he read in childhood and again in maturity they have said less. A look at these tales shows how faithfully they mirrored the childhood sorrows, anxieties, and wishes that continued to stir his imagination.

In *Surprised by Joy* Lewis singles out *The Story of the Amulet* as the Nesbit tale that "did most for me" (p. 17). This still-popular book, published when he was seven, features four children whose "poor, dear Mother" is convalescing in Malta after being "very ill" with her new baby. Their father is away reporting the Russo-Japanese war.[31] Besides their nurse, their only housemate of note is an Egyptologist whom they consult as surrogate father and eventually make famous by using the Amulet to reveal to him scenes from ancient civilizations. Once the two halves of the Amulet are joined, their parents return, and the Egyptologist becomes one with the apparition of a learned but amoral Egyptian priest.

Because Lewis read the tale before and after his mother's death, its motifs of restored health and family reunion changed from wishes to dreams. While away, the children's father was engaged in work that meant nothing to them and was powerless to help their mother. The Amulet takes them back in time, but never to the Far East. After living with yet also apart from a father temporarily unmanned with grief, Lewis never wholly enjoyed his companionship. Even during his father's terminal sickness, also from cancer, he lamented feeling pity but not love for him.[32] Though outwardly reconciled with his father, he became so in spirit only after purchasing The Kilns with his inheritance and returning to the Anglican faith.[33]

Nesbit's tale foreshadows the Chronicles of Narnia in its themes

30. On Morris, see *Surprised by Joy,* 132, 137, 145; see also Lewis, "William Morris," in Lewis, *Rehabilitations and Other Essays,* and Carnell, *Bright Shadow of Reality,* 47, 50, 78-79, 93, 95, 134, 161; Hooper and Green, *Biography,* 44-45, 107, 293; Walsh, *Literary Legacy,* 12. On MacDonald, see Lewis, ed., *George MacDonald: 365 Readings,* xxvi-xxxii; *Surprised by Joy,* 152, 154; Carnell, *Bright Shadow of Reality,* 48-49, 67-68, 95, 106n.; Hooper and Green, *Biography,* 45, 63, 105, 111, 144; Manlove, *Modern Fantasy,* 55-98 passim.

31. Nesbit, *The Story of the Amulet,* 12-13.

32. *They Stand Together,* 305 (July 1929).

33. On Lewis's conversion experience (28 September 1931), see Hooper and Green, *Biography,* 116, and other biographies; on his move to The Kilns (10 October 1930), see *Brothers and Friends,* 68.

of four children separated from their parents, magical journeys into other worlds, and guidance there by a nonhuman mentor — in *The Amulet* by the monkey-like Psammead, in *The Silver Chair* by the "Marsh-wiggle" Puddleglum. Coincidentally, in Nesbit's tale the baby whose birth led to the mother's separation from her children is nicknamed "the Lamb," a synonym for Christ.

The even deeper relevance of Haggard's mythopoeic novels *She* and *Ayesha* explains why Lewis read them so intently at Wynyard and in adult life found them compelling despite their inadequate diction. Their hero Leo Vincy (Latin for "lion" and "subduing" or "restraining"), who lost his mother in infancy and his father in boyhood, is brought up by the Cambridge don Holly, who transmits to Leo his interest in mythology and anthropology. While in Africa, they hear of a beautiful white woman, rumored to be immortal and all-powerful over living and dead, who rules from a mountain above the plain of Kor (Latin for "heart"). Guided blindfold through a cleft in the rock face, they sleep in a sepulchre, then pass though caves filled with corpses to find her wrapped in graveclothes. Ayesha, whose full name signifies "she who must be obeyed," sees Leo as a reincarnation of the beautiful Greek youth Kallikrates. Brooking no rival, she banishes and later strikes dead a native girl whom he loves, while he lies near death from a mysterious illness, then revives him with a magic cordial. Though she wins his love, she cannot mate with him. Indeed, she communicates better with Holly, who alone has seen her undraped and who has found her fluent in the classical tongues and Arabic. Once exposed to a flame symbolizing life, she withers with age.

In the sequel, *Ayesha,* the now middle-aged Leo is with the aged Holly in a Central Asian lamasery when they hear of a "Priestess of Hes" ("she") dwelling within a mountain. En route, they stay with a drunken Khan whose beautiful wife Atene falls in love with Leo. Though she guides them across a river to save them from her jealous husband, it is the veiled priestess who rescues them from the Valley of Dead Bones, sentences their foe to death, and visits Leo in a dream. Again pursuing him, while rejecting advances from Holly, she still cannot mate sexually with Leo, whose kisses restore her "wild, ethereal beauty."[34] After she has

34. Haggard, *Ayesha* (1905), 261. In *Ayesha* eighteen years have gone by in the lives of the characters since the events in *She* (1887).

rescued him from the assault of skeletons reanimated by Atene, he dies on her breast, leaving Holly to return and report the events.

Only in *Ayesha* is the priestess-queen called "Mother," yet her significance for Lewis as a recently bereaved boy cannot be missed. The multilingual queen ruling from her faraway mountain muffled in her shroud and surrounded by the dead surely recalled Lewis's mother, his first teacher of Latin and French. Even more closely, the tales predict the future course of his life: obedience to a surrogate mother, avoidance of sexual partnership,[35] and membership of all-male colleges that were originally staffed by celibate clergy equivalent to the white-robed priests through whom Hesea rules. Less obviously, it predicts not only its young reader's proficiency in Classics but his celibate life and austerely furnished college rooms. He was also, of course, a convivial don, but those elements in his life that were matters of compulsion rather than preference all have analogues in Haggard's mythopoeic novels. So has his most psychologically profound novel, *Till We Have Faces,* which he claimed to have been composing half his life:[36] its veiled queen Orual, to whom Holly's ugliness has been transferred, her tutor "the Fox," and her beautiful sister Psyche. While obvious inferences from names like Kor (Latin *cor*) and At[h]ene can be left to the reader, in his name (Latin *leo* and *vinci*) the hero appears to foreshadow Aslan in Narnia.

Lewis himself described the appeal of other stories read in childhood, by Beatrix Potter, Matthew Arnold *(Sohrab and Rustum),* H. G. Wells ("Country of the Blind," *First Men in the Moon*), and Jonathan Swift (*Gulliver's Travels* in full). As he admits having related the autumnal imagery of "Squirrel Nutkin" and the death of Balder (in Longfellow's *King Olaf*) to his mother's impending death,[37] we can likewise apply his unusual response to *Sohrab and Rustum:*

35. Despite Hooper's support (*All My Road Before Me,* 9) of A. N. Wilson's conjecture (*C. S. Lewis,* xvi, 58-59) of sexual relations between Lewis and Mrs. Moore, I remain skeptical, as it seems inconceivable that in the 1920s a woman with an adolescent daughter slept with a young man, yet all lived *en famille* and attended church together, without guilt.

36. In a letter of 21 February 1956 to his then publisher Jocelyn Gibb.

37. *Surprised by Joy,* 19-20.

> I hardly appreciated then, as I have since learned to do, the central tragedy; what enchanted me was the artist in Pekin . . . the cypress in the queen's garden, the backward glance at Rustum's youth . . . the hushed Chorasmian waste.

Arnold's poem prompted "a passionate, silent gazing at things a long way off."[38] Schoolboys commonly pass over psychological encounters in favor of martial ones. What is surprising is Lewis's fascination not by those, nor by the Asian names and setting, but by the poem's "distance and calm," "grave melancholy," and such details as the Chinese artist's "ivory forehead and pale hands." Lewis's account recalls the nostalgia and passionless gravity of James Joyce's Stephen Daedalus after rejecting a call to the priesthood. *Sohrab and Rustum* directed Lewis's imagination not forward to an adolescent boy's duel with his father but backward to his childhood paradise with his mother. Furthermore, it suggested to him the role in life of an artist or observer rather than participant. Again, female mythological figures that enchanted him in adolescence — the Maenads, Helen, Deirdre, Maeve, and Brynhild — represent womanhood distanced and idealized by Lewis the Dreamer.[39]

Like many teenagers Lewis reacted against authors his father urged upon him, notably Lord Macaulay, but not against the Victorian or any other period as such. He enjoyed the "moderns" of his boyhood, William Butler Yeats or Walter de la Mare, rejecting only the self-proclaimed modernists who came into prominence after his return from the war. Though Lewis inherited his father's powers as raconteur and his mother's collection of Victorian novels, from neither did he inherit his love of romance and fantasy. On buying an Everyman edition of the *Canterbury Tales* in 1916, he was enthralled by the *Knight's Tale,* and especially by the dying Arcite's cry, "Mercy, Emelye," but found the other tales coarse, garrulous, and lacking the "romantic charm" of *Sir Gawain and the Grene Knight* or the *Morte d'Arthur.* Upon finding the Everyman edition to be a modern and abridged version, he lost interest, telling Greeves that he could not bear to have "anything but

38. *Surprised by Joy,* 48.
39. *Surprised by Joy,* 97.

what a man actually wrote."[40] An edition of *Troilus and Criseyde* found in October did not disappoint him, but his markings in the 1928 edition from which he taught are purely editorial — notes on manuscripts, variant readings, or emendations — giving no indication either of youthful romanticism or of the scholar-detective's fascination so evident in his famous article "What Chaucer Really Did to *Il Filostrato.*"

The romantic and the scholarly reader, the Dreamer and the Mentor, combined in 1932, when Greeves lost patience with Froissart's *Chronicles.* Enjoyment of such a book, Lewis advised, required its treatment as a "hobby," to be "set about" by inscribing "a map" and "genealogical tree" in the end papers, running headlines above pages, and compiling a final index of underlined passages. He marvels that so many enjoy "developing photos or making scrap-books," yet so few tackle books as systematically. "Many an otherwise dull" but prescribed work "have I enjoyed in this way." Because "one is *making* something," it "acquires the charm of a toy" while retaining "that of a book."[41]

A scholarly reader can deceive himself into mistaking his absorption in a "game" for the spell a great work casts on its readers. Lewis's students sometimes found that a poem or romance did not fulfill the expectations aroused by his lectures.[42] To say this is not to convict him of the scholar's other fallacy, valuing a work according to the labor its interpretation has cost. In his library, the works that give the clearest evidence of his "game," Sidney's *Defence of Poesie* and Milton's *Areopagitica,* would not normally be considered "dull." One that might, Mill's *System of Logic,* he presumably marked while teaching philosophy at University College (1924-25). His headlines, footnotes, and underlinings in a 1922 reprint of "On Liberty" show a deeper interest in Mill's ethic and psychology than in his political theory.[43]

The sometimes heavy annotations to his Bohn edition of Milton's

40. *They Stand Together,* 109 (May 1916) and 140 (October 1916).

41. *They Stand Together,* 438.

42. In *C. S. Lewis at the Breakfast Table,* D. S. Brewer in "The Tutor: A Portrait" calls the *Allegory of Love* "remarkable and splendid, although misleading" (p. 47), a criticism developed in Peter Bayley's "From Master to Colleague" (esp. 81-82).

43. Sidney, *Defence of Poesie . . . ,* ed. Albert Feuillerat (1923); J. S. Mill, *A System of Logic,* 3rd ed.; Mill, *Political Economy;* Mill, *"Utilitarianism," "[On] Liberty,"* and *"Representative Government."*

prose, signed in January 1927, raise several questions. In the front papers of volume 1, Lewis sets out a program of reading for an essay or lecture, to include items from all three volumes.[44] In those of volume 2, he lists pages indicating such characteristics of Milton as humor, disrespect for authority, and traditional wisdom. These annotations, together with page headings to the essays on the English Reformation and church government and *Areopagitica,* suggest some work of major proportions. If he ever undertook one, why did he abandon it? Alternatively, did these annotations form part of his preparation to lecture on the Renaissance? Some heavily annotated essays seem too far from the mainstream of English literature for use in tutorials. Perhaps to get through them he needed to play his "game" more heartily than usual.

A further question arises because most pages of volume 1, including those containing the *Defence of the English People,* remain uncut, and in volume 2 Lewis gave up annotating *The Tenure of Kings and Magistrates.* This further underlines Lewis's lack of interest in politics. Was he in this instance a "literary" or an "unliterary" reader, as defined in his *Experiment in Criticism* (1961) — that is, did he read for enjoyment or for use, and would the answer "both" invalidate his distinction?[45] Admittedly he never read as the "unliterary" do, just to kill time, but did he at times read solely for use works that others would read out of curiosity?

The evidence indicates that he read in different ways at different times of his life. The copy of MacDonald's *Phantastes* that enthralled him in 1916 has no markings. His centenary edition of *Lilith* (1924) has a fair number, listed with quotations in the endpapers. These seem to represent his rereading so as to interpret the book for Greeves in 1933. Viewing *Lilith* as directed against the illusion of religionless

44. John Milton, *Prose Works,* ed. J. A. St. John, 3 vols. (London: Bohn, 1848). These items included the final prayer in *Of Reformation in England* (vol. I); the introduction to Book II of *Reason of Church Government, Areopagitica* (vol. II); autobiographical portions of *Apology for Smectymnus,* some chapters of *Doctrine and Discipline of Divorce,* and an address to Parliament in *Tetrachordon* (vol. III).

45. *An Experiment in Criticism,* esp. 5-7, where Lewis describes as "unliterary" those who read only acknowledged classics; he also discusses the professional use of texts by academics and reviewers. The distinction is not extended to the reading of polemics.

philanthropy, he finds there a first utterance of that world into which introspection leads the mind, a demand for spiritual death, in the sense of surrender to the divine will. Two underlinings bear out this theme, as does the marking of a passage on the half-converted soul symbolized as a runaway horse.[46] He marked far more intensively MacDonald's literary essays, especially remarks on imagination and form as expressions of the divine Creator.[47]

Some markings in J. M. Manly's (undated) edition of the *Canterbury Tales* bear out a comment to Greeves on what a "glory-hole" a commentary on an "old author" can be. In the introduction he marked up a genealogy of Chaucer and information on Chaucer's knowledge of Italian, on medieval currency, on pronunciation of Chaucer's final "e," and on the music of the spheres. In a margin he suggests Quintilian as an earlier source than St. Jerome for making "a virtue of necessity."

All this goes to show that in his first decade of teaching Lewis annotated his books in preparation for tutorials and lectures, or else to collect ideas on a topic before writing on it. One can imagine him in a crowded lecture room declaiming with gusto the splendid phrases he marked up in the final prayer of Milton's *Reformation in England*.

In his final decade, at Cambridge, when much in demand as a reviewer, he inscribed in endpapers lists of pages and key words referring to usable quotations and main points in the argument, as if equipping himself to review upon a single reading. By this time he was so beset by fan mail, his wife's illness, and his own, that he read new books essentially for professional purposes.[48]

---

46. George MacDonald, *Lilith,* 217. Cf. the horse episode (ch. 21), with explication in *They Stand Together,* 460-61.

47. MacDonald, "On Imagination," odd-numbered pp. 1-41.

48. Markings in R. S. Loomis, ed., *Arthurian Literature in the Middle Ages,* comprise a few sidelines and underlines, but Lewis's review of the book (1960) was written mainly from his own knowledge and opinions. The markings in B. G. Davies's new edition of Sir John Hawkins's *Life of Samuel Johnson,* reviewed in 1962, are more detailed and applicable to review. In neither book do the markings approach the detail of earlier annotations, such as those of Douglas Bush's *"Paradise Lost" in Our Time* (reviewed 1947) or Logan Pearsall Smith's *Milton and His Modern Critics* (reviewed 1941). The lightest markings are in J. B. Broadbent's book on Milton, *Some Graver Subject* (1960), received about the time of Joy's death and not reviewed by Lewis.

Most of Lewis's annotations will be considered in chapters on his literary history and criticism, but we should first ask how he viewed his chosen craft of authorship. Had he been a cricketer, he might be imagined as first an amateur batting for the Gentlemen, then a professional batting for the Players, as can be seen in the correspondence with his publishers at Geoffrey Bles Ltd. In correspondence with Geoffrey Bles himself, the gentleman amateur gives place to the hard-headed professional. After Bles's retirement, Jocelyn Gibb became the managing director of the company; during Gibb's time the publishing giant Collins took over the Bles company in order to secure rights to Lewis's books.[49] Lewis learned to anticipate reviewers, to plan titles and formats — as a captain places his field — to make the desired impression upon potential buyers, and to comment upon each indication of how a book is selling. True to the original meaning of "amateur," he never dabbled, but wrote as one in love with his craft. What changed him into a market-wise professional was a conviction that for years he had been consistently underpaid by Geoffrey Bles. As he ruefully admitted to Gibb, a publisher of very different principles, a fool and his copy were soon parted.[50]

Since Lewis gave away two-thirds of his royalties from religious books, withholding the rest for tax, he had a higher motive for regret than personal chagrin. In Gibb's goodwill gesture of sending a hundred-pound cheque by way of apology, it is difficult to disentangle generosity from a wish to dissuade Lewis from his announced intention of entrusting future manuscripts to a literary agency. In remitting half that sum to charity, Lewis showed both Christian generosity and awareness of a possible ploy.[51] That Lewis continued to correspond with Gibb until just before his own death, exchanging gifts, visits, and eventually first names, reveals both his amateurism and his professionalism.

As early as 1926, he set out his authorial credo in his diary after his long narrative poem *Dymer* had been rejected by Heinemann. Some years later, he copied out the entry to console Greeves for the rejection of a novel. Even while writing the *Allegory of Love,* which made him famous

49. Information from Mrs. Lesley Walmsley, editor, Fontana Books division.
50. Letter to Jocelyn Gibb, 15 June 1955.
51. The agency was Curtis Brown. Letters to Jocelyn Gibb, 20 and 22 February 1955.

throughout academe, Lewis claimed to have "unmistakably failed" in the craft of verse-making he had practiced since childhood. Urging his friend to accept the defeat, he distinguished between an author's interest in his material and his thirst for celebrity, the early quenching of which was a token of divine mercy. Analyzing his reasons for wishing *Dymer* to be published, he eliminated love of money or of fame, even love of the poem. In the end, he had simply wanted to prove to the public, and to himself, that he was a true poet. The urge to excel others, overlaid during composition, had surfaced when a friend praised the completed poem. His only remedy lay in consciously suppressing self-worship by focusing on external reality. As he told Greeves, the moment a person called to write stops thinking of himself as "officially" an author, the resulting upsurge of ideas and images will compel him to take up his pen.[52]

In the first of these two letters, a claim to have taken more pains over devotional poems for friends than over anything intended for publication illustrates his literary code. As Joe Christopher has shown, in nearly every book Lewis somewhere alludes to a fellow Inkling.[53] He wisely refrained from submitting *Surprised by Joy* until Owen Barfield, his solicitor and fellow Inkling, had checked the manuscript to obviate any libel suit. Many students found him an impersonal tutor, but as author he subscribed to a tradition going back to the sonnets of Shakespeare and Donne, of writing with and for his friends.

In his famous — or notorious — inaugural lecture at Cambridge, Lewis described himself as a "dinosaur," or specimen of "Old Western Man," in being a bookman and Christian. Those who thought this a pose cannot have known how true it was. He never listened to broadcasts (other than his own), picked up newspapers only to do crosswords, attended no theatres, and read no magazines, only books and, as required, academic journals. Through books, Lewis tapped the memory of Western civilization. His communication with the contemporary world comprised an enormous and unremitting correspondence and the conversation of his male friends, most of whom were authors and fellow believers.

---

52. *They Stand Together,* 378-81, 385-87 (18 and 28 August 1930). Diary entry for 6 March 1926, quoted in *They Stand Together,* 381-84.

53. Joe R. Christopher, *C. S. Lewis,* 42, 60, 103, etc.

His correspondence opened to him the lives and thoughts primarily of women and children who read his religious books and Narnia stories. Most belonged to the English and American middle classes — teachers, academics, children; others were impoverished widows or spinsters to whom he had checks sent. He gave most freely of his time when asked for advice on writing or on spiritual matters, for in his prime Lewis became as compulsive a Mentor as in his youth he had been a Dreamer.

His other link with contemporary life was the conversation of students and friends. Sir Isaiah Berlin agrees that his account of Edmund Wilson as an Edwardian author mainly fits Lewis. Wilson typifies a generation of "full-blooded, masculine men of letters, with sometimes coarse (and even to some degree philistine) but vital personalities." Describing to Berlin and David Cecil (an Inkling) a dinner attended by Kipling, Wells, Belloc, Chesterton, Shaw, and others, Desmond McCarthy recalled their conversation as not about the topics of Bloomsbury — literature, the arts, friendship, ethics, personal relations — but about "royalties, publishers, love affairs, absurd adventures, society scandals and anecdotes about famous persons, accompanied by gusts of laughter, puns, limericks . . . banter, jokes about money, women and foreigners and . . . a great deal of drink." McCarthy compared the ambience to "that of a male dining club of vigorous, amusing, sometimes rather vulgar friends . . . the best-known authors of the time . . . so much disliked and disapproved of by Bloomsbury."[54] Though true of Lewis in company, this description naturally excludes the Inklings' talk of myths and beliefs, or of university and country life. John Wain, however, pointed to a hidden side of Lewis, a self-protective shyness beneath his over-heartiness.[55]

Yet another side appears in letters to Gibb soon after the recurrence of Joy's cancer. Under that stress, Lewis fussed endlessly over title pages and cover designs. Upon returning from their holiday in Greece (1960), he showed his usual urbane humor when refusing permission for a

---

54. *New York Times Book Reviews,* 12 April 1987, p. 41, excerpted from Sir Isaiah Berlin, "Edmund Wilson at Oxford," *Yale Review* (1987): esp. 143-44. Sir Isaiah Berlin agreed on the "Edwardian-ness" of Lewis in a letter to me dated 2 August 1987.

55. John Wain, "A Great Clerke," in *C. S. Lewis at the Breakfast Table,* 70.

Japanese version of *Miracles* that he thought likely to represent him as a fundamentalist, and when acknowledging the wit of Kathleen Nott's hostile review of his *Four Loves*. Within three weeks, as Joy lay in a nursing home, he was hectoring Gibb about the wording and format of the title and contents pages to the new edition of *Screwtape*. The peremptory "I'm afraid," a term inherited from his father, rang out as he overrode Gibb's objection to a paragraph in the preface. In the next letter, he apologized and accepted Gibb's suggestions.[56]

Whether he fussed about typography in Bles's time may never be known, the correspondence being lost. He and Gibb bickered for months over the title of *Till We Have Faces,* the poor sale of which was Lewis's greatest and least deserved disappointment, a disappointment all the greater because of Joy's large share in the heroine's characterization. The poor sales may to some extent have resulted from Gibb's rejection of Lewis's original title, "Bareface," which he thought suggested a western. Lewis eventually came up with a title acceptable to Gibb, but protested that every friend who had read the text preferred the original title.[57]

It is difficult to tell how far Lewis valued good sales for his own sake or for Gibb's. When exclaiming that the merger with Collins would increase royalties, or pressing Gibb to nominate two poor sellers, *The Abolition of Man* and the *Great Divorce,* for a proposed Penguin series, he was clearly self-interested. At other times, as when refusing to permit a proposed BBC dramatization of *The Lion, the Witch and the Wardrobe,* he was concerned about quality. In his best year for royalties, 1958, he showed his usual courtesy in retailing to Gibb the comment by Curtis Brown that Collins had handsomely atoned for the parsimony of Bles. In that year he received £3,319. In 1954, his first full year with Collins,

56. Letter of 12 May 1960 on Nott; letters of 17 June and 13 July 1960 on *Screwtape.*

57. Letter of 16 February 1956, defending "Bareface" as literally true of Orual at the start of the book and spiritually true at the end, and requesting cover design with faint outline of old woman's face signifying female deity Ungit, alongside stylized image of Aphrodite; letter of 11 April 1956, rejecting two cover designs and contrasting stiffness proper for Aphrodite with primitive sexual vitality for Ungit; letter of 21 February 1956 on title and requesting more blood lust in design for Ungit; letters of 20 and 26 April 1956, on title, the latter suggesting final title as acceptable to readers.

he had received £1,927, and for the first half of 1959 he received £1,350. Inflation has since made these earnings appear more modest than they were; the 1958 total probably exceeded his professorial salary. Even so, these figures do not take into account the smaller but considerable sales of the works he published through other firms.[58]

Romantic Yet Rationalist

Lewis began early, and never quite ceased, to play the roles of the Dreamer and the Mentor. His romanticism and rationalism were most at odds in his early manhood, as he treated Greeves to alternate rhapsodies and homilies, or as he disputed with Barfield. To see him revel nostalgically in a William Morris romance and then denounce Christianity as a "decaying superstition"[59] is like discovering a woodland cottage illuminated by sunset without and fluorescence within. In his boyhood Lewis embraced romanticism in two senses: alienation from his everyday world and intuition of another via glimpses of *Sehnsucht,* the fulfillment tinged with longing that he called "Joy."[60] A small boy who has in a sense lost both parents cannot but feel unhappy when shipped off to school in another country, but Lewis's Irishness, bookishness, and abhorrence of heat made his alienation more protracted. In 1914, he complained to Greeves that England was a "hot, ugly country," and Malvern College boys "coarse, brainless" Anglo-Saxons.[61] He reveled in the severe winters of 1916-17 (when the thermometer in the Kirkpatricks' hall read 7 degrees Fahrenheit) and 1939-40, but rarely failed to complain during a heat wave.

Lewis described his first visionary experience, on seeing Arthur Rackham's illustration to an article about Wagner's *Siegfried* and *Gotterdammerung,* as a feeling of being engulfed by "Pure Northernness" and of seeing "huge clear spaces hanging above the Atlantic in the

58. Notably *Allegory of Love* and *English Literature in the Sixteenth Century,* for which Oxford University Press gives yearly sales in the hundreds, compared with many thousands for religious and fictional works.
59. *They Stand Together,* 136.
60. *Surprised by Joy,* 12, 20, 62ff.
61. *They Stand Together,* 47 (June? 1914).

endless twilight of Northern summer, remoteness, severity." This he instantly connected with his emotion on reading, soon after his mother's death, of the death of Balder in Longfellow's *King Olaf.* He interpreted the intuition as the return of a lost "Joy": "the distance of the Twilight of the Gods and the distance of my own past Joy, both unattainable, flowed together into a single, unendurable sense of desire and loss, which suddenly became one with the loss of the whole experience," as he found himself back in his "dusty schoolroom."[62] He became obsessed with recovering this trance, which vanished as soon as he became aware of it. He seems unconsciously to have used the Norse imagery to clothe his past desolation with its austere beauty.

Like most visionary states, "Joy" could not be compelled, but this epiphany conditioned his whole cultural life. It imparted a passion for Wagner that lasted into his middle age. His letters to Greeves up to 1918, when he was wounded in battle, show him to be no less a devotee of music than of literature. As late as 1935 the symphonies of Sibelius induced in him a vision of "birch forests and moss and salt-marshes and cranes and gulls."[63] Yet those letters record attendance at only one live performance of a Wagnerian opera,[64] and none at symphony concerts. Just as he knew Shakespeare's plays from his Arden edition, so he knew operas and symphonies from his brother's record collection. As he enjoyed drama and music in private, so he preferred the early Communion service at Headington Church to better attended services.

From his first reading of it in 1914, Morris's *Well at the World's End* cast a spell over Lewis the Dreamer that was renewed at each rereading. Just why can be inferred from his comments and, as we shall see, from the romance itself. His devotion was neither to a person nor to a style, for the same author's *Roots of the Mountains* disappointed him by its lack of a "supernatural" element, notwithstanding its "beautiful old English," which "means so much to me."[65] When after his

---

62. *Surprised by Joy,* 62.
63. *They Stand Together,* 477-78 (December 1935).
64. He attended the opera with Barfield. Letters to Barfield, 6 May 1937, and following.
65. *They Stand Together,* 72-73 (May 1915).

father's death he settled in his own home both literally and spiritually, by purchasing The Kilns and becoming a Christian, he found Morris the most "essentially pagan" of poets in his evocation of this world's beauty, of the yearnings it excites but fails to gratify, and his "haunting sense of time and change." Only in Morris's *Love Is Enough* did he find a "light of holiness," which emanates from the renunciation of royal power for Love, an allegorical figure, by the hero of the interior story and which is signaled by the choruses that open with the title words. Philip Henderson represents the majority view in calling *Love Is Enough* one of Morris's "most enervated" works.[66] Certainly in this dreamy dialogue-romance it is difficult to tell what is going on. In Lewis's religious reading of it, he flung a bridge across the chasm within himself between the romantic and the realist. Some comments on Morris to Barfield in 1937 have an even more Christian flavor.[67] Since Lewis rarely mentioned *News from Nowhere* or the *Dream of John Ball,* he might be faulted by politically oriented critics for bypassing the "real" Morris. The greater part of Morris's immense output, however, consists of narrative poems based on Norse myths, so the interest of the young Lewis in the mythic poems and romances should not surprise us.

Why the *Well at the World's End* should have ravished Lewis more than *Sigurd the Volsung* needs explaining in view of his appetite for Norse mythology. Beyond the charm of its pseudo-medieval prose lies the unstated yet compulsive appeal of its plot and motifs. Lewis especially commended to Greeves books 1 and 2. The hero Ralph's proving his worth in chivalric combats and rescues would naturally appeal to a boy, but what sets Ralph apart from comparable figures in Malory's *Morte d'Arthur* is his disobedience to his father in leaving home to seek first adventure and then the Well at the World's End. Aflame with love for the woman who has drunk its rejuvenating waters, Ralph slays her rival lover, the Sun Knight, only to find her

66. Henderson, *William Morris: His Life, Work and Friends,* 128. E. P. Thompson, in *William Morris: Romantic to Revolutionary,* condemns the poem's mystical idealism, and Jessie Kocmanova, in *The Poetic Maturing of William Morris,* finds it inconsistent with Morris's Marxist materialism.

67. *They Stand Together,* 365-66 (July 1930), and letter to Barfield, 2 September 1937 (*Letters of C. S. Lewis,* 159), both discussed in my "The Light of Holiness: Some Comments on Morris by C. S. Lewis."

mortally wounded by that tyrant. When after that "evil hour in the desert" he sees her in a dream, "fair and fresh coloured as before the sword had pierced her side," she arouses in him no wild hope or desire, but an assurance of having won her love that would abide throughout his "long" and "perilous" quest. The Well that so many seek but so few find lies beyond the vale of Utterness and the mountains known as "the Wall of the World."[68] To the aging Morris, devoid of religious hope, Ralph's drinking at the wellspring of renewal probably represented a wish fulfillment. To the young Lewis, it was a further installment of that dream of reunion with his mother latent for him in H. Rider Haggard's novels, but with this difference: the older woman seen in a dream spurred Ralph forward to independent achievement, so that he drank the waters with a ladylove of his own age. Lewis first read the *Well* as an avowed atheist like Morris, but he discovered the "light of holiness" in *Love Is Enough* as a convert in whom Christian hope had replaced the unattainable dream. Having completed an essay on Morris that he later acknowledged as unsuccessful, he almost ceased to mention him in his letters.[69]

To claim that the *Well*'s primary appeal for Lewis was psychological is in no way to disparage a tale not easily put down, which has an anti-industrial theme congenial to Lewis.

When he first encountered MacDonald's *Phantastes,* the realist in him had for eighteen months been nurtured by W. T. Kirkpatrick, a late-Victorian rationalist in the mould of T. H. Huxley or John Morley. This formless tale of Faerie so excited Lewis that he at once prescribed it for Greeves, who found it hard going and warmed to it only on reaching the baptism in the Fairy Bath (chap. 11) and inset tale of Cosmo (chap. 13). Why did so incoherent a tale so enthrall Lewis? Nearly forty years later, he ascribed its appeal to its "cool, morning innocence."[70] Looking for some more tangible reason, we find a hero Anodos (Greek for "pathless"), who, haunted by his Shadow, wanders

68. *Well at the World's End,* bk. 2; the slaying takes place in ch. 10; the dream occurs on pp. 219-20; the Vale is described in ch. 32.

69. The essay was simply titled "William Morris"; see the comment in "On Criticism," *Of Other Worlds,* 53.

70. *They Stand Together,* 92-93, 96 (March 1916); *Surprised by Joy,* 145-46; Lewis, ed., *George MacDonald,* xxxiii.

through the land of Faerie and dies in combat. Already addicted to the *Faerie Queene,* Lewis may have felt challenged by the tale's strangeness and difficulties: the Alder tree that loves not men but their love; Cosmo, who dies on declaring his passion; Cosmo's magic mirror; and the cottage doors that open upon Memory, Dismay, Discovery, and the Timeless (chap. 19). The doors offer a clue, for if we read Dismay as "grief" and add the motifs of the downward staircase (chap. 17) and disappearance into the earth of the woman Anodos met in the White Hall of Phantasy (chap. 15), the episodes could once again have represented Lewis's early bereavement. Yet the woman no longer returns to this life, and by consenting to die, the narrator himself passes into the timeless condition. The imagining of both this transition and worlds beyond the one we know was to become a major preoccupation in Lewis's fiction and apologetics.

According to C. N. Manlove, MacDonald's fantasies enjoin self-renunciation: to find itself, the soul must abandon its divisive self-consciousness and return to the "unconscious tide of the universe" — hence the main theme of *Lilith,* that the soul is "dead" until it consents to death. Manlove calls MacDonald "an involuntarist," teaching that "one goes to sleep, and God takes over"; this is taught explicitly in the last fantasy novel *Lilith,* but implicitly in the very formlessness of the first one, *Phantastes,* which exemplifies Novalis's idea of the *Märchen* as a "dream-picture without coherence."[71] Since irrationalism and a yearning for absorption into the cosmos are quite foreign to Lewis, the appeal of *Phantastes* remains to be explained. An overcompensation for misery will not serve, for he had never been happier than at Great Bookham. Nor will general interest in the afterlife, for he had no religion, and letters prior to his army service show him regrettably uninterested in the suffering occasioned by the war.

The whole sequence of episodes involving the White Lady (chs. 15-19) offers our best clue. Having materialized from a statue in the hall of Phantasy, she reproaches Anodos for touching her then disappears into the earth. In a sequence Lewis was to imitate in *Perelandra,* Anodos follows her down a natural staircase leading to a subterranean country "in which the sky was of rock, and instead of trees and flowers,

71. Quoted in Manlove, *Modern Fantasy,* 60-61, 65.

there were only fantastic rocks and stones" (chap. 16).[72] With these mineral images of death MacDonald juxtaposes the taunting of goblins, whom Anodos allegorizes as "Selfishness." Having drawn an explicit parallel between his descent and dying, Anodos defies the icy sea-wind and waves, proclaiming that "The life within me is yet enough to bear me up to the face of Death, and then I die unconquered" (125). In a clear simulation of death, he advances in darkness along a promontory, then plunges into the waves, only to find himself supported as by "loving arms" and touched by a rainbow-colored boat that takes him on a "summer sea" through "southern twilight" to an island. As he traverses the enchanted sea, "a beloved form" seems to lie beneath him, and arms seem to reach up for him. While sleeping, he dreams of "faces that had vanished long ago," of love that "had never died," and "smiling lips" that "knew nothing of the grave." At last he wakes to find his boat "motionless by the grassy shore of a little island" (126-27). In this episode, death is transformed into rebirth, wintry northern desolation into southern abundance; but Anodos has brought about the rebirth by rejecting his fear of death.

Within the cottage on the island, Anodos meets a woman tall and spare, with ancient, wrinkled face and skin "like old parchment" but eyes "absolutely young," who like Haggard's Ayesha combines youth with immeasurable age and signifies maternal rather than sexual love. A "wondrous sense of refuge and repose" comes over Anodos as she sings him a long ballad of a knight's journey through a churchyard with the refrain "All alone I lie. . . . All alone, up in the sky." Upon meeting the ghost of his lady, whose dead baby has been transformed into an angel, the knight causes her to vanish by clasping her in a sexual embrace. The ghost concludes her visitation with her opening refrain, "And life is never the same again" (130-34).

The fusion of death with rebirth continues as Anodos goes out through the door of Dismay to be reminded of his drowned brother and bedfellow, whose death had brought a "strange conviction" of déjà vu (137). Finally, the old woman reveals that she had gone through the "door of the Timeless" to retrieve Anodos, whom she directs from her

---

72. *Phantastes* (1981 ed.), 119; subsequent references are given parenthetically in the text. Cf. the journey in *Perelandra*, chs. 14-15.

"island" across an isthmus to the mainland (144). As with similar motifs in the tales of Nesbit and Haggard, this episode appealed to the congenital interest of Lewis the Dreamer in life beyond the grave.

Though Manlove objects that the concluding chapters impose a Christian meaning upon the phantasmagoria of its opening half,[73] the seventeen-year-old Lewis probably saw the White Lady episodes less in religious than in personal terms. In addition to separation by death from his mother and by distance from his father and brother (Warnie was then in France), the episode's frequent warnings against sexual embraces doubtless reinforced his reluctance to engage in courtship. While furnishing his imagination ("the Dreamer") with motifs later employed in *Perelandra* and in the reanimation scene of *The Lion, the Witch and the Wardrobe,* it reinforced the rational and admonitory side of his personality that I have dubbed "the Mentor." This involves emotional inhibition, a Johnsonian commonsense morality, a renunciation of egoism, narcissism, and self-will, and MacDonald's own precept that "all a man has to do, is to better what he can" (171). The direction in which the episode was taking Lewis becomes clearer if we compare the epigraph to chapter 19, "I bear, uninterrupted, the consciousness of the whole of Humanity within me" (127), with Lewis's own saying that as a convert he felt himself "on the high-road home with all humanity," able to "compare notes with an endless succession of former travellers."[74] The world that mattered to him consisted of Christian or classical texts from all ages and the "humanity" that consisted of living and departed Christians or proto-Christians such as Virgil or Plato.

Because Lewis regarded literary discourse as the central expression of human culture, the mockery of Anodos by the fairies — "'He has begun a story without a beginning, and it will never have any end. . . . Look at him!'" (24) — may have had a deeper meaning for him than for most readers. By consenting to die, Anodos rids himself of the Shadow, which Manlove sees as self-consciousness, but which theologically connotes an ego that lives for itself alone.[75] In so doing, the

73. Manlove, *Modern Fantasy,* 76-77, 90-91, 96-97.

74. *They Stand Together,* 333-34 (January 1930).

75. Manlove, *Modern Fantasy,* 77: "The Shadow is the evil conscious self, which seeks to have . . . and destroys in having."

"pathless one" turns his own life into a "story" with a meaning and shape.

The analogy between authorship and divine Creation figures largely in the "Great War" disputations with Owen Barfield, in which Lewis, not yet a Christian, condemns the doctrine of the Incarnation as the absurdity of God walking into his own play. The arguments began during Lewis's first year at Magdalen, when, as "Mentor" by request, he analyzed in detail Barfield's B.Litt. thesis. Between 1925 and 1927 they exchanged long letters, of which six by Lewis but only two by Barfield survive. In them Lewis mainly objects to Barfield's view of poetic imagination as a vehicle of truth. In a briefer series of letters composed between 1925 and 1929, Lewis objects to the system of ideas of Rudolf Steiner called "anthroposophy" that Barfield had adopted. By November 1928, Lewis completed a formal dissuasive modeled on the medieval disputation and entitled "Clivi Hamiltonis Summae Metaphysices contra Anthroposophos Barfieldus." By then Barfield had supplemented his thesis with an introduction and an extra chapter and published it as *Poetic Diction*. Lewis had contributed to the book a frontal quotation from Aristotle and the key word in Barfield's assertion that poetry effected a "*felt* change of consciousness in the reader."[76]

Early in 1929 Barfield responded to Lewis's "Summa," as they called the tractate; then by midsummer Lewis sent "Replies to Objections" and a "Note on the Law of Contradiction." By agreement, these documents were all paginated in sequence. A break in pagination and the use of "God" instead of "Spirit" suggest that Lewis composed his essay on morality, "De Bono et Malo," not long before September 1931, when he returned to the Christian faith. Barfield's response, a substantial but unfinished tractate called "De Toto et Parte," expounds an ethic of self-realization. After beginning an acerbic "Commentarium" on this, Lewis lost interest and declined to resume the "Great War," being preoccupied with his *Allegory of Love* and *Pilgrim's Regress*.

Although its documents can at present be sampled only in articles

76. Quotation and attribution respectively in letters from Lewis to Barfield (2 February 1927) and Barfield to me (2 June 1977). Both are now in the Wade Collection.

and a monograph,[77] the "Great War" controversy offers the best evidence of Lewis's early mind-set and adoption of principles that became the keystone of his literary theory and practice.

Barfield contended that, by inducing a "change of consciousness," poetic language caused readers to grow not only in the power of perceiving resemblances but also in knowledge and wisdom. By restoring a lost unity between the perceiver and the perceived, its metaphors enabled them to know *(connaître)* rather than merely know about *(savoir)* things in nature. Primal man, whose unity with nature was inferable from words such as the Greek *pneuma,* signifying wind without, breath within, and spirit above or beneath, experienced the world as no less alive than himself, hence his figurative or "poetic" language. Next, mythology, "the ghost of concrete meaning," peopled heaven and earth with spirits.[78] Hyperion warmed Ge, and Demeter sprang up, where we speak of sun, earth, and growing corn. As an anthroposophist, Barfield claimed that ancient man neither invented gods nor projected human feelings but expressed a life and meaning inherent in Nature. During recorded history the rational or "prosaic" principle divided meanings into physical and nonphysical and so detached human consciousness from its cosmic and natural sources. Old, undivided meanings lingered in the Ideas or Forms of Plato, but the categories of Aristotle and the Scholastics completed the sundering, until nominalism obliterated any linkage between thoughts and things.[79]

Early poems conveyed human perceptions (and things perceived)

77. See Amos Franceschelli, "The Teachings of Rudolf Steiner with Especial Reference to C. S. Lewis"; Barfield, "C. S. Lewis and Historicism"; L. Adey, "The Barfield-Lewis 'Great War' "; James G. Colbert, "The Common Ground of Lewis and Barfield"; Charles Wrong, "Christianity and Progress"; Adey, *C. S. Lewis's "Great War" with Owen Barfield;* Stephen Thorson, "Knowing and Being in C. S. Lewis's 'Great War' with Owen Barfield"; Adey, "A Response to Dr. Thorson," with Thorson's "Reply." See also Patrick Grant, "The Quality of Thinking: Owen Barfield as Literary Man and Anthroposophist," and Grant, *Six Modern Authors and Problems of Belief,* 121-32; R. J. Reilly, *Romantic Religion,* 13-98, 106-8, 118, 131, 140; and G. B. Tennyson, ed., *Owen Barfield on C. S. Lewis.*

78. Barfield, *Poetic Diction,* 92.

79. Abstracted from *Poetic Diction,* ch. 4, sections 4-5, and ch. 5, section 1.

by imitative sounds and rhythms. In time, these "given" meanings gave way to meanings "achieved" in poetic metaphors. Barfield illustrates from derivatives of the Latin verb *ruo* (e.g., "ruin") how given meanings flow beneath later achieved ones, then resurge as poets seek to freshen their diction by returning to "Nature." In our scientific age, poets try to arrest the drift of words toward unambiguous meanings and abstractions. Typically, poets first create by allowing ingested material to well up from the unconscious, then use the contrary power of appreciation to correct and reorder the potential poem. Calling poetry "the progressive incarnation of life in consciousness," Barfield claims that pleasure is not poetry's object but its test, for, after their initial change of consciousness concerning the subject matter, readers become aware of the poem not just as an artifact but as a process.[80]

At the request of his publishers, Barfield added another chapter to *Poetic Diction* in which he developed three ideas that had occurred since Lewis read the thesis. (Since Lewis's notes have been lost, it is impossible to say what part Lewis's comments may have played in the development of these ideas.) The first was a definition of poetic criticism as "midwifery," bringing the reader from awareness simply of the finished poem to imaginative participation in its creation.[81] This theme has been developed, without acknowledgment, by poststructuralist critics. The second idea is that by tracing words to their figurative origins we can "unthink" the distinction between poetry and science implicit in Croce's view of poetry as meaningless emotion. Third, and most important, is Barfield's distinction between man as creator and as knower. Man's poetic, or "creative," principle produces both art and fundamental advances in knowledge. His prosaic, or "rational," principle produces at best understanding, and at worst pedantry, yet makes individual consciousness possible. The conscious self must identify with life through imaginative — that is, creative or "poetic" — activity, or else philosophy must stagnate. For this reason, Barfield savagely attacked linguistic analysis in his preface to the second edition (1952).

In dedicating the book to "Clive Hamilton" (Lewis's pseudonym when publishing *Dymer*), Barfield quotes Blake's aphorism "Opposition

80. Barfield, *Poetic Diction*, 181.
81. Barfield, *Poetic Diction*, 132.

is true friendship." Lewis had certainly provided both, but he had far more in common with Barfield than with materialists, positivists, or New Critics. Lewis began his first letter to Barfield by agreeing that reason grasps relationships rather than things in themselves and that reason, sensory experience, and habits of thought provided a practical substitute for direct knowledge of reality. He did not agree that they could provide access to a "supersensible" or timeless reality, and he illustrated his objection with comic sketches showing human figures labeled "Reason" and "Experience" directing Barfield toward "Reality," and a tree-belt representing a land of chimeras approached by Steiner's "Occult Science," a system of willed meditation that claimed to train the mind to know the supersensible by perceiving its own thought processes.

Imagination, Lewis maintained, does not enable us to make true statements, though we can make none without it. It can at different times convince us of entirely opposite beliefs: that human beings count for little in the cosmos and that they were made in the image of its creator. A nominalist to his core, Lewis always doubted the meaning of "Truth" as distinct from "true statements."

Lewis the Mentor was equally skeptical about the anthroposophical belief in the unity of the perceiver with the object perceived, for he simply had to believe in a material world independent of his own mind. Imagination equips us to form mental pictures of things, but assertions about the phenomena themselves must be subject to logical and empirical verification. Beneath his joking threat to cut his throat should reality turn out to be purely subjective lay the same unease that impelled Dr. Johnson to refute Berkeleyan idealism by kicking a stone. In Barfield's view, the primal unity of humankind with nature gave way to a detachment from nature illustrated in the bifurcation of *pneuma* into the spiritual and corresponding but physical entities spirit and wind.

This brings us to Rudolf Steiner's system called "anthroposophy" and Lewis's reasons for trying to dissuade Barfield from it in the "Summa." Though raised a freethinker and given a technical education, Steiner (1861-1925) enjoyed mystical experiences in childhood that convinced him of a spiritual world as real as the material one. Having a natural tendency to trace lines of thought back to their origins — science to alchemy, Christian mysticism to Neoplatonism and Plato himself, Scholasticism to Aristotle — he studied philosophy under Brentano and developed a system of training based on the phenomenology of Brentano and that of another student of Brentano, Husserl.

The first of three creative periods in Steiner's life began when a professor compared Steiner's phenomenology (attention to thinking, as distinct from things thought about) to Goethe's tracing of color to its invisible source, light. At twenty-three, Steiner was invited to edit Goethe's scientific writings. His second creative period came at the turn of the century, with his conversion to Christianity. Having previously attacked both the Christian ethic and Kant's "categorical imperative" as "philistine embodiments of duty in external codes,"[82] Steiner now blended his existentialist belief in moral freedom, based on disciplined thinking, feeling, and willing, with insights from the Christian and Hindu scriptures. His third and best-known creative period followed his expulsion in 1912 from the Theosophical Society for refusing to recognize the young visionary Krishnamurti as Christ reincarnate. He immediately founded the Anthroposophical Society, on the principles of seeking enlightenment from Western as well as Eastern mystics and of treating Christ's Incarnation as the focal point of human history and thought.[83] Anthroposophy, or "human wisdom," was to reunite the human ego with an external world no less spiritual than material. Its disciples must make the "world-content" into their own "thought-content" and know external Nature by learning to "know her within."[84] Next, they must attend to their acts of thinking and making choices, rather than to thoughts or moral laws themselves. By contemplating themselves as objects, they would free themselves to make fully conscious decisions and open themselves to external impressions.

Steiner's teaching in this third phase can best be drawn from the only book of his that Lewis read, *The Way of Initiation,* otherwise translated as *Knowledge of Higher Worlds, and Its Attainment* (1917). An initiate first develops *imagination* by meditating upon some object, such as a seed, that has no personal associations, thus becoming aware

82. Steiner, *Philosophy of Freedom,* 140.

83. A. P. Shepherd, *A Scientist of the Invisible: An Introduction to the Life and Work of Rudolf Steiner,* 67-74.

84. Steiner, *Philosophy of Freedom,* 14.

of the formative or "etheric" forces responsible for the growth of both the seed and oneself. Next one attains *inspiration* by emptying mind and heart so as to open them to the cosmic or "astral" forces that form human feelings and relationships. Aware of oneself as "a link in the whole of life," the initiate learns, by renouncing egoism, competitiveness, and the propensity to use people, to discern the spiritual element that informs all human relationships. Eventually the seeker will enjoy a vision of the whole human drama past, present, and to come. The initiate finally develops *intuition* by exercising the will in relating to the spiritual forces responsible for cosmic, as distinct from personal or historical, evolution. Having attained equilibrium in freeing himself from calculation, unbridled passion, sentimentalism, impulsiveness, and lust for power, the anthroposophist enjoys clairvoyant awareness of the natural and social worlds and their spiritual ground. Faith has vanished into "knowledge and insight, which nothing can undermine."[85] As ancient myths show, primal humankind enjoyed this clairvoyance, which Hindu seers still attain in death-like trances. Christ opened initiation to all by training disciples to enjoy clairvoyance while remaining fully conscious. They lived together in willed love *(agape)* rather than kinship or passion *(storge* or *eros)*. The Fall, which resulted from attacks by "Ahrimanic" beings upon human spiritual ("etheric") awareness and by "Luciferic" beings upon social ("astral") awareness, had exposed humanity to destruction through materialism and self-serving passion, yet made possible human freedom and dignity.

This bare-bones account of a system as all-embracing as Freudian psychology has ignored anthroposophy's practical achievements in organic gardening, education, art, and physical culture, of which at that time Lewis was apparently unaware. Despite the obvious appeal of *Knowledge of Higher Worlds* to Lewis the Mentor, he had four motives for attacking Steiner's system: distrust of spiritual authoritarianism, discomfort at the notion of realities conveyed by myths and fairy tales, disbelief in angels and demons, and unwillingness to accept that the mind could profitably observe and direct its own operations. He had grown increasingly distrustful of all forms of introspection since 1923, when he saw a spiritualist brother of Mrs. Moore sink into raving

85. Steiner, *Knowledge of Higher Worlds, and Its Attainment,* 187.

lunacy. Lewis's reaction took the forms of a willed extraversion and an Ulster Protestant distrust of spiritual authoritarianism that remained with him for most of his life. Steiner's literalism regarding myths, as Lewis complained in his diary, spoilt many a folktale for him.[86] In one of the "Great War" letters he coined the word "bulverism" for the argument that his doubt of Ahriman's existence revealed how this demon of materialism was manipulating him. The error, as he later explained in his Socratic Society paper "Bulverism," lies in assuming without proof that one's opponents cannot rationally disagree with one, then supposing them to have been got at.[87]

Lewis's fourth motive, distrust of thinking about one's own thought processes, stems from a distinction he came across in 1924-25, while serving as *locum tenens* for his old philosophy tutor, in Samuel Alexander's *Space, Time and Deity* (1920). It explained for him why he had so often failed to reexperience "Joy" by rereading a book or revisiting a place. The mind, said Alexander (using the terms in a special sense), "contemplated" objects or other people, but "enjoyed" its own sensations and feelings, which it could not at the same time contemplate and enjoy.[88] Realizing that he had been vainly trying to enjoy and to contemplate his experiences at the same time, Lewis henceforth distinguished between enjoying and subsequently contemplating an experience, whether of Joy or simply of reading. Just as Barfield distinguished between the initial and subsequent effects of reading a poem, so Lewis saw the teacher intent upon "practical criticism" as expecting students not to surrender to and afterward think critically about a text, but to do both at once.

Alexander expounded an emergent evolution of mind from neural reactions, and of deity from mind, by means of a "nisus" or creative tendency that caused space-time to engender matter, matter to engender life, and living structures to engender mind. In his "Summa," Lewis replaces space-time by "Spirit," Hegel's synonym for the Absolute or

---

86. Diary, 7 July 1923; "The Lewis Family Papers," VIII, 136, quoted by Franceschelli.

87. Lewis, "Bulverism," originally published in 1941.

88. Alexander, *Space, Time and Deity*, I:12ff. In Christian mysticism, "contemplation," like Alexander's "enjoyment," refers to illuminative experience itself.

God. Just as in Alexander's view matter, by indwelling creativeness, brought forth mind, so in that of Lewis Spirit hastened to embody itself in matter, and the human spirit in artifacts. Since authorship and appreciation demand an interplay between enjoyment of feelings or sensations and contemplation of external objects, Lewis, like Alexander, condemns introspection.

In the "Summa," therefore, Lewis develops an objectivist ethic and aesthetic. Excluding issues specific to anthroposophy, Part I, "Being," presents life and the cosmos as wholly interconnected. The individual enjoys his own being, within Spirit, and contemplates his neighbors. Likewise, ultimately Spirit "is" the individual. Lewis illustrates the soul's ability to enjoy itself within Spirit by a literary analogy in which Shakespeare stands for "Spirit," Prince Hamlet for the individual, and the remaining characters for other souls. By "soul" Lewis means the entire person, whose existence has no meaning outside a material world and society. Artistic subcreation requires the poet to separate and contemplate an element in his own psyche, as Shakespeare did his Iago-element, but to construct minor characters (such as Rodrigo) from without. The determinant is whether the dramatist "enjoys" — that is, inwardly undergoes — the character's experience. To this Barfield objects that the separation of enjoyed and contemplated characters is too arbitrary (in which pigeonhole would Cassio fit?). At all events, only the first kind of creation, that of Iago, represents the cosmic creation by Spirit. Like individual souls, such characters take on a life of their own.

Lewis rules out any notion of Spirit as the Judeo-Christian providential Deity controlling its creatures. Instead, Spirit represents a knowing and sentient nature or cosmos, begetting all things and seeing them as mutually related. In that case, it makes no sense to think of Spirit as incarnate in any individual. Nevertheless, as Shakespeare finds self-limitation easier when creating Prospero than when creating Caliban, so the spiritual life becomes more evident in some souls than in others. The touchstone is whether the soul indulges its passions or sees itself within the context of Spirit. Here Lewis acknowledges dependence on Kant's categorical imperative that enjoins the willing of actions that would be good for all to will. In this sense, the soul lives best that dies to its own will, as to some degree do all that live under law.

In Part II, "Value," Lewis constructs a hierarchy of activities that constitute two stages of the spiritual life. Just as morality requires an effort to will as Spirit wills, in the common interest, so science, history, art, and philosophy, in ascending order, require an effort to see objectively, as from Spirit's viewpoint. Science occupies the lowest rung, originating as it does in the passions of curiosity and desire for material improvement. History ranks above science because it requires qualitative study of places, people, and events and resists abstraction. Art ranks above science because it creates a more total system of relationships and above history because it is yet more concrete. But art is not synonymous with imagination, which it rather serves. This point Lewis may have observed from Wordsworth's *Prelude,* from which at that time he read a portion daily, as if it had been the Bible. By schooling the soul in disinterested activity, art gives it a foretaste of the spiritual life. Philosophy excels other modes because it implants both knowledge of the soul's relation to Spirit and capacity to view the world with detachment.

The second stage of the spiritual life requires the soul not only to see the world and other creatures disinterestedly, but also to will their being. This stage has three elements: charity, memory, and imagination. Lewis memorably describes this stage as becoming a window for Spirit to see through. That an author raises a work to a higher power by viewing characters with both sympathy and detachment, as Shakespeare does Lear, is evident enough; but a splendid passage on imagination ("Summa" II, xiii) sheds further light on the value of charity. Imagination resembles "Joy" in being at once desire and satisfaction. It includes art and memory, in that it ideally involves both total comprehension of its objects within a system and their recognition as by déjà vu. In describing the latter, Lewis employs language reminiscent of Coleridge's famous gloss in which the Ancient Mariner "yearneth towards" the moon and stars, "and everywhere the blue sky belongs to them, and is their appointed rest, and their native country, and their own natural homes."[89] The imagining soul likewise owns yet renounces ownership of its objects, charging all with life as the life of Spirit flows beneath the surface of all things. Imagination therefore raises work in science, history, art, and philosophy to a higher level. Likewise, charity raises

89. Coleridge, *Ancient Mariner,* IV.

memory, as well as art. Thirty years later, Lewis was to argue in his *Four Loves* that family affection, friendship, and erotic love attained their fullest potential only by admixture of *agape,* or charity.

Lewis conveys objectivist values in a further sense. Just as Spirit must incarnate itself in creation, so the artist necessarily incarnates himself in using the materials of his craft, the moralist in beneficent action. In both his criticism and his fiction, Lewis always sought to discredit romantic notions of the artist as a "genius," or higher order of human being, a Nietzschean "superman" exempt from the moral law that binds the rest of humanity. In his *Experiment in Criticism* (1961) and earlier essays on literary theory, he restricts the meaning of "artist" to that of a craftsman in a given medium — words, music, or stone — whose works, rather than personality, merit our attention. This impersonal view of criticism, this view of the literary work as an objet d'art within a genre, conditions his critical judgments, from the early disputation with E. M. W. Tillyard published as *The Personal Heresy* (1939) to his last critical book, *An Experiment in Criticism.* Likewise, his account of Satan in *A Preface to "Paradise Lost"* (1941) parallels his depiction of the villains Weston and Devine in his *Out of the Silent Planet* (1938) and *Perelandra* (1943), in depicting the antinomian, self-worshiping superman. More completely than elsewhere, in the "Summa" he condemns also what Alexander calls the "dangerous" practice of introspection.[90] At our most spiritual, we look outward and seek to incarnate ourselves in what we discover, make, or do.

90. Alexander, *Space, Time and Deity,* II:89: "The mind which broods over itself in dangerous practical introspection abandons itself to the enjoyment of itself."

CHAPTER 2

Literary Historian

The Allegory of Love

Lewis lost interest in continuing the "Great War" as he became increasingly preoccupied with writing his *Allegory of Love*. Although the research was suggested by his English tutor, F. P. Wilson, only Lewis could have carried it out.[1] He alone could have read texts in Latin, Middle English, French, and Italian with a historian's persistence and the fresh insight of a maker and lover of poems, translating at will into imitation medieval or Tudor verse. During the seven years he spent in its writing, at the rate of a chapter per year,[2] many a North American or European university would have required for tenure a stream of articles or a less time-consuming book. Oxford allowed him time to develop his complex argument from his already well-known lectures and his endless reading. Whatever the book lost with regard to the bibliography and full citations that graduate students now learn to provide, it more than regained in the inspired readings and arresting comparisons of a gifted lecturer.

1. George Sayer, *Jack: C. S. Lewis and His Times*, 145. My comment is anticipated by Peter Bayley, "From Master to Colleague," in Como, ed., *C. S. Lewis at the Breakfast Table*, 82.
2. The slow pace was owing to the demands of tutorials and lectures (letter to George Watson, 15 May 1962).

In his *Discarded Image,* published soon after his death but also based on the lectures, Lewis spoke of the "bookish or clerkly" medieval culture.[3] John Wain styled him a great "clerke," and his *Allegory* implies a bookish — and male — readership.[4] You catch the bookish flavor from his allusion to Fulgentius's "now famous (or notorious) *Continentia Vergiliana.*"[5] Lewis's assertion that "probably no reader" sees a phrase by Lydgate without recalling "*voces vagitus et ingens* in Virgil's hell" (*Allegory,* 242-43) implies a reader who, like Lewis, has absorbed the *Aeneid* into his marrow. That implied reader will also pick up the Johnsonian allusion in "When you are tired of Ariosto you must be tired of the world" (302), and, indeed, will see the world through books. Lewis assumes that the reader follows Greek and medieval Italian, understands what *Frauendienst* means,[6] but needs Lewis's translations from Old French poems.

Charles Williams, his editor, persuaded Lewis to change the original title, "The Medieval Love Allegory," perhaps thinking it inapplicable to the chapters on Chaucer and Spenser that some reviewers thought the best.[7] The full title, *The Allegory of Love: A Study in Medieval Tradition,* covers the definitions of courtly love, history and modes of allegory, and the dubious distinction between allegorical and symbolic poems.

The subject enabled Lewis to indulge the Dreamer's interest in poems based on dream visions. In this, his first and most influential academic book, literary history and criticism are intertwined. I shall separate them to the extent of discussing his lifelong engagement with the *Faerie Queene* in my ensuing chapter on Lewis's literary criticism.

The argument of the *Allegory* runs as follows. The cult of courtly love, with its marks of humility, courtesy, adultery, and quasi-religious devotion, sprang up in the provençal context of arranged marriages and landless knights. The first true love poems since the fall of Rome depicted love's ecstasy and suffering in characters personifying the lover's conflicting emotions. In his *De Arte Honeste Amandi,* Andreas Capel-

---

3. Lewis, *The Discarded Image* (paperback ed.), 5.

4. See John Wain, "The Great Clerk," in Como, ed., *C. S. Lewis at the Breakfast Table.*

5. Lewis, *The Allegory of Love,* 84. Subsequent references are given parenthetically in the text.

6. Service to one's lady.

7. Such as G. Bonnard or G. L. Brook (see the bibliography).

lanus described the signs and improving effects of love and laid down rules for (adulterous) courtship. Building on a Roman allegorical tradition preserved in sermons, poets represented love and courtship in figures derived from the classical deities.

Supremely, in the *Roman de la Rose,* Guillaume de Lorris showed the suitor being admitted to the Garden of Love by the lady's squire Fair Welcome (Bialacoil), after overcoming her guardians Jealousy, Gossip, Shame, and Danger. Against Reason's advice, he seeks to rescue the imprisoned Fair Welcome and win the Rose, signifying the lady's love.

Even Chaucer, not usually an allegorist, drew on this tradition in *Troilus and Criseyde.* Cupid shoots arrows of desire into Troilus, who conquers Criseyde with the approval of Venus, goddess not only of love but of Nature philoprogenerative. He suffers the obsessive longing and insomnia that Andreas listed among the signs of love.

Between Chaucer and Spenser, English and Scottish poets — Gower, Lydgate, Dunbar, Douglas, and others — combined the erotic with the older moral allegory. In the *Faerie Queene,* Spenser achieved the most complete fusion. From the religion of love he established the tradition of romantic love consummated in marriage that continued to nourish English literature down to the twentieth century. His lover knight, schooled in virtuous and gentle discipline, was to evolve into the English ideal of the gentleman.

At this time (1928-36), Lewis accepted the conventional division of European history into Dark and Middle Ages, but treated the Renaissance in cultural rather than chronological terms. Distinguishing Renaissance allegory from medieval by its decorative rather than psychological use of Cupid, Priapus or Pleasaunce, he regarded Chaucer as "too true a child of the Middle Ages" to resent the "alien" features of his Renaissance-style source for the "Parlement of Fowles," Boccaccio's *Teseide* (*Allegory,* 174-75). In his well-known but at this time only academic article, Lewis advanced the thesis, undisputed for half a century, that the *Troilus* was a medievalization of Boccaccio's *Il Filostrato.*[8] To consider Chaucer's Italian

8. Lewis, "What Chaucer Really Did to *Il Filostrato.*" David Wallace, *Chaucer and the Early Writings of Boccaccio,* maintains that "medievalizing" originated not with Chaucer but with Boccaccio, but calls *The Allegory of Love* "a splendid pioneering effort."

precursor "Renaissance" implies a cultural and geographical distinction. With "medieval" literature he associates a courtship that is "noble" in being idealistic as well as aristocratic, with "Renaissance" literature a courtship that is frankly, even cynically sensual. Yet he calls the *Troilus* "modern" because "successfully and perfectly medieval" (*Allegory*, 177), timelessly appealing because completely adapted to fourteenth-century English life. Troilus falls in love like any English nobleman nurtured on medieval romances, yet like a noble youth of any time.

Early reviewers mostly echoed Kathleen Tillotson's praise of the pages on *Troilus* as among the book's "noblest" and her praise of the "lucidity and sureness" with which Lewis defined allegory and romantic love. Equally typical was Oliver Elton's praise of his style as "imaginative" and "full of sap." Kathleen Tillotson's comment that "no one can read" the *Allegory* without "seeing all literature . . . differently" afterward, and G. L. Brook's that it offered "the . . . most illuminating" account so far of the "origin of courtly love and allegory" expressed the feelings of tutors and students in British universities for at least two decades.[9]

Yet even in 1936 several reviewers followed William Empson in objecting to the claim that, compared with the change to chivalric courtship of women, the Renaissance was "a mere ripple on the surface of literature" (*Allegory*, 4). In his highly favorable review, Empson also pointed out that the supposed uniqueness of provençal *cortezia (amour courtois)* could be refuted from Islamic and tenth-century Japanese literature.[10] Almost thirty years later, Peter Dronke pointed to chivalric images of love as an illness, as mania, and as coexistent with hate, in lyric poems of ancient Rome that Lewis undoubtedly did know.[11] The reaction had completely set in by 1949, when N. S. Brooke flatly contradicted Lewis's view of the "Bower of Bliss" episode in the *Faerie Queene*. While the substance of Brooke's dense and complex argument

9. See the reviews of *Allegory of Love* by Kathleen Tillotson, Oliver Elton, and G. L. Brook, all reprinted in Watson, ed., *Critical Thought I: Critical Essays on C. S. Lewis*, 96-98, 82-88, and 94-95 respectively.

10. William Empson, "Love and the Middle Ages," reprinted in Watson, ed., *Critical Thought I*, 79-81.

11. Peter Dronke, *Medieval Latin and the Rise of the European Love-Lyric*, excerpted in Watson, ed., *Critical Thought I*, 124-25.

must be considered in the next chapter, his essential contention is that Lewis misunderstood the poem's allegory, especially as regards Book II, "Temperance," in thinking that the Bower showed not perverted but normal sexual passion. In Brooke's view, as the House of Alma represented the human body properly governed, the winemaking episode of Book II typified the disordered liver, the fountain the misdirected heart, and the Bower the brain misused by the will as the "tool of desire." Brooke's unkindest cut was to charge Lewis with having subscribed to twentieth-century convention by viewing sexual passion as intrinsically good.[12]

The chapters on the *Roman de la Rose* and *Troilus and Criseyde,* so highly praised in early reviews, have drawn fire since about 1960 from both practitioners and opponents of historical criticism. D. W. Robertson, whose *Preface to Chaucer* (1962) took North American medievalists by storm as the *Allegory* had taken English medievalists, argues that Chaucer created not characters interacting in a fourteenth-century court but moral abstractions enacting theological paradigms in an allegorical setting.[13] Troilus illustrates irrational passion for a lady hitherto unknown who proves unworthy of his sacrifice of honor, position, and duty. Her garden, even its singing nightingale, is drawn not from an English landscape but from the Garden of Love in the *Roman.* His passion renewed by each assignation is the insatiable thirst of concupiscence recollected by St. Augustine. Once deserted by Criseyde, the vengeful Troilus vainly scours the battlefield for her new lover. After his death, from the "eighth sphere" he laughs at the folly of *cupiditas.* Chaucer undercuts his apparent sympathy with the lovers by Boethian allusions to the folly of pursuing a mutable rather than eternal good, by which Troilus exposes himself to the inconstancy of Fortune, as when the prisoner exchange deprives him of Criseyde. Insisting that such "Boethian elements" were "easily recognizeable to . . . Chaucer's audience" (*Preface,* 472), Robertson proves as bookish as Lewis, if rather more clerical.

English Chaucerians, in particular, have supported Lewis on the

12. N. S. Brooke, "C. S. Lewis and Spenser: Nature, Art and the Bower of Bliss," reprinted in Watson, ed., *Critical Thought I,* 105-19.
13. D. W. Robertson, *A Preface to Chaucer,* 34-36.

ground that Robertson treats the *Troilus* too much as a sermon and too little as a poem,[14] concluding with Lewis that the poem's climax and abiding impression is the ecstatic union of lovers whose separation is more pathetic than tragic. Yet Lewis calls Criseyde, "the ferfullest wighte" (*Troilus and Criseyde* II, 458), a tragic character in "the strictest Aristotelian sense" (*Allegory,* 189). The delight of so many readers, one might add, proves Pandarus no mere paradigm but a character.

Robertson avoids naming Lewis, but he strikes home in referring to "Romantic" readings of the *Troilus*.[15] Even the anti-Robertsonian E. T. Donaldson agrees with Robertson in finding the *De Arte Honeste Amandi* no love manual but an ironic exposé of carnal pleasure intended to amuse fellow clergy. Donaldson's most serious charge, one applicable to a bookman, is that Lewis confused "literary criticism with supposedly objective historical facts . . . derived mainly from the earlier literature he was examining."[16] In endorsing "myth" of courtly adultery, Lewis misled generations of students. The poem, after all, "concerns the love of a bachelor for a widow."[17]

Criticisms of the *Allegory's* "literary theory" (a term Lewis was among the first to employ)[18] may be distinguished from objections to its treatment of authors and central texts. Colin Hardie, for example, thought Lewis erred in treating Dante as an allegorist momentarily bewitched by courtly love; A. D. Nuttall thought him illogical in regarding *Piers Plowman* or even the *Pilgrim's Progress* as allegories, since they refer to an eternal world their authors and Lewis believed real.[19] Some readers complain that Lewis made minor allegorical poems seem

14. E.g., Elizabeth Salter, "*Troilus and Criseyde:* A Reconsideration," in John Lawlor, ed., *Patterns of Love and Courtesy,* 86-106. But Ida Gordon's *The Double Sorrow of Troilus* endorses Robertson's view.

15. Robertson, *Preface to Chaucer,* 50, 472. Robertson indirectly criticizes Lewis in "Chaucerian Tragedy" (in Richard J. Schoek and J. Taylor, eds., *Chaucer Criticism,* 2:102), quoting *Allegory of Love,* 189, to comment that Criseyde's is the wrong fear and the wrong love.

16. E. Talbot Donaldson, *Speaking of Chaucer,* 154-63. Excerpt in Watson, ed., *Critical Thought I,* 126-35.

17. Donaldson, *Speaking of Chaucer,* 156.

18. *Allegory of Love,* 22.

19. Hardie, "Dante and the Tradition of Courtly Love," in Lawlor, ed., *Patterns of Love and Courtesy,* 26-44; A. D. Nuttall, *Two Concepts of Allegory,* 27, 33.

more readable than they are. But on the central texts — the *Roman de la Rose, Troilus and Criseyde, Confessio Amantis,* and *Faerie Queene* — most academic readers, in the words of Charles Muscatine, "stand on his shoulders."[20] This is true even of Robertson insofar as Lewis established the tradition of reading Chaucer from a medieval reader's standpoint.

John Fleming has attacked Lewis's treatment of the *Roman.* While calling the book a "brilliant *tour de force,*" he notes the slip by Lewis of treating Bel Aceuil as a woman when the name governs masculine pronouns, and the graver errors of denying De Meun's allegorical intent and treating De Lorris not as moralist but as an "erotic mythologist" of courtly love.[21] Like his elder colleague Robertson, Fleming uses manuscript illustrations to undermine Lewis's reading of the *Troilus.* Having at least the authority of medieval book illustrators, Fleming appears immune from Ian Robinson's strictures on historicists for using nonliterary material, until one reflects on how many illustrators were monks or clerks in holy orders. D. S. Brewer, no Robertsonian, agrees with Fleming that as "*glossa ordinaria* for twentieth-century readers"[22] the *Allegory* misled generations of students, but Brewer thinks Lewis also erred in yoking together two distinct genres, allegory and love narrative.

While Lewis's theory of allegory will be further considered in the next two chapters, a few anomalies and quirks may be noted here. From the start, Lewis treats Ovid lightly but Andreas all too seriously. After pronouncing that a poet's biography has "little relevance for criticism" (115), he claims that no one can read certain lines in the *Temple of Glass* without recalling Lydgate's "secret tears" as a child forced into a monastery (*Allegory,* 242-43). (Here one wonders about his own at Wynyard School.) He begins his famous chapter on the *Faerie Queene* by forswearing political interpretation, yet, as an Irish expatriate, he

20. Charles Muscatine, *Chaucer and the French Tradition,* 130. Kathryn Kerby-Fulton, in "Standing on Lewis's Shoulders," describes this as a "well worn medieval metaphor."

21. John Fleming, *The "Roman de la Rose": A Study in Allegory and Iconography,* 43-45, 79.

22. Fleming, *The "Roman de la Rose,"* 80. D. S. Brewer, "The Tutor: A Portrait," in Como, ed., *C. S. Lewis at the Breakfast Table,* 41-67, esp. 47.

can see the figure of Artegall in Book V only as intended to justify the "detestable policy" of colonialization (349). He explains that medieval readers thought of Chaucer as translator and love-poet, but an early dislike seems responsible for his strange judgment of the *Canterbury Tales* as having "always been sterile" (163), despite the relevance of the *Franklin's Tale* to his case for a progressive idealization of spousal love.

In fact, when alluding to his own *Pilgrim's Regress* or Barfield's *Poetic Diction* or to an emblem in Warnie's regimental mess hall, Lewis rarely allows us to forget the human being behind the book.[23] This impress of personality is responsible both for the quirks and for some of the insights. Thus his comment on "modern ravings" (*Allegory,* 97) about sex organs, compared to the good sense of the twelfth-century author Bernardus Sylvestris, seems a dig at Havelock Ellis and Freud, and his comment on the "modern (or late) romance of marriage" (197) a dig at D. H. Lawrence and feminists. A gibe at New Critics for their "pernicious" practice of promoting one "excellence" by disparaging another (306) anticipates his plea in *An Experiment in Criticism* for readers to form their own opinions rather than be shamed into following their mentors. Yet his claim that Spenser's imagined figures have no "context in the objective world" (310) reads like a complaint by Eliot or F. R. Leavis, while his admiration for Spenser's "humble fidelity" to the "symbols" of folk literature and religion (312) is akin to that of Leavis for Bunyan. In viewing allegory as a "system of conduit pipes which . . . tap deep, unfailing sources of poetry in the mind of the folk" (120), Lewis conveys a Jungian insight via a homely analogy.

With the boldness of Leavis or I. A. Richards, Lewis discards the "poet's poet" cliché as an impediment to open-minded reading of Spenser (*Allegory,* 317) and finds the dead wife of Chaucer's *Book of the Duchess* better realized than the deceased in Milton's "Lycidas" or Arnold's "Thyrsis" (169). Yet he differs from the followers of Richards and Leavis in rejecting the lemon-squeezer mode of explication. The interpreter's "chief duty," he proclaims, is "to begin analyses and to leave them unfinished" (345). Here speaks a tutor content to let insights form in the minds of pupils.

The *Allegory of Love* shows other characteristics of the good com-

23. Further examples in Joe R. Christopher, *C. S. Lewis,* 25ff.

municator: end-of-chapter summaries, striking metaphors and analogies, Johnsonian epigrams, and a prevailing urbanity and lightness of
tone. Its images or analogies mostly come from common life — the
wild provençal vine tamed by Chaucer (197), the layers scraped from
the surface of Italian epic poems (308) — but the most memorable is
drawn from education: in the conclusions of the *Troilus* and *Morte
d'Arthur,* readers hear a bell summoning schoolchildren, "suddenly
hushed . . . back to their master" (43). The aphorism that on morality
men "more frequently require to be reminded than informed" (259)
looks back toward Johnson yet also forward to the universal moral law
of the *Abolition of Man,* but in his statement "Those who begin by
worshipping power soon worship evil" (189) we hear a contemporary
of Hitler.

The book also shows signs of the future popular theologian.
Apropos Jean de Meun, Lewis remarks that "good popularized doctrine
in verse" requires "clarity, mastery of the medium," and "appositeness
of metaphor" (142-43), the very qualities he was to deploy in the
apologetic broadcasts of his middle years. If "and the like" (143) refers
to his unrivaled power of analogy, he might have been assessing his
own capacity to write the *Problem of Pain* (1940) and the *Broadcast
Talks* (1941-42).

Responsible for both his wide appeal as a theologian and the
antipathy of some of his fellow academics was a populist strain of
imagery, at its best in his account of Pandarus as a "practical man" with
whom one may travel first class on third-class tickets and stay in fully
booked hotels (*Allegory,* 190), and at its worst in the sobriquets "Cissie
and Flossie" for two figures in the Bower of Bliss (331). Where admirers
perceived the ease and liveliness of a born teacher, academic opponents
detected popularism unbecoming a don. If none of these colleagues
would have stooped to "Cissie and Flossie," few could have risen to
this comment on some lines by Gower, in which

> we have the poetic history of that strange moment — familiar in the
> history of other passions as well as of love — wherein a man laying
> his ear close to his own heart, first hears the master passion itself
> there speaking with a doubtful voice, and presently hinting that it
> knows . . . itself to be all other than the tongue claims for it — that

its foundations are crumbling — that its superstructure is but a tissue of illusions and decaying habits, soon to dissolve and leave us face to face with inner emptiness. (220)

Such statements show a creative imagination beyond the mere understanding of texts and sources.

English Literature in the Sixteenth Century, Excluding Drama

Published in 1954, this, the largest and most controversial of Lewis's literary histories, formed part of the Oxford History of English Literature. I shall shorten its unwieldy title to the acronym OHEL, which Lewis used when humorously complaining of the immensity of his task, completed in a then-rare sabbatical year.[24] An expanded version of his Clark Lectures at Cambridge in 1944, OHEL is a more conventional literary history than the *Allegory of Love*. While it remains an unrivaled survey of its period, its attack on Renaissance humanism, its division of sixteenth-century literature into "Drab" and "Golden," and even the title of its long introduction, "The New Learning and the New Ignorance," seemed designed to provoke reviewers, among whom Yvor Winters attacked it the most savagely.[25] In view of the book's magnitude and detail, I shall consider only its introduction, methodology, and studies of Shakespeare and Sidney, again reserving that of Spenser for the next chapter.

Even more astounding than the range of Lewis's famous introduction are his assessments of Sir Thomas More, not Calvin, as a killjoy, of humanists as philistines, and of Francis Bacon as no pioneer of science but a "mere" empiricist who "achieved nothing" (OHEL, 3). Restricting the term *renascentia* to the study of classical Latin and the recovery of Greek texts, Lewis debunks the division of history into Middle Ages and Renaissance — a division that he himself used in

24. Letter to Sister Penelope, 10 January 1952. The sabbatical year for Lewis was limited to freedom from teaching.

25. Yvor Winters, review of *English Literature in the Sixteenth Century, Excluding Drama*, reprinted in Watson, ed., *Critical Thought I*, 212-18.

the *Allegory* — pronouncing the latter "an imaginary entity responsible for whatever the speaker likes in the fifteenth and sixteenth centuries" and gleefully stressing that he has reached page 55 without using the word.

One explanation of his skepticism follows from his assertion that since the phrase *medium aevum* came into use only in 1469, medieval authors and readers never saw the Christian Latin culture as an interlude between two civilizations. Another possible explanation is the well-known difficulty of dating, evident in the "medieval" Chaucer's indebtedness to the "Renaissance" Petrarch, or the contemporaneity of the post-Renaissance Rembrandt and late-Renaissance Milton.[26]

Lewis further startles us by asserting that humanist authors understood neither the medieval masterpieces they disparaged nor the classical ones they imitated. Constrained to "treat every great poem as an allegory or encyclopedia" (OHEL, 28), they could not enjoy medieval tales read literally. Because scholastic theologians did not write like Cicero, humanists ignored their ideas. They also killed Latin as a living language by insisting on a return to classical usage. They assumed a mask of Roman *gravitas* rather than Greek *sophrosyne,* for Hellenism came into its own only in the nineteenth century.

Lewis first began to feel skeptical about the sudden end of the Middle Ages when some work on Erasmus in 1928 took him back further than expected.[27] To judge from his annotations, three books chiefly influenced him to deny the orthodox view of the Renaissance: *Thomas More* by R. W. Chambers; *The Renaissance and English Humanism,* four newly published lectures that Douglas Bush sent to Lewis in 1941; and a 1945 reprint of Jakob Burckhardt's *Civilization of the Renaissance in Italy.*

In the book on More, Lewis inscribed a list of dates and references in the front pages, then underlined a statement that Tudor poetry was negligible until it began "its magnificent progress with Sidney and Spenser" (Chambers, 379). This may have influenced Lewis to think

26. The major poems of Chaucer (1340-1400) were written between 1385 and 1395, while Petrarch (1304-1374) is called "the most popular poet of the Italian Renaissance" *(Oxford Companion to English Literature).*

27. Letter to his father on 31 March 1928, in *Letters of C. S. Lewis,* 125.

of a Drab Age before the Golden. Despite his favorable portrait of More, Chambers accuses Elizabethan playwrights of falsifying evidence to present him as friend of the impoverished. Alongside the account of Utopian colleges as modeled on monasteries, Lewis scrawled a note of More's charge that abbots had enclosed common lands, a charge Lewis repeated in OHEL (57).

In the book by Bush, Lewis scrawled a derisive monosyllable on the Freudian reading of *Comus* but underlined the claim that Voltaire had started the "myth" of an exodus of scholars in 1453, although Italian scholars had been studying Greek for half a century (Bush, 14). His list of points by Bush included one to the effect that English humanists opposed not Christianity but individualism, and another criticizing the term "Middle Age" or thousand-year interregnum. He also sidelined (that is, marked with a vertical line in the margin) Bush's account of "literary rebels trying to write like the ancients" and devising "a code of dogmatic rules for the drama" (Bush, 37, 38). All of these he used in OHEL.

In his letter of thanks to Bush, Lewis defined the Renaissance exactly as in OHEL (55) and endorsed Bush's view of the sixteenth century as the golden age of magic and occultism. In Bush's text he underlined statements that astrology and witchcraft "flourished with fresh vigour" (Bush, 33) and that as the flame of humanism died down, science regained its late-medieval ascendancy (Bush, 131).

On some notable authors, Lewis's view differed from that of Bush. He marked Bush's account of Machiavelli as expounding medieval statecraft (Bush, 35ff.) only to confute it in OHEL (51-52), before asserting that *The Prince* was important only as the basis for the "machiavel," or cunning villain, in Tudor and Stuart drama. He already despised Bacon's empiricism, for in his letter he wondered at the common neglect of Hooker's "real thought" for Bacon's "dreams." While Bush emphasized Erasmus's respect for the piety and scholarship of English humanists, Lewis highlighted their pedantry and philistinism (OHEL, 29-31, 159-60). Later in OHEL, however, he wrote admiringly of More's *Utopia* and other literary works. According to Emrys Jones, Lewis confused English with Continental humanism, as Erasmus, the primary influence upon English authors, attacked the southern cult of Cicero and promoted a north-European humanism of sober practicality and common sense that underlay all that was best in English literature from More and Shakespeare to Pope and Johnson.[28] Had Lewis lived to read this, he could have pointed to the sterile imitations of classical tragedy by the English "university wits."

Among passages Lewis underlined in Burckhardt's book, the most relevant refer to the alliance of Italian humanists with despots, the insipidity of their histories compared with medieval annals, and the vulgar or trivial topics on which they exercised their classical Latin (Burckhardt, 132, 145, 157). In Burckhardt's view, those who wrote for citizens "had more of the spirit of the living language" (Burckhardt, 148). Lewis queried Burckhardt's claim that humanists began to think and feel like the ancients (Burckhardt, 120), since he thought medieval authors more akin to them. Having underlined Burckhardt's comment on the humanistic endorsement of astrology, he compared this to the pseudoscientific determinism of modern ideologues (OHEL, 6, 14). Most significantly, he underlined a quotation from Castiglione to the effect that good speech resembled classical prose (Burckhardt, 230), for Lewis always advised prospective authors to test a draft by reading it aloud.[29] To him, good writing resembled fluent and lively speech. His power to command attention from students and nonacademic readers alike came from an ear for speech that he shared with Chaucer and, among moderns, Bertrand Russell.

Later, in 1958, Lewis recorded on the title page his disappointment upon rereading Burckhardt. In his annotations, he ignored anything favorable to Italian humanists, as if using the book to support a view already formed. He apparently overlooked Bush's disapproval of Burckhardt for popularizing the word "Renaissance," coined in 1855 by Michelet. Lewis employed linguistic relativism to discredit the term "Renaissance," claiming that all such terms involve hindsight: Romans and Greeks never saw themselves as ancients, nor did medieval people see themselves as medieval. The humanists, however, congratulated themselves upon living in a *renascentia,* upon having restored sound learning by breaking with all ages since the fall of Rome. "Our legend of the Renaissance" had therefore originated with them. Since their touchstone of civilized writing was classical usage, they acted as "judges

28. Emrys Jones, *The Origins of Shakespeare,* 8-11.
29. For example, letter to Joan Lancaster, in *Letters of C. S. Lewis,* 291-92.

in their own cause." A difficulty with this view is that Lewis and Bush saw the Renaissance as a "legend" because English Protestant scholars had associated it with the Reformation and the rise of science, and Catholic scholars with the "destruction of a humane and Christian culture by kill-joys and capitalists" (OHEL, 56). In either case, however, the concept meant more than the study of classical literature.

Lewis employed two other strategies in OHEL to discredit the term. The first was to show the scientific and social revolutions in full swing before the sixteenth century. Scientific discovery he ascribed not to Bacon's program for empirical research but to the testing of deductions by Arabic and medieval mathematicians (OHEL, 3). Enclosures and the new class of landed gentry, together with restriction of grammar schools to their children, began in the Middle Ages (OHEL, 56-60).

His final and more radical strategy was to deny the whole notion of a *Zeitgeist* or time-spirit as no more real than "pictures seen in the fire" (OHEL, 64). Since what survives is a matter of chance, the "content" of any age is unknowable. We tend to see patterns in the periods we know least.

Lewis's disbelief in the Renaissance seems less eccentric now than it did in 1954. Even then, Wain called it "not unusual" save in its "wholeheartedness,"[30] citing a Victorian parallel. The 1886 and 1972 printings of *Encyclopedia Britannica* reveal a volte-face. In the 1886 edition J. A. Symonds admitted the difficulty of dating, but confidently asserted that a "whole change . . . came over Europe at the close of the Middle Ages." The "Revival of Learning" was a "function of that vital energy . . . that mental evolution," which begot "the modern world . . . its new conceptions of philosophy and religion . . . re-awakened arts and sciences . . . manifold inventions and discoveries . . . altered political systems" and "expansive and progressive forces."[31] In the 1972 edition, Lynn Thorndike treated this view as a misconception emanating from Voltaire, Michelet, and the "once-influential book by Burckhardt." She taxed Symonds and Walter Pater with having dreamed up

30. John Wain, "Pleasure, Controversy, Scholarship," reprinted in Watson, ed., *Critical Thought I*, 201-5.

31. John Addington Symonds, entry "Renaissance" in *Encyclopedia Britannica*, ninth edition, 1886.

a third great age, after those of Greece and Rome. Twentieth-century scholarship has discredited the shafting of all things medieval, according to Thorndike. Italian humanists were visiting Constantinople fifty years before the alleged exodus; gunpowder, the compass, and science in general date back at least to the thirteenth century, and only printing was new. Confirming all that Lewis said on the humanists' obsession with classical style, Thorndike magisterially concluded:

> It is necessary to reject Michelet's redefinition of the Renaissance as the discovery of the world and of man, together with . . . vague terms and intangible conceptions such as the medieval . . . and . . . modern mind. . . . Instead, one should return to the original conception of . . . a revival of classical Latin belles-lettres and the recovery of Greek classical belles-lettres.[32]

This brings us to a curious lapse on Lewis's part. For his introductory lectures to medieval literature and his *Allegory of Love,* he read and annotated the 1922 edition of Etienne Gilson's *Philosophie au Moyen Age,*[33] but not to the end. The pages of Gilson's chapter "Le Retour des Belles-Lettres . . ." remain uncut. Lewis took what was relevant for his *Allegory of Love,* but he overlooked Gilson when working toward OHEL. What, therefore, did he miss? After describing Petrarch's enchantment with Cicero and Augustine, and his realization that their ethical codes and that of Virgil were all compatible, Gilson ascribes the "return of belles-lettres" not to any influx from Constantinople but to Italian patriotism. Taking a step refused by Dante, Petrarch distinguished between Italian culture and non-Italian "barbarism," singling out for attack the Scholastic tradition represented since the twelfth century by the University of Paris. To him, the best pagan authors and early Fathers (all Italian) stood for wisdom and love, the Scholastics of Paris for sterile disputation about words and eschewing of literature for theology. In Italy, literature faced a different foe, the zealotry of monks such as Savonarola. Boccaccio defended poetry on the ground that the

32. Lynn Thorndike, entry "Renaissance" in *Encyclopedia Britannica,* fourteenth edition, 1972.
33. There is a general reference to *Philosophie au Moyen Age* in Lewis's discussion of medieval Aristotelianism in *Allegory of Love,* 88.

Scriptures were full of poems, poetic imagery, and underlying meanings. In pagan poems Mussato found philosophy, even theology, beneath a veil of allegory.

By the time of the deaths of Petrarch (1374) and Salutati (1406), the final victory of literature was assured. As Petrarch's ideas found acceptance elsewhere, patriotism grew into an identification of barbarism with Scholasticism and of literature with Latin eloquence rediscovered. Had Lewis read on, he might have viewed humanist allegorical interpretation as a defense of literature against attacks by theologians and philosophers, comparable to Sidney's argument that poets taught by giving pleasure. Whether or not he would have agreed with Gilson's account of anti-medievalism, he would have had to deal with its political significance, the rejection of a common latinate culture in favor of cultures based on separate countries or languages. Though he and Gilson agreed on the fourteenth-century revival of classical belles lettres in Italy, Gilson supplied a more coherent rationale for the activities and aberrations of humanist scholars.

In common parlance, the term "Renaissance" still denotes a new culture. Does it remain in use by educational vested interest, or as a matter of convenience, or has it some legitimate meaning that Lewis and Thorndike failed to see? Though far from indifferent to art or music, Lewis rarely attended exhibitions or concerts, had not left the British Isles since 1918, and during vacations explored the countryside rather than cities. Continuity between medieval and Renaissance architecture being nowhere more evident than in Oxford, he perhaps failed to see the import of the multifariousness that his introduction so fully documents. Save for the classical revival, the Renaissance represented less a rebirth than a dispersion. The various strands of European culture no longer needed to cohere as in the past. Before the time of Columbus, maps showed Jerusalem at the center of a flat earth and Paradise in the east. By 1620 the captain of the *Mayflower* used Mercator's projection.[34] Artists painted not only religious but, increasingly, secular subjects. The best Tudor buildings were not churches but palaces, manor houses, or colleges. For all the fanaticism, life no longer came to a focus in the church. Plays with secular plots took place in secular theaters, while

34. Daniel F. Boorstin, *The Discoverers,* 101-2, 154-56, 273.

"sugar'd sonnets" dealt with secular passions — of whatever kind. Shakespeare felt no pressure to write poems like oranges, in which the literal sense concealed the fruit of "moralitee and hoolyness," but could write them like apples, the peel contributing to their flavor and nutrition. As a bookman, Lewis failed to appreciate how rulers, merchant venturers, artists and craftsmen, poets, and scientists trusted in God but went about their business independently of each other and usually of the church. To speak of an unchristening of Europe would be nonsensical, but in Protestant countries, at least, authority and sacredness were in varying degrees transferred to monarchs and class hierarchies, while a collective quest for salvation turned into a multitude of individual and sectarian quests. Our descendants may, like Lewis, regard the Industrial Revolution as the more wholesale break with the past, but the European Renaissance seems likely to retain connotations beyond the confines of literary history.

George Sayer records the delight Lewis took in claiming to shocked friends that "the Renaissance, as generally understood, never existed," and that "there was nothing whatever humane about" the humanists, who were "intolerant and philistine."[35] Based on the context, this must have been between 1944 and 1953. In *Surprised by Joy*, begun by 1948, Lewis says that the longer he investigates "the evidence the less trace" he sees of the "vernal rapture" that supposedly "swept Europe in the fifteenth century."[36] As his letter to Bush shows, he had made up his mind on the Renaissance by 1941. If his evidence consisted of the literary texts used for the Clark Lectures and OHEL, he read them in the light of his disrespect for the humanists save as editors. It seems likely that he thought of the labels "Drab" and "Golden" (in preference to "Plain" and "Decorated") while preparing the lectures, for they have the ring of a star lecturer's shock tactics. In that case, was he engaging in the pejorative assessments he deplored in the Leavisites?

Lewis first qualifies his distinction as suiting verse better than prose, which is generally inferior. He applies the term "Drab" to writing from the 1540s to the late 1570s, earlier works being "Late Medieval." In those decades, "for good or ill, poetry has little richness either of

35. Sayer, *Jack*, 195.
36. Lewis, *Surprised by Joy*, 61.

sound or images," the best verse being "neat and temperate," the remainder "flat and dry," while the prose is "artificial" and "cumbersome." Verse of the "Golden" era is "innocent or ingenuous." He offers the example of sculptors who, having learned to shape a beautiful face and body, are for a time happy to do just that. "Men have at last learned how to write; for a few years nothing more is needed than . . . the strong, simple music of the uncontorted line" in poems loaded with whatever is "naturally delightful" in the environment or "female form" (OHEL, 64-65).

Even if the antithesis between plainness and ingenuousness is not self-contradictory, the denial here and later (OHEL, 318) that the terms "Drab" and "Golden" are pejorative and eulogistic can hardly be taken seriously. We need not dispute Lewis's case for an evolution from plain or dull to rich and concrete writing, thence to the elaborate and ingenious style of Shakespeare's last plays or of metaphysical poems. Nor does it follow that he treats "Drab Age" authors unfairly. While disapproving of Ascham's humanist aesthetic, he heartily endorses his advice on teaching and much enjoys his literary persona. He finds Gascoigne a minor poet but an important critic, whose *Certain Notes of Instruction* prompt him to reflect on the common preoccupation of "Drab," "Golden," and metaphysical poets with making artifacts, namely poems, rather than communicating actual experience.

The label "Drab" defeats its purpose in the learned discussion of the Book of Common Prayer. Having pigeonholed Cranmer as an expert compiler of committee reports (OHEL, 194-96), Lewis must resolve the difficulty that Cranmer produced a literary masterpiece in the Drab Age by focusing on the technical problems of translating the Latin liturgy. After showing how Cranmer lowered the emotional temperature of the medieval language, he concludes that the Prayer Book owes much to the "Drabness" of its time, for "Sobriety is the reverse side of Drabness." Faced with the "artistry" of its Latin originals, the book tempers and fortifies them, "as they transfigure it." It indulges no "merely natural" emotions, and "even religious feelings it will not heighten till it has first sobered them." At its best, "it shines with a white light hardly surpassed outside the New Testament" (OHEL, 221).

The tone of the Prayer Book seems akin to that of Lewis's own apologetics, which it clearly influenced. More to our purpose, he equivocates by finding in a work so full of resplendent prose — witness the Litany, Collects, and General Thanksgiving — a sobriety that is the obverse of drabness. Can prose exalted enough to fit his description be in any sense drab?

In this instance the critic and worshiper prevail over the categorizing historian, who draws a withering broadside from Yvor Winters. In Winters's view, Lewis would have done better to employ the sixteenth-century terms "plain" and "sugared" or "eloquent"; but in any case Lewis erred by dealing with the poetry in terms of schools — Petrarchan or metaphysical — rather than singling out the best in every style. Winters even taxes Lewis with having failed to discover "what poetry is" and being incompetent to find "the best poems," which have more in common with each other than with their supposed schools. This illustrates a difference of purpose between the New Critic and the literary historian. Where Winters would have produced and justified a list of the "best" Elizabethan short poems, as a mentor of students Lewis aimed at empowering them to make choices.

Unlike Lewis's condemnation of humanism, the label "Drab" originated in literary experience: reading too much verse in poulter's measure. Just as Lewis the critic treats More's *Utopia* and *Dialogues of Comfort* more sympathetically than Lewis the historian treats More's scholarship, so Lewis rarely reads the "drabbest" verse without sensing where it comes to life.[37] Save for pages on Wyatt (OHEL, 223-30) that Davie, and doubtless Winters, found painfully unappreciative, his willing ear makes him a more reliable critic of minor poets — and of all prose authors — than he sometimes is of major poets in the "Golden" era.

Where Lewis was an authority, as on Spenser and the late medieval Scots, he continues to enlighten us. In areas where he was not, however, as on sonnet sequences by Shakespeare and others, he had to decide whether as historian to provide information and survey previous work, as critic to record personal impressions, as commentator to explain allusions, or as theorist to consider principles of composition. To some extent, the scheme of the Oxford series met his difficulty by requiring a historical chart and annotated bibliography. He could therefore con-

37. See OHEL, 232-35, 244, 260-63, 269-71.

fine his text beyond the introduction to criticism and theory. Though now in need of updating, the bibliography remains a tour de force, and the chart is indispensable for many students now ignorant of European history. While Winters complains of a failure to single out "the best poems" for critical comment, he also concedes that treatment by historical setting and stylistic tendency is inevitable in a literary history. As he says, the place for studies of individual poems is the critical essay rather than an already monumental book.

Reserving Spenser for fuller study in the next chapter, we can now sample Lewis's practical criticism in OHEL from his discussion of Shakespeare's sonnets and his theoretical criticism from comments on Sidney's *Defence of Poesy.* In Lewis's personal copy of the 1926 reprint of Shakespeare's sonnets,[38] he underlined portions of the introduction concerning Shakespeare's reputation in his own time, subsequent attacks, and Johnson's defense. In Lewis's notes in the frontispiece he sorts the sonnets into groups according to addressee, paramount feeling, and/or topic. Thus sonnets 1-17 urge a man to marry and procreate, 18-19 concern perpetuating his memory, and 20-26 record the mutual love of the speaker and his male friend. Lewis's notes here are considerably franker on the man-to-man relationship than is the account in OHEL. Sonnets 43-65 tell how the speaker loves and misses his absent friend. Only sonnets 127-52, under Lewis's briefest heading, concern heterosexual love. The final heading, on imagery in the sonnets, corresponds to numerous underlinings in their texts. Lewis sidelines a number of well-known sonnets that he discusses in OHEL. Beneath a few he cites parallels from other Elizabethan sonnet sequences or from Ovid. Beneath sonnet 107, already heavily marked, he notes internal evidence for a date soon after the death of Queen Elizabeth, and under sonnet 123 evidence for Southampton, rather than Pembroke, as Shakespeare's patron.

Little of this analysis appears in OHEL; nor, as Davie complains, is much included from research available to Lewis on the poet-patron relationship.[39] Lewis did structural analyses of five sonnets in his notes

38. Probably the facsimile edition (London, 1926).
39. Donald Davie, "Entering into the Sixteenth Century," reprinted in Watson, ed., *Critical Thought I,* 206-11.

in the frontispiece (sonnets 12, 18, 30, 33, 66); only three of these (sonnets 66, 18, 33) appear in OHEL, in sentences that correspond exactly to the brackets, numerals, and side-notes of the analyses (OHEL, 507), while the other two figure in the study of key words (OHEL, 502). The best defense against a charge of prudery about Shakespeare's supposedly homosexual love of his patron, which the praise of the sonnets as "Golden" verse at its "highest and purest" might indicate, is that the book's studies of sonnet sequences mark a transition from Lewis's early dislike of biographical inference from a literary work to his eventual preoccupation with various kinds of love. Thus he refuses to treat Sidney's *Astrophel and Stella* as autobiographical, and he points to the unlikeliness of Shakespeare's urging a homosexual partner to marry. Even though some sonnets express a love beyond normal friendship, Lewis claims that the sonnets are unique in being reflections on love itself. The opening of sonnet 144, which he sidelines and briefly mentions (OHEL, 502, 506-7), epitomizes his argument:

> Two loves I have of comfort and despair,
> Which like two spirits do suggest me still:
> The better angel is a man right fair,
> The worser spirit a woman colour'd ill.

The "better" love Lewis sees not as homosexuality, pederasty, or simply friendship but as charity, a spiritual love that wishes the other's good. Having exalted it as early as 1928, in the "Summa," and later in his *Four Loves* (1960), he claims that *agape*, coexisting with love between relatives, spouses, friends, or comrades, will raise such love to its highest power. Here he also finds Shakespeare's contemplative treatment responsible for the "stillness" and universal validity of the sonnets. His argument surely deserves respect on account of the anonymity that has made the sonnets so tantalizing to biographers. Being anonymous, the friendship that comforts the speaker in sonnet 30 comforts any reader. Even the cynical "My mistress' eyes are nothing like the sun" (sonnet 130) has this detachment and anonymity in its gentle ridicule of conventional love-poems: "I never saw a goddess go,/My mistress, when she walks, treads on the ground."

As Shakespeare's sonnets best represent the poetry of the Golden

Age, so Sidney's *Defence* represents its theory. Summarizing Sidney's argument (OHEL, 344-47), Lewis says that drawing directly on Aristotle, the elder Scaliger, and Minturno,[40] and indirectly on other humanists, Neoplatonists, and classical poets, Sidney formulates the code and taste of young noblemen of his time, based upon their common view of life. Above devotional or philosophical poetry, that taste exalts the fictive kind, which can evoke images of a life beyond fallen man's will to attain. Poetry owes its improving effect not to practical teaching or exemplary characters but to its power over the passions that govern human action. Sidney's Christian idealism leads him to prefer heroic poetry (as Northrop Frye would say, Romance) to tragedy, comedy, or satire.[41]

Sharing both Sidney's preference and its religious basis, Lewis naturally sympathizes with the *Defence,* yet he also notes humanistic errors and prejudices, such as a misreading of Aristotle's *Poetics* that underlay the cult of dramatic unities, or disapproval of Spenser's *Shepherd's Calendar* on account of its departure from classical precedent. Stressing the essay's incompatibility with modern tastes and beliefs, he venerates it as the natural outcome of a coherent philosophy and aesthetic that Sidney shared with his peers.

Lewis may have annotated his copy of the Feuillerat edition of Sidney's *Defence of Poesy* as early as 1923, but more probably during the late 1920s, as his headlines summarizing Sidney's arguments resemble the section headings of the "Summa." It was at that time, in all probability, that he borrowed Nichol Smith's copy of *De Poeta Varietiis* (1569) by Antonio Sebastian Minturno, since he recorded its author and date in the Latin names and numerals he then most affected. Some phrases from his frontispiece analysis and running headlines for Sidney's treatise recur in OHEL. This methodical annotation, which, as he told Greeves in 1932, enabled him to enjoy reading dull books, may partly account for his cool commendation of the prose that has charmed so many readers of Sidney's *Defence*. For once, Lewis failed to surrender himself to the text.

40. Julius Caesar Scaliger (1484-1558), *Poetices;* Antonio Sebastiani Minturno, *De Poeta Varietiis* (1469). See OHEL, 19, 343.
41. Northrop Frye, *The Anatomy of Criticism.*

The Discarded Image

In 1962, Lewis told Sayer he was "making a book out of" his "Prolegomenon to Medieval Studies," the lectures at Oxford in the 1930s that guaranteed him capacity audiences. He also used his parallel "Prolegomenon to Renaissance Studies." The combined courses did not fill lecture rooms at Cambridge, for, as he explained, "People in Cambridge can't stand a great deal of that sort of thing."[42] He decided, therefore, to make the book "a good deal shorter" than the lecture series. Paradoxically, the benefits of compression made A. N. Wilson wish it a good deal longer.[43] Lewis did not live to see *The Discarded Image* published, yet in completing it he triumphed over ill health.

The subtitle, *An Introduction to Medieval and Renaissance Literature,* suggests a continued denial that the Renaissance represented a new civilization. In condensing the lectures into a book, Lewis chose not to discuss Tillyard's *Elizabethan World Picture* and A. O. Lovejoy's *Great Chain of Being.*[44]

Ian Robinson's attack on *The Discarded Image* shows why Lewis felt the climate at Cambridge so unsympathetic to historical criticism. Robinson finds "three quite different aims" in the book: to supply a "mass of background knowledge" of which parts will "rise temporarily into the foreground"; to supply a "map" for consultation before rather than during a reading of literary texts; and to assure the reader of having "understood a medieval poem by seeing it as its original audience saw it." The last, he claimed, "we can simply never do" since the "original audience" is as much a construct of the modern imagination as the poem itself.[45] Lewis's "decisive fallacy," according to Robinson, is to think it possible to construct any "map" save by reading poems and relating them to each other.[46] The same critic has since questioned the whole notion of a "world picture" shared by original readers,[47] alluding

---

42. Sayer, *Jack,* 246.
43. A. N. Wilson, *C. S. Lewis: A Biography,* 151.
44. Both titles are included in OHEL's bibliography.
45. Ian Robinson, *Chaucer and the English Tradition,* 269.
46. Robinson, *Chaucer and the English Tradition,* 267.
47. Robinson, unpublished essay (1980) in my possession.

to background-and-period expositions by scholars such as Tillyard, Lovejoy, and Basil Willey.

The attack on Tillyard's book, in particular, has been taken up by a number of New Historicists on the ground that in identifying the social structure with a "collective mind," derived from a "notion of unchanging, universal human nature," Tillyard objectified a historical construct of the ruling class.[48]

In an early review of *The Discarded Image,* John Burrow distinguished between Northrop Frye's view of cosmologies as purely literary constructions, or fantasies, and Lewis's account of the Model as both beautiful and, to medieval scholars, factually true.[49] John Holloway points out that in representing its supersession as pure loss, Lewis does less than justice to the "bleak integrity" of science.[50] When Lewis first gave his "Prolegomena" lectures at Oxford he led academic fashion, but by the time he was completing *The Discarded Image* he trailed behind it. Noting that (in 1980) "Lewis still has his disciples," Alice Kaminsky implies that, even in medieval studies, old historical criticism is in retreat.[51] To swim against the tide being Lewis's favorite exercise, any judgment must be a matter of opinion.

The basis of Robinson's criticism is that reading always takes place in present time — that by trying to adopt a medieval viewpoint Lewis overlooked what was universal in the texts in question. In his *Preface to "Paradise Lost"* Lewis calls this the "Doctrine of the Unchanging Human Heart," in which he disbelieved, as do the New Historicists.[52] Nowhere in *The Discarded Image* does he claim that all medieval people subscribed to or even knew of the medieval cosmic "Model." Philosophers tried to account for observed phenomena, theologians strove to settle questions concerning God and man, devotional writers attempted to expound the spiritual life, peasants worked to till their fields. The

48. Victor Shea, "New Historicism," in Irena R. Makaryk, ed., *Encyclopedia of Contemporary Literary Theory,* 131.

49. John Burrow, "The Model Universe," reprinted in Watson, ed., *Critical Thought I,* 223-27.

50. John Holloway, "Grand Design," reprinted in Watson, ed., *Critical Thought I,* 228-30.

51. Alice Kaminsky, *Chaucer's "Troilus and Criseyde" and the Critics,* 198.

52. Lewis, *Preface to "Paradise Lost,"* chap. 9.

Model chiefly delighted artists and poets, hence Donaldson could charge Lewis with treating evidence from literary texts as objectively valid. A compound of Neoplatonic and Christian ideas, the Model combined Ptolemy's planetary system with a structure of parallel hierarchies: angelic, biological, social, and psychological. Above, the concentric spheres of the seven planets surrounded the Primum Mobile. Beyond these sang the nine choirs of angelic beings defined by Pseudo-Dionysius, and beyond them was God. Below, the natural order consisted of mineral substances endowed with mere existence, plants endowed with the capacity for growth and reproduction, animals endowed also with passions, and man endowed also with reason. The social order of kings, nobles, and populace reflected the angelic, as did the psychological triad of body, soul, and spirit.

The Model formed the basis of so many medieval poems insofar as it was a literary and artistic construct. Lewis inferred it not only from Boethius's *Consolation* and the *Celestial Hierarchies* of Pseudo-Dionysius but also from poems by Dante, Chaucer, and others based on the "Dream of Scipio" in Cicero's *Republic,* and poems by Lucan, Statius, and other Romans. To argue that Lewis imposed his scheme upon poems better understood without it is beside the point: he read it not into but out of medieval poems and their classical sources. The scheme's chief value to the present-day reader is in illuminating features of medieval and Renaissance texts that may seem obscure or superfluous, such as planetary influences that in *Troilus and Criseyde* or the *Knight's Tale* typify pagan deities.

As an additional benefit, the Model, which in Lewis's view endured until at least 1700, sheds light on the psychological terminology of Prince Hamlet, on Shakespeare's assumptions concerning royal and paternal authority, and on the behavior of fairies and lovers in the *Midsummer Night's Dream.* Lewis may have overstated his case, for had paternal authority remained beyond dispute, the right of the young to choose their mates could hardly be a major issue in that comedy or in the Robin Hood ballads. If critics sometimes misuse the Model by projecting upon the audiences of Chaucer and Shakespeare a too-uniform disapproval of Troilus or Falstaff, the fault does not lie with Lewis, who offered it only as an aid to exegesis. *The Discarded Image* helps readers understand sizeable portions of medieval and Renaissance texts that they might otherwise overlook or misread.

One shortcoming, the book's evasiveness concerning cultural evolution, was characteristic of Lewis. Barfield's "abiding impression is that the very notion of *development* of any sort was somehow alien to Lewis's mind."[53] Lewis's statement "In modern, that is, evolutionary thought Man stands at the top of a stair whose foot is lost in obscurity; in this [the Model], he stands at the bottom of a stair whose top is invisible with light"[54] is as undeniably logical as it is irresistibly eloquent. A remark by Boethius to the effect that "all perfect things are prior to all imperfect things" (cited in *Discarded Image,* 85) deepens the contrast between the doctrines of creation and evolution. In his epilogue, Lewis explains what is familiar to any student of Romanticism, the imagery of progressive change in authors from Goethe to Keats and its parallel in philosophers of the Enlightenment, as the ambience in which Darwin developed his theory. But to add that "when changes in the human mind produce a sufficient disrelish of the old Model" another "will obediently turn up" (*Discarded Image,* 221) is to brush off not only biological and geological evidence for evolution, but the very notions of scientific research and testing.

Less obviously, when exposing the naivete of Swinburne's picture of a fourth-century world "grown grey" from Christian asceticism, Lewis contradicts himself. Ascetism and mysticism, he says, were common to pagan and Christian alike. "It was the spirit of the age" (*Discarded Image,* 47). Whether he took this from his old lecture notes or wrote it afresh in 1962, in OHEL (64) he had denied the validity of *Zeitgeists.* Yet their validity is implicit in the book's very title and subject matter, which refer to an "image" or representation conventional at a particular time, but since "discarded."

A bookman to his core, Lewis describes images of Fortune's wheel from reproductions in a book translated in 1953.[55] Yet his exposition of the medieval Model lives most gloriously when from his vast reading

---

53. Owen Barfield, "C. S. Lewis and Historicism," n. 2, reprinted in *Owen Barfield on C. S. Lewis,* 67-81. Lewis's evasiveness with regard to evolution is noted in Christopher, *C. S. Lewis,* 36.

54. Lewis, *Discarded Image,* 74-75. Subsequent references will be given parenthetically in the text.

55. J. Seznec, *The Survival of the Pagan Gods.* See *Discarded Image,* 87n.

he constructs a visual image of the sky as beheld by imaginative viewers. The medieval cosmos, being finite, has a "perfect spherical shape, containing within itself an ordered variety." To behold "the night sky with modern eyes is like looking out over a sea that fades away into mist, or looking about one in a trackless forest — trees forever and no horizon. To look up at the towering medieval universe is much more like looking up at a great building." Because we find space confusing or terrifying where our forebears found it "overwhelming in its greatness but satisfying in its harmony . . . our universe is romantic, and theirs was classical" (*Discarded Image,* 99). In *Out of the Silent Planet* (1938), conceivably written in the same decade as the originating lecture of this passage, Lewis describes the hero's voyage to another planet not in architectural terms but with the same awe mingled with at-homeness. Though incomprehensibly vast, the heavens teem with life.

Cross-references can be made to other works as well as to the space trilogy. When looking up with Pseudo-Dionysius at the angelic hierarchies above man, Lewis appears scornful of Milton's angels for having "too much anatomy and too much armour," like the gods of Homer and Virgil (*Discarded Image,* 75). Neoclassicism has come between the Model and the postmedieval poet. In the fifteenth chapter of *A Preface to "Paradise Lost,"* however, he treats the bodily forms and appetites of the angels as acceptable, even inevitable, given Milton's Renaissance Platonism. Here it looks as though Lewis revised his opinion after writing the opening chapter of OHEL. In many places, as in explaining the mathematical basis of the Copernican theory, the church's stand against astrological determinism, and planet worship (*Discarded Image,* 103-4), the *Discarded Image* bears out OHEL. It does not always bear out the *Allegory of Love,* for Lewis admits having mistakenly attributed the frequent reiterations of planetary characteristics to the paucity of books, rather than, as he now thinks, to the pleasure of recognizing common knowledge. Lewis perhaps indulges the pleasure of recognition in tracing back the Boethian image of Philosophy as a woman young yet old (*Discarded Image,* 80), like H. Rider Haggard's Ayesha.

What awes one about the *Discarded Image* is the ease with which Lewis passes from demonstrating the ordered immensity of the medieval cosmos, noted from Isidore and Alanus, to tracing our image of the cosmos as a "shoreless sea" in Pascal and Milton, to explaining anomalies in Chaucer's or Dante's aerial vision of earth as due to the medieval artist's lack of perspective. His distillation of the medieval cosmos from his literary travels exhilarates by its breadth and scope. What he expounds in the lectures, he imagines in Ransom's voyage through the night sky. In historical imagination, as in his power to hold his readers, Lewis rises above any number of subsequent scholars who might now see his inaccuracies or know facts and sources unknown in his time.

CHAPTER 3

Practical Critic

TO DO JUSTICE to all of Lewis's criticism would require a separate book. A chapter permits only some indication of its range and a look at his studies of Spenser and Milton and their subsequent reception. The bibliography in *C. S. Lewis at the Breakfast Table* lists ten critical books, thirty-one articles, and forty reviews, together with three collections of essays on literary topics.[1] Of his ten introductions or afterwords to books by others, about half concern literary topics. The twenty-two essays in Walter Hooper's selection include three on medieval and five on Renaissance topics, four on Romantics and Victorians, one each on Bunyan, Addison, and Jane Austen, and six on matters of literary history or theory.[2]

1. The books are items numbered 4, 7, 10, 14, 19, 27, 34, 37, 41, 48; the articles are items numbered 4, 5, 7, 8, 9, 11, 19, 24, 25, 57, 70, 72, 80, 82, 84, 86, 88, 89, 91, 101, 104, 119, 122, 123, 125, 127, 130, 138, 139; the compilations are *Rehabilitations and Other Essays* (1939), *They Asked for a Paper* (1962), and the posthumous *Studies in Medieval and Renaissance Literature* (1966) and *Selected Literary Essays* (1969), both edited by W. Hooper.

2. "The Alliterative Metre," "What Chaucer Really Did to *Il Filostrato*," and "The Fifteenth-Century Heroic Line" are on medieval topics. "Hero and Leander," "Variation in Shakespeare and Others," "*Hamlet:* The Prince or the Poem," "Donne and Love Poetry in the Seventeenth Century," and "The Literary Impact of the Authorized Version" concern Renaissance subjects. (There are also seven essays on medieval and six essays on Renaissance topics in *Studies in Medieval and Renaissance Literature*.) Essays on Romantics and Victorians include "Shelley, Dryden and Mr

As significant as their range is their chronology. Between 1932 and 1939 Lewis published the *Allegory of Love, The Personal Heresy* (with E. M. W. Tillyard), *Rehabilitations and Other Essays,* and six articles. His other publications in these years consist of *The Pilgrim's Regress, Out of the Silent Planet,* and essays for university or college magazines. During the war he turned to religion and fiction, his critical work consisting of invited lectures on *Paradise Lost* and *Hamlet.* Among established academics this is not uncommon, but Lewis was unusual in continuing to write on religious or moral rather than literary themes. As will be shown in Chapter 8, though he still produced academic books, the subjects of his invited essays reflect his religious conversion.

Of the remaining critical books, *An Experiment in Criticism* and *Studies in Words* will be considered in the next chapter, and *The Abolition of Man* partly there and partly in conjunction with *That Hideous Strength.*

The Faerie Queene

Lewis's criticism of this poem should have worn better than that of *Paradise Lost,* since it represents an engagement that continued throughout his career, rather than a final conviction reached early on. Over thirty years, his view of the poem underwent a considerable change. To observe this is not to fault him for inconsistency but to praise him for honestly recording his maturing response. In particular, he moved from expounding the poem's structure in purely literary terms to expounding it in terms equally applicable to literature, the visual arts, and sixteenth-century popular culture. He also came to distinguish between the viewpoints of its characters and those of its implied readers.

From the "Prolegomena" lectures Lewis fashioned the chapter on Spenser in the *Allegory of Love;* from the Cambridge lecture notes Alastair Fowler completed the posthumous *Spenser's Images of Life*

Eliot," [Toast to] "The Memory of Sir Walter Scott," "William Morris," and "Kipling's World." Writings on literary history and theory include "De descriptione temporum," "Bluspels and Flalansferes: A Semantic Nightmare," "High and Low Brows," "Metre," "Psycho-Analysis and Literary Criticism," and "The Anthropological Approach."

(1967); in between came OHEL, three essays, and a review. Since each served a different purpose, a line of development is not easily traced.

In the *Allegory of Love,* Lewis is concerned with the poem's genre and supersession of courtly by spousal love. Thus he treats the procession of Deadly Sins as medieval allegory, although in *Spenser's Images* he treats it as pageant. He also details motifs and devices derived from Italian epics and those owed to English folklore and Spenser's own temperament. At this point in the poem's critical history, Lewis felt it essential to expound the structure of each book as a kernel of allegory surrounded by romances with types as characters and by some merely fictional episodes. He saw the Cantos on Mutability as allegorical kernels unsurrounded, and Arthur's quest for Gloriana as part both of the poem's "continuing allegory" and of the surrounding romances.

Later expositions by Lewis show improvement or extension rather than fundamental change. In "Tasso" he infers from the intricacy of medieval art that Spenser expected readers to recall the Bower of Bliss while in the Garden of Adonis. Having first seen the Bower as a place of sterile titillation and the Garden as a place of natural fertility (*Allegory of Love,* 326), he cites Tolkien for the view that industrialism has conditioned us to think of beauty and evil as mutually exclusive.[3]

In OHEL Lewis admits having undervalued the poem's structural innovation, its unique polyphony of stories. He expounds the structure of each book while claiming that Spenser intended to create an illusory impression of "pathless wandering" (381), a phrase conceivably suggested by MacDonald's hero Anodos. Though conceding that particular stories lack direction, he completes the revaluation begun by his dismissal of the traditional view that Spenser was primarily a stylist, or "poet's poet" (*Allegory of Love,* 317), by extolling the structure of the *Faerie Queene* as its greatest strength.

It is not easy to draw a line between the "political" interpretation Lewis eschews and the historical information he supplies. He conjectures (OHEL, 356, 382) that Spenser modeled his Arthur upon the hero not of Malory's *Morte d'Arthur* but on the hero of *Arthur of Little Britain,* and that Spenser called him "Prince" after the son of Henry

3. Lewis, *Studies in Medieval and Renaissance Literature,* 116-18.

VII. At this point he asserts what in *Spenser's Images* he denies, that Arthur represents the Aristotelian virtue of Magnanimity. "Allegorically, we are told, he is Magnificence," which "means Aristotle's Magnanimity" (OHEL, 382). As Jan Kouenhoven points out in the most substantial attack on Lewis's criticism of the *Faerie Queene,* Lewis here substitutes for *megaloprepeia,* or "magnificence" in the sense of public benefaction, the quite distinct virtue of *megalopsychia,* or high-mindedness as opposed to pettiness or self-seeking.[4]

More characteristically, Lewis views Gloriana as both a type of the divine glory and a compliment to Queen Elizabeth. Rather than infer her characteristics from those of the Queen, he infers the nature of the compliment from the fictional traits. Arthur's quest for Gloriana he explains platonically as that of the soul for a perfection beyond this world. Syncretism being typical of Spenser's age, Lewis finds traces of other current ideologies, from occultism to Calvinism. Here he merely touches on what in *Spenser's Images* was to become his main theme: the centrality in the poem of pageantry and iconography.

In a 1941 essay for sixth-form students (grades 11 to 12 in the U.S.), Lewis associates the poem with folk-romances, morality plays, the *Morte d'Arthur,* and *Pilgrim's Progress* as likely to reward the simple, receptive reading of an adolescent.[5] Even in OHEL, he insists that, for readers willing to immerse themselves in the story, Spenser has supplied all the guidance they need (388). This seems at odds with the pessimistic conclusion (393) that, Spenser's world having passed away, so may "his fame," and also with his admission at the outset of *Spenser's Images* that he now thinks the poem "perhaps the most difficult . . . in English," because it requires from its reader both simplicity and sophistication (1). Its incompleteness he now sees as fatal to its being read simply as interwoven stories. Conversely, modern readers are ill-equipped to appreciate its sophisticated blend of pageant, masque, mythography, emblem, and iconography. Lewis mentioned these forgotten arts in OHEL, but in these final lectures he approaches the *Faerie Queene*

---

4. Jan Carel Kouenhoven, *Allegory as Metaphor: The Organization of the "Faerie Queene,"* 12-13. For Greek terms, see Aristotle, *Nichomachean Ethics,* IV, ii, iii.

5. Lewis, "On Reading 'The Faerie Queene,'" reprinted in *Studies in Medieval and Renaissance Literature,* 146-48.

much as D. W. Robertson, Jr., does the *Canterbury Tales*.[6] One footnote in the portion completed before his death, on the "False Cupid," expounds the five arrows in Robertsonian vein as "Beauty, Simplicity, Courtesy, Companionship and Fair Seeming" (*Spenser's Images,* 18-19). Unlike Robertson, however, he neither neglects the poetic texture nor assumes an original readership conditioned by ascetic theology. Moreover, the *Faerie Queene* is explicitly allegorical.

While his conclusions about Spenser's living images, or tableaux, usually take further the insights of the *Allegory* or OHEL, he switches his focus from the structure of narrative and allegory to the representation of life through statues, temples, gardens, tableaux, and ritual. Thus to explain the choice of "massy gold" for the statue of Cupid, he cites an earlier allusion to its sinister significance when arguing that Cupid is an idol that for a time misled Britomart in her quest for "chaste," that is spousal, love. From the unbinding of the Cupid-statue's eyes to watch Amoret being tortured, he infers Cupid's enmity to the marital affection signified by her marriage to Scudamour. The wounded dragon under the statue signifies that Cupid imperils the female chastity that dragons guard in myths such as the "Garden of the Hesperides." The arrows signify the adulterous desire treated by Ovid and the poets of courtly love (*Spenser's Images,* 18-27). Here again he comes close to Robertson's way of expounding Chaucer, but with regard to an admittedly allegorical text.

Lewis sees antitypes to Cupid in the embrace of Amoret and Scudamour (which originally concluded Book III), in the Temples of Venus and Diana (IV, x), and in the figures of Belphoebe and Amoret. Discussing the Temple, he expounds from III, vi, how after their reconciliation Venus and Diana jointly fostered Belphoebe and Amoret and so discovered that Sol had begotten both upon the virgin Chrysogonee (i.e., "Goldbirth"). Like the goddesses, the sisters present two apparently conflicting aspects of woman, the chaste huntress and the future wife (*Spenser's Images,* 48-50).

The opposition between the Bower of Bliss and its antitype, the Garden of Adonis, forms part of a larger one between localities typifying good and evil. Responding, perhaps, to being taxed with insensitivity to the Bower's beauty, he finds there an art that simulates with intent

6. D. W. Robertson, Jr., *A Preface to Chaucer.*

to deceive, while he sees in the Garden nature and love themselves (*Spenser's Images,* 36-51). Expounding Spenser's mythography, he finds in the Garden the earthly Venus giving form to Adonis, who represents "matter" (51-52). Thus the Garden signifies cosmic creation as described by the Neoplatonist Ficino, in which the heavenly Venus gives form to Nature. Places representing evil are either titillating but barren, like the Bower, or else solemn and empty, like the House of Busirane; those representing good are fertile, cheerful, and full of lovers. In Spenser, energy is never the attribute of evil, which can provoke, imitate, or, as with Pyrochles, merely fume, but can never beget or create. Spenser otherwise represents evil in ravenous warriors, figures diseased, deformed, or hideous, and empty caves or houses, whether derelict or sumptuous. Beyond the central characters, Spenser represents good in simple folk or even in beasts like Una's dwarf and ass. In the dance of the Graces on Mount Acidale, he shows spontaneity and order as two complementary aspects of good. The poem's many tyrants exemplify the abuse of order, and some figures represent bestial disorder.

Without using two terms that have never caught on among literary critics, Lewis applies Alexander's distinction between the "enjoyed" and the "contemplated" as developed in the "Great War."[7] Once the naked dancers on Mount Acidale know themselves observed by Sir Calidore, they vanish. In his "Summa" (I, vii), Lewis argued that whenever Shakespeare looked up from his manuscript, Hamlet ceased to exist. The characters could enjoy (i.e., experience) themselves but could contemplate (observe) only each other. Only the author could both enjoy each speaker in turn and contemplate the entire court. After distinguishing five figures of evil in the *Faerie Queene,* Lewis remarks that any of them might tempt a character to sleep or die. In narrative portions, however, readers observe each tempter as a being of the specified kind (*Spenser's Images,* 73). In other words, the character enjoys (experiences) the temptation while the reader contemplates the tempter. Similarly, the character beholding a pageant finds it incomprehensible while the reader needs no explanation. So Spenser expresses his belief that in this world we see things "not truly but in equivocal shapes" (82). The Red Cross Knight merely sees seven figures in procession; the reader sees the whole realm under sin

7. Samuel Alexander, *Space, Time and Deity.*

and the Knight imprisoned by the pride he enjoys. The Knight follows his Dwarf out of a corpse-strewn cell; the reader sees him leave a world enthralled to sin and the Devil (29-30). The distinction resembles that which any theorist might draw between the character's restricted view and the reader's more informed one.

Lewis rejoins to critics of Spenser's "Faceless Knights" that the romance genre demands flat characters, since the inner self that a realistic novelist might disclose via reported thoughts must appear in the events. Florimell's fear and confusion appear in her flight and subjection to Proteus. A middle ground between the flat characters of romance or fantasy and the rounded ones of realistic fiction appears in Britomart's dream of the Church of Isis, which Lewis explains as her means of recognizing her role. As Isis she must temper the severe justice of Osiris — that is, Artegall — with mercy and "equity" (*Spenser's Images*, 99-104).

Lewis exemplifies the historical critic who employs his learning to elucidate and place a literary text within its period and genre. To this day, most Spenserian scholars echo the praise of Lewis by Graham Hough, who found in the *Allegory of Love* "my first real guide to the reading" of the *Faerie Queene,* or that of Paul Alpers, who calls Lewis "the most influential modern critic of Spenser."[8] What has survived best is Lewis's account of Gloriana, about whom few critics have much to say. Least immune to attack has been his distinction between allegory and symbolism, which A. D. Nuttall criticized in *Two Concepts of Allegory.* Five years before Nuttall, though more sympathetically, Hough questioned this distinction, finding symbolism compatible only with belief in some transcendent reality, but allegory equally compatible with belief or unbelief.

Lewis's most celebrated contrast has been that between the Bower and the Garden. Rosemary Freeman found his distinction between nature and art too simple, for elsewhere in the poem Spenser "demonstrates the power of art to take over . . . where nature left off."[9] Hough

---

8. Graham Hough, *A Preface to "The Faerie Queene,"* 6; Paul Alpers, "The Rhetorical Mode of Spenser's Narrative," in Peter Bayley, ed., *Spenser, "The Faerie Queene": A Casebook,* esp. 128.

9. Rosemary Freeman, *"The Faerie Queene": A Companion for Readers,* 174.

thought the soundest feature of Lewis's contrast in the *Allegory of Love* that between sterile sexuality in the Bower and generative Nature in the Garden and the Temple of Venus.

Hough differs from Lewis on some points — for example, rejecting Lewis's division of the poem into "Fragment A" (I–III) and "Fragment B" (IV–VI). But so far the only critic to have totally rejected Lewis's readings has been Jan Karel Kouwenhoven, who expounds the poem as allegory pure and simple; she sees the poem as only apparently a narrative and not at all about characters, as in Shakespeare or Homer. Compared with Robertson on the *Canterbury Tales,* she supports her case with far more detail from the text.

Though I have neither the space nor the expertise to consider all of Kouwenhoven's eighteen objections to Lewis's view, her first, that in saying the poetry taps "sources not easily accessible to discursive thought" Lewis implies by "ironic circumlocution" that it is "silly beyond description,"[10] seems merely tendentious. Some half-dozen, however, do expose limitations in Lewis. One such limitation is a "blind faith in the ways of romance" (Kouwenhoven, 4) evident in his claim that structural defects need deter only readers averse to romance. Lewis, she contends, reads the poem "rhetorically" as carefully planned, yet also "Romantically" as an organic growth, in order to explain supposed misstatements in Spenser's Letter to Raleigh. That document in no way suggests a "writer fumbling for safe generalizations". (6-7). Kouwenhoven also questions whether Lewis's "anachronistic" picture of the poem as by "an inspired *vates*" has any sounder foundation than his "animus against humanist poetics" (6-7). This parallels the Robertsonian charge against Lewis, of "Romantic" misreading of Chaucer.

Without calling Lewis dishonest, she passes on to the grave charge mentioned earlier, concerning his interpretation of Prince Arthur's "Magnificence" in the Letter as synonymous with "Magnanimity" or pride. To be valid, Aristotle's

> alleged catch-all ought to derive its content from virtues . . . similar to the poet's. It does not, as Lewis is well aware. He has precipitated

10. Kouwenhoven, *Apparent Narrative as Thematic Metaphor,* 4.

his "sympathetic" reading of the Letter on the assumption that it
need not significantly fit the poem. (Kouwenhoven, 12-13)

Moreover, Lewis, being "much given to high-handed solutions," mis-
interprets the Prince's attraction to Florimell as indicating that she is
an aspect of Gloriana. By using the first-person plural, Lewis "aligns
the reader with Arthur; hinting that we, too, are committed to a
perpetual search for a 'Faerie Queene,' during which we are to catch
only tantalizing glimpses of glory" (Kouwenhoven, 19).

Had Lewis lived to read this, he would presumably have responded
that *megalopsychia* epitomized the virtues of a great man, such as Aristotle had in mind. By the same token, however, the Christian ideal of
saintliness rules out pretensions to greatness, for humility, condemned
by Aristotle, is among its principal virtues. So unless Spenser was trying
at once to picture a Renaissance prince and a Christian saint, a matter
Lewis failed to consider, Kouwenhoven's charge appears valid. It is
otherwise with her attack on Lewis's use of the lecturer's "we," a man-
nerism deserving a rebuke but hardly a witch hunt.

Two further charges raise issues concerning Lewis's critical position
and stature. The first is that, having unsoundly assumed continuing
general belief in courtly love, as medieval practice and literary theme,
he then "by sleight of hand" (Kouwenhoven, 99) incorporates wedded
love into his definition of chastity and makes its supersession of courtly
love the theme of the *Faerie Queene*. Here, surely, Lewis can at worst
be charged with anachronism in applying to Spenser's poem Milton's
praise of wedded love in *Paradise Lost*.[11]

That Lewis misread the *Roman de la Rose* was, as we have seen,
the contention of Fleming. But Kouenhoven uses the charge to question
Lewis's reading of the *Roman* as presenting "by means of personifications" the love story of the Dreamer and his Lady. Rightly noting that
when the personifications were present, the characters were absent, since
the Lady and her Pride could not walk the same stage, he should have
seen that "the stage will not support a lover either." Lewis also "perfectly
well" realized "that not all the personifications qualify as moods of lover
and lady," and so he "ought to have questioned his conception of

---

11. *Paradise Lost*, IV, 750-70.

Guillaume [de Lorris]'s mode" rather than that poet's "execution" (Kouwenhoven, 120). Though tangential to Spenserian scholarship, her charge that Lewis ignored contrary evidence must be taken seriously. If asked how she can know what Lewis "perfectly well" saw, she could reply that what is obvious to her should have been obvious to Lewis, and so question his critical competence. However, since she does not indicate which personifications Lewis ought to have found inapplicable to the moods of lovers, or her grounds for saying he knowingly disregarded them, one must suspend judgment.

The other part of this charge is that by "contrasting the natural sex of the Garden with what he sees as its artificial perversion in the Bower," Lewis "equates it with chastity by sleight of hand. Sex does become chaste through marriage," which, however, "is not a natural relationship but a divine institution" (Kouwenhoven, 99). Married love, adds Kouwenhoven, "cannot plausibly be treated as courtly love dialectically *aufgehoven* [elevated]" (181).

The gratified desire of spousal love and sublimated desire of courtly love certainly appear different in kind, but as a Platonist the author of *The Four Loves* might conceivably reply that, whether physically fulfilled or not, the nearer love approaches perfection the more it includes of *agape*, a selfless willing of the other's good. Even so, courtly love as Lewis describes it precludes the daily give-and-take of married life to which he applies the Greek term *storge*,[12] for familial or comradely affection.

Kouwenhoven also disputes Lewis's assertion that the characters experience but do not understand the "wonders, beauties and terrors" of their world, while the reader both enjoys and contemplates their experience, retorting that "Spenser's characters do not have points of view of their own. It is just not true" that the reader sees through Britomart's eyes.

> The poet describes [erotic images] directly, dropping Britomart altogether. . . . There is only one point of view, the reader's. . . . The poem addresses us as sick unto death, caught in original sin. Yet for all his [imagined] affinity with Spenser, it is Lewis who impedes a

12. Lewis, *The Four Loves*, 33.

unifying response, by childishly relishing the marvels of romance for their own sake and thus playing off the fiction against the meaning. (Kouwenhoven, 93-94)

The word "childishly" highlights the kernel of this charge, the immaturity of clinging to the earliest experience of the *Faerie Queene* as a series of wondrous tales. Though not borne out by *Spenser's Images*, with its premise that the poem must be read at once simply and with sophistication, the charge echoes W. W. Robson's assessment of Lewis's criticism as limited by immaturity.[13] In the main, the immature Lewis may be identified with the Dreamer, the mature with the Mentor; yet all perceptive criticism requires imagination as well as rationality and experience.

Kouwenhoven appears to oversimplify the process of composition. To the poststructuralist critic, as to Lewis, there need be nothing improbable about a tension within Spenser between the Puritan allegorist and the fantasist, or even the political propagandist. Like Robertson on Chaucer, she reduces a multivocal poet to a univocal one. Her attack, however, brings into question Lewis's hitherto unchallenged preeminence among interpreters of the *Faerie Queene*. Neither his work (as he ruefully acknowledged) nor hers appears likely to rescue Spenser from the position of scholar's poet to which twentieth-century criticism has consigned him.

Paradise Lost

In his Ballard Matthews lectures given at the University of Wales in 1941 and published as *A Preface to "Paradise Lost,"* Lewis argued that Milton relates the fall of the rebel angels and of humankind according to the central Christian tradition, in a poem that exemplifies "secondary epic" and therefore requires a weighty, hierophantic style, as in Virgil's *Aeneid.* Fallen through injured pride, Satan tempts Eve while disguised as a serpent, then by divine fiat dwindles into one when about to "relate his triumph" to his cohorts. Adam and Eve, no savages but king and

13. W. W. Robson, "C. S. Lewis," *Cambridge Quarterly* 1 (1966).

queen of Paradise, commit the primal sin of disobedience through her pride and his excess of spousal love.

During the past half-century, Lewis's main and subsidiary contentions, which underlie his *Screwtape Letters* (1942), *Perelandra* (1943), and *That Hideous Strength* (1945), have been attacked, defended, and in part discredited. Among Miltonists, his criticism of the poem's style enjoys more respect than that of its theology and characterization.

In the lectures, for the substance of which Lewis drew heavily upon some wartime lectures at Oxford by Charles Williams,[14] he attempted to remove impediments to the poem's appreciation by twentieth-century students. Chief among these were an empathy with Satan under "Romantic" influence and attacks on the poem's "grand" style by Eliot and Leavis.

The chapter refuting Eliot's contention that the style was best judged by a poet lost its point in 1947, when Eliot modified his aspersions on Milton's language.[15] In *Revaluation* (1936) Leavis had contended that for all the "magnificent invention" of the opening books, "we feel" a growing "dissatisfaction" with the "routine gesture" and "heavy fall" of the verse, yet eventually yield to the ritual's "inescapable monotony."[16] With exceptions, such as the account of Mulciber's fall, Leavis finds the style so apt to call attention to itself, so remote from "any English that was ever spoken," as to suggest an impoverished sensibility (Leavis, 51). This "defect of intelligence" and "of imagination" is accompanied by a "dominating sense of righteousness" and "incapacity to question or explore its significance." The poem's "moral passion" owed too much to "innocence — a guileless unawareness of the subtleties of egoism — to be an apt agent for projecting an ordered whole of experience" (Leavis, 58). Leavis must have further exasperated Lewis by tracing Milton's poetic defects to his early imitation of Spenser (Leavis, 56).

14. Williams complained of unacknowledged borrowing in a letter now included in the Wade Collection.

15. In T. S. Eliot's 1947 Henrietta Hertz Lecture to British Academy, reprinted as "Milton II," in Eliot, *On Poetry and Poets*. Cf. "Milton I" (1936) in the same volume. Eliot now regarded Milton as having an adverse influence on eighteenth-century rather than on modern poets.

16. F. R. Leavis, *Revaluation*, 43-44.

Lewis rejoined that the poem was being criticized for its intended and proper solemnity. Milton had endeavored "to enchant us," yet his critics complained that the poem "sounds like an incantation."[17] Satan's address to his countless followers was condemned for sounding like an oration. Leavis and he were agreed on "the properties of Milton's epic verse," which Leavis well described, but "he sees and hates the very same that I see and love" (*Preface,* 130). Even this polite response drew a surprising amount of discussion, yet Lewis saved his sting for his three concluding paragraphs. In the first, he compared critics disliking Milton's "civil" style to barbarians shut out of China by the Great Wall. In the second, he described "more respectable" readers too accustomed to realism to accept "passions organized into sentiments." These he answered by pointing to the selectiveness inherent even in stream-of-consciousness novels such as those of Joyce. In the third, he extended the Great Wall analogy by likening Eliot to an ascetic gone forth into the desert, who condemns richness only to invite license in the next generation.

Though excluding both Leavis and Eliot from the "contemptible class" of barbarians, Lewis had fired the first shot in his war with the Leavisites. Leavis himself did not retaliate, and in fact he charmed Lewis by welcoming him to Cambridge in 1955. This was the year after Lewis had attacked the sixteenth-century humanists, whom Leavis had also condemned in his essay on Milton. Both insisted upon personal encounter with a text, rather than judgment by reputation. Lewis valued music, ritual, and fantasy, while Leavis prized immediacy and fidelity to experience.

An arbitrary division of books discussing the *Preface* into those published before and since 1970 reveals a shift in the focal points of attack and defense. The chapters on the rebel angels and Adam and Eve soon came under attack from A. J. A. Waldock in 1947. Disputing Lewis's contention that pure evil is easier to depict than pure good, Waldock thought either extreme equally difficult to embody.[18] The issue of Satan's character was taken up in 1960 by John Peter, who objected to Lewis's making theological points by wrenching incidents from their poetic

17. Lewis, *Preface to Paradise Lost,* 130. Hereafter cited as *Preface.*
18. A. J. A. Waldock, *"Paradise Lost" and Its Critics,* 72-75.

contexts.[19] In defense of a celebrated "Romantic" reading, William Empson (1961) denied that by approving Satan's sense of injured merit Shelley endorsed immorality or anarchy.[20] The ensuing debate led to a gain in understanding, for in 1962 Davis Harding traced the reader's sympathy to support for the underdog, the "seductive" poetry allotted to Satan, and, above all, the fact that Satan's viewpoint is the predominant one in the opening books.[21] Stanley Fish in 1967 saw the "speciousness of Satan's rhetoric" as detectable only by hindsight.[22] But Lewis's principal defender was John Steadman. In his 1976 book he envisaged Satan as at once absurd, heroic, and the traditional "father of lies," using rhetoric conformable to Renaissance critical doctrine.[23]

Lewis's standing as a Miltonist was questioned more profoundly by attacks on his view of Adam and Eve. Waldock taxed him with denying the reader's impressions, which are "the facts of the poem" (Waldock, 26). Eve fell, Waldock says, by disobedience, not pride, as Augustine taught. Adam ate the forbidden fruit out of love for her, not just because "fondly overcome with female charm" (*Paradise Lost*, IX, 999; Waldock, 46ff., esp. 51-52). In persuading him to eat, she could hardly, as Lewis had insisted, be accused of murderous intent, being ignorant of what death was (Waldock, 63).

Empson gave Lewis back-handed praise for "accidentally" realizing that Milton had made credible the consequences of Eve's disobedience by depicting it as the act of a "great lady" in some medieval romance (Empson, 163). Yet Lewis's "practical" suggestion that Adam should have chastised and then interceded for her was unhelpful, for, as in classical tragedy, Adam must take the "most sublime" course by joining her in sin and exile (Empson, 189). Few if any critics have accepted Lewis's distinction between marital love and "uxoriousness," or his claim that Adam owed God a "higher duty" than he owed to his wife (*Preface*, 122-23).

On the poem's genre and style, Peter pressed further the strictures

19. John Peter, *A Critique of "Paradise Lost,"* 126-27.

20. William Empson, *Milton's God,* 17-19.

21. Davis P. Harding, *The Club of Hercules: Studies in the Classical Background of "Paradise Lost,"* 42.

22. Stanley Fish, *Surprised by Sin: The Reader in "Paradise Lost,"* 5-6.

23. John M. Steadman, *Epic and Tragic Structure in "Paradise Lost,"* 132-33, 227-31.

of Leavis by describing *Paradise Lost* as a "tertiary" epic, far more remote even from elevated speech than was the *Aeneid* (Peter, 111). Christopher Ricks in 1963 elegantly epitomized the dispute by saying that: (1) Lewis and Leavis agreed on what the poem was but not on what it should be; (2) Lewis and Empson agreed to revere the poem yet disagreed on what it was or should be; and (3) Empson agreed with Leavis on the criteria for good verse but thought *Paradise Lost* met them.[24] For his part, Ricks warmly commended Lewis's view of its latinate syntax as appealing more to the reader's feelings than to logic, and wished more of the *Preface* had been devoted to stylistic criticism (Ricks, 86).

Like J. B. Broadbent (1960),[25] Ricks described Lewis as the most "influential" traditionalist reader. He even agreed with his much-disputed view of Raphael's prophecy as an "untransmuted lump of futurity" in two final books marred by "curiously bad" writing (Ricks, 78-79; *Preface*, 125). Fish listed a number of objections to that phrase, and he saw an assessment of the poem's concluding books as contingent on the interpretation of its beginning and middle, noting that Lewis's condemnation of their style "still finds its adherents."[26] In William Kerrigan's view (1983), "evaluating the final two books . . . has replaced explaining Satan's heroism as the dominant problem . . . [of] *Paradise Lost.*" "There is," he adds, "no clearer instance in which the modern Miltonist enjoys an understanding . . . superior to that of his predecessors," including Lewis.[27] While some still condemn the style of the poem's concluding books, most critics — from Lawrence A. Sasek, who in 1962 defended the prophecy as educating the listening Adam, to Ronald Macdonald, who in 1987 saw it as essential to the poem's scheme[28] — have agreed with Kerrigan to regard Lewis's phrase "untransmuted lump of futurity" as a misjudgment.

24. Christopher Ricks, *Milton's Grand Style*, 8-9.
25. J. B. Broadbent, *Some Graver Subject*, 291.
26. Fish, *Surprised by Sin*, 301; Fish cites Lewalski, Prince, Sasek, Summers, and MacCallum.
27. William Kerrigan, *The Sacred Complex*, 271-72.
28. Lawrence W. Sasek, "The Drama of *Paradise Lost*, Books XI-XII," in *Studies in English Renaissance Literature*, ed. Waldo F. McNeir (Baton Rouge, 1962), cited in Burton Jasper Weber, *The Construction of "Paradise Lost,"* 244; Ronald Macdonald, *The Burial-Places of Memory: Epic Underworlds in Vergil, Dante, and Milton*, 176.

Critical attention has also shifted from the personality of Satan, on which Lewis's view has lately won qualified support,[29] to the poem's intent and genre. Building on arguments by Ricks and Fish, D. R. Danielson (1982) taxes Lewis with three errors regarding "Edenic sex." The first was to impose "traditional categories" so as to establish "Milton's orthodoxy." Having like Augustine attributed "concupiscence" to the fall, Lewis "can only squirm" at unfallen sexuality in the poem, accusing Milton of inconsistency. The second was inapplicably to impose "postlapsarian categories" by ascribing the unfallen Eve's blush to a "modesty or bashfulness" distinct from bodily shame, despite its consistency with the Pelagian account of prelapsarian sex dismissed by Augustine. The third was to conclude from the similarities between unfallen and fallen sexuality that the fall had made no fundamental difference. Following up Fish and particularly Ricks, Danielson argues that Milton represents the "innocent happiness of unfallen sexuality." Readers who are unable to overcome "guilty responses" by appreciating this will "remain uneducated by" the "contrast between then and now."[30]

Burton J. Weber (1971) claims that by believing the fall to be historical Lewis failed to recognize it as a fact of moral experience. Empson taxes Lewis with contempt for the evolutionary beliefs of twentieth-century students, while Wayne Shumaker (1967) praises Lewis as among the "most elegant" of twentieth-century theologians seeking to save the Genesis myth by subtilizing it into "God's metaphor."[31] Detecting a "whiff of New Criticism" in Lewis's refusal to recognize the relevance of the blind poet's situation and experience,

29. Among those who support Lewis's view are Michael Lieb, *The Dialectics of Creation: Patterns of Birth and Regeneration in "Paradise Lost,"* 26; Weber, *The Construction of "Paradise Lost,"* 16nn.1-2; William Riggs, *The Christian Poet in "Paradise Lost,"* 15-16. G. K. Hunter, *"Paradise Lost,"* 90, generally agrees with Lewis but thinks the dice are loaded against Satan on doctrinal grounds. Murray Roston, *Milton and the Baroque,* 54-55, thinks Lewis's view of Satan is historically valid but inadequate to explain the character's appeal.

30. Dennis R. Danielson, *Milton's Good God: A Study in Literary Theodicy,* 184-88.

31. Weber, *The Construction of "Paradise Lost,"* 175-76; Empson, *Milton's God,* 88-89; Wayne Shumaker, *Feeling and Perception in "Paradise Lost,"* 8-9.

Charles Martindale (1986)[32] points toward a new understanding of the poem by J. P. Rumrich.

In *Matter of Glory* (1987), significantly subtitled *A New Preface to "Paradise Lost,"* Rumrich argues that God wishes to preserve glory and Satan to recover it. Lewis, he contends, has wrongly equated primary epic with an adolescent quest for personal honor and secondary epic with service to God in maturity. The true contrast should be between the quest of Achilles for immortal glory, even in death, and that of Aeneas for the glory of Rome.[33] Echoing Lewis's title by way of compliment, Rumrich traces Lewis's limitation as a Miltonist to a "horizon of expectations" that excludes not only the "concern" of all epics with glory but also Milton's radicalism and "materialism." Unlike Lewis, who sought consensus among theologically conservative readers, Milton made no attempt to expurgate his "heresies," which included "materialism" — that is, a female aspect of God implicit in the material Chaos from which heaven and earth were formed (Rumrich, 7-8).[34]

Without claiming to rival Lewis in "style, lucidity or general literary expertise," Rumrich explains the threefold allusion in his title as implying that, like Lewis, he considers "the meaning of the whole poem as well as its cultural basis." He follows "roughly the same course . . . from Milton's philosophy" to "particular interpretive issues" but offers an "alternative understanding" of the poem's "relations to its precursors" and of its "theology" as related to Milton's intended meaning (Rumrich, 7-8). But, like Martindale and L. J. Damrosch (1985),[35] Rumrich finds Milton's poems, and *Paradise Lost* in particular, inseparable from their author.

From Tillyard to Rumrich, therefore, scholarly interpretation of the poem has come full circle; but as Rumrich admits, few interpreters since Lewis have considered every aspect of the poem. None, I suggest, could have done so within so brief a book.

32. Charles Martindale, *John Milton and the Transformation of Ancient Epic*, 65.
33. John Peter Rumich, *Matter of Glory: A New Preface to "Paradise Lost."*
34. "Heresy" in Rumrich's view, not mine.
35. Leopold J. Damrosch, *God's Plot and Man's Stories: Studies in the Fictional Imagination from Milton to Fielding*, esp. 120.

CHAPTER 4

Literary Theorist

FOR REASONS THAT will become apparent during this chapter, after discussion of theory in *The Allegory of Love* three works of critical theory, *An Experiment in Criticism*, *Studies in Words*, and *The Abolition of Man*, will be considered in reverse order of writing.

The Allegory of Love

In her survey of *Troilus* criticism, the nonhistoricist Alice Kaminsky defines the historical critic as one reconstructing the past to discern what an author "intended to create," and so becoming his "contemporary."[1] Despite their "different interpretations" of poems, she continues, Lewis and D. W. Robertson "agree that they can decipher the secrets of the past as Chaucer meant us to know them." Chauncey Wood, an ardent Robertsonian, approves Lewis's effort to "recreate the historical, social and literary circumstances" in which Chaucer read *Il Filostrato*, but thinks his reading not historical enough. To him, Chaucer's emphasis on the royal rank and duties of Troilus is a veiled comment on the adultery of Edward III.[2] Wood's definition of historical criticism appears almost identical to that of New Historicism, but

1. Alice Kaminsky, *Chaucer's "Troilus and Criseyde" and the Critics*, 16.
2. Chauncey Wood, *The Elements of Chaucer's "Troilus,"* 31-32, 35.

whereas the old historical critics considered ideas and beliefs found in books, sermons, or works of art, the new consider the economic, linguistic, and social context in which a literary work was produced.[3]

Ian Robinson attacks Lewis as *too* historically minded, insisting that "poetry can only live in the reader, in the present." Though "in a voice from the fourteenth century," Chaucer speaks to us "here and now." Deploring attempts to substitute for "present reading" the "more verifiable discipline of history,"[4] Robinson applies to the *Canterbury Tales,* in particular, the Leavisian principle of relating texts to medieval English poems rather than to theological works by Augustine or Boethius. He vents his fury chiefly upon Robertson for treating poems as "prose paraphrases of themselves, made to fit a conviction of what they *must* be saying" (Robinson, 274), arguing that we still read Chaucer, because of his *un*likeness to his contemporaries.

Robinson objects, in my view justly, to Robertson's insistence that to understand Chaucer's poems readers must familiarize themselves with possible sources from Augustine to Boccaccio (Robinson, viii) that most will find more difficult than the poems. In his late essay "De Audiendis Poetis," however, Lewis suggests that to confine readers to a twentieth-century view puts them in blinkers of another kind.[5] One might illustrate from the sorts of nuances a modern playgoer misses in Shakespeare's chronicles if ignorant of the Elizabethan view of kingship. Lewis's whole endeavor, as lecturer and literary historian, was to enrich rather than supplant first-hand reading, in which he believed no less than Robinson, Leavis, or I. A. Richards. To regard only literary texts as relevant to literature begs the question of works raised to literary eminence by their merit rather than their intent. Among these, in Chaucer's time as in ours, were the *Consolation* of Boethius and the *Confessions* of Augustine. Robertson erred not by attending to these but by insufficiently attending to Chaucer's poems. Lewis cannot be accused of failing to read the *Troilus* as a love poem. A more serious charge is implicit in Robinson's view that

3. Louis A. Montrose, "The Poetics and Politics of a Culture," in H. Aram Veeser, ed., *The New Historicism,* 30.

4. Ian Robinson, *Chaucer and the English Tradition,* 266-67.

5. Lewis, *Studies in Medieval and Renaissance Literature,* 1-17, esp. 1-3. "De Audiendis Poetis" was written late in Lewis's career as the introduction to a book that was never completed (see Hooper's introduction to *Studies,* vii).

reading always takes place in present time, that as a historical critic Lewis overlooked what is universal in the substance of works that have endured.

In *Two Concepts of Allegory* (1967), A. D. Nuttall mounted the first systematic attack on another aspect of Lewis's literary theory. He detected a shift of ground between Lewis's distinction of allegory from symbolism and his explanation of the allegorical practice of Guillaume de Lorris. Lewis first expounds allegory as a way of exploiting the "equivalence between the immaterial and the material" (*Allegory of Love,* 44-45). An allegorical poet starts from immaterial but indisputable realities (such as anger and the temperance to restrain it), personifies each, and plausibly represents inward conflict as a duel. A symbolic or sacramental poet, to whom phenomena echo their counterparts in the invisible world, presents the divine love in the erotic. The allegorist works from the "given" of his real passions to the "fiction" of their imagined conflict, the symbolist from an imperfect and to that extent unreal passion in the material world to its "real" counterpart in the eternal.

In expounding de Lorris (*Allegory of Love,* 113-15), Lewis starts from his account of allegory as representing the inner life, then contends that de Lorris differed from Chretien de Troyes by rejecting the "fantastic" world of knightly adventures for the "real" world of psychological events. Nuttall objects that Lewis makes a false distinction, as neither mental nor transcendental realities can be described save in metaphorical terms. The medieval poet, nurtured in a strongly theological culture, inevitably blurred the line between *allegoria* and *figura,* the type and what it prefigures.[6] If Moses prefigured Christ, then Moses was *allegoria* (in current parlance "signifier") and Christ *figura* ("signified"). That Christ, the figured, was more "real" would not prove that Moses was fictional. Though Lewis might deny any mystical element in medieval allegory (Nuttall, 48), the figure and the figured were more similar than he allowed. "Where allegory is exciting, it is . . . because of a peculiar impression of validity in the images," a quickening of "our apprehensions . . . by a feeling akin to recognition," so that "the strange equivalence of outer and inner is at once set in motion" (Nuttall, 32). Lewis, adds Nuttall, writes "like an Elizabethan Neopla-

---

6. A. D. Nuttall, *Two Concepts of Allegory,* 24ff., citing Erich Auerbach, *Scenes from the Drama of European Literature* (New York, 1959).

tonist once he comes to details of the poem" (Nuttall, 33), indicating that de Lorris presents the "magic" of the beloved's eyes as it "exists not . . . outside the human mind, but outside any school of poetry" (*Allegory of Love,* 129). Nuttall finds examples of allegory as defined by Lewis in "frigid" eighteenth-century "allegorizings"; but he defines his own object as "to show that allegorical poetry is more curiously and intimately related to life than was allowed by the petrifying formula of C. S. Lewis" (Nuttall, 159).

The most recent reflections on this subject occur in an essay by Marius Buning, published in 1991.[7] Buning, who regards *The Allegory of Love* as Lewis's "most important work of criticism," treats its subject as "the kind of allegory or picture language . . . concerned with man's inner struggle . . . between virtues and vices" first exemplified in the *Psychomachia* of Prudentius. Citing Nuttall and other critics,[8] he suggests that Lewis took a "narrow view" of allegory, confining it to the first two kinds listed by Northrop Frye, "naive" and "continuous" (the others being "freistimmig" or free-style, "doctrinal," "implicit," "ironic," and "indirect"). Like many Romantic critics, Lewis preferred symbolism or sacramentalism, that is, the treatment of the material as in some degree embodying the ideal or eternal. In Buning's "linguistically oriented view," allegory is "a form of polysemy, or multiple meaning, structured in such a way that the reader is encouraged to look constantly for further significance above and beyond the literal surface of the fiction."[9] There, for the present, the debate rests.

An Experiment in Criticism

By 1960, when Lewis finished writing *An Experiment in Criticism,* the teaching of F. R. Leavis had so pervaded British university and school

7. Marius Buning, "*Perelandra* Revisited in the Light of Modern Allegorical Theory," in Peter J. Schakel and Charles A. Huttar, eds., *Word and Story in C. S. Lewis,* 277-98.

8. Especially Northrop Frye, *The Anatomy of Criticism;* Paul De Man, *Blindness and Insight;* Peter Piehler, *The Visionary Landscape: A Study in Medieval Allegory;* and Angus Fletcher, *Allegory: The Theory of a Symbolic Mode.*

9. Buning, "*Perelandra* Revisited," 278-79, 281, 283.

departments of English as to be dubbed "Leavisianity." Noel Annan shrewdly comments that it appealed to students from the working and lower middle classes by persuading them that close reading of a few texts forming the "great tradition" would give them sound judgment, discrimination, and a feeling for the texture of human life. It was the equivalent of salvation by faith alone. No longer need they master ancient or foreign literatures or plough through source-texts, like their contemporaries who received a traditional education at the "public" schools and ancient universities.[10] Lord Annan oversimplifies the class divide, for Leavisites taught in private-sector schools too, but, as he perceives, literary study according to the new gospel required more rigor and concentration, but much less time. As a training for life, it promised greater rewards than either the blend of classics, ancient history, and philosophy known as "Greats" and entrenched at Oxford since the Renaissance, or the philological and historical study of English literature from the Anglo-Saxons to the Romantics that Lewis and Tolkien had helped to establish at Oxford. Richards and Leavis had set new standards for sensitive and independent reading of texts, but what Lewis tried to counteract in the *Experiment* he soon after epitomized as the "insolence and self-righteousness" abounding "in literary circles," which reminded him of seventeenth-century theological disputations.[11] He saw a more limited role for literature than did Leavis, for as a Christian he could neither regard it as his main source of values nor equate critical with moral perception.

In the *Experiment,* Lewis brought together convictions recorded earlier. The capacity for experiencing a "change of consciousness" through reading, a point contributed to Barfield's *Poetic Diction* (1928), he now saw as a mark of the "literary" reader (*Experiment,* 3). In "Different Tastes in Literature" (1946), he had distinguished between the "literary" who reread valued books and the "unliterary" who read a book but once, to use it as a vehicle for daydreams,[12] a propensity he now labeled "Egoistic Castle-building" (*Experiment,* chapter 6). To

10. Lord Noel Annan, *Our Age: Portrait of a Generation,* 315-27, esp. 320-21.

11. Lewis, "The Vision of John Bunyan" (1962), in *Selected Literary Essays,* esp. 152.

12. Lewis, *Of This and Other Worlds,* 153-61.

this form of self-indulgence he had confessed himself prone in 1946, when distinquishing the novels of that "fine and neglected artist" Forrest Reid (target of a Leavisite critic) from those of Marie Corelli, which he therefore dared not read again.[13] In the same year, he expressed a preference for editorial scholarship over the evaluative criticism he already thought harmful when practiced in schools.[14] In "On Three Ways of Writing for Children" (1952), he condemned the use of "adult" as a term of literary approval, while agreeing that authors ought not to evade the facts of death and violence.[15] But his fiercest, if most oblique, assault upon the influence of Leavis was "Lilies That Fester" (1955),[16] in which he derided the concern for culture that Leavis and Eliot had inherited from Arnold. He argued that when enjoying a symphony the heroine of E. M. Forster's *Howard's End* unreflectingly senses a "whole world" through music, but belief in culture, like that in religion, would distract her from "the things culture and religion are about." "Appreciation" being "more evident" in a schoolboy's unforced enjoyment of fantasy or science fiction (and that of Lewis the youthful Dreamer) than in the reading practiced by students wishing to join a cultured minority, he feared replacement of the old ruling class by a new managerial elite trained to regurgitate acceptable opinions in examinations. He overstated his case, for even now a good degree in English, if attainable by this means, is no passport to a boardroom or Whitehall. But in 1960 to be a Leavisite had become as advantageous in securing university and school English posts as it had been a hindrance a generation before. Whether one views the Leavisites as an elite based in Cambridge that had superseded one based in Bloomsbury or sees Lewis as promoting an elite of his own based in Oxford depends on one's judgment of the *Experiment in Criticism.*

One can sympathize with both sides, for Leavis and Richards[17]

13. Lewis, "Different Tastes in Literature." F. R. Leavis contributed an introduction to Peter Coveney, *Poor Monkey* (1957); reprinted in America as *The Image of Childhood* (1967), 269.

14. Lewis, "The Parthenon and the Optative" (1946), in *Of This and Other Worlds,* 142-46.

15. Lewis, "On Three Ways of Writing for Children," in *Of Other Worlds,* 22-34.

16. Lewis, "Lilies That Fester," in *They Asked for a Paper,* 105-19.

17. I. A. Richards, *The Principles of Literary Criticism,* 183.

hoped that, once disabused of insincere reverence, young people might grow in mind and spirit by grappling with works of genuine merit. Lewis saw a willing suspension of judgment, unforced surrender to the work, as prerequisite for a heightening of consciousness in the reader. His Calvinistic distinction between the "literary" minority and the "unliterary" majority, a division "foreshadowed in the nursery,"[18] offended a reader of my acquaintance who had neither read Leavis nor heard of *Scrutiny* — and whom Lewis's care to avoid equating literary sensitivity with moral or intellectual superiority failed to mollify. To some extent the book's structure is to blame, for not until the third chapter does Lewis explain that the unliterary reader uses a work while the literary reader receives it. Nor until the eleventh chapter does he define his "experiment" as judgment of a work according to whether it is read primarily by repeat readers who incorporate its characters, incidents, words, and images into their own consciousness or by once-only readers seeking diversion or self-gratification.

So imprecise a definition inevitably involves inconsistencies and begs questions. Those books that reward "literary" reading must eventually appear as a list, even if longer and more variable than that of the "Great Tradition." That most readers kill time while a minority lose themselves in enjoyment makes one wonder which practice is more consistent with psychological and spiritual maturity. In the chapter on myths, even Lewis shifts his ground by explaining that virtually any retelling conveys the essence of a great myth, but that the unliterary do not receive from it "one-tenth . . . of what reading has to give" (*Experiment,* 48). In claiming that only the literary perceive a work's aural qualities, he fails to consider how unliterary believers might respond to dramatic or liturgical representations of, for example, the Passion.

He distinguishes the literary by their devotion to works couched in language, which therefore convey meaning. The inartistic need not use paint or stone, but because the unliterary must use language they cannot but be influenced by whatever terms and ideas they encounter. Like Orwell, Lewis finds the influence of "castle-building" stories in magazines for schoolboys and women very harmful. Richards and Leavis

18. Lewis, *An Experiment in Criticism,* 13.

would surely have agreed, but they took much further the question of how texts and genres could influence people for good or ill. To say with Lewis that the most effective inoculant against infection by false values inherent in bad literary texts is "a full experience of good" (*Experiment*, 94) begs the question of how we distinguish the two. The best, he implies, is whatever continues to refresh the few, while the worst is whatever distracts or drugs the many who need continual change. Since Leavis would evidently have agreed, why were they at odds?

Primarily, they thought very differently about the act of reading. Lewis remained in part a Dreamer even while functioning as Mentor to students and readers. It is difficult to imagine Leavis in any other role than that of Mentor. Complaining that English literature courses have made students think of reading as a virtue or therapy rather than a pleasure, Lewis calls the attitude to reading instilled by New Criticism "Puritan conscience . . . without the Puritan theology," accompanied by a suspicion of enjoyment conducive to Puritan "intolerance and self-righteousness" (*Experiment*, 10). This leads him to examine two meanings of "serious," grave and whole-hearted. To read seriously, he maintains, is to read in the spirit in which the author wrote (*Experiment*, 11). Many New Critics would reject this as the "intentional fallacy." His examples — Rabelais, Chaucer's comic tales, and Pope's "Rape of the Lock" — point his argument without excluding gravity where appropriate. While Lewis argues by naming extreme instances, Leavis examines relevant passages. Lewis assumes consensus and wide reading, while Leavis expounds his convictions by close illustration from a narrower range of texts.

Ultimately their difference was a matter of religious principle. With Lewis, reading was akin to prayer: one emptied oneself before a text as a devotee before God. "Those of us who have been true readers all our life seldom fully realise the enormous extension of our being which we owe to authors." To read was to escape from the prisons of self and period so that, as Lewis beautifully concludes his *Experiment*, "in reading great literature I become a thousand men and yet remain myself. . . . Here, as in worship, in love, in moral action, and in knowing, I transcend myself; and am never more myself than when I do" (*Experiment*, 141).

The one prison he failed to mention was the masculine gender.

Until his late marriage, in every allusion to the reader he presumed the male sex. Only after his marriage did he modify the cerebral and combative tone of his critical and theological argumentation. In "Queenie," a partner in critical writing as well as in life, Leavis had the advantage of him.

Leavis treats the unknown text as a plant or potion to be tested until its effect is known, then endorsed or condemned. In a world without Providence, readers must either attain a mature understanding of human life and nature or be stunted and blinkered by commercial puffery, the popular press, or literature unworthily so called. The very title *Scrutiny* characterizes the Leavisian approach to reading. Had Lewis founded a journal, he might have called it *Exploration.*

How could two learned critics with so much in common enjoin reading to such opposed effects? One reason was the security of Lewis, born into the professional class and educated via the Oxford "Greats" program that had so long groomed young men for the clerisy and public service, in contrast to the bitter struggle of the lower-middle-class Leavis to win acceptance at Cambridge in and for the modern discipline of English literature, conceived as he thought honest and relevant to twentieth-century society. The one class had the world before it and Providence as its guide; the other had to exercise tough-minded vigilance lest it be gulled into subservience to the old ruling class and big business.

A study of Richards's *Principles of Literary Criticism* reveals more profound though not total disagreement between him and Lewis. Richards sees the effect of art not as momentary poignancy or intense pleasure, still less as amusement, but as the organization of feelings and impulses in its viewer, listener, or reader toward fullness and mature growth. In this sense the recipient, like Lewis's literary reader, is permanently affected. Even a *Divine Comedy,* however, can lose this potency once it has become remote from contemporary understanding and belief.[19] On the principle that great art heightens consciousness Lewis would have agreed — though without calling this "Vigilance" as opposed to anaesthesia (Richards, 184) — but on literary obsolescence his faith in scholarly exposition, and his enjoyment of swimming against

19. Richards, *Principles,* 197-98, 222.

the tide, compelled him to dissent.[20] Richards asserts that neither time nor changing beliefs need doom works accessible to the young or unsophisticated, whose understanding of *Macbeth,* the *Pilgrim's Progress,* or *Gulliver's Travels* may deepen with maturity and education. But Dante, Milton, Baudelaire, or Henry James would from the outset prove beyond them (Richards, 211-13). Unlike Leavis, Richards thought even the most sophisticated readers likely to lose interest in a novel by Henry James once they had fathomed its difficulties.

Richards noted an increasing allusiveness in contemporary poets, whereas Lewis saw the audience for modern poets shrinking daily owing to their esoteric language. Two contemporaries Lewis enjoyed, Yeats and de la Mare, Richards thought esoteric because the one had taken refuge in theosophy and the other in dreams (Richards, 197, 266).

Despite some agreements — for example, Richards disposes of a Freudian interpretation of the Abyssinian maid in "Kubla Khan" by the scholarly source-hunting method Lewis labeled "Dryasdust" (Richards, 29-30) — Lewis condemns in his *Experiment* a principle fundamental to Richards and Leavis: that inferior works make readers less fit to respond to the best (Richards, 204), and that only critical "Vigilance" could avert the "pernicious" effects of reading inferior works: blunted sensitivity and distorted responses to experience (Richards, 230). Richards uses the term "Vigilance" to denote both the heightening of consciousness Lewis so eloquently described four years later ("Summa," II, xiii) and the watchfulness that the critically enlightened must exercise lest the public be "inveigled" (Richards, 236) into accepting stereotyped or mediocre art. Lewis's acerbity against the "Vigilant school of critics" (*Experiment,* 124ff.) arises from his belief that they perceived art and life as one — that while he disapproved of pornography yet enjoyed and valued poems by Ovid, they condemned in art what they disapproved in life. Had he recently reread the *Principles,* he might have been piqued by its strictures on the "timidity" of critics who avoid contemporary writing (Richards, 220) and its dismissal of both "transcendental" accounts of artistic creation (255) and that exchange of emotional and physical suffering by which Lewis had relieved his wife's suffering (175).

20. Cf. "Zeitgeistheim" in *Pilgrim's Regress* and Lewis's account of discovering Dante's "Paradiso" with Barfield in *They Stand Together,* 325-26.

Like Leavis, Richards put a premium on maturity and attacked the "childishness" of Hollywood films, yet he never joined Leavis and Eliot in attacking Spenser, Milton, and Shelley. But by pointing to some bad works still in print *(Hiawatha* or *Lorna Doone)* and insisting upon the power of even the slightly substandard to inoculate readers against the best, Richards emboldened other iconoclasts. By 1960, Lewis protested, the index of approved works and authors had diminished beyond all reason (*Experiment*, 127).

Though the *Experiment* received mainly favorable reviews,[21] as polemic it probably has the life-expectancy of the now-waning Leavisite movement. Why, one wonders, do its positive insights seem as lost upon the postmodernist critics, and in particular the reader-response theorists who now dominate university departments of literature, as they were upon the structuralists before them? Students seeking guidance on myth, romance, or fantasy turn to Northrop Frye or Tsvetan Todorov rather than Lewis. Impersonal reading cannot be the cause, for, like any New Critic or deconstructionist, Lewis taught students to focus on texts rather than on their authors. Nor is the present unpopularity of old-style historical criticism applicable to this book. Can the explanation be that his principle of judging a text by the kind of reading it invites only superficially resembles current reception theory?

Susan Suleiman has identified six kinds of reception theory.[22] The first, exemplified by Roman Jakobson and Wayne Booth, is "rhetorical." Jakobson argues that texts emit ethical or ideological messages for their reader to decode. To this Lewis would rejoin (*Experiment*, 82-83) that texts consist not merely of content *(logos)* but also of form *(poiema)*. At the same time as the *Experiment*, Booth argued that the values and beliefs of a work's "implied author" determine those understood by its "implied," or envisaged, reader. This comes close to Lewis's contention (*Experiment*, 85-93) that a good reader sits still before the work and

21. Notably by Frank Kermode, in *New Statesman*, 3 November 1961. But W. W. Robson was more critical, asserting that Lewis "attempted, in a regrettably indirect manner, to counter the influence of Leavis," and that the conclusion of *Experiment* is "worthy of a better book" ("C. S. Lewis," 263).

22. Susan R. Suleiman, introduction to *The Reader in the Text*, ed. Susan R. Suleiman and Inge Crosman, 3-45 passim.

listens. Booth's concept of an "implied" author and reader has been criticized as an interpretive construct warranting a consistent rather than a valid reading. The "traditional" historical reading, which Suleiman excludes from any form of reception theory, would forearm Lewis, if not Booth, against that objection.

Suleiman's second form of reception theory comes from "semioticians" and "structuralists," who analyze and clarify the implicit codes and conventions so as to specify the "inscribed" audience and its role in making the work readable. These theorists then identify the aesthetic and cultural conventions by which readers understand a text and which its author uses to help or frustrate them. When advising readers to enter into the "spirit" in which a text was written (*Experiment*, 11), Lewis says in part and in general what Roland Barthès spells out in detail. Like Todorov, however, Lewis hopes to reach an objectively valid interpretation. He would probably criticize this group of theorists for focusing upon the reader's intellectual processes to the exclusion of the aural, emotional, and imaginative.

This seems indicated by Suleiman's third category, "phenomenological" reception theory, exemplified by Wolfgang Iser, who attends mainly to the aesthetic perception that enables a reader to form an idea of the work as a whole. Only when so "realized," according to Iser, does a text come alive. In arguing that until it is sympathetically read (*Experiment*, 104) a printed text remains only potential literature, Lewis gives preference to readers' attitude over their act of imagination.

Lewis would undoubtedly have disagreed with Suleiman's fourth group of theorists, described as "subjectivist" and "psychoanalytic." Among these, Norman Holland reconciles Freudian with New Critical practice by presenting the content of a text as unconscious fantasy striving to defend against anxiety, with the text's form as the defense mechanism. Abandoning all claim to objectively valid interpretation, Holland attributes both content and interpretation to the reader rather than the author. A possible link with Lewis lies in Jonathan Culler's objection that Holland assumes the reader's ego to be autonomous. So indeed does Lewis, but his celebrated conclusion to the *Experiment* describes the literary reader as voluntarily relinquishing his identity and so enlarging it by opening himself to identities created in the text.

Nor would Lewis wholly dissent from Suleiman's fifth group of reception theorists, who consider reading as a collective act determined by the social and historical context of readers. However, whereas these critics assume present-day readers to be conditioned by class, education, and ideology, Lewis considered the author and original readership time-conditioned by then-prevalent religious and philosophical ideas, and, with Frye and Todorov, saw most literary works as originating in earlier works.

Suleiman calls her final kind of reception theory "hermeneutic," though its practitioners are usually known as "deconstructionists." Geoffrey Hartmann distinguishes his "negative" hermeneutics both from "positive hermeneutics," which claims objective validity for a single interpretation, and from New Criticism, which focuses on the text to the exclusion of the author. Jacques Derrida claims to show objective interpretation to be impossible by undermining the unity of any text, thereby showing that its meaning is undecidable. Jacques Lacan and Hillis Miller reach the same goal by undermining the unity of the self, whether of author or reader — so in effect one assemblage of conflicting voices vainly strives to make sense of another. Thus negative hermeneuticians, or deconstructionists, claim to have destroyed the "metaphysics of presence" assumed by Western philosophers since Plato. If Lewis compared literary reading to prayer or meditation as an act of self-renunciation, he never doubted the existence of the renouncing subject or literary object. He would therefore have opposed this school of criticism as vigorously as he did the linguistic-analysis philosophy in which it originated.

The first three kinds of reception theory and the fifth, then, overlap the arguments of the *Experiment* yet leave substantial differences of focus and direction. With the Freudian criticism and logical positivism from which the fourth and sixth kinds of reception theory developed Lewis waged war throughout his career. In the "Great War," while maintaining the individual's existence and distinctness from the world, he had humorously told Barfield he would commit suicide if proved wrong.

In his *Experiment,* Lewis differs from almost any current literary theorist in using plain terms and everyday analogies so as to communicate with the undergraduate or indeed any book lover. Addressing literary readers as "we" and "the few," he proclaims them a minority not identifiable by degree or occupation. He would probably have included the majority of reception theorists, and all deconstructionists, among the "unliterary" who use rather than receive literary works. So long as academic critics write for initiates only and value interpretation as highly as authorship, Lewis's criticism will remain out of favor.

By insisting, like Richards, that a poem, play, or novel is something made *(poema)*, Lewis opposes any idea of it as the product of its social, linguistic, or literary context rather than its author (*Experiment*, 82). He does not, however, identify a traditional myth with any version or teller, but insists on the independent life of the tale. Moreover, some tales by known authors, such as Shakespeare or Dickens, live in many minds as myths, independent of their texts. Stories by George Mac-Donald, H. Rider Haggard, and J. R. R. Tolkien have the universality of myths, though, as it were, "manmade" myths, a literary kind the Inklings called "mythopoeia."

Much has been made of Lewis's approving allusions to works by his friends and favorite authors and his derogatory references to those of D. H. Lawrence and Henry James. The latter (*Experiment*, 61, 91, 113, 126) can be discounted as barbs aimed at Leavisites. A few references to books by Haggard and John Buchan are more than counter-balanced by those to universally esteemed works of Chaucer, Shakespeare, Scott, Austen, or Dickens. But he tends to draw upon a few favorite works, like *Great Expectations,* rather than spreading references throughout an author's works. In early chapters, as in his auto-biography, he refers to works beloved in childhood: illustrations by Beatrix Potter and Arthur Rackham, Norse myths, *Treasure Island,* or Wells's *First Men in the Moon* (*Experiment,* 14, 15, 29). Yet before finishing this series of allusions he brings in Renaissance paintings and Gertrude Stein (*Experiment,* 18, 19, 27-28), and he is soon alluding to authors from classical times to the twentieth century: Homer, Racine, Hawthorne, Kafka, Dostoevsky, and Tolstoy (*Experiment,* 42-43, 38, 59-60). If he also brings in Mervyn Peake's Gormenghast trilogy and Tolkien's *Lord of the Rings,* is this more reprehensible than citations by Leavis of, say, T. F. Powys?

In his allusions, however, Lewis falls between two stools, being neither so specific as Leavis nor so systematic as Frye. What in the end limits the value of several definitions in the *Experiment* is a lack of range, focus, and depth. For example, his working definition of a fantasy as "any narrative that deals with impossibles and preternaturals" (*Experiment,* 50) begs the question of what we should regard as possible or natural and seems superficial beside those given or cited by Todorov.[23] Discussion in Lewis's chapter on fantasy is confined to the reader's motives and responses; but Todorov takes account as well of a fantasy's "syntactical" aspect, its performance, and the reader's response, along with its "verbal" (structure and style) and "semantic" (themes and meaning) aspects. Lewis discusses such motives for reading fantasies as wish-fulfillment or daydreaming, distinguishing between "disinterested" or constructive daydreaming by the literary reader and egoistic or self-indulgent dreaming by the unliterary reader. Todorov demonstrates how and how far specified texts induce "hesitation," or uncertainty, in the hero and/or reader. In his best-known and only perfect paradigm, James's *Turn of the Screw,* are the ghosts real or imagined by the narrator?

In his *Anatomy of Criticism,* Frye defines relationships between the reader and hero in a myth, legend, or fairy tale, along with "high" and "low" mimetic and "ironic" literary works. He also discusses how works in each genre reach their publics: by dramatic performance, singing, recital, or silent reading. Like Todorov, Frye writes for teachers of literature, while Lewis writes for these but also for any educated readers. By comparison, Lewis's discussion of fantasy is lightweight.

Partly on account of its slightness, the *Experiment in Criticism* has received less attention than its tolerant stance and highly readable arguments merit. To have rivaled the critical works of Todorov and Frye, it would have needed to be on the scale of the *Allegory of Love.* In the few years left him after Joy's death, Lewis's health and morale would not have permitted such an undertaking. A further reason for the book's neglect lies in the fact that it was directed against an offshoot of New Criticism that is virtually confined to students, teachers, and academics within the British Commonwealth. In North America or Continental Europe, the teachings and cult of Leavis have never ac-

23. Tzvetan Todorov specifies hesitation (i.e., uncertainty), either in the hero or in the reader, as the defining characteristic of fantasy, whether or not the situation is real (*The Fantastic: A Structural Approach to a Literary Genre,* 25ff.).

quired the influence they had in Britain. Even Lewis's admirable chapter on realism is directed against a preference less evident in North America, one for "realism of content" over "realism of presentation," hence a prejudice against modern fantasies by Tolkien and others.

In that chapter, Lewis makes a useful distinction between probable situations, as in *War and Peace* or *Middlemarch,* and probable responses to improbable situations, as in *King Oedipus, Great Expectations,* or *Hamlet.* Recognizing works of quality in either kind, he says roundly that truth to life in the sense of "realism of content" ought not to be required (*Experiment,* 66-67). His target here may be Marxist critics, for Leavis thought fairy tales of great value to children. Like Orwell, Lewis thought superficially realistic school stories did children far more harm than any fairy tale.[24] He maintained — as Leavis would surely have agreed — that no work can deceive a reader about life unless it claims to be realistic (or, perhaps more accurately, unless it is received as such).

In the chapter as a whole, Lewis writes with a wit and passion inspired by the Dreamer's love of traditional romances and fairy tales. To brand the taste for these "immature," he urges, is to overlook both the value of literary escape from the here and now described in a famous essay by Tolkien[25] and the best aspects of childhood: its energy and insatiable curiosity, its willingness to suspend disbelief and to give rein to imagination.

Studies in Words

Published in 1960, *Studies in Words* originated in a rather unsuccessful lecture series at Cambridge. Its brief preface is dated June 1959, but four essays intended for a further semantic study ("World," "Life," "I Dare Say," and "On the Fringe of Language") were added as concluding chapters to the posthumous second edition.[26]

24. George Orwell, "Boys' Weeklies."
25. "On Fairy Stories" (orig. 1939 lecture).
26. Lewis, *Studies in Words.* All references are to the second edition (1967). For information on the additional chapters, see Joe Christopher, *C. S. Lewis,* 30-31, where the original title of the last essay is given as "I Dare Affirm."

In the original edition Lewis traces the usage of *nature, sad, wit, free, sense, simple, conscience* (and *conscious*), with their synonyms, from classical or biblical to early twentieth-century literary contexts. The book amply documents the value of the expository criticism that in the *Experiment* Lewis calls "Dryasdust," after Scott, and which includes literary etymology. A unifying argument or narrative being out of the question, the reader can at best expect coherent literary histories of well-chosen words, but save for *sad,* Lewis selected words that anyone might think central to major texts. For example, virtually every author of note between the sixteenth and nineteenth centuries attaches partic- ular importance to *nature* in one of the senses listed by Lewis, from an astonishing range of classical, Old English, and Middle English texts. No word unlocks so many branches of learning as *nature* and its synonymns *kind* and *physis.*

Lewis calls a present-day meaning that readers can fallaciously assume the "dangerous sense." Inevitably, *free* was used most in political or ideological contexts, as in contrast to *vileyne,* later *villain,* an ety- mology especially pleasurable to Marxist critics. This is the only instance in *Studies in Words* of history *in* as distinct from *of* words, Barfield's topic in a well-known book.[27] As a rule Lewis takes his examples not, like Barfield, from the Oxford dictionary but from his own reading. Overt use of the dictionary, when *conscire* is used as an English verb (*Studies in Words,* 187-92), induces tedium and confusion. Its promi- nence in the entry on *conscience* in the *Oxford Dictionary of English Etymology* suggests that he discussed it with the editor, his Oxford colleague C. T. Onions.

So far as the book is controversial, its targets are semantic errors by William Empson, mostly in matters of detail: for example, Empson's claim that [common] sense is a metaphor, or that "wit" in Pope's *Essay on Criticism* always means "verbal joker."[28] A further target is a passage in *The Meaning of Meaning* in which Ogden and Richards scouted the view that Shakespeare's characters and utterances were true to life, and in which Empson thought they insisted too much on the purely "emo-

27. Owen Barfield, *History in English Words.*
28. Lewis, *Studies in Words,* 9, 93-96; William Empson, *The Structure of Complex Words,* 257, 87.

tive" function of poetic diction.[29] In another case, Lewis and Richards are at cross-purposes. While honestly grappling with the criteria of badness, says Lewis, Richards condemns any poem that evokes "stock responses." In that case, he urges, what about Gray's *Elegy?* But Richards has been discussing the stereotypes of magazines and films, whereas Lewis is thinking of common experiences and attitudes that continually recur in ballads, folktales, and poems that are, like the *Elegy,* of a proverbial cast.[30] To Richards, reading or hearing a poem is an intensely individual experience, to Lewis often a collective one. While both thought it harmful to believe in those fantasies that pass for popular "realistic" fiction, Lewis took much less interest than Richards in other forms of commercial art.

Of all Lewis's critical works, *Studies in Words* appeals to the most narrowly academic readership. Only its term "dangerous sense" and its vigorous attack on adverse reviewing in the chapter "At the Fringe of Language," added in the second edition, recall the lawyer's son who so enjoyed unarmed combat.

The Abolition of Man

Readers equipped to follow its erudite yet elegant definitions may prefer the tone of *Studies in Words* to the combativeness of *The Abolition of Man,* originally three wartime lectures at the University of Durham, but most, one imagines, will find the latter book livelier and more disturbing.[31] The present dominance of literary departments by various forms of postmodernism makes Lewis's forebodings concerning a certain New Critical textbook seem more justified now than even a few years ago, although he overreacted to that book itself.[32] In *The Control of Language,* Alec King and Martin Ketley, two Oxford graduates teaching in an Australian grammar school, used the Ogden-Richards dis-

29. Lewis, *Studies in Words,* 314; Empson, *Structure of Complex Words,* 6-8.

30. Lewis, *Studies in Words,* 328; Richards, *Principles,* 203.

31. Lewis, *The Abolition of Man, with Special Reference to the Teaching of English in the Upper Forms of Schools* (originally Riddell Memorial Lectures, 1943).

32. Cf. Doris Myers, *C. S. Lewis in Context,* 72-73, who finds the book "less radical" than Lewis supposed.

tinction between "referential" and "emotive" prose as the basis for a series of analyses designed to teach critical reading and exact writing; in their preface they acknowledge Ogden and Richards's *Meaning of Meaning* as their inspiration.[33]

Lewis pounced upon their illogical judgment that the adjective "sublime," describing a waterfall, denoted Coleridge's feeling concerning himself, to charge the authors with forearming students against a proper emotional response to nature, such as awe or personal insignificance (King and Ketley, 17; *Abolition*, 23-24, 30-31). He also notes their failure to exemplify good descriptive writing when exposing the persiflage of a tourist brochure as an instance of the New Critical tendency to train students to recognize spurious but not genuine writing. Though right in this instance, his assessment is highly selective, for in support of the principle "Show, not tell" the authors analyze many passages of real merit, in chapters Lewis might not have read.[34]

Though he avoids naming the book, its authors (to whom he refers as "Gaius" and "Titius"), or their critical mentors, the direction of his attack becomes unmistakable when he charges a similar text by "Orbilius"[35] with exposing an anthropomorphism about horses as the "willing servants" of colonists without pointing to the real relationships of horses and their masters. The book in question, E. G. Biaggini's *Reading and Writing of English* (1936), has a preface by Leavis and commends works by the Leavises and by Denys Thompson, a contributor to *Scrutiny* and compiler of the once widely used English school textbook *Culture and Environment.*

Lewis's more general apprehensions expressed in his second and third lectures seem particularly applicable to the present tide of deconstructive, feminist, Marxist, and New Historical criticism in academic departments. In the second, he fears that students might be conditioned not only against awareness of nature and wildlife but also against those

33. Alec King and Martin Ketley, *The Control of Language: A Critical Approach to Reading and Writing.*

34. Myers, *C. S. Lewis in Context,* says that Lewis annotated his review copy only to the end of chapter 6, that is, only the portion he attacked.

35. Gaius Titius was an orator and tragedian noted by Cicero for his subtleties; Lucius Orbilius Pupillus was a teacher known as a "bitter critic of contemporary characters and conditions" *(Oxford Classical Dictionary).*

universal moral principles he calls "the Tao" and documents from the *Encyclopedia of Religion and Ethics.* The antiscientific strain in the *Abolition of Man* pervades *That Hideous Strength,* completed a year or two later. In the same lecture he attacks the assumption by Richards that the self-preserving instinct, or even awareness of good, necessarily leads to desirable action. Pointing out (*Abolition,* 41) that neither implies self-sacrifice for the good of others, he condemns the folly of training "men without chests," that is, devoid of altruistic feeling or moral principle,[36] yet expecting from them conduct on which their civilization depends for its continuance. In the third lecture, he condemns the dismissal by King and Ketley of writing intended to appeal to the reader's feelings; in a note in his copy of their book he appends a list of great authors who do so.

No less ominously, people unaware of objective values and constraints, even of external Nature, will be prone to manipulation and conditioning. In its examples of linguistic conditioning, *The Abolition of Man* anticipates Orwell's "Politics and the English Language." But it is postmodernists, rather than the New Critics of Lewis's day, whose curricula and teaching condition students against objective literary, moral, and religious values by treating all such values as expressions of class and ideology. In our time, the closing of the academic mind is a very real prospect. So, however, is its opening, inasmuch as literary theory in its technical rather than ideological sense offers common ground to students of different literatures and academic disciplines.

Lewis and Some New Critical Reviewers

Although the prime target in the *Abolition of Man* was a seminal book by Ogden and Richards, in his final years Lewis became almost paranoid about the influence of Leavis. In one letter he refers to that critic's "yahoo howls," a phrase presumably prompted by Leavis's notorious attack on C. P. Snow's lecture "The Two Cultures," and to "severities"

36. The phrase occurs in a letter to Lewis from his father dated 7 May 1917, in which he mentions rowing as "putting a chest on a man" (George Sayer, *Jack,* 68).

about Leavis in a book by George Watson.[37] In another, Lewis mentions the supposed Leavisite dominance of the *Cambridge Review,* in which from 1935 until after Lewis's death only two articles were at all hostile to Lewis, one condemning the chapter on Eliot in his *Preface to "Paradise Lost"* and the other complaining of his preoccupation with that poem's religion to the neglect of its art.[38]

His defensiveness might have been rooted in several reviews by L. C. Knights in *Scrutiny*. One review of *Rehabilitations and Other Essays* accuses him of "spurious thinking" and of using his "learning and ingenuity" to foster complacency in middlebrow readers. Yet more damaging were charges of being less interested in his subject matter than in rationalizing an attitude and of browbeating those critics of the Oxford English syllabus who sought to replace its useless erudition by training of individual taste and critical intelligence.[39] So inspiring a teacher as Lewis must have felt wounded by this. As the fact that the *Rehabilitations* essays were not republished in his lifetime suggests, the barbs of Knights found their mark.

As Knights acknowledged two years later, when reviewing the *Preface to "Paradise Lost,"* Lewis henceforth responded to criticism by naming opponents and treating their arguments with more respect.[40] Applying Leavis's attack on Milton's style to the description of Eden

---

37. Letter to George Watson, 12 May 1962. Watson says of Leavis, in *The Literary Critics* (1962), 194:

> Even the technical and linguistic pre-suppositions of his criticism, . . . such as his repeated insistence upon . . . "concreteness" and "specificity" or for the realization of "feeling" in poetic language, do not cease to be uncertain because they are passionately held. . . . The most serious charge to be made against his criticism is twofold[:] . . . he has hurried towards value-judgements, especially in his later work, without respect for the . . . delicacy and complexity of literary values, and he has not known enough about anything — or cared much about finding out.

38. Regrettably, I failed to note the date or receipient of this letter. *The Cambridge Review,* published from 1935 to 1978, had no bias toward any critic or school, and indeed published several articles by or respectful of Lewis.

39. L. C. Knights, "Mr. C. S. Lewis and the Status Quo," *Scrutiny* 8 (1939-40): 90-92.

40. L. C. Knights, "Milton Again," *Scrutiny* 11 (1942-43): 146-48.

commended by Lewis, Knights charges him with insensitivity to "obvious qualities" in the verse. To applaud its hieratic style, he contends, is to overlook the absence of what is organic, deeply felt, or genuinely natural.

In this comment Knights modifies Richards's view of poetic language as purely emotive. In a later article in *Scrutiny* Leavis castigates Richards for his "pseudo-scientific" and "neo-Benthamite" *Principles of Literary Criticism.*[41] According to Leavis, Richards erred in ignoring a poet's knowledge-by-experience, his *connaissance,* of nature and human life. It is astounding that Lewis, who so valued this, could overlook its importance to Leavisite critics.

In the same article, directed against *Essays in Criticism,* Leavis deplores that journal's setting of scholarship against criticism. Admitting that any intelligent critic of, say, seventeenth-century verse must take into account that age's usage and poetic conventions, Leavis distinguishes this from the claim of the medievalist Rosamund Tuve that students can make no judgments before acquiring an immense apparatus of scholarship. Critics should concern themselves with literary matters, not social history at large. Impractical as that stipulation may be, had Lewis known of it he must surely have judged it an error on the right side. The principle that critics should stick to literature underlies Ian Robinson's book on Chaucer, which, as I suggested in Chapter 2, treats Lewis's poetic criticism far more sympathetically than his history of ideas.

Future literary historians may accept the distinction between emotive and referential language yet convict Richards of sustaining a false dichotomy between the languages of poetry and science, of feeling and of knowledge. While honoring Lewis for taking a stand against technocracy and critical authoritarianism, they may regret his failure to exploit the weakness in Richards's case by upholding — whether with Barfield or with Leavis — the case for literature as embodying, through perception of analogies and resemblances,[42] the kind of knowing implicit in the French verb *connaître,* as distinct from purely intellectual knowing *(savoir).*

41. Leavis, "Education and the Universities: A Sketch for an English School," *Scrutiny* 19 (1950-51): 162-83, esp. 183.
42. Cf. Gregory Wolfe, "Language and Myth in the Ransom Trilogy," in Schakel and Huttar, eds., *Word and Story in C. S. Lewis,* 64-65.

CHAPTER 5

Fiction Writer for Adults

BETWEEN 1933 AND 1957, Lewis published seven works of fiction for adults and seven for children. All are allegories or fantasies save for *Till We Have Faces,* a psychological novel based on the myth of Cupid and Psyche. The most explicit allegory, *The Pilgrim's Regress* (1933), is often dismissed as a conversion story,[1] but it upset its few reviewers far less than *That Hideous Strength* (1945), a satire of technocracy with the added irritant of thinly disguised caricatures of colleagues.

In the novels a movement is discernible from naive allegory in the *Regress* to psychological realism in *Till We Have Faces,* via science fiction in the space trilogy. As Lewis pointed out with regard to his preference for Orwell's *Animal Farm* over *Nineteen Eighty-Four,* admixture of genres rarely satisfies like pure form,[2] hence the quasi-realistic fable *That Hideous Strength* has pleased critics less than the purely mythopoeic *Perelandra.* The trilogy shows an element of improvisation, for Lewis enters as a character at the end of *Out of the Silent Planet* and both before and after Ransom's voyage in *Perelandra,* but the narrator of *That Hideous Strength*

---

1. Cf. John Henry Newman, *Loss and Gain* (1848); Ronald Knox, *A Spiritual Aeneid* (1918); and Thomas Merton, *The Seven-Storey Mountain* (1948), abridged as *Elected Silence* (1969).

2. In his essay "George Orwell" (1955), Lewis writes concerning *Animal Farm:* "A myth . . . allowed to speak for itself . . . says all its author wants it to say and (equally important) . . . doesn't say anything else."

remains anonymous. In that novel, even Ransom becomes a marginal and mythic figure. By contrast, the Chronicles of Narnia show a coherent characterization and design. Most though not all fictional works by Lewis involve a dream-vision, a sudden dislocation of the protagonist into another world or society, a journey toward enlightenment and self-completion, and the assertion of hierarchical order against anarchy or preying of the strong upon the weak.[3] But *Till We Have Faces* has no villain or demon, only a predatory element within Orual, the central figure.

A further element in most of the novels is the prominence given to the language employed by characters.[4] This is natural in view of their most common feature, dislocation to a wholly unfamiliar environment. Lewis's general aims have been defined as (1) to resensitize readers to the spiritual realm,[5] (2) to bring them from misery to felicity,[6] and (3) to convey "valuable meaning" through pleasant instruction.[7] The first aim one can accept without demur as of a piece with that of Lewis's sermons and apologetics, most of which were intended to enlighten listeners conditioned by their secular culture. That the second aim is responsible for the loyalty of readers is disputable, since most of us react negatively if we feel we have been got at. Yet again the aim seems undisputable and in keeping with Lewis's medieval scholarship. The third, while open to the same objection, is identical with the function assigned literary works by Sidney. As several critics note, and as the following study will show, each novel represents a different genre of fiction.[8]

---

3. Colin Manlove, in "'Caught Up into the Larger Pattern'" (in Peter J. Schakel and Charles A. Huttar, eds., *Word and Story*, 256-76), lists a number of elements or techniques that recur throughout Lewis's fiction: dislocation, either physical or philosophical (258); "stress" on "spiritual growth" (263); breaking out of enclosures (264); emphasis on "meeting others" (265); a "journey out of the self" (265); "individual or local actions" being "predetermined" (267); and the intertwining of "fiction and reality, accident and design" (268).

4. Gregory Wolfe, "Essential Speech," in Schakel and Huttar, eds., *Word and Story*, 58; Doris T. Myers, *C. S. Lewis in Context*, 50, 82-83, 88.

5. Wolfe, "Essential Story," 65.

6. Paul Piehler, "Myth or Allegory?" in Schakel and Huttar, eds., *Word and Story*, 212.

7. Donald E. Glover, "C. S. Lewis and the Tradition of Visionary Romance," in Schakel and Huttar, eds., *Word and Story*, 171.

8. Esp. Manlove, "'Caught Up into the Larger Pattern,'" 275.

Allegory: *The Pilgrim's Regress* (1933)

In his preface to the third edition (1943),[9] Lewis castigated his first novel for its uncharitable temper and an obscurity compounded of allusions to interwar criticism and culture, names comprehensible only to readers with a classical education, a private understanding of the major target "Romanticism,"[10] and a mistaken assumption that idealist philosophy constituted the main highway to Christian belief. To readers of *Surprised by Joy* or the "Great War" disputations, that now little-trodden path will be familiar.

In this wartime edition Lewis added explanatory chapter heads that are often more explicit than or even inconsistent with his text. Before the second chapter of book 2, for example, he tells us that John gives up his religion "with profound relief" and at once "has his first explicitly moral experience." In the text, John bounds along crying "There is no Landlord" or "black hole" (hell), but to me his delight in the beauty of mountains, sunlight, and castle on looking back at Puritania is more striking than his moral experience, a dialogue in which Mr. Vertue dissuades him from misusing his new freedom by killing birds (51-53). Later the preface claims that Mother Kirk represents not the Church but Christianity in general, yet in the text (100) she calls herself the Landlord's "daughter-in-law," hence the Bride of Christ.

At times headline, narrator, and allegorical symbol are at odds. The reductionist Gus Halfways calls his sister Media a "brown girl," or sexual temptress, a rebuke described in the headline as the "modern literary movement" debunking "Rapture" before it could become "Lust." Nothing in the context indicates any racist overtone to "brown girls." Her name, but not her friendly conversation, suggests a heroine of magazine romance. Next, the headline of the section in which Gus is showing off his motorcycle ironically remarks, "The poetry of the Machine Age is so

9. I am using the Fount paperback edition of *The Pilgrim's Regress* (1977; reprinted 1986). Subsequent page references are to this edition.

10. Lewis explains "romanticism" as feelings of "intense longing" evoked by nature and the "marvellous in literature" (11-12). Senses of "romantic" not germane to *Pilgrim's Regress* include adventure stories, "Titanic" heroes and emotions, "abnormal" feelings or imagery, egoism and subjectivism, and primitivism.

very pure." From the text (book 2, chap. 8), it is not clear why Gus views his idol as "real art," in contrast to the "self-deception and phallic sentiment" of traditional deities who were really "brown boys and girls whitewashed" (62), since in real life lovers and fast vehicles seem quite compatible. The text signifies only a worship of the machine and its speed. Any reader capable of following the classical and literary references does better to use an early edition without headlines. The novel was originally written in two weeks during August 1932, with a small, highly educated readership in mind.[11] The headlines represent Lewis's attempt to make it more widely comprehensible.

As in Bunyan's masterpiece, the narrator who dreams the events remains stable while the hero develops. Likewise the hero's name suggests a representative figure, though of a post-Christian age. But whereas the adult Christian of *Pilgrim's Progress* flees the wrath about to overtake the City of Destruction, the puzzled adolescent John quits the Puritania of his childhood, ruled by an alternately benign and threatening Steward on behalf of an unseen Landlord.[12] Though interrupted by various dangers and entrapments, Christian's journey is linear, toward a Celestial City visible only near the end. John seeks a paradisal Island already glimpsed, and perhaps suggested by Yeats's "Lake Isle of Innisfree." He first travels westward through a tableland typifying contemporary culture, then northward to the land of the Pale Young Men, typifying interwar reactions against Romanticism; he then travels vicariously further north in the report of his companion Vertue, to the abode of Mr. Savage, where dwell tribes typifying Communist, Nazi, and Fascist regimes. Next, he goes vicariously south in Vertue's report of slaying the Dragon responsible for contemporary cults of sex, drugs, and the occult. Finally, after he is carried by Mother Kirk over the Grand Canyon of sin and unbelief, John turns back east toward the mountains and Castle that are now imbued with the celestial goodness and beauty he had envisioned in his Island. He has made a circuitous journey that is at once a progression through adolescent rebellion toward mature

11. See Kathryn Lindskoog, *Finding the Landlord: A Guidebook to C. S. Lewis's "Pilgrim's Regress,"* xxvi-vii.

12. Lindskoog traces the term "Landlord" to Herbert's "Redemption" (*Finding the Landlord*, 46-47).

acceptance of moral choice and discipline and a regression from contemporary secularism toward a more central and traditional Christian faith than the distorted versions represented by Puritania and Mr. Broad [Church]. As in Bunyan's allegory, the hero's journey represents his own conversion and quest for salvation, while its localities and their denizens represent the world he observes during that quest.

For several reasons, to expect of Lewis's *Regress* the earthiness, drama, and broad application of its great precursor would be unfair. First, the City of Destruction and path descending toward Hell even from the gates of the Celestial City derive from that prime source of Christian eschatology, the book of Revelation, while the black hole and ambivalent Steward come out of Lewis's childhood experience of Protestantism as preached by his grandfather and practiced in Ulster. Second, while everyone is at some time mired in the Slough of Despond or imprisoned by Giant Despair, only the well-educated ever feel imprisoned in Darkest Zeitgeistheim by Sigismund (Freud).[13] As remarked in the 1943 preface, the intellectual traveling toward Christianity via the idealism of Bradley or Bosanquet is a rarer being than Lewis realized while writing. Third, though not without tense moments, John's quest can have none like the trial in Vanity Fair, for the angriest disputation in a free society lacks the edge of a struggle against persecution.

Admitting these differences, what qualities of Bunyan's allegory can we legitimately expect in the *Pilgrim's Regress?* Lewis wrote the tale when nearing the end of his exposition of the medieval love-allegory. Thirty years later, in his "Vision of John Bunyan," he described allegory as giving "one thing in terms of another," but he vigorously condemned its treatment as a "cryptogram" based on ideas already familiar and therefore superfluous. Its scenes, characters, and dialogue should have their own validity: rather than decoding a vale as humility, the reader should be refreshed by humility as by a "green valley." Bunyan's writing succeeded (as Leavis had remarked) because of his ear for "popular idiom and cadence" and because each sentence depended on the whole context.[14]

13. Lindskoog suggests that the reference may be to the fourteenth-century Emperor Sigismund, who gave Jan Huss a false promise of safe passage (*Finding the Landlord,* 31).

14. Lewis, "Vision of John Bunyan," in *Selected Literary Essays,* 148-50.

Although Lewis's subject matter precluded the down-to-earth quality of Bunyan's writing, we can ask whether his symbols — the scenes, characters, and dialogue — live independently of any key and without encoding what is already familiar. Given Lewis's statement in his 1943 preface (20-21) that despite "obscurities" due to "autobiographical" elements, he had attempted an allegory of general significance, we can enquire whether it is more autobiographical than he admits.

So far as the story shows John — that is, "Jack" Lewis — growing up by losing his fear of confinement in a "black hole" and his distress at the Steward's fickleness, then by exposing false reasoning and parasitic lifestyles, it is confessedly autobiographical. The same is true of John's quest, but his sexual indulgence represents male lust in general, doubtless observed in wartime. Having the raw intensity of recent experience, unmellowed by time and humor, the *Regress* in several ways enhances our understanding of the reluctant and primarily intellectual conversion traced in *Surprised by Joy*. Nothing in the autobiography corresponds to John's protest when urged to follow Vertue: "He is mad, sir," or the Man's (Christ's) reply: "No madder than yourself" (179-80). In the narrative context, John is right, for Vertue has just made threatening gestures and hurled a boulder at him from crags above the vale of Wisdom (Idealism). When the Christ-figure calls John mad for wishing to return there, he is justified only by the reader's presumed belief in the Island and dissatisfaction with Wisdom's austere and chill hospitality. Again, John's tears on beholding his father's ruined cottage show the *Regress* autobiographical at a deeper level than *Surprised by Joy*, for Lewis told Greeves that he "could cry" at feeling pity but not love for his dying father.[15] Even Lewis's admission in the preface of having lost his temper in the portrait of the Pale Young Men scarcely removes the disguise in that episode of his antipathy to T. S. Eliot and the Anglo-Catholic movement.[16] The names of the Young Men include not only Neo-Angular but also Humanist and Neo-Classical, thus typifying two major targets in OHEL, written many years later.

15. Letter of 25 July 1929, in *They Stand Together*, 305.
16. First evident in letters to Eliot dated 19 April and 2 June 1931, on Eliot's slowness in considering an essay Lewis submitted for *Criterion*.

The crucial episodes for our consideration are those symbols conveying Lewis's view of modern intellectual trends. By his own admission, the least satisfactory are John's encounters with the Pale Young Men (book 6, chaps. 2-4, 7) and the children of Wisdom (book 7, chap. 10). Even without a sweeping headline on the "strange bedfellows" made by anti-Romanticism, Freudianism, and "Negativism," it is difficult to suspend disbelief when Mr. Neo-Angular attributes his generosity in sharing his supper with John and Vertue to "dogma, not feeling." Having abandoned "the humanitarian and egalitarian fallacies," Mr. Neo-Classical refuses to share his, and Mr. Humanist hopes the wanderers have not brought the "romantic virus" (124). What could better fit Lewis's condemnation of cryptogrammatic allegory[17] than Neo-Classical's praise of a cubical piece of beef and square biscuit, or the Pale Young Men's responses to John's question concerning their common principles? After replying together, "Catholicism, Humanism, Classicism" (125), they admit that, since only Neo-Angular believes in the Landlord, their real bonds are in being sons of Mr. Enlightenment, who begat Sigismund upon his first wife Epichaerecacia and the Pale Young Men upon his second wife Euphuia[18] (terms known to a mere handful of readers), and in their common hatred of Mr. Halfways and his music, presumably jazz.

By contrast, Mr. Sensible's servant Drudge, though likewise a literary "humor," lives independently of explanation. Given his master's complacent parasitism and abuse, it makes sense for him to leave with John and Vertue, then join Mr. Savage further north. Yet to attribute the interwar growth of Communism and Fascism to economic deprivation does not explain the alienation of Drudge from Sensible. The missing element lies in Mr. Sensible's link with the Oxford tradition of gracious living by what the struggling young Lewis called a "scarlet conclave of old men."[19] Many years later, he identified Mr. Sensible with a line of essayists and critics from Montaigne to Arnold and

17. In his 1962 broadcast, "The Vision of John Bunyan," later published in *Selected Literary Essays.*

18. The Greek term *epichaerecacia* means pleasure in the suffering of others *(Schadenfreude); euphuia* refers to shapeliness or attractiveness.

19. "The Lewis Family Papers," compiled by W. H. Lewis, VII, 293-94 (summer 1923). Told that securing an English post could take twenty years, Lewis humorously considers poisoning a member of the "conclave."

Saintsbury.[20] More broadly, Sensible represents the English upper-middle class, the Eloi of H. G. Wells's *Time Machine,* who could not survive without their drudges the Morlocks. Yet neither the Eloi nor, presumably, the dons showed Mr. Sensible's combined civility to John and harshness to Drudge. Even late-Victorian aestheticism does not explain the "touch of mythical life" (preface, 19) in Mr. Sensible, the self-interested moralizing on the impending demise of his dog: "We must take our life on the terms it is given us. . . . [T]he great art of life is to moderate our passions. . . . Confound that Drudge. Hi! whoreson, are we to wait all night for our supper?" Or Mr. Sensible on the Canyon: "Surely a modest tour along the cliffs on *this* side . . . would give you much the same . . . scenery, and save your necks" (108-9).

While theological liberalism is better realized in the modernist bishop of the *Great Divorce,* both Mr. Broad (Church) and Mr. Sensible come alive in discourses conceivably based on oracular platitudes heard by the young Lewises at their father's gatherings. Whether North and South have the "mythical life" claimed in the text (preface, 19) is debatable. The barren landscape that John and Vertue traverse seems as real as the Canyon, yet too featureless to be associated with the Pale Young Men, with hard-line ideologies, or even with the tribes of Savage, whose mountain lair, with its hint of Berchtesgaden, is simply reported by Vertue. Again, the southern swamp described to John is hard to associate either with decadent Romanticism or with occultism, still less with Nazism, as Lewis claims (preface, 18).

John's Island (book 1, chap. 2) carries more conviction, being glimpsed as a hitherto unseen stretch of road; heard as a bell, a plucked string, and a voice saying "Come"; seen as a primrose-filled wood; and finally revealed by the lifting of mists (33). If it appeals less than Aslan's country, still unseen at the end of the Narnian Chronicles, this is because its mountain nymphs and enchanters who neither act nor reappear fail to arouse the emotion easily transferred from Aslan to his home.

The preposterous dialogue of the children of Wisdom (book 7, chap. 11), a catalogue of idealist philosophers and gurus, illustrates the book's central weakness as a lack of focus, a disposition to shoot in all

20. Letter to W. L. Kinter, 30 July 1954.

directions, the same defect that mars another fantasy born of anger, *That Hideous Strength.* In the end, the *Pilgrim's Regress* remains of interest as the first fantasy novel by Lewis, with anticipations of the *Screwtape Letters* in its devil Wormwood and of OHEL in its characters Humanist and Neo-Classical. Yet it enabled him to embody his conversion experience and perceptions of the surrounding culture in images and symbols, notably the circular journey, that he would later develop in his space trilogy and Chronicles of Narnia.

The Space Fiction Trilogy

Exactly when Lewis first read David Lindsay's *Voyage to Arcturus* (1920), which he called "shattering, intolerable, and irresistible,"[21] is not known. That pessimistic visionary novel has several features in common with the *Pilgrim's Regress* and the space novels, as the following thumbnail sketch will show.

At a seance, the hero Maskull ("Man's," also "mask") and his companion Nightspore are persuaded by the mysterious intruder Krag to undergo transportation to Tormance, the sole inhabited planet of the solar system Arcturus. Deserted by the others, Maskull traverses symbolically named landscapes where he is influenced by exponents of various ideologies or moral attitudes. In the first, Joiwind and her husband Panawe practice a love that precludes the killing and eating even of plants. Elsewhere Maskull encounters male dominance, female sexuality, materialism, and medieval asceticism. When Krag has presided over his death on the ocean, Maskull is replaced by Nightspore, who experiences the nihilistic vision that ends the book. Beyond the music of Muspel (the warm paradise of Norse mythology), for which Maskull and others have yearned, a final nothingness defeats both Muspel and Surtur, the creator and provider figure in Tormance.

How far Lewis derived the idea of an allegorical journey from Lindsay, from Bunyan, and from personal experience is uncertain, but two parallels between *Pilgrim's Regress* and *Voyage to Arcturus* are worth remarking. The first is that, when led toward three statues representing

21. Lewis, "On Science Fiction," in *Of Other Worlds,* 71.

distinct identity, love, and religious desire, Maskull faces a chasm marking a subterranean transept, along which his ascetic guide Corpang (literally "heart-pain") leads him to the left and by implication to the west. The second parallel occurs once the encounter with the statues has convinced Maskull that Thire, the deity symbolized in the third, is not the supreme power, so that life is at bottom "wrong."[22] As they emerge from underground, and Corpang fears having no guide in the outside world, Maskull reasons that, as he has come from the south where he met Joiwind, they should continue north. Although in the *Pilgrim's Regress* south and north represent cults of self-indulgence or self-deception rather than nature-worship versus nihilism, there are clear parallels with John's westward quest for the Island and Vertue's northern and southern journeys.

A number of parallels between *Voyage to Arcturus* and *Out of the Silent Planet* are also evident. At the initial seance in *Voyage to Arcturus,* a body materializes that Krag identifies with Surtur, the shaping spirit on Tormance, yet also with Surtur's shadow Crystalman, which on every dead face imprints his "awful grin" (210). To reach the ruined house, workshop, and tower at Starkness, from which he will travel in a space-torpedo, Maskull must walk with Nightspore and Krag seven miles from the nearest station. At the beginning of *Out of the Silent Planet,* the "Pedestrian" identified as Ransom is walking to Sterk when a woman persuades him to rescue her son from the workshop where Weston and Devine have built the spaceship in which they transport Ransom to Mars in the youth's stead. Lindsay's cosmonauts travel naked, as do Ransom, Weston, and Devine when troubled by heat. An obvious parallel between Tormance and Malacandra is the perpendicular mountain range in each planet. Maskull's view of the night sky when climbing the launching tower, however, is much slighter than Ransom's sidereal vision from the spaceship, drawn from Lewis's medieval reading.[23] The apparent parallel between Panawe's surprise at Maskull's identification

---

22. David Lindsay, *A Voyage to Arcturus,* 221.

23. Esp. Isidore of Seville, *Etymologiae,* III. In his two-volume edition of this work, Lewis annotated in detail vol. 1, pp. 47, *De Magnitudine Solis;* 48, *De Magnitudine Lunae;* 53, *De Lumine Lunae;* 58-59, on eclipses; and 71, on names of stars. In *Etymologiae* III, lxxi, he underlined the explanation of Greek sun and moon myths and cults.

of enlightenment with development of tools and Oyarsa's disbelief in the technocratic values of Weston and Devine may result from their common basis in *Gulliver's Travels.*[24]

Though scenically resembling Lewis's Malacandra (Mars), Tormance, like Perelandra (Venus), is a new planet. If Maskull's descent to Wombflash Forest recalls the subterranean vision of Ransom at the end of *Perelandra,* Nightspore's penultimate vision of evolving species (283) vividly contrasts with Ransom's awe and delight at the richness of subterranean life. So does Maskull's X-ray vision of animals, in which "naked Life" passes into his own body, then a "crustacean" re-forms there, hard and ugly (191).

The question as to why Lewis felt inspired by the cosmic pessimist Lindsay has no simple answer. As well as a tendency to borrow devices and motifs, he also had a critic's capacity to "enjoy" an author's view of life, however different from his own. He found no less inspiration in the scientific positivist Wells's *First Men in the Moon.*[25] Maskull's extreme reverence for Joiwind as a "blessed spirit" and his condemnation of Gleameil's self-indulgence in leaving her husband and children to pursue an otherworldly vision (175), her awareness that she will not return, and the pathetic farewell scene, suggest that Lindsay's fantasy, like those of Nesbit and Haggard, touched the ever-sensitive spot of Lewis's grief for his mother. Soon after publishing *Out of the Silent Planet,* he claimed to have begun to write it on finding that a pupil took planetary colonization seriously. He also expressed surprise that no reviewer had commented on its implicit theology. Ten years after publishing *Perelandra,* he said that Lindsay's *Voyage* had suggested the enrichment of Wellsian scientific and Vernian voyage-romance with spiritual experience.[26]

24. David Downing, *Planets in Peril: A Critical Study of C. S. Lewis's Ransom Trilogy,* 126, cites a list of parallels by Jeanette H. Lytton: protagonists find themselves in unknown surroundings through the treachery of fellow voyagers, meet rational beings, learn their language, communicate their own culture, and finally leave for home.

25. Downing lists parallels with Wells's book: physicists building a craft; the younger one being mercenary; antigravity device; sound of meteorites on hull; steel shutters to exclude light; voyagers fear aliens whom they themselves endanger (*Planets in Peril,* 124).

26. Letters to Sister Penelope, 5 August 1939, and to W. L. Kinter, 28 March 1953.

Among several echoes of the *Voyage to Arcturus* in other books by Lewis is Krag's invitation for Maskull to visit "Crystalman's country" (24), recalling heaven as "Aslan's country." Where Lindsay shows the divinity on Tormance as in Hindu fashion both creative and destructive — Surtur and Crystalman — as a Christian Lewis embodies the creative power of good in Aslan or Maleldil and the destructive power of evil in the White Witch, Queen Jadis, or Wormwood. Behind the haunting music of Muspel is a final nothingness that Lewis was to experience only when grieving for Joy *(A Grief Observed)*.

A few motifs of the *Regress* can be traced in *Out of the Silent Planet,* and, indeed, *Perelandra*. One is structural: the hero's journey and his return enriched by tuition and experience. From an early description, Ransom can be seen to resemble Lewis in age and build.[27] Another is the association of divinity with an island, to which John is summoned by music and Ransom by the "sweet" yet "seemingly remote" voice of the Oyarsa.[28] The name of Oyarsa's locality, Meldilorn, is a clever compound of "mel" (sweetness), "eldil" (angel), and "[for]lorn."[29] The use of names as signifiers also recalls the *Regress*. Thus the scientist's name Weston is a pun on "western," while those of Ransom and Devine allude directly and ironically to the Christian deity.[30] That of Augray (augurer) signifies the role of sorns as scientists and savants, and that of the dim-witted youth Harry, for whom Ransom is the substitute, conceivably refers to the phrase "Tom, Dick, and Harry" for the unlearned, and perhaps ironically to a colleague's nickname.[31] Several names and words being of Viking origin, Malacandra has a northern flavor.[32]

Lewis's other major source-text is *Paradise Lost,* and beyond that Genesis. But whereas the averted fall of Eve forms the central motif of

27. Downing, *Planets in Peril,* 102.

28. *Out of the Silent Planet* (London: Pan, 1968), 138. Subsequent references are to this edition.

29. Cf. Mr. Mell, David Copperfield's flute-playing teacher.

30. The name of Devine, whose main interest is in exploring for precious metals, also evokes use of a divining rod.

31. T. D. ("Harry") Weldon.

32. Downing, *Planets in Peril,* 25: *hrossa* (horse); *handramit* (lowland); *harandra* (highlands).

Perelandra, in *Out of the Silent Planet* the fall of Satan is narrated by Oyarsa to Ransom to explain the "silence" of Thulcandra (Earth), its isolation from the divinely governed solar system. A subtler allusion to the poem is Weston's reproach of Ransom for creeping into his "back-yard like a thief" (28).[33]

Whatever the book's merit as science fiction, it undoubtedly repays what Lewis called "literary" reading. The rereader notes the structure of chapters: five chapters (9-13) on Ransom's education by the *hrossa,* culminating in the plot's central episode in the middle chapter (13), when Ransom's disobedience to the *eldil's* command results in the death of his benefactor Hyoi; then five chapters on his meeting with the Oyarsa at Meldilorn (17-21), which culminate in the comic humiliation of Weston, a rough parallel to that of Satan in the tenth book of *Paradise Lost.* One notes also the parallel between the meeting of the fallen angels in the opening books of Milton's poem followed by Satan's journey to Eden, and the meeting of Ransom and the scientists in chapters 1-2 followed in turn by the journey to Malacandra, where Ransom intrudes with fatal result upon the paradisal *hrossa* community. Although it is Weston who slays Hyoi, whether out of fear, for meat, or for collection as a specimen, Ransom instigated the fateful *hnakra* hunt by telling the *hrossa* of his encounter with the *hnakra.* Again, two chapters (3-4) on the journey in the spacecraft are balanced by the two on Ransom's transportation by Augray to Meldilorn (15-16).

The only internal evidence in *Out of the Silent Planet* that Lewis was planning further space novels occurs in Oyarsa's final charge to Ransom (chap. 21). Although "heavenly years" are not as those of Earth, the current year "has long been prophesied as" one of "stirrings and high changes and the siege of Thulcandra may be near its end" (166-67). The entry of Lewis as narrator in the conclusion and epilogue of *Out of the Silent Planet* but at both the beginning and the end of *Perelandra* suggests that the planning was haphazard. The principal defect of *Out of the Silent Planet,* inconsistency in the character of Weston, further suggests improvisation. A renowned physicist would be unlikely to travel in a personally constructed spacecraft with the gold-hunting Devine, let alone dream up a naive project for colonizing another planet

33. Cf. Satan's entry into Eden, *Paradise Lost,* book 4, lines 188-92.

and explain it in pidgin English. Both in Weston's humiliation by the linguist Ransom and in his ducking by command of Oyarsa ("Much water and many times"), Lewis took the bookish schoolboy's revenge on the science master, to the detriment of his literary art. During the temptation episodes of *Perelandra,* Weston becomes the more sinister and more credible Un-man.

Lewis wrote only one draft, with minor revisions, of his "holiday" fiction, and, like many a part-time novelist, he learned his craft on the job. Had he, like the perfectionist Tolkien, completed and revised his trilogy before offering it for publication, it would have been a finer work. Yet the public response to *Out of the Silent Planet* and *The Screwtape Letters* must have encouraged him to persevere.

A second reading shows the trouble Lewis took to make *Out of the Silent Planet* a credible scientific romance. During his journey to the habitations of the *séroni,* Ransom realizes how the breathable air on Malacandra lingers in the *handramits* or depressions corresponding to the "canals" of Mars (103).[34] Though the power of Malacandra's forests to keep its atmosphere warm would now be disputed, the bones of extinct animals and birds on its frigid surface indicate a credible evolution of an old planet. Darwinian competition is ruled out, however, by an orderly distribution of functions among the planet's few species and by common obedience to orders from the Oyarsa (archangel) via his *eldila* (angels). Thus the elongated *sorns,* the planet's scientists and savants, live separately in their caves without engaging in verbal and professional combat like academics on Earth. In the denser atmosphere at water level the *hrossa* are the poets and singers of Malacandra, as well as its food gatherers, hunters, and tradespeople. Below ground dwell the planet's artisans and craftsmen, the *pfifltriggi.* Each of the three species has its own language, but the common language is that of the *hrossa,* since the science and knowledge of the *sorns* are conveyable in any language and the art of the *pfifltriggi* can easily be observed, but poetry can be conveyed truly only in its original tongue. Having

34. Lewis said later: "When I . . . put canals on Mars I believe I already knew that better telescopes had dissipated that old optical delusion . . . [that is] part of the Martian myth . . . in the common mind" ("On Science Fiction," in *Of Other Worlds,* 69).

no overlapping functions, the species use each other's gifts, as when the *sorns* depend upon *pfiffltriggi* to manufacture their instruments.

The principle of order rather than competition likewise obtains in mating and reproduction, so the *hrossa* feel sexual desire only before begetting the few young needed to maintain a stable population. The *sorns* who question Ransom during a break in his journey with Augray diagnose lack of order and hierarchy as the cause of Earth's isolation and miseries. One *sorn* says that human beings have "no Oyarsa," Augray that each tries to function as "a little Oyarsa," and an old *sorn* that humans "have no *eldila*" (119). In comparing human self-dependence to a woman trying to beget her own young, the same speaker betrays a masculine prejudice that seems implicit in Lewis's coinage "Maleldil" (Male-eldil?) for the cosmic deity. The name has otherwise been explained as "Lord of the Covenant" and "Lord of Hosts."[35] The name "Mal[e]acandra" for this planet where Ransom speaks only with males has a different explanation, for on Perelandra (Venus) he will converse with its female inhabitant.

Because of this breakdown of order on Earth, Weston owns loyalty to no species but his own, yet he is commended by Oyarsa as being above the mere self-interest of Devine. Weston's annoying pidgin English is apt to deflect attention from the subtle link between his scientific humanism and his Nietzschean excuse for killing Hyoi, that the good of the "lower" species must yield to that of the "higher." At the time of writing, this principle was being invoked in defense of Nazi racism and aggression. One might say that, just as in Europe racism and "might is right" were filling a vacuum left by the breakdown of old hierarchies of church and class, so in Thulcandra the scientist Weston and the technocrat or plutocrat Devine were intent on filling the power vacuum resulting from the lack of an Oyarsa and *eldila*. Yet one remark by Weston limits the use of this analogy. He tells Ransom that he and Devine are acting "upon orders" in kidnapping him. Likewise, the Oyarsa of Malacandra tells Ransom his version of the Judeo-Christian myth, that Thulcandra's planetary Oyarsa has rebelled against Maleldil and is now bound to Thulcandra, ruling it as he pleases. In the trilogy, therefore, what historians might see as a phase in the evolution of

---

35. Downing, *Planets in Peril*, 41, citing Joe Christopher, *C. S. Lewis,* and Evan Gibson, *C. S. Lewis: Spinner of Tales.*

Europe's future, from a system of interlocking monarchies to a federation of democracies, becomes a conspiracy between applied science and the powers of evil. In the mid-twentieth century the new order proclaimed by the Axis powers looked much more like a demonic conspiracy than an interregnum. The species on Malacandra obey the Oyarsa[36] but respect each other's functions and lifestyles, without competition or pecking order, and in this sense enjoy at once the benefits of monarchy, theocracy, and democracy. They are denied only the "progress" accruing from applied science and economic competition. An unacknowledged or else unwitting inspiration of Lewis's trilogy was William Morris's *News from Nowhere.*

By a nice irony, the philologist Ransom can adapt to life on Malacandra as the scientists cannot. In learning the *hrossa* speech and grammar, he shows a true scientific curiosity that eventually enables him to shed the fear instilled by Weston's and Devine's account of meeting *sorns.* Indeed, he shows himself their superior in a practical sense, by acting as interpreter in their dialogue with Oyarsa, an episode that brings out the best and the worst in Lewis.

As Ransom traverses the island, the mixture of the familiar and the strange creates a sense of awe. On the seemingly empty slopes, crowned by a grander set of monoliths than at Stonehenge, the air is filled with "silvery" whispering that his guide explains, speaking in hushed tones as in a church: "The island is all full of *eldila*" (125). Counterbalancing this awe is the comfort of the warmest air Ransom has felt on the planet, as on an autumn day at home. Ransom's mingled awe and trust will set off Weston's arrogance and unease, but in the meantime Ransom has been learning about the planet's history from its sculptured monoliths and about the lifestyle of *pfifltriggi* from Kanakaberaka. Among the *pfifltriggi,* he is told, females count for most, but among the *séroni* for least. By concluding a chapter (chap. 17) with this observation, Lewis gives prominence to a custom by which women became artisans rather than academics.

36. The name "Oyarsa" derives from *ousiarch* (Governor) in Bernardus Silvestris, *Cosmosrophia* (Downing, *Planets in Peril,* 69; Myers, *C. S. Lewis in Context,* 55). Fuller discussion of sources can be found in Roger Lancelyn Green and Walter Hooper, *C. S. Lewis: A Biography,* 162.

Before Weston and Devine arrive on the island, Ransom speaks frankly of their "bentness" to an Oyarsa who admits having underestimated this, and so establishes a rapport that gives point to Ransom's (mis)interpretations of Weston during his translation of Weston's speech. When Weston pleads that superior civilization confers a right of conquest over the *hrossa*, Ransom translates medical skill literally as knowledge of how to stop pain, law more pejoratively as killing, imprisoning, and settling disputes, armaments as knowing methods of killing and, most pejoratively, commerce and transportation as exchanging goods and carrying "heavy weights very quickly a long way. Because of all this . . . it would not be the act of a bent *hnau* if our people killed all your people" (158).

As he proceeds, Ransom finds the abstract terms of Weston's vitalist rhetoric less and less translatable into the concrete speech of the *hrossa*. "Life is greater than any system of morality" becomes "it is better to be alive and bent than to be dead." Then the translator becomes enmeshed in Weston's self-contradiction, for the innate superiority of later creatures through the relentless progress of "Life" that will enable humans to colonize other planets and escape death turns into propositions of increasing absurdity from "the best animal now is the kind of man who makes the big huts and carries the heavy weights" to the human species perpetuating itself by killing "all the *hnau*" in one planet after another (159).[37] When commended by the Oyarsa for not seeking merely his own good, Weston sidesteps the problem of individual mortality by responding, "Me die. Man live" (160). The ensuing dialogue between an Oyarsa baffled by loveless humanism and a scientific humanist baffled by Oyarsa's failure to appreciate the ethic of "loyalty to humanity" ends in the judgment that Satan has taught humanity to transgress all moral injunctions save a minor one, "love of kindred," which he has twisted into "a little blind Oyarsa" in Weston's brain (161). Here Lewis unintentionally anticipates a current theory on the origin of psychopathic behavior.[38] In diagnosing humanity's major sin

---

37. Cf. Myers, *C. S. Lewis in Context*, 50.

38. In a CBC news magazine interview, Dr. Robert Hare (department of psychology, University of British Columbia) described his research as indicating that congenital absence of conscience and empathy results from abnormal circuitry in brain.

as its fear of extinction due to planetary decay, the Oyarsa grafts ecological awareness upon Judeo-Christian mythology.

Not only for the name "Oyarsa" but also for several earlier details Lewis drew on traditional myths and images. At the Rise, the right-hand path led to the house, the left (Latin *sinister,* "on left") to the laboratory. During the voyage, the night sky revealed not empty but deep space, a cosmos or "heavens" filled with life as in medieval astronomy. To this Lewis adds his own comment on totalitarian regimes and scientific humanism, in the picture of Earth as a "megalomaniac disc" that Ransom mistakes for the moon. Here the Mentor jogs the Dreamer's arm.

John Wain's judgment that all Lewis's novels for adults are just "bad"[39] is a ludicrous oversimplification. What limits *Out of the Silent Planet* is the immaturity noted by W. W. Robson: the pun "thick" applied to Weston's body and to his moral intelligence, so inconsistent with his stature as a physicist; the schoolboy humor of ducking Weston to bring him to the proper frame of mind for serious dialogue; even the piquant finale to Ransom's return to Earth, his very Lewisian request for a "pint of bitter" (177). What partially redeems it is the Dreamer's awe at the mystery and beauty of the quasi-medieval cosmos, recalling some memorable accounts in the lectures that were the basis of *The Discarded Image.*

Turning our attention to *Perelandra,* several intended comparisons can be made between its opening and that of *Out of the Silent Planet.* In the earlier novel, the Cambridge don Ransom traverses flat farmland at sunset after a thundershower; in the later, the narrator, the Oxford don Lewis, crosses the flat Worchester Common (suggesting the spacious grounds of Worcester College, quite near Oxford Station) in a gloomy autumnal dusk. The dreariness of the first landscape is in the main objective; that of the second more evidently projects the narrator's self-doubt and fear as he approaches Ransom's cottage. Likewise nourished on Wellsian science fiction, he fears *eldila* as Ransom feared *sorns.* Like Ransom he has left his haversack behind, though on the train. As the narrator fears nervous breakdown, then lunacy itself, the

39. John Wain, "The Great Clerk," in James Como, ed., *C. S. Lewis at the Breakfast Table,* 74.

landscape becomes increasingly symbolic: an abandoned factory and boarded-up house yield to "crossroads" by a "Wesleyan chapel" as belief returns in Ransom's account of Malacandrans and eldila.[40] When Lewis plucks up courage to enter the blacked-out cottage (the first of many allusions to the war), he stumbles over a white coffin, Ransom's second space vehicle. As Ransom's intended reproach (of Weston and Devine) came out as a feeble protest, so that of Lewis turns into "Thank God you've come" (15), after which the narrator's fears subside.

Primarily the openings differ in that Ransom's Perelandran voyage and return take place within the first two chapters, so that our attention is directed less to his adventure than to its import, which is more explicitly Christian than that of *Out of the Silent Planet*. In fact, the author neither describes the voyage nor attempts plausibility. On Venus, or Perelandra, Ransom is not troubled by problems with breathing or temperature, while Weston steps ashore in pith helmet and shorts, equipped with camping stove and canned food. Without explanation, Weston's pidgin English has been replaced by fluent Old Solar, the language Ransom learned to speak on Malacandra (19-20).

A second difference lies in allusions during *Perelandra* to the Inklings, some incidental, some important, and one fundamental though implicit. The name Humphrey (Havard) for the doctor who attends the returned Ransom exemplifies the first, the epithet "Dark Lord" for Earth's devil the second.[41] The most subtle allusion, Weston's metamorphosis into the diabolical "Un-man," derives immediately from Weston's having toyed with a dark Power beyond his comprehension, and ultimately from Barfield's explanation (in the "Great War") of Steiner's distinction between "Lucifer," the devil appealing to human pride and wish for knowledge, and "Ahriman," the devil of materialist technocracy.[42] In *Out of the Silent Planet*, Weston acted as Lucifer and

40. I am using the reprint of *Perelandra* entitled *Voyage to Venus* (London: Pan, 1960). Subsequent page references are to this edition.

41. Tolkien read drafts of *The Lord of the Rings* to Lewis before the writing of *Out of the Silent Planet* and to the Inklings in wartime (Humphrey Carpenter, *Inklings*, 65-66, 135ff.). Dr. R. E. Havard, one of the Inklings, was nicknamed "Humphrey" (Carpenter, *Inklings*, 138).

42. Ahriman is the chief of Zoroastrian evil spirits. See the discussion of the "Great War" between Lewis and Barfield in Chapter 1 above.

Devine as Ahriman; in *Perelandra* we meet only Weston as the Luciferic Un-man tempting the Lady to assert her maturity by staying on the Fixed Land.

Just when does the one become the other? Ransom first realizes Weston's demonic character upon finding him tearing a frog with his fingernails (99-100). Yet after vainly trying to convert Ransom from Christianity to a mishmash of emergent evolution and a Nietzschean faith in progress via supermen, Weston falls into a convulsion signifying demonic possession. His word *nisus* (84), for the amoral Life Force responsible for human "progress," is a key word in Alexander's *Space, Time and Deity,* on which Lewis drew for his "Summa." There, however, it refers to an emergent godhead. The gradual transition from "he" or "Weston" to "it" or "the Un-man" takes place during the central chapter that begins with the tearing of frogs. The term "Un-man" has a range of literal and figurative meanings: an inhuman being that inhabits Weston's body; its attempt to "un-gender" Ransom and the Lady by inducing cowardice and female chauvinism, respectively; its subversion of human dependence on Maleldil; and its being the antitype of Christ the Son of Man (Maleldil the Younger). The name "Ransom," incidentally, was an afterthought, the hero's original name being "Unwin."[43] At what point Lewis first conceived of him as the Perelandran equivalent of Christ is not known.

For all its admixture of fact and supposed authority,[44] *Perelandra* reads best as mythopoeic fantasy. The Green Lady and her lizard, possibly suggested by Spenser's Una and her dragon, inhabit an unfallen planet. While slaying and incinerating the Un-man, Ransom suffers a foot wound equivalent to Achilles' heel. The Lady sees herself as a child becoming "older" through instruction rather than experience. To Ransom she appears in turn as a "goddess," a "Madonna" (57), an unfallen Eve, and finally as Queen and bride to the planet's King. Yet from the

---

43. Lewis first offered *Out of the Silent Planet* to Allen and Unwin, hence the change of name (Downing, *Planets in Peril,* 52).

44. In a footnote near the end of chapter 1, Lewis cites a source from "Natvilcius" (*Oxford English Dictionary:* " *nat wilc,* meaning 'anon'") on the "form in which eldils appear to our senses," with an invented literary reference, Latin quotation, and translation.

first, she speaks to him as princess to noble, bidding him greet his "Lady and Mother" for her. His quasi-medieval response "Our Mother and Lady is dead" (59) refers in the story to Eve and in its author's life to his childhood bereavement, but could mislead by apparently referring to the Blessed Virgin. The Green Lady's account (58) of being driven from King Tor by "waves" conveys little until near the end, when Tor refers to dependence on Maleldil as throwing oneself "into the wave" (195). Retrospectively, this converts the sundering into a means of exposing the Lady to temptation and spiritual growth.

The obviousness of green as a sign of the Lady's innocence throws into relief the problem of Ransom's piebald skin. Why she nicknames him "Piebald" need puzzle us no more than why white men were called "Palefaces," save that Ransom is untypically innocent of human vices and corruptions, while the equally innocent King Tor has no significant color. We can explain Ransom's color either literally, by his voyage with one side exposed to the sun, or symbolically, by his disobedience while hunting with the *hrossa*. By the opening of chapter 12 (138), he observes his skin to be uniformly ivory, so that if first seen now he would not be called "Piebald." At this time he has resolved to kill the Un-man and been advised to sleep by the Younger Maleldil, who said, "My name also is Ransom" (135). In the final chapter (chap. 17), Queen Tinidril uses "Piebald" simply as a name. All this suggests that Ransom was piebald literally and in two senses figuratively: innocent on the side turned toward Earth, in comparison with its ruling Power, and sinful on the side facing the heavens; and, until his decision to kill the Un-man, not fully integrated as a servant of Maleldil. When finally interpreting the events, King Tor muses that were a man cleft in twain, and half turned to earth, his "living half must still follow Maleldil" (195). By now the division has become a choice between body and soul, matter and spirit. In 1951, Lewis congratulated an American reader on being the first to see the development in Ransom's character since *Out of the Silent Planet;*[45] he later added that Ransom typified Christ only insofar as any Christian should.[46]

The symbols of the Floating Islands and Fixed Land are even more

45. Letter to W. L. Kinter, 28 November 1951.
46. Letter to W. L. Kinter, 28 March 1953.

complex. To stay afloat is to accept and subject oneself to the "wave" sent by Maleldil. By implication, to stay on land is to set up on one's own.[47] From his reading and his arguments with Barfield, Lewis undoubtedly knew of Coleridge's distinction between *natura naturata* ("nature natured") and *natura naturans* ("nature naturing"), between being open to change and growth and being (in the Lady's case prematurely) set in one's ways. Barfield's distinction between poetry as the primal language and prose as that of rational and scientific man[48] is hinted at when Ransom looks for Weston but also for food on the Fixed Land. He finds nuts with kernels tasting "austere and prosaic" after the fruit of the floating islands (90). Near the end of the book, the eldils comment on the Great Dance in psalmodic or liturgical prose, while the King, rather than the Queen, interprets events in plain prose and blesses Ransom on his way. As Lewis remarked, he gained more from Barfield than Barfield from him.[49]

Technically, a distinct gain in sophistication is apparent in the early narration of Ransom's journey and return and a gradual shift during the third chapter from the narrator's viewpoint to Ransom's. Conversely, in the final chapters the viewpoint shifts back, beginning with "He remembers lying still" (170), when Ransom is waking in the cave. A paragraph later, the narrator comments on Ransom's mental confusion and his own difficulty in conveying the recovering Ransom's impressions. During the penultimate chapter (chap. 16), constant reminders of Ransom as observer and speaker, with eyes still attuned to the soft light of Perelandra, emphasize Ransom's subjectivity. His impending return has been signaled by his discovery of the "coffin, open and empty" (179), in allusion to Christ's empty tomb. As the Christ of Perelandra, Ransom has risen again from the underworld. Now he will return to his own world.

In the final chapter, the Coronation and Great Dance maintain interest and bring Ransom's tale to a climax even though our early knowledge of his safe return forfeits suspense. The royal tributes locate

47. Downing, *Planets in Peril,* 130, citing the *Faerie Queene* on the instability of islands, sees Spenser and Lewis as employing symbol in opposite ways.

48. Discussed in A. Owen Barfield, *Poetic Diction,* 139ff.

49. Lewis, *Surprised by Joy,* 161.

Ransom's achievement in the planet's recent past while predicting its future, when Ransom will no longer play a central role. Critics have disagreed about the eldilic pronouncements. Though a few think them wordy,[50] most find them to attest both the grandeur and the paradoxical nature of Maleldil.[51] In two ways they represent the author's attempt to grapple with the formless infinitude of the modern cosmos. Its "centre" is "where Maleldil is," that is "in every place. Not some of Him in one place and some in another, but in each place," even if minute beyond conception, "the whole Maleldil" (201). Only the Bent Oyarsa is "nowhere." In the cosmic plan represented as a "Great Dance," "plans without number interlock." To the "darkened mind," the cosmos may seem chaotic "because there are more plans than it looked for" (201-2). By implication, being "darkened" by the Fall, the human mind will never comprehend the cosmos, so what is now called "Chaos theory" represents that mind's utmost limit.

A more difficult problem for the author is how to maintain interest in a fall averted, by definition a non-event. One means of doing so is the mythopoeic narrative.[52] Another is the quasi-musical ABA structure of the three temptation scenes.

In the first of these, in chapter 7, Weston's effort to pervert Ransom's Christian faith and ethic is preceded by his arrival, threatening of Ransom with a revolver, and the Lady's departure, and then followed by his fit and Ransom's disposal of the weapon.

In chapter 8, Weston's first session with the Lady is more subtly framed. Beforehand, Ransom wakes from a dream of being back on Earth feeling nostalgic for Perelandra: "The dream (for so it seemed to him) of having lived and walked on the oceans of the Morning Star rushed through his memory with a sense of lost sweetness that was well-nigh unbearable." Here Lewis the Dreamer beautifully evokes the *Sehnsucht* that impelled John to set out on his Pilgrim's Regress. But aches and pains, hunger and thirst bring Ransom back to reality. Weston

50. Myers describes these passages as "wordy and magisterial" (*C. S. Lewis in Context,* 71).

51. E.g., C. N. Manlove, *Christian Fantasy from 1200 to the Present,* 250.

52. Myers cites Margaret P. Hannay's list of parallels and differences to demonstrate that the story follows *Paradise Lost* rather than Genesis (*C. S. Lewis in Context,* 58, 61).

has gone to menace the Lady with some more diabolical scheme than colonizing Malacandra. After eating the fruit and nuts of the Fixed Land, Ransom finds awaiting him a giant fish sent to transport him — like the air-fish of MacDonald's *Golden Key,* an allusion to the ancient fish symbol for Christ.[53] Thus before the temptation begins it has been located within the continuing warfare between God and Satan. The dialogue ends in the Lady's praise of Maleldil, not Weston, for her prospect of becoming as the eldils. From Weston's irritated response, "I will sleep now," Ransom intuits a diabolical presence, "something that was and was not Weston." He also senses that not he but Maleldil has triumphed in this moment, not in the creation or redemption, but in a "disaster averted" (96-97). Thus the chapter's conclusion alludes to its beginning, confirms the eschatological import of the temptation, and encapsulates the entire action of the novel. By this quasi-musical structure and cross-reference of themes, Lewis compensates the reader for the absence of that suspense which is proper to science fiction.

He also fixes the reader's attention by means of statuesque or frozen images, as in a pageant. The most impressive are faces. Weston, as he looks up from tormenting a frog, has the unrelenting gaze and "expressionless mouth" of a corpse, which rebuff any thought or feeling about it (100). The voice emanating from that face claims not merely to be "older" than Ransom in wisdom and experience, but to have heard the eternal councils of "Deep Heaven" (108), so identifying the Un-man with Satan. The Lady's face, observed by Ransom as temptation begins to take effect, shows neither sorrow nor confusion, yet an increased "hint of something precarious" (102). After the Un-man's claim to antiquity, her face dispels Ransom's panic as, "deep within" her "innocence," which has endangered yet protected her, she gazes up "at the standing Death above her, puzzled, but not beyond . . . cheerful curiosity" (108).

In the third temptation scene (chap. 10), the most complex allegorical tableau, the Un-man's retelling of countless legends of great women produces on the Lady's face an expression "like a tragedy queen," seen by Ransom in a flash of lightning, as in gothic novels.

53. The Greek word for fish is *ichthus;* early Christians drew the symbol of a fish to stand for *Jesos Christos, Theou [H]uios* (Jesus Christ, Son of God).

That single lightning flash shows him the Un-man sitting bolt upright, the Lady raised on one elbow, the lizard lying awake at her head, a grove of trees beyond, and great waves against the horizon. He wonders how the Lady can see those jaws moving as if munching rather than talking and not know the speaker to be evil (115). Every detail in the scene functions as a signifier: the storm, of crisis; the lizard, of watchfulness; the grove, of potential idolatry; the waves (as the Un-man has alluded to them), of historical change; the jaws, of lust that consumes its prey. Here, in the most medieval of Lewis's novels, medievalness reaches its apogee. To speak of "medievalism" would imply the conscious nostalgia of *That Hideous Strength*.

Yet even in *Perelandra*, many passing references to the war and several features of the tempter's technique anchor the central conflict within the dark age of twentieth-century totalitarianism. While generally following the Augustinian formula of suggestion, delight, and (almost) consent, and Satan's temptation of Eve in *Paradise Lost*, the Un-man uses conditioning devices, bonding with the Lady as "we" versus Ransom as "he," then cutting the ground out from under Ransom by sneering at his Christian morality and compassion for other creatures as being out of date. The Un-man later shifts from apparently rational argument with the Lady to arousal of heroine-worship by telling her tales of great women. His turning of Augustinian theology against itself by arguing that Maleldil seeks the Lady's growth through postlapsarian experience *(felix peccatum Evae)* is traditional enough, but his incessant suggestion as the Lady sleeps belongs to the age of secret police interrogation and of the sleep-teaching predicted in Huxley's *Brave New World* (1932).

Equally contemporary was Ransom's relief in venting "lawful hatred" of the Un-man, but in the Un-man's appeal to incipient feminism against cosmic male dominance the novel was in advance of its time. An impediment to its continuing reception is the prospect that present and future readers, especially female, may endorse what it condemns. Why should a masculine deity deny the Lady her heroines, mirror, and robe? One response that seems valid within both the planetary context and present-day sensibility is Ransom's horror at the slaughter of birds to make the robe. From the Un-man's dissection of the living frog to his vicious ripping out of feathers, the author's own horror at human cruelty to other species finds intensifying expression. In this regard, as Filmer points out, Lewis was an early environmentalist and champion of animal welfare.

Whether owing to wartime conditions or to its author's renown, the text received less copyediting than it should have had. In a novel so full of Christian symbolism, for Ransom to smash the Un-man's skull in the name of the Trinity is, I suppose, acceptable. But his boast of pursuing Weston with "hounds . . . of the Spartan kind, so flew'd, so sanded" (145) strikes even this lover of the *Midsummer Night's Dream* as schoolboyish.

If such imperfections, and the occasional use of Ransom as the author's mouthpiece, have denied *Perelandra* the popularity and acclaim of the *Lord of the Rings,* the tautness and focus of its temptation episodes, the beauty of its imaginary world, the strangeness of its subterranean creatures, and its triumphal Great Dance, which recalls a memorable account by Lewis of reading Dante's *Paradiso* with Barfield,[54] make it Lewis's most successful space fantasy.

By common consent *That Hideous Strength* is his least. Several critics have condemned its admixture of incompatible material and implausible characters, while Roger Lancelyn Green and Walter Hooper think it "a Charles Williams novel written by C. S. Lewis."[55] As A. N. Wilson points out, however, it has seeds of greatness.[56]

Although its preface is dated Christmas Eve, 1943, internal evi-

---

54. Lewis wrote: "*Paradiso* . . . has opened a new world for me . . . a mixture of intense, even crabbed, complexity in language and thought with, *at the very same time,* a feeling of spacious, gliding movement, like a slow dance, or like flying . . . like the stars — endless mathematical subtlety of orb, cycle, epicycle and ecliptic, unthinkable and unpicturable, and yet . . . the freedom and liquidity of empty space and the triumphant certainty of movement" (*They Stand Together,* 325-26).

55. See Chad Walsh, *The Literary Legacy of C. S. Lewis,* 128; Corbin Scott Carnell, *Bright Shadow of Reality,* 103ff.; Manlove, *C. S. Lewis: His Literary Achievement,* 80ff. Humphrey Carpenter comments on the schoolboyishness of *That Hideous Strength,* which he calls the "worst and most enjoyable" of the space novels *(Inklings,* 220). Green and Hooper's comment is found in *C. S. Lewis: A Biography,* 174; Joe Christopher challenges their statement, claiming that Lewis's characters are more Christian than those of Williams (*C. S. Lewis,* 102).

56. A. N. Wilson, *C. S. Lewis: A Biography,* 191. Cf. Green and Hooper, *C. S. Lewis: A Biography,* 178-79.

dence confirms Wilson's statement that Lewis wrote the novel in the final two years of the war. The preface shows that by 1943 he had resolved to write a "fairy-tale" beginning with commonplace characters and scenes, set in a university, and eventually featuring "magicians, devils, pantomime animals, and planetary angels."[57] The progression from natural to supernatural is that of Williams, the mixture of humans and animals that of the Boxen (and Narnian) stories. Its central theme, suggested by a conversation with a scientific colleague, resembles that of an unnamed tale by Olaf Stapledon since shown to be *The Star-Maker* (1937), one of the "hellish" books to which Lewis refers in correspondence.[58] The only conscious borrowing was of Numenor or the "True West" (misspelt as "Numinor") from Tolkien's *Silmarillion*, then known only to the Inklings.

Coincidentally, the ending, when Ransom is about to depart for Perelandra, presages Williams's sudden death (9 May 1945). The new elements in Ransom — his quiet authority over a group of adherents, unintended sexual attraction, and failing vigor — were, as Carpenter points out, characteristic of Williams.[59] So too was the Arthurian theme in the novel: Ransom's new name Fisher-King, his exposition of the "Logres" or spiritual aspect of British civilization, and his collaboration with the resuscitated Merlin to undo the demonic conspiracy of the National Institute of Co-Ordinated Experiments by assembling the unlikely Company of St. Anne, a name Lewis claimed to have chosen for its euphony and plausibility[60] rather than for its association with the Blessed Virgin's mother.

The Company consists of an Arthurian scholar and his childless wife, known to the heroine Jane Studdock as "Mother" Dimble; Jane's house cleaner, Mrs. Maggs, whose husband is in jail for theft; Arthur Denniston, a rival applicant for Jane's husband Mark's fellowship, and

57. *That Hideous Strength*, 7. I am using Macmillan's paperback edition (1965). All page references are to this edition.

58. On the emergent deity in *Star-Maker*, Downing (*Planets in Peril*, 53) cites Lewis's letter to Arthur Clarke in 1953, describing the book as "devil-worship." For a possible reference to *Star-Maker* in a letter to W. L. Kinter, 15 September 1953, see p. 258 in Chapter 9 below.

59. Carpenter, *Inklings*, 198.

60. Letter to W. L. Kinter, 15 September 1953.

his beautiful wife Camilla, named after the swift-moving virgin queen of Aeneas's rival; and the skeptical MacPhee, modeled on Lewis's private tutor Kirkpatrick and, like most Victorian rationalists, on the side of the angels. Oddest of all, the Company includes Mr. Bultitude the bear, who does the smashing at the headquarters of N.I.C.E.

Without Merlin and the Company, only Ransom would be left to help the *eldila* foil an evil technocracy's plan to usher in the second Dark Age prophesied by Churchill as the consequence of a Nazi victory, one "made more sinister and perhaps more protracted by the lights of perverted science." Several practices of the Nazi regime had been anticipated in works by Stapledon and by J. B. S. Haldane, who wrote a stinging criticism of the trilogy.[61] A weakness fatal to the plot's credibility is that N.I.C.E. operates and is destroyed only within Edgestow, yet threatens civilization throughout the planet. In Williams's *Place of the Lion* (1931), much admired by Lewis, the apocalyptic events occur piecemeal throughout most of the book, and the lion, eagle, and other creatures are mostly seen at some distance, with a resultant gain in credibility.

As Chad Walsh remarks, *That Hideous Strength* is "intellectually overstuffed."[62] It pillories everything Lewis disliked about twentieth-century life, from feminism, relativism, and reductionism to vivisection, technology, and philistine development. As a nineteenth-century invention, the slow train that Jane takes to St. Anne's is exempt from censure. In Devine, elevated to Lord Feverstone, Lewis earned opprobrium for supposedly satirizing a leading Magdalen "progressive," T. D. ("Harry") Weldon.[63] At the meeting when the Fellows of Bracton College decide to sell Bragdon Wood to N.I.C.E., Feverstone humiliates Canon Jewel, a relic of the time before 1914 when the old were respected. Their names, signifying treasure and lust for it, typify allegorizing almost as explicit as in the *Pilgrim's Regress*.

61. J. B. S. Haldane refers to self-improvement of the human species and colonizing of planets in "Possible Worlds" (see Downing, *Planets in Peril*, 39); Haldane's critique of the trilogy is found in "Auld Hornie, F.R.S.," *Modern Quarterly* 1 (Autumn 1946): 32-40.

62. Walsh, *The Literary Legacy of C. S. Lewis*, 118.

63. Stated to me in 1969 by Colin Hardie, then Fellow of Magdalen College.

Most personal and place names have obvious meanings: the College's "Brag-don" Wood, its "dry" Newton Quadrangle and "beautiful, Gregorian" (20) buildings; Edgestow, in Old English "the place of the sword," and the village of Cure Hardy, formerly Ozanna le Coeur Hardi; Hingest, the scientist and amateur antiquarian; Curry, the ambitious college principal; and Jules, the titular head of N.I.C.E., whose egoism and outdated science represent a cruel swipe at H. G. Wells, the propagandist of scientific positivism, and Jules Verne, the pioneer of science fiction.[64]

More subtle nomenclature points to issues in the two parallel plots. The college was named after a medieval jurist who condemned the overriding of law by rulers.[65] As the surname "Stud-dock" denotes, in the marriage of Mark and Jane procreation, indeed passion itself, are in suspension. Even without her real-life progenitor's "crush" on Lewis,[66] Jane's brief passion for Ransom makes sense within her story. Her clairvoyant dreams make her invaluable to the Company of St. Anne's and prospectively to N.I.C.E., which practices occult as well as secular "science." While Jane comes and goes freely from an old country house, Mark is by double bind detained in a florid mansion built by an Edwardian *nouveau-riche*. Its name "Belbury" refers both ironically to the anti-Christian proceedings of N.I.C.E. and directly to its Pavlovian conditioning.[67]

In the last lecture of his *Abolition of Man* Lewis foresaw positivist conditioning against nature and moral law by willful misuse of words, to which Jane would be less susceptible on account of her literary education. Practiced by a totalitarian bureaucracy, such misuse of language as calling the center for overcoming aesthetic and moral scruples the "Objective Room" was what Orwell soon after dubbed "Newspeak."

64. Green and Hooper (*C. S. Lewis: A Biography*, 174) suggest that Lewis may have been thinking of Blewbury, at Oxford, once considered as a site for a proposed atomic energy plant. Downing (*Planets in Peril*, 138) thinks Jules's name alludes to H. G. Wells and Julian Huxley, coauthors of a "polemical" book on evolution entitled *The Science of Life* (1929).

65. Henry de Bracton, *De legibus et consuetidinibus Angliae* (On the laws and customs of England), cited in OHEL, 48. See Myers, *C. S. Lewis in Context*, 89.

66. Jane Flewett, an evacuee who acted as housemaid for Lewis. See Wilson, *C. S. Lewis: A Biography*, 186ff., esp. 189.

67. Downing, *Planets in Peril*, 137.

At Belbury, the white-bearded Frost, probably modeled on Freud, seeks to condition Mark into embracing "objective" morality, and Filostrato to imbue him with a hatred of nature. The latter's name has been traced to the Greek philosopher Philostratus, whom Lewis later quoted as attributing art to imitation not of nature but of the ideal (OHEL, 320). It could also allude to Boccaccio's poem on idolatrous passion, on which Lewis wrote his first academic article.[68] Mark's passion for getting on by knowing influential people is more idolatrous than the obsession of Williams's Damaris Tighe, whose medieval scholarship consists of observation without insight. As Lewis said later, the plot consists of a triple conflict, between grace, nature, and anti-nature.[69]

Some names are paired by *jeu d'esprit,* for example those of Grace Ironwood, who first interviews Jane at St. Anne's, and the ungracious Steele, to whose department Mark is assigned. The name Wither for Mark's interviewer at Belbury appears arbitrary until we contrast his behavior with that of Grace. Where she is laconic but direct, he is full of half-promises and circumlocutions. While her surname implies fertility as well as resolve, his implies decay, and his language and demeanor evince the constant shifts of front Lewis somewhere remarks as characteristic of evil. That crude incarnation of police terror, Fairy Hardcastle, typifies the book's tendency to shoot at too many targets. Her first name alludes ironically to her masculinity and directly to the book's subtitle. At first sight "castle" implies her role as ogress. Or does it refer to Belbury itself, that make-believe research institute where those in favor enjoy bondage with unease and those out of favor a cell? Yet she threatens Mark not like a Gestapo or KGB agent but like a Hollywood gangster, and Lewis's sneer at her lack of corsets signals his dislike of fat and bossy women.

Lewis set his first space novel in summer, his second in autumn, and his third in late autumn and winter, sometimes with multiple reference. In chapter 5, headed "Elasticity," the fog appears the morning after the Fairy has told Mark that "making things clear" is anathema to Wither but that Mark's new job consists of writing N.I.C.E. propaganda (97). Next morning Mark sees Wither's once courtly face shift

68. Lewis, "What Chaucer Really Did to *Il Filostrato.*"
69. Letter to W. L. Kinter, 30 July 1953.

from "dreamy distaste" to a "cat-like smile" hiding a "snarl" while he defines elasticity as requiring Mark to do whatever N.I.C.E. orders, at a much reduced salary (119-20).

In chapter 5, Denniston tells Jane he enjoys autumnal fogs, yet in the next chapter fog descending over all midland counties becomes a symbol at once of darkness over Logres and of a loss of character and integrity in the national culture due to industrialism. How far Lewis realized that autumnal fogs were caused by pollutants is uncertain, for his choice of a midland rather than northern setting might reflect the influence of the Birmingham-bred Tolkien. At the funeral of Hingest, the fog muffles the construction noises and curses of the workman as the deaf Canon Storey reads the service. The objurgations jar with the venerable phrases of the Prayer Book, as do the quarrelsome voices with the respectful faces of the dead man's upper-crust relatives, as if signifying the demise of a local, hierarchical, and implicitly Christian society (126).

At the end of chapter 6 Lewis patently echoes Wordsworth and Arnold. After the famous Professor Frost has met Jane's husband in the library of N.I.C.E. — a reward for Mark's collaboration — Jane fulfills her precognitive dream by seeing that luminary in a street, outlined against the fog. Shocked, she takes the next train to St. Anne's, where the fog turns into a white mist, above which she sees far-off hills whence flows the river, here unpolluted.[70]

Doubleness and contradiction are woven into the plot: in constant juxtapositions of episodes at Belbury and at St. Anne's; in contradictions between intention and outcome, as with the College dinner following the death of Hingest and defection of Mark, which ends with the smashing of the Henrietta Maria window (93); and in the dinner at Belbury when, like the builders of the Tower of Babel, or like Milton's Satan returned in triumph, the speakers can only utter nonsense syllables (343-46). The Company of St. Anne's can accommodate differences without quarrels, rivalries, or conflicting aims, but among the Fellows of Bracton progressives fight traditionalists, while in N.I.C.E. an inner ring tempts, manipulates, and divides members intent on joining it.

70. Cf. Wordsworth, *Prelude*, book 8, lines 272-76; Arnold, *Sohrab and Rustum*, lines 875-92.

As with the previous space novels, the middle chapter marks a turn in the action. Before chapter 9, the "hideous strength" of N.I.C.E. carries all before it yet remains apparently rational. During that pivotal chapter, "The Saracen's Head," Jane dreams of Mark revering the head of Alcasan with his masters, yet of his distaste for the "new man" it represents. Mark envisions the soul of Wither "dissipating itself . . . through formless and lightless worlds" (188) by irreversible entropy, yet moments later Wither obstructs his departure from N.I.C.E. MacPhee tells Jane of the kidnapping of Ransom by Weston and Devine, agents of the demonic powers behind that pseudoscientific institution (190-92). David Downing sheds light on the connections between the demonic powers and N.I.C.E. by tracing successive episodes at Belbury to the circles of Dante's *Inferno*.[71]

In the remaining chapters, as Merlin emerges from his agelong sleep to destroy N.I.C.E., its increasingly absurd rulers honor a tramp in mistake for him and reveal their godless institution for the Tower of Babel (or babble) it really is. By making N.I.C.E. a grab bag of all manner of things he disliked, Lewis made it more intriguing yet less credible. In 1944, he warned students of King's College, London, that seeking membership of power-wielding elites or "inner rings" could prove both futile and expensive.[72] This comment, along with the membership fee and initiation rite sprung on Mark at Belbury, points to Freemasonry as one target. Another was anthroposophy, hinted at by the fact that the room where Filostrato teaches Mark "objective" (i.e., amoral) values has the asymmetrical design of the Goetheanum, Steiner's temple of "Occult Science" (chap. 14).

As their idol, the rulers of N.I.C.E. choose the guillotined head of Alcasan, a French chemist and murderer. By keeping its brain alive, they mystically perpetuate the power of science and technology, despite having murdered their only genuine scientist.[73] The idol anticipates the central processing unit of a mainframe computer, which both stores

71. Downing, *Planets in Peril*, 94-97. For example, Mark's being asked to decoy Jane to Belbury in chap. 9 is connected with canto 38, on traitors, in the *Inferno*.

72. "The Inner Ring: An Oration" (1944).

73. Lewis later named MacPhee and Hingest as the only genuine scientists in the book. (Notes for Fr. Peter Milward, 1955, in the Wade Collection.)

an institution's accumulated data and does calculations beyond the human brain's capacity. But what Filostrato, Frost, and Wither adore is the human brain and mind, so taking the positivist "religion of humanity" to its logical extreme. Filostrato's detestation of nature and Cosser's wish for radical change at Cure Hardy symbolize those assaults on nature and historical continuity that Lewis saw as consequences of the "great divide" in human culture,[74] signified jointly by the Enlightenment and the Industrial Revolution.

Yet the motif of the Head originated in conversations and dreams long before either the space novels or the Cambridge inaugural lecture. In his diary for 29 May 1923, Lewis recorded talking with his fellow student Jenkins concerning their projected play about a scientist injecting a corpse to keep its brain and nerves alive. Other relevant features of its plot were the discovery of the corpse kept frozen in its coffin, the scientist's intention of making the heroine his next victim, and the central incident of her deliverance. Lewis also mentions Jenkins's sighting in the Bodleian Library of a man with a long red beard whom they decided to use as model for their scientist.[75] In February 1923, Lewis had dreamed of being brought by an old lady to see her sick son, whom they found drowned; when the corpse revived and threw a fit, they had to drown him again.[76] Soon afterward, Ms. Moore's syphilitic brother "Doc" Askins went mad, and Lewis dreamed of his return from the asylum. In July, he dreamed of the Disembodied Head. Later, in 1930, he dreamed of finding a charwoman's head in a kitchen cupboard.[77] Out of these dreams and incidents emerged the motifs of the Head of N.I.C.E., the old woman's appeal to Ransom on behalf of her son in *Out of the Silent Planet,* Jane's precognitive dreaming, and the whole "scientific" cult of a brain divorced from imagination, feelings, and senses. MacPhee mentions experiments with keeping animal heads animated, and Grace Ironwood mentions a German experiment in keeping a criminal's head alive (195). If outmoded by the computer and by genetic engineering, the disembodied head motif and the dreams

74. Lewis, *De Descriptione Temporum,* in *Selected Literary Essays,* 3.
75. "The Lewis Family Papers," VIII, 121; *All My Road Before Me,* 238.
76. "The Lewis Family Papers," VIII, 46.
77. *They Stand Together,* 377.

suggest an apprehension by the young Lewis of becoming a kind of Cheshire cat, with developed intellect but undeveloped heart.

The space trilogy also embodies a well-founded fear of the "New Order" that the totalitarian powers of its time sought to establish. The title of the fourth chapter of *That Hideous Strength*, "The Liquidation of Anachronisms," reveals an equal fear of Fascist and of Communist secret police, the euphemism being common to both. An "anachronistic" but kindlier way of life is observed by Jane en route to St. Anne's and by Mark at Cure Hardy. A city dweller by birth but countryman by inclination, Lewis preferred the ever-fading old order represented by Chaucer's Knight and Shakespeare's Adam. We should view his attack upon scientific positivism as expressing both his fear of totalitarianism and his hankering after a preindustrial culture in which old age was respected, workers were treated as neighbors rather than "hired hands," and servants "sweat for duty, not for meed."[78] However unattainable, what Alice Chandler calls a "Dream of Order"[79] inspired nineteenth-century authors from the conservative Scott to the Marxist William Morris, and this dream persists in the retreat of the affluent from the city to the refurbished "cottage." A. N. Wilson also notes anticipations of present-day environmentalism.[80] By 1952, Lewis thought real-life horrors had outstripped those of his satire.[81]

At a deeper level, Lewis sought in his space novels to reconcile Newtonian cosmology and biological discovery with the Judeo-Christian cosmic and terrestrial hierarchy. While flying to Malacandra, Ransom views no trackless immensity but "the heavens and all the powers therein" of the *Te Deum;* the crablike creatures of Perelandra he sees not tearing each other in the slime but drawing each other in procession. Amid the turmoil of war against a pseudoscientific ideology, the overabundance of material in *That Hideous Strength* implies the Dreamer's compulsion to infuse past and present, personal and cultural, with the

78. Shakespeare, *As You Like It*, act 2, scene 3, line 58.
79. This "Dream of Order" could be Christian, feudal, or socialist, as opposed to anarchic Victorian capitalism. Chandler, *A Dream of Order.*
80. Wilson, *C. S. Lewis: A Biography*, 190.
81. Letter to Miss Montgomery, 10 June 1952.

"dateless, timeless peace of life in a really regular household" that Lewis wistfully admired about Ruskin's childhood.[82]

Theological Satires

The Screwtape Letters

Of all the books Lewis wrote in wartime, *The Screwtape Letters* reached by far the widest public. A. N. Wilson estimates total sales at a million, George Sayer at two million.[83] By common consent, the least popular was the *Great Divorce* (1945). While neither would be considered a novel, both are fictions with themes and attitudes akin to those of the trilogy.

The obscure Danish book *Letters from Hell*,[84] which Lewis started reading in 1916 but found disappointing, may have left some impression, but the idea for *The Screwtape Letters* came after a church service in July 1940, his first idea for a title being "As One Devil to Another." He expounded it to his brother as a series of letters from a retired devil advising a young one how to undermine the faith of his first "patient." The strategy is to avoid logical arguments, which the patient might contravert, in favor of playing a manipulative "heads I win, tails you lose" sort of game. For example, Wormwood is advised to lead his "patient" to think that the failure of a prayer for patience proves prayer to be futile but to convince him that success should be set down to autosuggestion.[85] By May 1941, when the letters began to appear weekly in an Anglican newspaper called *The Guardian*, Lewis had named his demonic author and the letters' recipient, embarked on a range of moral and spiritual issues facing the unnamed "patient," and

82. *They Stand Together,* 488, referring to Ruskin's autobiography *Praeterita.*

83. Wilson, *C. S. Lewis: A Biography,* 179; George Sayer, *Jack: C. S. Lewis and His Times,* 165.

84. G. A. Thisted, *Letters from Hell* (1885); the English translation (1911) included a preface by George MacDonald. For Lewis's comment on this book, see *They Stand Together,* 12.

85. Letter to W. H. Lewis, 20 July 1940, in *Letters of C. S. Lewis,* 188; see also W. H. Lewis, "C. S. Lewis: A Biography," 285.

begun a simple plot. Having initially drawn a young man into a worldly and flippant circle, Wormwood, the junor devil, suffers successive defeats as his patient falls in love with a Christian girl, comes under the influence of her family and friends, and finally departs for a better world while courageously performing air-raid duties. The events take place from the outbreak of war to the peak period of German bombing in 1940-41. In his final letter, printed in November 1941, Screwtape relishes the prospect of eating his beloved nephew and protégé Wormwood.

In keeping with the comic intent, other devils have suggestive names: Slubgob, the principal of the infernal seminary; Glubose, who tempts the patient's mother into over-particularity, the obverse of gluttony; and Slumtrimpet, the girl's attendant fiend, who reports a tendency to ridicule unbelievers that can be indirectly used to maneuver the patient into spiritual pride. The name "Wormwood," based on the fallen star in the Apocalypse that turns river waters bitter, alludes also to Hamlet's taunt at his uncle in the Play scene.[86] Other than "torture," what meaning resides in the name Screwtape depends on whether Lewis knew the North Americanism "screw" for cheat or exploit. Presumably he derived "tape" from "tapeworm" and "red tape."

The two names relate to the book's subtext, the tutelary bond of uncle and nephew that, like all demonic loves, turns into backbiting and cannibalism. The first sign of its deterioration comes in the opening of letter 12, where Screwtape turns from urbane encouragement to reprehension because Wormwood has allowed the patient to repent his dalliance with a circle of "scoffers" and worldlings before undergoing a second conversion. Wormwood's error was to permit two solitary pleasures, reading and a walk to an old mill, which have led the patient to reflect on his current way of life. The second hint of the superficiality of the affection between uncle and nephew comes in the opening of letter 20, where Screwtape rebukes Wormwood for pushing sexual temptation on the patient too persistently, which has provoked "the Enemy" (God) to put a stop to it. As Screwtape tells his nephew, once the patient finds that such attacks end if they are not succumbed to, he will become more resistant.

86. Revelation 8:10-11; *Hamlet,* act 3, scene 2, line 193.

Having indulged in donnish humor in one letter at Slubgob's inefficient teaching of sexual temptation (letter 18), Screwtape hopes in the next for Wormwood's silence about his own aspersions on a colleague for whom he now professes "the highest respect" (letter 19). Never a campus politician, Lewis was alluding to common-room squabbling at Magdalen by "stormy spirits" whose absence on war service was a relief.[87] As in business and politics, backbiting goes on beneath a veil of polite goodwill.

When comparing divine and demonic attitudes toward love in letter 18, Screwtape perceives the Enemy's notion of a love requiring the good of both partners as self-contradictory, for to him love is inherently competitive, the stronger preying upon the weaker. In *That Hideous Strength*, Lewis would juxtapose episodes of scheming and backbiting at Belbury with episodes of mutual support at St. Anne's.

That the really self-contradictory concept of competitive love inspires both uncle and nephew is shown in letter 22, when Screwtape vows revenge on Wormwood for reporting his "unguarded" reflections on Slubgob to the secret police. In the same letter, Screwtape denounces the Christian with whom Wormwood has let his patient fall in love in one of Lewis's finest passages of invective: "Not just a Christian, but such a Christian — a vile, sneaking, simpering, demure, monosyllabic, mouse-like, watery, insignificant, virginal, bread-and-butter miss! . . . She makes me vomit. . . . We'd have had her to the arena in the old days." Yet this "little prude" is "ready to fall into this booby's arms like any other breeding animal." Screwtape wishes God would "blast her for it, if He's so moonstruck by virginity." But he recognizes that God hides a love of pleasure behind "those fasts and vigils and crosses." Screwtape bitterly contrasts this divine hedonism with the "high and austere mystery" of the "Miserific vision" in Hell.

Screwtape renews his attack on Wormwood for allowing the patient to enter the girl's household, whose "very gardener" is acquiring the "deadly odour" of Christianity. The household's "pretence" of *agape* recalls an unnamed author's account of heaven as a region "'where there is only life and therefore all that is not music is silence.'" Screwtape bursts into a rhapsody on Hell as a kingdom of "Noise" and "dy-

87. *They Stand Together*, 497.

namism," expressing whatever is "exultant, ruthless, and virile." "Noise" shields the demons from "qualms, . . . scruples, and impossible desires." Already they have "made great strides" upon Earth in turning the whole cosmos into "a noise," and Heaven's "melodies and silences . . . will be shouted down in the end." The foaming Screwtape is reduced to dictating the remainder of the letter as (with obvious reference to book 10 of *Paradise Lost*) he turns into a centipede. In its verve, misogyny, antimodernism, farce, irony, and allusive humor, this is the most spirited and varied of the letters.

The most coherent sequence comes in the final letters. The patient's death is prepared for by Screwtape's professed indifference to the civilian casualties that make Wormwood rejoice (letters 24 and 28). It is critical — from Screwtape's point of view — that the patient survive the war; then Wormwood might lead him on a long decline into midlife disillusion, marital discord, and despair at besetting sins. Screwtape also asserts the fiendish value of perverting longing for heaven into a utopian dream, Communist or scientific, in order that love of this world may grow in the patient's heart. In a swipe at a Leavisian buzzword, Screwtape suggests that this "creeping death" can be cultivated by teaching humans to call it "Maturity" (letter 28). Having learned that the patient's town is to be bombed and that the patient will be imperiled by air-raid duties, he urges Wormwood to tempt him to cowardice, perverting terror and pity into hatred. To subvert the patient's courage, Wormwood should instill fantasies of self-preserving action, then when a crisis really comes "rush" him into cowardice (letter 29).

Hearing of the patient's exemplary courage and modesty in his first raid, Screwtape begins the penultimate letter by threatening his nephew "bring us back food, or be food yourself" (letter 30). The food symbol inverts the Eucharist and heavenly banquet and forewarns readers of the patient's end. Screwtape's most psychologically penetrating and amusing advice, surely based on Lewis's experience in the trenches, is to feed the patient with false hopes of relief and false expectations that the ordeal will soon be over, so that disappointment can be produced before the patient becomes too fatigued to worry at all and lapses instead into "humbled and gentle weariness." Disappointment leads to anger, thence to cowardice.

The time for intellectual dissuasion being past, Wormwood must befuddle his client into believing his horror and fear at the sight of human entrails to be "real" and feelings kindled by "happy children or fair weather" merely sentimental and "subjective."

The concluding letter is among Lewis's finest pieces of writing. It begins with a sinister burlesque of Victorian ululation ("My dear, my very dear, Wormwood, my poppet, my pigsnie") and of incestuous desire ("I have always desired you, as you . . . me. The difference is that I am the stronger"). Its spare rhythms create a vivid picture of the rage and despair in Hell at the loss of the patient's soul: "The howl of sharpened famine . . . re-echoes . . . through all the levels of the Kingdom of noise." Lewis imaginatively elaborates assertion into image: "There was a sudden clearing of his eyes . . . as he saw you for the first time, and recognized the part you had had in him . . . you had . . . no longer. . . . as if a scab had fallen from an old sore . . . as if he shuffled off . . . a defiled, wet, clinging garment. . . . [It] is misery enough to see them in their mortal days . . . splashing in hot water and giving little grunts of pleasure. . . . What, then, of this final stripping, this complete cleansing?"

To read the *Screwtape Letters* purely as a story is to overlook moral and psychological insights too numerous to elaborate here. Yet the book has the apparent randomness of a portion of life lived in imagination, rather than the systematic character of a moral and spiritual treatise. It switches back and forth between and reintroduces topics: academic and theological modernism (letters 1, 7, 10, 15, 23, 27, and 28); (Anglican) church services and parties (2, 7, 16); family life (3, 24); prayer (4, 27); charity (6, 26); love and/or lust (19-21); spiritual aridity (8, 9); worldliness and laughter (9-11). A number of topics appear in only one letter — gluttony (17), anger (21), noise (22), spiritual pride (24), craving for novelty (25) — while death and survival, fear, and fatigue appear in several letters (28, 29, 30). This list reveals an increasing tendency to dwell on inner and moral experience, yet Lewis indulges his likes and dislikes — such as hatred of noisy modern music and machinery — from beginning to end. Critics who find in his writing a lack of inwardness cannot have given the last three letters, in particular, the attention they deserve. Yet Lewis drew upon only three sources of inner experience: warfare in 1918, domestic life at the Kilns, and senior common room factions at Magdalen. Though certainly relevant to the reader's experience of bombardment and of family rows, these leave untouched large areas of adult life, such as the fluctuations of love, which Lewis knew only at second hand.

How long the book will be read and by whom is an unanswerable question. A more useful one is this: Who has read it so far, and as what? We can safely assume that most readers so far have been literate Christians in Britain and North America. Whether they read it as a "spiritual classic" is more doubtful. Like many Victorian novels, it first saw print as a magazine serial but, as analysis shows, one nearer the randomness of the *Pickwick Papers* than the classical form of *Great Expectations*. Great devotional works like the *Imitation of Christ* or Law's *Serious Call* have a clearer structure.

The inevitable lack of argumentative sequence in letters supposedly written as the war progressed in no way lessens their comic impact. Ironically, in view of its condemnation of coteries, the *Screwtape Letters* has allusions now as in-group as any by Evelyn Waugh, Kingsley Amis, or David Lodge. I am thinking of digs at Leavisite and Freudian critics and at Anglo-Catholic or modernist churchmen, endorsement of the traditional Anglican parochial system, and even use of biblical and Miltonic myths about fallen angels. The upper-crust circle of the patient's girl need not preclude the book's survival — witness Jane Austen — and still less need its ridicule of Marxist and Wellsian utopianism. As with the space novels, what finally limits the *Screwtape Letters* is over-hasty publication.

The additions Lewis made to the *Guardian* text can be illustrated from letters 25-30. On the cult of the future, he adds with Johnsonian common sense that the demons have conditioned us to envisage the future as a "promised land" that only "favoured heroes attain," rather than as something we all reach at "sixty minutes per hour" (letter 25). With equally Johnsonian Toryism he inserts earlier in this letter that in the arts the modern craving for novelty has led to new extremes of "lasciviousness, unreason, cruelty and pride." In the next letter (26), three insertions add depth and point to Screwtape's observations on love. The first describes love as an ambiguous state that seemingly resolves difficulties that are actually merely shelved under its "enchantment." In the second, Screwtape adds that lovers, being doubly blind, believe sexual "excitement" to be permanent and mistake it for the "charity" requisite for the "mutual self-sacrifice" involved in lasting marriages. Nearly twenty years later, in his *Four Loves,* Lewis maintained that *agape,* or "charity," is a component in the benign forms of friendship, familial, and sexual love. His third insertion was the advice remarked earlier on disguising vindictiveness and self-righteousness as "Unselfishness."

The more important of two insertions in letter 27 shows Barfield's influence in purging Lewis of chronological snobbery, when Screwtape claims that the demons have prevented the moderns from correcting errors of their own by persuading them to ignore the ancients. In the following letter the second of two insertions is on the confusion of utopian dreams with longing for heaven. An insertion describing the demons' "dilemma" — that to promote justice and charity is to do God's work, but to promote the opposite results in wars or revolutions that awaken humans from their "moral stupor" (letter 29) — makes almost credible the ensuing assertion that God makes the world "dangerous" in order to bring moral issues into prominence.

Read and reread, the *Letters* prove not only more amusing but more psychologically penetrating than any of Lewis's other fiction for adults except for his *Great Divorce* and *Till We Have Faces.* Yet he hated having to dwell so long on evil, and set little store by this, his first best-seller. In 1952, when his friend Sister Penelope wrote him that she still had the manuscript, he advised her to sell it for charity.[88]

The Great Divorce

In his diary for 1933, Lewis proposes to write a book based on a patristic allusion to the *refrigerium,* or excursion to Paradise, permitted the damned.[89] He published the work in weekly installments under the title "Who Goes Home?" which Blès persuaded him to change, because the title had been used before. It is also the closing formula

88. Letter to Sister Penelope, 10 January 1952.
89. Diary entry for 16 April 1933, in W. H. Lewis, "C. S. Lewis: A Biography," 102. No indication is given of where the patristic allusion can be found.

of a parliamentary session. He chose the title *The Great Divorce* to challenge Blake's denial of any absolute division between good and evil.[90] For every reader unfamiliar with Blake's *Marriage of Heaven and Hell,* a thousand would have missed the original title's intended allusion to MacDonald's metaphor of the spiritual life as homecoming; yet the original title better conveys the preoccupation of almost every visitant in the *Great Divorce* with finding or clinging to a home on Earth.

The book has been praised for its spiritual insights and for its satire of both theological modernism and domestic power play, and also for involving "this ever-diverse pair — atomically rational Lewis and mythopoeic Lewis," in my terms the Dreamer and Mentor.[91] The book's most abiding image, however, is surely its grey city, the dingy essence of any British industrial megalopolis at that time, with its ever-spreading suburbs, chitchat, and status seeking. Almost equally memorable, not as recognition but as surprise, is the account of Heaven: the foot-piercing grass and sharp river foam, the selfless inhabitants more sociable but also more substantial than their visitors. Lewis builds his fantasy upon a principle since defined by Eric Rabkin as reversal of ground rules.[92] Heaven is not dreamlike or aerial but ultrasubstantial, while Hell is a city of nightmare populated by "Ghosts." Arrested development and fixation characterize not the believing "Solid Ones" but the unbelieving visitors. One Lewisian prejudice remains intact, in that Hell is urban and Heaven rural.

As if to anticipate recent accounts of near-death experiences, the bus to Heaven is driven by a "being of light," one of the book's three informants, who tells the passengers they can stay in Heaven and even if they return can repeat the trip at will. The second informant, an

---

90. Preface (dated April 1945) to *The Great Divorce,* 5. Page references are to the Macmillan paperback edition (1946).

91. Wilson describes *The Great Divorce* as "Lewis at his very best . . . approaching a masterpiece" (*C. S. Lewis: A Biography,* 202); Walsh calls it "one of the closest approaches to Dante's masterpiece . . . achieved in this century" (*The Literary Legacy of C. S. Lewis,* 80); and Sayer says it is "perhaps the most profound and nearly perfect of all his works" (*C. S. Lewis and His Times,* 185).

92. Eric Rabkin, *The Fantastic in Literature,* passim, and the introduction to *Fantastic Worlds: Myths, Tales and Stories,* 22ff.

"intelligent" passenger, describes the city and its inhabitants to the narrator. The third informant, George MacDonald, comments on encounters between visitants and their friends or relatives in Heaven. As the parallel with Virgil implies, the *Divine Comedy* supplied models for the book in general, as it did for the Driver, the Tragedian, and the Lady.[93] A medieval dream-vision, the book comprises two sequences of dialogues featuring six males and five females, followed by an encounter between husband and wife. MacDonald enters (chap. 9) at the end of the first encounter between a female Ghost and one of the Spirits. Just before the encounter between husband and wife, a lecher — the only Ghost who affirms his willingness to stay — allows a Spirit to kill the lizard symbolizing his lust (chap. 11).

Although Lewis felt self-condemned by this fantasy, specific biographical allusions — such as whether he ever saw the tall and well-built Bishop Barnes of Birmingham — are red herrings. The bishop grown fat by denying the faith he ought to have taught represents modernist clergy in general. Again, the failed poet at the start is not Lewis but any would-be artist unable to accept criticism or adapt to his environment. Similarly, the figures of the Tragedian and Dwarf into which Sarah's husband has split represent any neurotic diminished by clinging to imagined past glory. Like any of the other visitors, the husband can stay if he will renounce what keeps him from joy.

While the Christian paradox of losing one's identity by clinging to it fits most visitants, the *Great Divorce* is primarily the work of Lewis the moralist, or Mentor. One need not believe in Christianity to agree that the possessive mother loved her son too little (chap. 11), or that the ambitious wife who nagged her husband into a nervous breakdown failed to accept him as he was (chap. 10). In agreeing to "forgive him as a Christian" but "not forget" the wife echoes Jane Austen's Mr. Collins. Similarly, the poet, the intelligent man, the male cynic, the nagging wife, and the bullying husband would be recognized by believer and unbeliever alike.

93. The Driver is identified with the Angel at the gates of Dis; the Tragedian and wife parallel Dante and Beatrice in *Purgatorio* (letters to Kinter, 28 March 1953 and 30 July 1954).

Christian belief and ethics play a clearer role in the woman Ghost's protest at the lack of privacy and modesty in Heaven (chap. 8), in MacDonald's entry (chap. 9) just in time to prevent the narrator from becoming infected by the hopeless cynicism of the Hard-Bitten Ghost, and in the reformed lecher's growth into a giant riding a stallion. To equate the bishop merely with Mr. Broad, the Victorian liberal of the *Pilgrim's Regress,* is to miss the point of his insistence on returning to read a paper to the Theological Society. Even when dazzled by the whiteness of his former protégé, he maintains that Heaven all about him is a metaphor for some state forever sought and never found, and that Christ was a youthful idealist who would have outgrown his early teachings. The bishop wants forever to discuss and in that sense contemplate the bliss that Dick eternally enjoys. Not coincidentally, his Society meets on Fridays, the church's weekly fast-day in memory of the Crucifixion.

Less obvious but more profound are the psychology and placement of the dialogue of a Ghost named Pam with her brother about her desire to see and speak with her son Michael. To her, parental love is our "highest and holiest feeling" (p. 93); to her brother, this love of her murdered son, being unredeemed by the love of God, has become an idol. The mother feels the son born of her body to be hers eternally; her brother realizes that he naturally grew away from her. Her angry denial of having overcompensated for an unplanned pregnancy by excessive mother-love concludes ironically: "I hate and despise your God. I believe in a God of love" (95).

Assuring the troubled narrator that hope remains for Pam, MacDonald claims that although "something in natural affection . . . will lead it on to eternal love," its corruption is worse than that of "natural appetite" (96-97). His further explanation of the fact that the worst is a corruption of the best is immediately followed by the appearance of the Ghost carrying the red lizard of lust on his shoulder. From this juxtaposition and the ensuing contrast between Sarah and her former husband, the narrator sees family affection *(storge)* and sexual passion *(eros)* as idols unless transmuted by *agape,* the self-giving, undemanding love lauded by St. Paul. Fifteen years later, in *The Four Loves,* Lewis affirmed the necessity of charity if affection, passion, and friendship were to achieve their potential for good.

Most critics have overlooked the subtle admixture of Christian theology and ethics with dynamic psychology in the sublimation of sexual desire during the lizard-shedding episode. Because salvation hinges on a willingness to grow and change by forgiving the wrongs on which the lost eternally harp, the grey city is Hell for those who insist on returning to it, but Purgatory to those willing to stay in Heaven.

For several reasons, the *Great Divorce* has remained less popular than Lewis's other theological fantasies. Its episodic plot is deprived of suspense and climax by MacDonald's commentaries. The episodes dated by Lewisian antimodernism work against those featuring recurrent human types. Defective plotting and, again, failure to edit out what was ephemeral or personal have kept on the sidelines a picture of the urban wasteland and its fragmented society that deserves a wider audience.

Psychologized Myth: *Till We Have Faces*

Though the least popular when published, and still not widely known, *Till We Have Faces* (1956) is now widely recognized by academics as Lewis's best novel for adults. It alone can be fully appreciated, though not fully understood, without prior knowledge of his life and times or sympathy with his beliefs. Its poor sales profoundly disappointed Lewis, for the originating myth had been in his mind since at least 1923, when he began a poetic version, and the novel was his joint creation with his future bride. His emotional investment is patent in letters to Gibb in the spring of 1956. Defending the original title, "Bareface," he pleads that everyone he has consulted prefers it.[94] Indeed, "Bareface" would have attracted more browsers in bookstores. As he explains, its central figure, Orual, went physically barefaced in childhood and by the time she finished her tale in her old age was psychologically bared. Somewhat testily, he rejected two wrapper designs, insisting on the representation of the goddess Ungit by a band of red rock inscribed with the wrinkles of a hideously aged female face, and of Aphrodite's statue by a figure

94. Letter to Gibb, 21 February 1956.

like the early Greek original in being stiff rather than provocative.[95] Finally, to spare Joy embarrassment, he had the dedication printed on a different page from the frontal motto "Love is too young to know what conscience is."[96]

As a Christianized version of the "Cupid and Psyche" myth related by Apuleius in the *Golden Ass, Till We Have Faces* belonged from the start on shelves labeled "Literature" rather than "Popular Fiction." Its increasing respect among "literary" readers, whether or not postmodernist, is traceable to its original and powerful presentation of a familial affection that destroys in seeking to possess, to its interwoven symbols, and to its characterization and dialogue. Even the apparent male chauvinism of Psyche's protest to Orual, "I am a wife now. It's no longer you I must obey,"[97] is inherent in the myth. In substituting for Cupid a "Brute" associated with sightings of lions, Lewis draws less upon the fairy-tale "Beauty and the Beast" than upon his own recently completed Chronicles of Narnia, for the Shadowbrute is never seen save by Psyche and is heard only by implication as the divine "voice" prophesying to or passing judgment on Orual. Psyche's loss of her mother, her dependence on the Fox for counsel not forthcoming from her father, and Orual's possessiveness as mother-substitute, together with an unhandsome woman's resentment at her lot, conceivably originated in shared confidences between Lewis and Joy Davidman as virtual co-author. But the reader need not know all this to follow the plot.

One of the three principal changes Lewis made in Apuleius's story was the replacement of Cupid by a "Brute." The second was the replacement of Venus by the inscrutable Ungit, whom Lewis fashioned partly, as Doris Myers has shown, from the Eastern Mediterranean Great Mother, or fertility goddess,[98] and partly from the hideous and inscrutable mother figure who confronts the hero of his poem *Dymer,* on which he was working in 1923 when he drafted a never-to-be-

---

95. Letter to Gibb, 11 April 1956.
96. Letter to Gibb, 2 May 1956.
97. *Till We Have Faces,* 127. Page references are to the Eerdmans paperback edition (1966).
98. Myers, *C. S. Lewis in Context,* 193-98.

finished poem on Cupid and Psyche.[99] The elimination of Venus enabled him to set the action entirely in this world and retell the myth as a novel. As Myers has shown, he took as much trouble as any historical novelist to supply a plausible setting: an imaginary kingdom, probably in the Caucasus, adjoining Greece in the Hellenistic era. He also gave his narrator some of the vocabulary and pragmatic attitudes of England's "Virgin Queen Elizabeth."[100] Not much of this would be apparent at first reading.

Finally, Lewis eliminated the two sisters in Apuleius's story, who, being jealous of Psyche's palace, persuade her to break her promise to refrain from looking at her husband, replacing them with one half-sister who relates the story from her own viewpoint. It is this device, above all, which turned *Till We Have Faces* into a psychological novel. This should endear it to the present generation of critics, for to a large extent it is a book about writing a book. Beneath its given events — the marriage, transgression, and banishment of Psyche — runs a subtext created by Lewis.

Receiving no answer to her enquiry as to why the gods who have deprived her of Psyche inhabit "dark places" (249) and speak only in hints, Orual realizes that they can reveal themselves only to mortals with "faces" (294), that is, with developed and complete identities, able to face themselves as they are and have been. Orual has ruled Glome justly and intelligently but veiled her face, so making herself distant and awesome. Suppressing her love of nature and the arts, she has become a workaholic, and thereby overlaid if not killed her own soul. "The Queen," she recalls, "had more and more part in me and Orual had less and less" (226). Having confirmed her power by mortally wounding her opponent Argan in the "inner leg," she has become masculine in swordsmanship, ruthlessness, and power of decision. Her repressed femininity has prompted her to monopolize her beloved counselor Bardia, and so deprive him of family life. (To Lewis's surprise,

99. The unfinished poem is written in a notebook and mentioned in Lewis's diary, 9 September 1923; see "The Lewis Family Papers," VIII, 163-64. The confrontation between the hero and the mother figure in *Dymer* is found in canto 3, stanzas 23-25. *Dymer* will be discussed in more detail in Chapter 7.

100. Myers, *C. S. Lewis in Context*, 201-2.

the publisher's readers failed to perceive the passion for Bardia evident in her emotions when they lay back to back while returning from her first visit to Psyche, when he kissed her hand as Queen, and when he wished her a man.)[101] She dares do all things save expose herself and let those she loves lead their own lives. But *qui s'excuse, s'accuse.* In writing her life story as a charge against the gods, she discovers her own guilt in using Psyche and Bardia as objects of possessive love. In baring her face and confronting her past, she undergoes a death of her old self after hearing from Bardia's widow Ansit how overwork has destroyed him.[102]

It follows from Orual's story that nobody at court save Psyche is a complete human being. Driven by passion, the King shows poor judgment in wedding the daughter of the declining King Cap-had (my hyphen) and precipitates rebellion and accompanying disasters by having Tarin castrated after finding him in bed with his (unmarried) daughter Redival, herself driven by sexual passion and self-interest. The wise and unpossessive Fox, tutor to the sisters, chose slavery because he feared to die. Even the brave, practical, and decisive Bardia dares not examine his own heart, nor his conventional religiosity, which is tantamount to superstition, nor will he face Orual to demand time for his home life. Yet the health of that home life is thrown into question by the Fox's remark that Ansit keeps Bardia "tied to" her "apron strings" and "rules him like her slave" (146). Even the original Priest of Ungit, so awesome in his bird-mask, is stricken with blindness by the plague that besets Glome.

On a mythic and religious level, Ungit offers through the Priest to relieve the kingdom of its apocalyptic drought, famine, pestilence, and threatened war consequent upon the sin of King Trom. The condition she sets is that the King must sacrifice his youngest and loveliest daughter, Psyche, to Ungit's son, the Shadowbrute. That willing victim has already shown herself not only beautiful but selfless, a lover of nature, art, and the fellow mortals she heals. Psyche exemplifies the positive virtue of disinterested love that Lewis upheld in a famous

101. Letter to Gibb, 16 February 1956.
102. Cf. Manlove, who calls the book "a steady dislocation of certainties of the central character" ("'Caught Up into the Larger Pattern,'" 262).

sermon[103] and later in his *Four Loves.* Three centuries before Christ, she anticipates much that Christ taught and did, yet Lewis intended her to signify not Christ but the naturally Christian soul. She endures death, only across its narrow river to be resurrected glowing with life and to perceive robes and palace where Orual sees only rags and rocks. (Lewis was coming round to Barfield's view that the observer's attitude modifies the reality observed.)[104] Her name, the Greek word for "soul," connotes imagination and awareness of the spiritual within the material. In disobeying her husband's injunction she forfeits joy, love, and home. Orual, her tempter, unconsciously acknowledges this when interpreting the chains that rattle in the wind as Psyche lamenting her exile.

Just how the sacrifice relieves Glome of pestilence and famine is not clear. In the Christian mythos, Christ's sacrifice frees the believer of guilt and misery resulting from the fall, but in this retelling of the Cupid and Psyche myth only an allegorical explanation seems at all feasible: Glome representing humanity, Psyche the human soul and precursor of Christ offered to the god of love, their union the condition of human happiness and well-being. Yet in *Till We Have Faces,* the god of love was begotten of the inscrutable Ungit, whose egg-shaped temple has functioned as nature's womb.

For their curse to be lifted, the people of Glome must obey Ungit's promptings by sacrificing Psyche. But in their rulers they need the Fox's wisdom and Bardia's practicality rather than the caprice of King Trom. Insofar as she combines their virtues and employs the Fox and Bardia as advisers, Orual is their best ruler, yet at the price of foregoing Psyche's love of nature, the arts, and her fellow humans. She sacrifices herself for the kingdom by overlaying her own soul. Significantly, only Orual and the Fox use the name "Psyche," while the King, Redival, and Bardia use her given name, "Istra." The name used is an index of the user's immersion in the tribal culture of Glome.

An alternative reading of the story is suggested by Lewis's unfinished poem of 1923. Denouncing as a half-truth Apuleius's account of Psyche being given to a dragon by order of the jealous Venus, it hints

103. "The Weight of Glory" (1942), preached in St. Mary the Virgin, Oxford, and published in *The Weight of Glory and Other Addresses* (1949).
104. Peter J. Schakel, *Reason and Imagination in C. S. Lewis,* 42-43.

at her release by Zephyrus, deity of the wind. Its initial mention of the prevailing drought suggests that Lewis intended weaving in a fertility myth. The poem continues by alluding to the palace and to the injunction forbidding Psyche to see her lover. It then denounces Apuleius's tale of two plain sisters persuading Psyche to commit breaches, here unspecified, of the kingdom's laws. As in the book, where Psyche sees a palace, her visitors see only moorland. Finally, weeping shapes separate into Psyche and her twin brother Jardis, handsome to the point of effeminacy, who reports her story. The importance of the poem is twofold: by implication Psyche is rescued from death; and her story is reported by a hermaphrodite figure whose name, modified to "Jadis," Lewis was to use for the Witch in two Narnia stories.[105] In the novel, the tempter and reporter merge into Orual, and it is hinted that the West Wind has delivered her from her chains to her bridegroom. The final version, therefore, is polysemous, suggesting at once Psyche's death and her resurrection, rescued by a fertility spirit, and her translation to the palace, where she transgresses the injunction.

As several commentators note, Orual grows spiritually after recording Psyche's story and her own.[106] In Colin Manlove's view, this inward change constitutes the novel's plot.[107] Even before her self-criticism in part II, her use of the new Priest Arnom as counselor in place of the aged Fox implies that she now finds a place for religion. Moreover, her two self-exposures, the first intended by the King to show her an unfit bride for the Brute by making her behold herself in the court's only true mirror, the second when she removes her veil to show that unattractive face to Bardia's widow, imply that she has accepted the ugly woman's fate.

As to why the book remains little known among readers at large, reasons so far suggested are that despite some violent incidents its major development takes place within Orual herself,[108] that because she is using a foreign language Orual's style is somewhat "stiff and artificial,"[109] that its origin in classical myth does not recommend it to

---

105. *The Lion, the Witch and the Wardrobe* and *The Magician's Nephew.*
106. Principally Manlove, *C. S. Lewis: His Literary Achievement,* 199, 208-9.
107. Manlove, "'Caught Up into the Larger Pattern,'" 272.
108. Manlove, "'Caught Up into the Larger Pattern,'" 272.
109. Schakel, *Reason and Imagination in C. S. Lewis,* 7.

readers no longer familiar with Greco-Roman lore, that its title signifies little to most readers, and that its Christian values are implied rather than spelled out.[110] By the same token not only Orual's self-undermining narrative but the mirror, veil, and other symbols central to the structure make *Till We Have Faces* the most palatable of Lewis's novels to the present generation of critics. These other symbols include light and dark, water and wine, surgery, the spider and web, the Shadowbrute himself, the palace and Grey Mountain, the womb, egg, and parent figures. In addition, the recurrent metaphor of pregnancy involves several features of Orual's book congenial to poststructuralist criticism: reflexivity, ambivalence, and dependence upon reader-response from the "wise" Greeks to whom Orual hopes it will be conveyed.

As Mara E. Donaldson has pointed out, Lewis employs metaphor in a sense defined by the Christian deconstructionist Paul Ricoeur, to signify both likeness and difference between tenor and vehicle.[111] To illustrate, in perceiving Glome as a web with herself at its center, gorging on the stolen lives of Bardia and others, Orual perceives a characteristic of absolute monarchies. Yet the most autocratic ruler cannot organize the entire life of each subject, nor as the liberal reformer gifted in delegating authority has Orual stolen lives as willingly as did her father, that capricious autocrat King Trom. Again, the divine use of her autobiography to "probe" her "wound" (254), and of Ansit's accusations as divine surgery (266), certainly describe a radical and painful spiritual healing. Yet the "surgery" leaves her awaiting death after a stroke (308), while the "two strokes of a razor" (255) that made possible Tarin's diplomatic career rendered him a self-satisfied eunuch.

By lumping similes, metaphors, and other images under the general term "symbols" we can observe two sets of antitheses: revelation versus concealment, and the nurturer versus the predator. In the first, the mirror is played off against the veil, light against dark, the Brute's "palace" against the Temple of Ungit. When Orual offers herself for sacrifice in place of Psyche, the King compels her to behold her face in the mirror, implying that her physical appearance matters to the

110. Myers, *C. S. Lewis in Context*, 213.
111. Mara E. Donaldson, *Holy Places Are Dark Places: C. S. Lewis and Paul Ricoeur on Narrative Transformation.*

Brute as to a bridegroom and that every other mirror at court flatters the self-beholder. Since the court's one clear mirror does not harm the vain Redival, it must wound Orual only because she hopes to be offered as a god's bride, in substitution for Psyche.

This experience shapes Orual's nightmare, in part II, of falling into the "black hole" (274-75), an image first used in the *Pilgrim's Regress*.[112] Forced by her father to see her own "ruinous" face, she associates herself with Ungit, Batta, and a spider gorging on stolen lives in the web of Glome (276). In this dream the two patterns of symbolism coalesce. Orual realizes her inward change during her reign, from "Maia" (name for a mother and nurse-goddess), or possessive nurturer of Psyche, to a predator not upon the kingdom she has ruled wisely and justly but upon Bardia and his wife. The change began when she ceased to hear the well's rattling chains as Psyche weeping.

Wandering in the neighboring kingdom of Essur, Orual hears of a local deity named Istra (Psyche) veiled in black for winter and in white for spring. In Glome, the white veil preserves Orual's respect and conceals her ugly face. In the other kingdom, returning sunlight brings a fertility restored to Glome only by the sacrifice. The significance of veiling is complicated by the description early in the book of the sacrificial victim's face as a "lifeless mask" (80) like that of a temple prostitute, and by the masking of Orual as a soldier for her duel with Argan. In Glome, the Queen's white veil signifies incorruptibility, whereas in Essur, the two veils signify Istra's death and resurrection. But to Orual, the meaning of her own veil varies with the context. When the King orders the girls to be veiled lest they frighten his second bride, Orual realizes her own ugliness (11). When she tells the Fox that she has persuaded Psyche to disobey her husband's injunction, she omits to mention her glimpse of the palace and emotional blackmail of Psyche by stabbing herself. Rebuked for the lesser offense she has disclosed, she resolves never more to show a man her face. Here the resumed veil hides her possessiveness, which destroys the beloved like the "dark, secret love" of Blake's "Sick Rose." Refusing the King's order to doff her "frippery" (181), she removes it only when her destructive passion has been exposed by Bardia's widow (262). By showing her face no

---

112. Recurrences of this image are listed in Downing, *Planets in Peril*, 92-93.

incitement to adultery she restores the veil's former significance, as Lewis's original title "Bareface" would have emphasized.

This brings us to the signifiers light and dark. In Glome, "holy places are dark places" (50), and Ungit is associated with what is earthy and instinctive. On the Grey Mountain, Orual sees Psyche in sunlight and, having pressured her into disobedience, has a vision of herself dead, followed by a bright light within which a stern yet "sweet" voice (173) terrifies her even before lightning flashes apocalyptically reveal falling rocks and trees and a flooding river. The vision reveals to Orual that the god has realized Psyche's disobedience. The beauty of his countenance undoes her less than its "passionless and measureless rejection" of all that she has "thought, done or been." He pronounces his bride's exile and, by implication, that of Orual, who "also shall be Psyche" (173-74). At once both light and voice give place to lamentation.

From her infancy, Psyche's face has brightened the room she was in. Following her illness, it wears a "new and severer radiance" (33). The association of Psyche, the Shadowbrute, and the Mountain with light and revelation and of Ungit and the veiled face of Orual with darkness, concealment, and unawareness, the apocalyptic symbolism of the curse upon Glome and the disobedience of Psyche imply a contrast between supernatural and natural — in Nietzschean terms "Apollonian and Dionysian" — religion. The Greek statue that Orual installs in the House of Ungit inspires no popular devotion, for the numinous reaches the people via the old image and worship.

To a large extent, Lewis succeeds in grafting Christian upon pagan mythology. Psyche is sacrificed on what becomes a "Holy Tree" (98, 139). The river that separates her from Orual is just six feet wide, as if to connote death and the human body. The little apocalypse on the Mountain frightens Bardia's taciturn substitute Gram yet never becomes known in Glome, a parallel to the finale of *That Hideous Strength*. The eucharistic symbol of what Psyche perceives spiritually as wine and Orual materially as springwater works within the general context of the "palace" that Orual sees only as rock (a biblical symbol of Christ). The god's rumored appearance as a leonine "Brute" fits into the pagan and the Judeo-Christian myths. Even the name "Shadowbrute," first used after Psyche has agreed to be sacrificed, fits when understood in Jungian, Platonic, and Christian terms to imply that the Brute is both the "shadow" aspect of the personality and a shadow or type of Christ. Even the Priest calls the sacrifice the "Brute's Supper" (49). Within the tales of "Cupid and Psyche" or "Beauty and the Beast" the name is best understood in Jungian terms, as denoting the Bride's need to accept the animal element in love.

Where the graft of Christian upon pagan symbolism does not take is at the god's injunction that Psyche may not see his face. To forbid a Christian to behold Christ her bridegroom has no meaning either on Earth where she cannot or in heaven where she forever will. So an act of disobedience that is meaningful only in the pagan myth and the fairy-tale has consequences that are meaningful only in the Christian mythos. That is the central weakness of Lewis's wisest and best story for adults. Admire as we must the ingenuity of substituting the silent Gram (Greek for "letter") for Bardia, or the perceptiveness of Lewis (or of Joy) when Psyche angers Orual by insisting that she knows her husband as no virgin could, the story of *Till We Have Faces* comes unglued at its central injunction. A lesser implausibility, the Brute as the son of Ungit, can be defended in that the religion of Ungit confers superhuman fearlessness upon its Priest when the King holds a dagger to his breast.

In her old age Orual sets down her quasi-legal case against the gods, neither fearing their vengeance nor expecting their answer. She writes in Greek, hoping that some palace guest might convey the manuscript to "wise men" in the "Greeklands," who will judge its indictment with the open minds of those educated in a superior culture. Since her expectation exposes her own conduct to similar judgment, her case undermines itself as it proceeds. Before the sacrifice, when admitted to Psyche's cell, she resents being comforted like a "child." Realizing this, Psyche calls her "Maia," as she had in her infancy (67), thus proving herself the more perceptive and mature of the two. This impression is confirmed by her mingled realism and compassion in anticipating her tormentors as "cruel men, cowards and liars, the envious and the drunken," who cannot discern good from evil. Choking at Psyche's detachment, protesting even as Psyche asks her to promise that she will not kill herself, "for the Fox's sake," as the three had been such "loving friends," Orual asks herself bitterly, "Why must she say bare *friends?*" (68-69). No discerning reader can miss the implied mourning for the loss of quasi-maternal power over Psyche.

Orual's momentary vision of the Palace prompts her to beg forgiveness of its god and of Psyche for having presumed to "scold" and "comfort . . . as a child" one grown "far above" herself (132-33). Her admission understates what took place, for when told that she stood before the Palace "gate," she exclaimed that they must flee "this terrible place." Misinterpreting this, Psyche responds, "You do see it [the Palace] after all," upon which Orual asks the "fool's question 'What?'" even though she knows the answer. In writing this episode, on which her "charge against the gods" chiefly rests, she tries to convey the exact truth. Did she at that time believe in the invisible "Palace"? Surely no Greek reader can take this seriously. "But it's different in Glome. There the gods are too close to us." In saying "there," not "here," she puts herself in the place of readers she presumes to be too rationalistic to realize the sense of the numinous that Psyche had gathered from the word "terrible." Feeling "infinite misgiving" as "the whole world" and her sister with it slipped from her grasp, Orual screamed, with her father's rage, "There's nothing there!" Having roused Psyche to momentary fury, and led her to call her Orual instead of Maia, a name not used again until their final reconciliation, Orual shouted, "You're trying to make yourself believe it," and shook her sister "as one shakes a child." In the act of writing, Orual realizes that she was "lying," for she knew not whether Psyche had gone mad or really saw "invisible things" (117-18). Thus the process of writing steadily undermines both Orual's case against the gods and her rationalism absorbed from the Fox.

The symbol of pregnancy relates at once to the course of Orual's life, the divine creation, and the act of writing. She comes to view her absorption in her office as a pregnancy in reverse, by which she "locked Orual up or laid her asleep . . . deep down inside . . . curled there. . . . [T]he thing I carried in me grew slowly smaller and less alive" (226), in contrast to the New Year ritually born from the egg-shaped House of Ungit. When about to write, Orual is "with book" (247), a favorite saying of Lewis. Upon completing her indictment, confident that the gods "have no answer" (250), she remarks, "I made my book and here it stands" (248), an allusion to Browning's paradigm of the self-refuting monologue, "My Last Duchess," that seems incompatible with the pregnancy image of writing.

Within days of its supposed completion, Orual hastens to recant her indictment while time permits. The change in herself, she sees, began with the "writing itself." Understanding her past self very differently, she must record "passions and thoughts" she had "forgotten," for she speaks "before judges and must not lie" (253). The change from "Greek traveller" and "wise men" (3-4) to "judges" can only be one from human to divine arbitrament. The divine surgery, that self-contemplation (in a clear mirror) inseparable from true autobiography, has brought her to view her conduct from a divine standpoint, as if from the Mountain where she once stood with Psyche. As Lewis said in his "Summa," she now views her life "as Spirit sees it."

In this sense, the divine prediction "You also shall be Psyche" can be associated with Psyche's four tasks in the myth. Orual compares her autobiographical writing to sorting seeds of grain (256) and envisions Psyche gathering with ease the golden wool of wisdom that has cost Orual such labor (283-84). Orual's dream of descending to the underworld with King Trom (whose name is "mort" in reverse)[113] alludes to Psyche's third task, fetching water from the Styx (273-76); Orual's attempt to drown herself the next night is stopped by the god (279). The god's final pronouncement, "You also are Psyche" (308), indirectly alludes to the fourth task, bringing back beauty from Persephone, in that Orual's final vision of herself as Ungit or Batta leads to a self-renunciation that transforms her ugly face and soul to resemble those of her sister. This is how we should interpret the final vision in which, silenced by joy, Orual hears a voice announce, "The god comes to judge Orual," and is shown herself in a pool, distinguishable from Psyche only by garments, as the voice proclaims, "You also are Psyche" (307-8).

Admittedly the Fox, as a rationalist who depite himself loves the old poems and myths, belongs to the Hellenistic culture after Aristotle, but Orual's conflicts with Psyche and Ansit arrest and convince the modern reader just because they can arise in any age or society. When Orual calls on Bardia's widow the conventional three days after his death, she addresses her as woman to woman rather than monarch to subject. After she unveils, the two at first embrace weeping, then draw apart in mutual estrangement. As Ansit levels her accusations, her

113. Carol Ann Brown, "Who Is Ungit?" 1-5.

sentences become briefer, her words plainer and more pointed, until they reveal that she has overcome her own possessiveness. "I was his wife, not his doxy. He was my husband, not my house-dog. He was to live the life he thought best and fittest for a great man — not that which would most pleasure me." As she continues to speak, she seems at first possessive about her son, now in Orual's service: "He will turn his back on his mother's house . . . will seek strange lands, and be occupied with matters I don't understand, and go where I can't follow, and be daily less mine — more his own and the world's." But then she surprises Orual by her rhetorical question, "Do you think I'd lift up my little finger if lifting it would stop it?" To Orual's astonished query she responds, "Oh, Queen Orual, I begin to think you know nothing of love," then partially retracts, saying, "Yours is Queen's love, not commoners'. . . . Like the Shadowbrute. They say the loving and the devouring are all one, don't they?" (263-65).

For Psyche to sleep with an unseen husband is peculiar to the myth, but who that thinks a sister or daughter deceived by a villain would not share Orual's exasperation during her second visit?

> "Neither he [the Fox] nor I nor Bardia . . . believes for a moment in your fancy that it is the god. . . . [E]very man and woman in Glome . . . would say the same. The truth is too clear."
>
> "But what is all this to me? How should they know? I am his wife. I know."
>
> "How can you know if you have never seen him?"
>
> "Orual, how can you be so simple? I — how could I not know?"
>
> "But how, Psyche?"
>
> "What am I to answer to such a question? It's not fitting . . . and especially to you, Sister, who are a virgin."
>
> That matronly primness, from the child she was, came near to ending my patience. It was almost . . . as if she taunted me. (161-62)

When forced into agreeing to look at the Shadowbrute, Psyche pronounces, with the sad finality of anyone constrained to take a detestable decision:

> I know what I do. I know that I am betraying the best of lovers and that perhaps, before sunrise, all my happiness may be destroyed

forever. This is the price you have put upon your life. Well, I must pay it. (166)

As a novelist Lewis is at his best when the universal takes precedence over the particular and personal.

Thus the novels have come full circle[114] from the God of the Island in *Pilgrim's Regress,* whom John at last finds at the home from which his journey began, to the God of the Mountain, whom Orual finds in finding herself. The journeys differ in that John's is a round tour of the early twentieth-century world and its ideas, while Orual's is an interior voyage through her past life. In a double sense, Lewis, like the central figures of his first and last novels, was to find Joy during his tragically brief partnership with his virtual co-author in this, his best because his most soul-searching novel.

114. Manlove, " 'Caught Up into the Larger Pattern,' " 274.

CHAPTER 6

Children's Storyteller

O F ALL THE BOOKS by Lewis, the Chronicles of Narnia have
attracted and retained the largest readership. Critics have explored
their plots, characters, and genre, religious and moral teaching, language, biblical and literary sources, structural devices, symbols, and
motifs, not to mention the geography of their imagined worlds.[1] Just
as it seemed that nothing new could be said about them, I read David
Holbrook's *Skeleton in the Wardrobe*.[2] After so many encomia on the

---

1. Among others, Donald E. Glover, *C. S. Lewis: The Art of Enchantment*, and
Evan Gibson, *C. S. Lewis: Spinner of Tales*, discuss plots and characters; Michael
Murrin, "The Multiple Worlds of the Narnia Stories," in Peter J. Schakel and
Charles A. Huttar, eds., *Word and Story*, 232-55, examines the Narnia stories in
connection with German art fairytale genre; and Dabney A. Hart, *Through the Open
Door: A New Look at C. S. Lewis*, discusses Lewis's use of myth. Among those writers
who examine religion, ethics, and language in Lewis are Doris T. Myers, *C. S. Lewis
in Context*, 112-81; Jim Pietrusz, "Rites of Passages"; John D. Cox, "Epistemological
Release in *The Silver Chair*," in Peter J. Schakel, ed., *The Longing for a Form*, 159-70.
Charles A. Huttar, "C. S. Lewis's Narnia and the Grand Design," in Schakel, ed.,
Longing for a Form, 119-35, and Kathryn Lindskoog, *The Lion of Judah in Never-
Neverland*, examine Lewis's use of motifs, especially biblical motifs. More comprehensive studies of the Chronicles include C. N. Manlove, "'Caught Up into the Larger
Pattern,'" in Schakel and Huttar, eds., *Word and Story*, 256-76; Paul F. Ford, *A
Companion to Narnia;* Hooper, *Past Watchful Dragons: The Narnian Chronicles of C. S.
Lewis;* and Peter J. Schakel, *Reading with the Heart: The Way into Narnia.*

2. David Holbrook, *The Skeleton in the Wardrobe*. Page references will be given
parenthetically in the text.

stories, this book acted as a shot of adrenalin, but when a Leavisite critic attempts assassination by psychoanalysis, no friend of Narnia can stand by and do nothing.

Holbrook gives two reasons for thinking the tales unfit for children. The first is that Lewis was insufficiently mature to handle the "deeply disturbing material" (Holbrook, 173) that welled up from his unconscious as he wrote. Queen Jadis the White Witch *(Magician's Nephew; The Lion, the Witch and the Wardrobe)* and the Witch of the Green Kirtle *(Silver Chair)* emanated from Lewis's mother, who had not only rejected him by dying but had earlier failed to confer a secure identity through creative play. Aslan, the Christ of Narnia (whose name Lewis derived from the euphonious Turkish word for lion),[3] bounded into Narnia "out of Lewis's own unconscious" (Holbrook, 55), originating in Rev. Robert Capron, the flagellating principal of Wynyard School ("Belsen"). Having identified with the aggressor, the "unhappy child" (Holbrook, 11) surviving within the distinguished academic turned Capron into a punitive deity.

Holbrook goes on with the happy freedom of an amateur psychoanalyst to convert Mrs. Lewis's "cheerful and tranquil affection" *(Surprised by Joy,* 9) into maternal coldness and inadequacy, and her nine-year-old son's grief into a castration complex (Holbrook, 36, 48-49). He infers a presumption that her cancer had resulted from marital intercourse (Holbrook, 65), that her "Bad Breast" is represented in the spires and turrets of the White Witch's castle (Holbrook, 36, 68, 73), and that a Narnian lamp-post represents the paternal penis (Holbrook, 67). In response to such an interpretation, the uninventive scholar can only protest that from at one time daily readings of Wordsworth's *Prelude* Lewis was fully conscious of the maternal role in forming a child's identity, and that he nowhere wrote of being thrashed at Wynyard, only of his unsought status as Capron's "pet."[4]

Admittedly the most convincing villains in the tales are female, and the heroes include three orphan princes. Compared to Queen Jadis, King Miraz *(Prince Caspian)* is a paper cutout of Hamlet's wicked uncle, and Uncle Andrew *(Magician's Nephew)* a clown. Since Jadis the Queen-

---

3. Letter to W. L. Kinter, 28 October 1954.
4. See *Surprised by Joy,* 26; *Letters to an American Lady,* 117 (6 July 1963).

Witch existed from before the creation of Narnia, her name probably derives from the French word *jadis* ("formerly," "once upon a time") rather than from "jade" ("nightmare") as Holbrook suggests (Holbrook, 65). She brought about the ruin of the ancient city of Charn, introduced evil into the world on the day of Narnia's creation *(Magician's Nephew),* and practiced "Deep Magic from the dawn of time" (*The Lion, the Witch and the Wardrobe,* chap. 13). As I have argued, Lewis's anti-feminism and need of a surrogate mother did result from his childish perception of being abandoned by his mother and the added shock of being sent so soon to boarding school. But this does not license conjectures about his babyhood for which neither *Surprised by Joy* nor the letters of Mrs. Lewis offer any support, so as to turn her into a witch. Nor will supposed parallels with psychiatric patients prove much about Lewis.

There is more to support Holbrook's belief that Capron's cruelty inflicted lasting damage. Lewis describes with horror seeing a classmate caned (*Surprised by Joy,* 28), an experience I recall as being more distressing than being caned in person. But Lewis's own attribution of his first religious convictions — and terrors — to the faith of clergy at the Anglo-Catholic church near the school (*Surprised by Joy,* 33) implies an identification with them rather than with the clerical sadist Capron.

As regards the "minatory" (Holbrook, 34 et al.) figure of Aslan, it is important to note that punishments in the tales usually involve religious symbolism. Thus the metamorphosis of Eustace into a dragon *(Voyage of the "Dawn Treader")* alludes to a biblical image of the devil (Revelation 12:3-9). The peeling of the dragon skin down to the boy's heart, which Holbrook converts from singular to plural (Aslan "lacerates and unpeels people": Holbrook, 30), represents conversion and repentance. Its good effects can be seen in Eustace's satisfaction in helping his fellow voyagers while still a dragon and in his newly developed sense of humor once restored to human shape. Aslan's mauling of Aravis *(The Horse and His Boy)* is also an external sign of a need for inward change, for it brings home to her the punishment of the slave-girl she deceived into abetting her escape. When Shasta comes to her defense, Aslan at once departs. In the same book, Prince Rabadash's transformation into a donkey is reversed on condition of good behavior, a fact that Holbrook conveniently ignores. Like the dwarf's taunting of Edmund, " 'Turkish delight for the little prince'" (*The Lion, the Witch and the Wardrobe*, chap. 11), it represents reform by ridicule. To call Aslan a "minatory figure" is to miss much that children love about him: the golden mane and silky fur, the playful rolls and graceful steps.

Holbrook's second major criticism is that Lewis acts duplicitously in presenting his own nightmares as fairy tales, his own misogyny and paranoid view of the world as Christian teaching. If, as Lewis maintained, his fictions grew out of mental images[5] (as Holbrook adds, from his unconscious), he had no hidden agenda. If he found the world a cruel place through which his characters needed guidance, so do many children in tough schools or adults outside the secure enclaves of the prosperous. On Lewis's own submission, the win-or-lose situation of Britain in the 1940s was what his experience had led him to expect (*Surprised by Joy*, 32), but that says as much about his battle experience in 1918 as about his schooldays at Wynyard. By combining his antipathy to "coarse, brainless" boys at Malvern who had inflicted "abject misery, terrorism and hopelessness" (*They Stand Together*, 47, 55) with his tirades about homosexuality between "Bloods" and "tarts" (*Surprised by Joy*, chaps. 7-8), one might guess at sexual abuse that an adolescent would be too embarrassed to report yet surely too grownup to repress into his unconscious, but that would be only conjecture.

Although Lewis was worried by a headmistress's prediction that his *Lion, the Witch and the Wardrobe* would confuse and terrify children,[6] in fifteen years of teaching the stories to students who mostly read them first as children, I recall not one complaint of their inspiring fear or hatred. Some objected to talking animals and some, justifiably, to the strictures on coeducation in the *Silver Chair*, a book dated by its author's prejudice against "progressive" schooling and parenting, not to mention the absurd headmistress of Experiment House. Such, however, is often the case with children's classics. Consider the Victorian idea of a healthy diet in *The Secret Garden*: eggs, butter, and lashings of cream. Or compare the "delight and joy" that Isaac Watts's *Divine and Moral Songs* gave eighteenth-century children with their denunciation by a twentieth-century historian appalled by their images

5. Lewis, "Sometimes Fairy Stories Say What's Best to Be Said."
6. Letter to Ruth Pitter, 28 November 1950.

of hell.[7] Indeed, That Lewis himself received countless enquiries from both children and adults is a tribute in itself.

To judge the Chronicles of Narnia from figures and symbols taken out of context is to distort them. To read the tales as wholes, whether individually or in sequence, is to realize the equal importance of symbols that originated in mid-twentieth-century life, in medieval and Renaissance literature, and in Lewis's own past.[8] Captain Maugrim the wolf *(The Lion, the Witch and the Wardrobe)* may embody a castrating mother-figure, as Holbrook claims (Holbrook, 65), but as head of a tyrant's secret police he signified a very real threat when Lewis began the tale (1939), or even when he published it (1951). The medieval swords and arrows of Narnian warfare are even less likely to terrify or brutalize children than the six-shooters of old-time westerns. As with the final slaughter in Homer's *Odyssey,* obsolete weaponry and the written word filter violence through the reader's imagination. It may be of interest to note that the villainess of Morris's *Water of the Wondrous Isles* is also called a "Witch," and the heroine addressed as "Daughter of Adam" (Morris, 469). In the case of educational or racial prejudices, as in the portrayal of dark-skinned, garlic-smelling Calormenes *(Last Battle),* such elements risk provoking protest and so spoiling the illusion for adult readers, but whether they annoy or puzzle the young one must vary with the individual.

It may be useful to consider the Chronicles' probable meaning, influence on, and attraction for young readers. Details noticed by young readers may depend on whether the books are read at random, as must often happen, or in a deliberate order: either the order in which the books were completed *(The Lion, the Witch and the Wardrobe; Prince Caspian; Voyage of the "Dawn Treader"; Horse and His Boy; Silver Chair; Last Battle; Magician's Nephew);* the order of their publication *(The Lion, the Witch and the Wardrobe; Prince Caspian; Voyage of the "Dawn Treader"; Silver Chair; Horse and His Boy; Magician's Nephew; Last Battle);* or the order of chronology from the creation to the end of

7. Frances Hodgson Burnett, *The Secret Garden;* Isaac Watts, *Works,* 1:xix; Esmé Wingfield-Stratford, *A Victorian Tragedy,* 57-58.

8. In *C. S. Lewis: His Literary Achievement,* 120-86, C. N. Manlove traces allusions in the Chronicles to literary sources in all periods.

Narnia *(Magician's Nephew; The Lion, the Witch and the Wardrobe; Horse and His Boy; Prince Caspian; Voyage of the "Dawn Treader"; Silver Chair; Last Battle).*[9]

Those who read in the order of writing are more likely to perceive the progression from early childhood to old age in the protagonists and in the Narnian landscape.[10] Having briefly begun writing *The Lion, the Witch and the Wardrobe* late in 1939, Lewis resumed in the summer of 1948. From that point, the whole series took him six years, long enough for some changes of perspective to emerge. In *The Horse and His Boy,* written in 1950, the Calormene sovereign, Prince Rabadash, and the Grand Vizier use the rhetorical formulae of the Arabian Nights. In *The Last Battle,* written two years later, the worshipers of Tash bow to the ground like Muslims, yet the Calormene officer Emeth uses plain English and is welcome in Aslan's country because he has obeyed the universal moral law that Lewis elsewhere called "the Tao." Imagination and, no doubt, reflection on the author's own *Abolition of Man* have modified a stereotype and a dogma. The continuing concern in the Chronicles with the effects on children's values of positivist conditioning has been very fully explored by Myers.[11]

In *The Lion, the Witch and the Wardrobe,* the four Pevensie children are evacuated from London during the war to the house of an old bachelor known as "the Professor." While hiding in a wardrobe to escape a tour of the house led by the housekeeper, they find it to be a passage into another world and so stumble into Narnia by seeming accident. Yet in Aslan's good time they find themselves to be Narnia's long-expected sovereigns.[12] The youngest of the children, and the first to enter Narnia, is named after Lucy Barfield, to whom the book is dedicated, whose first name has the root meaning "light."[13] Lewis concluded the book by anticipating "further adventures" in Narnia, and at once began *Prince Caspian.* As that book opens, the Pevensies are waiting at a junction for the trains that will

9. All information concerning the order and dates of the stories is taken from tables in Ford, *A Companion to Narnia.*

10. Myers, *C. S. Lewis in Context,* esp. 125.

11. Myers, *C. S. Lewis in Context,* 112-81.

12. On the blurred distinction between accident and design, see Manlove, " 'Caught Up into the Larger Pattern,' " 262.

13. Manlove, *C. S. Lewis: His Literary Achievement,* 135.

take the girls to one school and the boys to another, when they are summoned back to Narnia by a horn blast. The horn signals a cross-over not only from childhood to pubescence but also from present time to the author's inner journey, for Prince Caspian's medieval education is analogous to Lewis's own development from predilection for folklore and romance to rejection of modernism and secular humanism. When finally returned to the station platform, Peter and Susan have grown too old to visit Narnia again.

The past in the enchanting *Voyage of the "Dawn Treader"* is more cultural than personal. The two youngest Pevensies, Edmund and Lucy, are spending the summer with their aunt and uncle. Their cousin Eustace has had a modern, permissive upbringing by parents who taught him to call them by their first names instead of "Mother" and "Father" and has attended a school resembling Summerhill or Dartington Hall. While discussing a picture of a Narnian ship that is hanging in a back bedroom, all three children suddenly find themselves aboard the ship, which is called the *Dawn Treader* (a name signifying discovery and enlightenment). Once at sea, Eustace is reeducated by experience in a world that is predominantly symbolic and mythological. Transformed in the "Lone" Isles into a dragon, he suffers the isolation that awaits a spoilt child, then has his dragon skin peeled off down to his heart, so as to become a caring and sharing person. Lewis attributes the boy's greed and egoism to his permissive upbringing. The more spoiled the child, the deeper and more painful his reformation.

Following Eustace's transformation, the voyage takes us even further into a timeless world of myth and symbol. The finding of a Narnian lord's corpse on the isle called Goldwater by King Caspian but Deathwater by the idealist Reepicheep (chap. 8) doubtless originated in the Midas myth but represents opposed values. A psychological symbol, the rescue from Dark Island of an exiled Narnian lord nearly driven mad by the terror of nightmares coming true (chap. 12) implies a lack of trust remarked by Bacon: "Men fear death as children fear to go in the dark."[14] When the *Dawn Treader* approaches the Utter East to set Reepicheep down near Aslan's country, Caspian's lust to follow recalls Sir Percival's obsessive quest for the Grail in Tennyson's *Idylls of the King*.

14. Francis Bacon, "Of Death," in *Essays,* 4-6.

In the next tale Lewis wrote, *The Horse and His Boy*, which features an adolescent boy and girl who break free of wicked stepparents, discover their true identities, and eventually become King and Queen of Archenland, Lewis juxtaposed three cultures. In the southern empire of Calormen, the ruler, crown prince, and Grand Vizier address each other in the language of the *Arabian Nights*. In Archenland, law and custom rule even its king, who hunts like a medieval monarch. The free-spoken Narnians who accompany their Pevensie sovereigns from the north seem idealized Vikings.

The ensuing *Silver Chair* draws upon the medieval quest-romances, and beyond them the myth of Orpheus. The "Underland" inhabited by the Witch's inhibited and silent subjects blends elements from the Greek Underworld, the Judaic Sheol, and the modern totalitarian state. Once liberated, Prince Rilian experiences a compulsion to descend to the still lower region of Bism, a desire compounded of curiosity about an alien world and a momentary death-wish. This overcome, his ascent to Narnia blends liberation from confinement by a possessive foster mother with joyous awakening to life and freedom. His confinement explains both his outbreaks of violence[15] and the general rejoicing at the Green Witch's death. His relief resembles that of Lewis when Mrs. Moore died, shortly before he began this book.[16]

At the beginning of the book, Eustace Scrubb and Jill Pole have entered Narnia from a shrubbery where they hid from Jill's tormentors at Experiment House. The sea voyage in the *Dawn Treader* that has changed Eustace forever took place during the recent school holidays, so he is still about nine years old. At first, his classmate Jill behaves like a schoolchild, posturing at the cliff edge until Eustace tries to rescue her. When Eustace falls off himself, Aslan blows him down to Narnia (21-22).[17] Unaware that the lion is Aslan, Jill is terrified of him. She

15. Cf. the violent outbreaks of Knight in William Morris, *Water of the Wondrous Isles*, 258. It may also be noted that in Morris's book as well as in *Silver Chair* the villainess is called "Witch" (Morris, 343, etc.) and the heroine is addressed as "Adam's Daughter" (Morris, 469).

16. George Sayer points to Lewis's inviting friends to stay at Kilns again, resuming exercise, and improving in health (*Jack: C. S. Lewis and His Times*, 203-4).

17. Page references given parenthetically in the text for all of the Narnian Chronicles refer to the editions cited in the bibliography.

tries to excuse herself for her part in Eustace's fall but soon bursts into tears. Isolated and thirsty, she has no choice but to follow Aslan's direction to drink from the only stream. Humbled and submissive because of her recent fear and guilt, she accepts the quest to search for the lost Prince Rilian and listens carefully to Aslan's explanation of four signs to follow. Jill and Eustace mature quickly during the journey and adventures that follow. Imprisoned in the giants' castle, Jill simulates childish giggles and behavior to deceive the Queen and attendants into allowing her to explore the castle and find an escape route.

Since even children so mature for their age could not have coped alone with the Queen-Witch in Underland, Lewis gave them a mentor. The transformation of his gardener Fred Paxford and perhaps his old tutor Kirkpatrick[18] into Puddleglum the Marsh-wiggle was a stroke of genius. As with Dickens's Mark Tapley, Puddleglum's demeanor varies with his circumstances. He is pessimistic when all seems well, soberly confident in Aslan's instructions when the children are bewildered, and prompt and courageous in stamping on the Witch's fire as its hypnotic fumes begin to lull the Prince and children into acquiescence. Already the drug has made them deny the sun's existence, just as secularism and materialism dispose moderns to deny God. In that sense, Underland signifies the post-Christian culture.

The remaining books have both theological and personal meaning, the latter more affecting for young readers. Having ended his first story with the resurrection of Aslan and the defeat of the Witch, Lewis relates Narnia's apocalypse in the most fully theological story, the *Last Battle,* which he began last and finished in the summer of 1953. In the next few months he finished *The Magician's Nephew,* begun in 1949 and resumed for part of 1951. He probably wrote the central chapter of *Magician's Nephew,* relating Narnia's creation and fall, before starting the *Last Battle.* The opening and closing episodes of *The Magician's Nephew* are saturated in his personal history, from the attic passage and "end room" of Little Lea and the magic rings of Nesbit's *Amulet,*[19] through the occultism of the "adept" Uncle Andrew, which recalls the

18. Respectively, Hooper, *Past Watchful Dragons,* 81-83; Myers, *C. S. Lewis in Context,* 151.

19. Cf. Manlove, *C. S. Lewis: His Literary Achievement,* 170.

"Great War" against Steinerism (though the would-be magician also combines the ruthlessness of Weston with the greed of Devine),[20] to the poignant episode of Digory healing his mother by feeding her the apple. The last fulfills a wish not granted Lewis in childhood. Was he right to grant it to Digory, whom Aslan has prepared to live without his mother? Yet child-readers might be depressed by a conclusion so inconsistent with the mercy of Aslan, who has invited the prayer he grants. Her death would, moreover, make nonsense of the quest for the apple of life or, as the Witch claims, eternal youth. Lewis concluded the tale as Nesbit concluded her *Amulet*, for no sooner has Digory healed his mother than his father returns rich from the East.

Thus the Chronicles take the Pevensies from Lucy's first entry into Narnia in *The Lion, the Witch and the Wardrobe* to their final entry into the "real Narnia" in Aslan's country in *The Last Battle*, via a stable that alludes to the Nativity. After the final destruction of the old Narnia, the creatures who love Aslan enter the new Narnia through the doorway, while the others disappear into Aslan's dark shadow. Among those who enter the door are a Calormene and many creatures from folk-literature, all of whom have in common good hearts and the power of speech. But only three of the four Pevensie children join the rush "farther up and farther in," for Susan has succumbed to the lure of teenage pleasures and fashions and is "no longer a friend of Narnia." After their first adventures in Narnia, the only collective undertaking by all four is the rescue of Prince Caspian. This completed, the adolescents Peter and Susan can no longer return to Narnia. At the end of *The Voyage of the "Dawn Treader,"* Edmund and Lucy are told that they will not visit Narnia again, and Eustace and Jill take the central roles in *The Silver Chair* and *The Last Battle*. Aslan's explanation to the three Pevensies at the end of *The Last Battle* that they and their parents left the "Shadowlands" of earth by means of a railway accident may have been suggested to Lewis by a pile-up of three trains at Harrow on 8 October 1952 in which more than a hundred passengers died.[21]

20. Myers, *C. S. Lewis in Context*, 171.
21. Armin Schneider and Ascanio Mase, *Railway Accidents of Great Britain and Europe*, 67-73. The enquiry into the accident resulted in the installation of automatic signaling.

In representing puberty as closing the door to Narnia, Lewis seems to have had in mind the teenager's rejection of fairy tales as "kids' stuff."[22] Narnia resembles the worlds of myth and fairy tale in which everything, whether Narnian or English, is alive and existentially meaningful for the central figures. Aslan's country includes a "real" Narnia but also a "real England," thus uniting imagination and reality as in the Platonism Professor Digory Kirke commends in his old age, or the Neoplatonism of Steiner and Barfield.[23] When the creatures of Narnia enter Aslan's country with their human visitants, all distinction between fact and imagination disappears.

Looking at the tales in the order of the chronology of Narnia, one begins with its creation in *The Magician's Nephew,* continues with its redemption in *The Lion, the Witch and the Wardrobe* and its golden age under the four Pevensie sovereigns in *The Horse and His Boy,* and proceeds through the quest-voyages to its decay and apocalypse in *The Last Battle.* In keeping with Lewis's principle of smuggling in Christian doctrine, this sequence approximates the Christian mythos,[24] beginning with the creation and fall *(Magician's Nephew),* continuing with the sacrifice of Aslan on the Stone Table and his resurrection *(The Lion, the Witch and the Wardrobe),* followed by the Narnian equivalent of Exodus *(The Horse and His Boy),*[25] then by a mission to retrieve lost lords and journey toward heaven *(Voyage of the "Dawn Treader"),* a descent into Sheol *(Silver Chair),* and the apocalypse *(Last Battle).* This order would self-evidently put more weight on Lewis's theological overthought than on his personal underthought. How much of it is gathered upon a first reading must vary with the reader's age, education, and acquaintance with the Bible.

Only readers well-versed in English literature and recent history will discern some sources and allusions. To illustrate from his creation and apocalyse narratives, in the *Magician's Nephew* the Deplorable Word of Jadis, a female equivalent of the Dolorous Stroke in Malory's

22. In "On Three Ways of Writing for Children," Lewis blames modernist critics for promoting this attitude.

23. On Platonism in the Chronicles, see Myers, *C. S. Lewis in Context,* 151, 180-81, and Murrin, "The Multiple Worlds of the Narnia Stories," 232.

24. Cf. Manlove, *C. S. Lewis: His Literary Achievement,* 124, where he describes the Chronicles as "Christian history."

25. Manlove, "'Caught Up into the Larger Pattern,'" 267.

Morte d'Arthur, turns the city of Charn into a charnel house and is the antithesis of God's creative word "Let there be light." The story proceeds from the undoing of creation within the Witch's world to her failure to tempt Digory to disobey Aslan and take an apple to revive his mother with the forbidden fruit. As Aslan later explains, this would have been giving it to her "at the wrong time, in the wrong way" (chap. 14). After eating the apple, Digory's mother falls into a sweet, drug-free sleep, but she is pronounced cured only after Digory has buried the apple core in the garden (chap. 15). To understand why Digory would have brought disaster upon himself by eating the apple we must combine several passages, from the rhyme over the golden gates (chap. 13) to Aslan's explanation. According to the rhyme, those who enter the garden over the wall to "steal" apples will find their "heart's desire" but also "despair." This implicitly echoes the contrast in *Paradise Lost* between the Devil's climb into Eden over the wall and a pilgrim's entry into Heaven through the golden gates. The injunction breached by the Witch, "Take of my fruit for others or forbear," helps Digory resist her temptation to eat an apple himself and share eternal youth and power with her, as king and queen of Narnia or Earth. Digory prefers to "go to Heaven" after his allotted span. The Witch then tempts him to steal an apple and take it immediately to cure his mother. If he does not, she argues, he will always feel guilty for having failed her — the charlatan's argument to a cancer patient's relative. Though hesitantly responding that his mother has taught him to keep promises and not to steal, Digory finally refuses when urged to abandon Polly (his Eve).

Aslan's "Well done" (as to the faithful servant in Matthew 25:21) remains Digory's sole reward until he has planted the apple that will protect Narnia and seen the misery of his Uncle Andrew, the would-be magician, who has endured being planted and watered by animals who think him a type of tree. As the astonished boy sees a perfumed tree grow from the apple, Aslan explains that its smell nauseates the Witch, just as long life and power bring misery upon the evil-hearted. Had someone plucked the fruit and sown the seed unasked, he would have made Narnia into a cruel world like Charn. In the same way, it is the apple Digory plucks at Aslan's direction from the new-grown tree that heals his mother. The text both upholds religion against amoral magic and implicitly contrasts the divine order with slave empires from the Egypt of the Pharaohs to the Soviet Union under Stalin.

The framework of the *Last Battle* consists mainly of theological symbols. We may dismiss as gothic machinery the thunderclap when Shift assures Puzzle that "Aslan never turns up nowadays" (chap. 1), yet the figures of the ancient ape and his ass combine a glancing blow at Darwinism with an allusion to the bestiary characterization of the ape (simius) as deceitfully imitative.[26] The name "Shift" connotes a fraudulent stratagem, a change of clothing, and the shifts of front Lewis thought characteristic of evil. Shift is often referred to as "the Ape" to emphasize both his subhuman status and the pretense implied in our verb "to ape." Shift's announcement that "true freedom" consists in obedience to him is his version of the "glorious liberty of the children of God" (Romans 8:21). It is also comparable to the enslavement by the Pigs in Orwell's *Animal Farm*.[27] The context becomes unambiguously theological when Jewel the unicorn calls on seven adherents of Aslan to proclaim the truth at Stable Hill and King Tirian commands the Narnians to make a stand by the "great Rock" whence they drink refreshing water (Isaiah 32:2).

The dream of Tirian, who is the seventh in descent from King Rilian, in which he sees the seven friends of Narnia dining together, is meat and drink to the numerologist. Since the Pevensies had been told that they cannot return to Narnia, they realize that they must have entered Aslan's country. The final entry to the "real Narnia" through the stable door, Aslan's "Well done!" to Tirian, the giant squeezing the sun that has swallowed the moon, and Aslan's order "Now make an end" complete the apocalypse.[28]

Why the Chronicles have attracted so many readers is a question best considered with regard to individual books, but first we should note two reasons evident from reading them in the order of their writing. The first is the progression from childhood to old age noted

---

26. Myers, *C. S. Lewis in Context*, 177.
27. Manlove, *C. S. Lewis: His Literary Achievement*, 182.
28. Manlove provides a list of apocalypse signs that appear in *The Last Battle* in *C. S. Lewis: His Literary Achievement*, 182.

earlier, which would obviously extend the age-range of readers and reward rereading. The second is an increasing subtlety in narration.

Lewis uses the narrator most explicitly in the first book completed *(The Lion, the Witch and the Wardrobe)*. The narrator warns readers of the foolishness of shutting oneself in a wardrobe, explains the White Witch's descent from Lilith, announces Edmund's desertion, partly blames his bad behavior on his schooling, hopes readers will not suffer the misery of Lucy and Susan after Aslan's death but will understand the quiet that follows their storms of tears, asks them to imagine the jubilant rides on Aslan's back, and promises further adventures in Narnia.

The events of *Prince Caspian* are conveyed by more varied means and with less use of the narrator. By describing Prince Caspian's childhood, education, and escape from King Miraz from Trumpkin's viewpoint (chaps. 4-8), Lewis compels the reader to contrast the dwarf's skepticism with Lucy's faith that the trees might speak again, as in Narnia's "good old days" (chap. 9). Conversely, Trumpkin displays alertness and promptitude in shooting the bear who would have eaten the contemplative girl. Yet Lucy and her convert Edmund wisely counsel the group to take Aslan's suggested way, while the practical Peter decides on the wrong one. All this is accomplished without authorial comment. Not until the thirteenth chapter does the narrator intrude, by explaining that it was stranger for the Prince to meet the great kings out of the old stories than for them to meet him. The narrator becomes omniscient only later in that chapter when reporting King Miraz's manipulation by his advisers into accepting Peter's challenge to single combat.

In *The Voyage of the "Dawn Treader,"* the narrator explains "port" and "starboard" and blames Eustace's "greedy, dragonish thoughts" for his transformation into a dragon, but otherwise merely adds details, as in the brief conclusion. Apart from the beauty of its imagined scenes and the intense longing communicated by the description of the sea near Aslan's country, the delight of this tale largely results from skillful use of Eustace as diarist, of Edmund as interpreter of Eustace's encounter with Aslan and transformation back into human form, of the magician Coriakin as cartographer, and of Ramandu's daughter as exponent of festal symbols and the means of disenchanting the sleeping lords.

The reader is expected to exercise judgment in reading the two portions of Eustace's diary. In the first portion, the "facts" he notes are always negative and the other voyagers always at fault. In the second, though Eustace still complains of his "unanswerable" arguments being ignored by Caspian, he records attempting to steal water and later receiving some from Lucy. Even young readers should see through her face-saving excuse that boys get thirstier than girls.

After his restoration to human shape, Eustace conforms to Todorov's theory of fantasy as "hesitation," wondering whether his nightmarish experience had been real or a dream, until Edmund assures him of its reality and identifies the lion as Aslan. Like Lucy, he saves the boy's self-respect by confessing his own treason in Narnia.

By unobtrusive shifts of viewpoint — to those of Eustace on Dragon Island and Lucy in the magician's library — Lewis provides constant variety without sacrificing clarity of outline. But the chief pleasure of the *Voyage* lies in the marvelous descriptions of the scenes through which the ship journeys and in Lewis's unobtrusive use of motifs by Malory, Tennyson, and Morris.[29]

In the next completed tale, the *Horse and His Boy,* Lewis makes skillful use of viewpoint. After the overheard conversation between the Tisroc and Ahoshta he departs from this well-worn convention by recording the very different reactions of the eavesdroppers. Implored to abandon her plan of escape, Aravis shakes her panic-stricken companion, threatens to rush screaming from the room to ensure their capture, and declares she would rather "be killed" than marry Ahoshta (chap. 9). As they part, that superficial socialite Lasaraleen, who might be any "flapper" of the 1920s, urges her to change her mind now that she has seen "what a very great man" her prospective husband is. In calling him a "grovelling slave" who has encouraged the Tisroc to send his son to certain death, Aravis articulates the likely response of young readers not bemused by rhetorical formulae.

Lewis is most inventive when using the Hermit to narrate the

29. For example, compare the Isles of Nothing, Kings and Queens, Young and Old, and Increase Unsought in Morris, *Water of the Wondrous Isles,* with the islands in *Voyage of the "Dawn Treader,"* and Utter Hay in Morris's book with the Utter East in the *Voyage.*

battle by interpreting its shapes reflected in his pool and the questions or comments of his listeners to flesh out his report. As he describes "a tall Tarkaan with a crimson beard," Bree interjects, "My old master Anradin!" When the Hermit says he sees "Cats" rushing forward, Aravis repeats, "Cats?" and the Hermit hastily explains, "Great cats, leopards and such" (159). His illustration of Edmund's "marvelous" swordplay, "He's just slashed Corradin's head off" (161), is too insensitive from the Hermit in his present way of life. Lewis regresses to his soldiering days in his commentary:

> Oh, the fool! . . . Poor, brave little fool. He knows nothing about this work. He's making no use at all of his shield. His whole side's exposed. He hasn't the faintest idea what to do with his sword. Oh, he's remembered it now. He's waving it wildly about. . . . It's been knocked out of his hand now. It's mere murder sending a child into the battle; he can't live five minutes. Duck, you fool — oh, he's down. (160)

When the breathless listeners cry, "Killed?" the Hermit replies, "How can I tell?" and continues to relate what he sees of the rest of the battle, leaving us in suspense until the narrative resumes with the words "When Shasta fell off his horse, he gave himself up for lost" (161). When last in Shasta's viewpoint, we shared his realization "If you funk this, you'll funk every battle all your life" (157). In a rare intrusion warranted by personal experience, Lewis justifies the switch to the Hermit's viewpoint by pointing to the futility of describing a battle from that of a single combatant.

The award-winning *Last Battle* shows Lewis at his best and worst as a storyteller. Introduced as the "last King of Narnia," Tirian is soon bound to an ash tree by Calormenes in league with the Ape. Watching the goings-on in front of the stable from afar, even Tirian wonders whether the stiff, silent creature shown to the frightened Narnians might after all be Aslan, until he recalls the Ape's "nonsense" about Tash and Aslan being identical (42). He recollects Narnia's past glories, recalling how children from another world had appeared in Narnia at every crisis. His reverie, amounting to a brief retrospect of the Chronicles, leads him to call out a plea for help for Narnia, even at the cost of his own life. Dawning hope prompts his appeal to all "friends of Narnia," upon which he is plunged into his dream or vision of the Seven Diners. When Peter challenges him, "If you are from Narnia, I charge you . . . speak to me," Tirian finds that he is unable to speak (45). Tirian's disillusionment as he wakes at dawn stiff with cold is among Lewis's subtlest touches; his misery is relieved almost at once by the appearance of Eustace and Jill, who untie him.

Peter's self-announcement as "High King" contrasts with the colloquial speech of Jill and Eustace and with Tirian's medieval salutation of Jill as "fair maid" (46). The ash tree and King Tirian's pronouncement "Narnia is no more" (85) on hearing of the death of Roonwit the Centaur link the Christian and pagan mythologies; in the Norse sagas the world is supported by an ash tree, and Tirian's pronouncement recalls the death of Baldir. The reporting of Roonwit's death by Farsight the Eagle echoes another Norse motif.

Too often, however, Lewis indulges in personal and contemporary intrusions. We can accept the children's entry to Narnia via the railway accident, which Eustace perceives as a "frightful jerk" (51) and later identifies as a collision (89), but when Jill says she would rather be killed fighting for Narnia than to "grow old and stupid at home . . . and then die in the end just the same" and Eustace replies, "Or be smashed up by British Railways!" (88), Lewis's apparent allusion to the Harrow accident has no place in the fantasy. In addition, at times his word choices can be misleading. As a working-class term for colored immigrants, the Dwarf's epithet "Darkies" for the Calormenes (116) has unintended overtones of racism.

An odd feature of *The Last Battle,* the Ape's retreat into alcoholism and his replacement as leader by the Ginger Cat, at first seems a mere contrivance for using his sad experience of Warnie's dipsomania and a mental image of a cat bolting from a stable. The cat motif, however, probably originated in the talking animals of the Boxen tales, for the surname of a pleasure-loving bear, the rakish Lieutenant James Bar,[30] was reused in *The Horse and His Boy* for the lord who set Shasta

---

30. In "Littera Scripta Manet" (unpublished) and "The Sailor" (in *Boxen,* 153-94).

adrift. The motif involving the Ginger Cat shows a subtle irony in that the Cat agrees with the Calormene captain Rishda that Aslan and Tash are only figments of the imagination, tells the Narnians that Aslan has swallowed up King Tirian, cynically persuades the dwarfs that there is no real Aslan (73-74), coolly offers to enter the stable, stalks in with feline primness (99), then moments later bolts into oblivion when confronted by Tash (100). Disbelief evaporates in the presence of evil.

While occasionally involving uncertainty (Todorov's "hesitation") as to the reality of an event or person, the fantasy more often uses reversal of ground rules, or what Manlove calls "upset expectations."[31] Thus Tirian, who talks and thinks as a medieval monarch, is struck by the strange, drab garments of the twentieth-century children. Combining reversal with word-play, Aslan explains that the hard-bitten dwarfs are so anxious to avoid being taken in that they cannot be taken out of this world and brought into a better one (135).[32] Their satisfaction that "the Dwarfs are for the Dwarfs" is more than a simple takeoff on communism or the triumphalism that accompanied the Labour landslide in the 1945 election. In contrast to Edmund, who attained "a kind of greatness" when breathed on by Aslan in *Prince Caspian* (153), these godless dwarfs, having forsworn the means of growth, must remain forever dwarfish.

A more fundamental reversal takes place in the final chapters. In "Night Falls on Narnia" (chap. 14), the falling stars, red moon near the sun, and creatures heading for the doorway to Aslan's country echo Revelation and the Flood myth. As in pagan myths, the falling and vanishing stars are people. As in what Lewis called the "myth" of evolutionary progress,[33] dragons and lizards inhabit Narnia — but at the end of time, not the beginning.

In chapter 15, as in his *Great Divorce,* Lewis endeavors to reverse the stereotype of heaven as a state of eternal torpor. Having reversed

31. Manlove, "'Caught Up into the Larger Pattern,'" 262.

32. Manlove (*C. S. Lewis: His Literary Achievement,* 136) mentions changing groundrules in *Prince Caspian* and fantasy as paradox plus reversal (185), but he sees this within extraterrestrial episodes rather than between real and imagined worlds.

33. Lewis, "The Funeral of a Great Myth," in *Christian Reflections,* 110-23.

the dark and lonely cosmos of post-Newtonian astronomers by encountering warmth and daylight beyond the stable door, the children find
themselves caught up with creatures factual and fabulous in a westward,
not eastward, rush when the Unicorn calls them "farther up and farther
in" (*Last Battle*, 155), a refrain that one critic has suggested might
otherwise connote returning to the womb.[34] The refrain is repeated
and the rush intensified in the final chapter, called (with Platonic
implication) "Farewell to Shadowlands." Here Lewis reverses the image
of heaven as a city, for the voyagers pass waterfalls and climb mountains.
The self-reflexive image that ends the Chronicles of Narnia, the story
in which every chapter is better than the last, suggests that heavenly
stasis is a conclusion never to be reached.

In these stories a childless academic managed to communicate
with children throughout and beyond the English-speaking world.
What proportion of child readers belong to his own social class has
never been determined. Nor to my knowledge has reader research
established why the Chronicles have been found such compulsive reading. For that matter, we do not know whether more children have first
heard them read by parents or read them independently. The following
suggestions, therefore, are merely speculative.

First, the attraction may derive from the narrator's identification
with children. In *The Silver Chair* the narrator presumes that his readers
attend better-disciplined schools than Experiment House, where the
need for just authority is appreciated. Presuming impatience with discipline near the end of term, he presents in *The Last Battle* the entry
into Aslan's country, where life resembles an everlasting holiday, as a
joyous running and bounding akin to the end-of-term fever at a hard-
working school. Second, the narrator assumes agreement on principles
that do not need to be justified to children: loyalty to schoolmates,
brothers, and sisters; dislike of bullies or tyrants, sycophants or flatterers.
Many an impoverished author must wish that to uphold such principles
would automatically guarantee sales in the millions.

Looking for inducements to read on, we find some in elements
common to all the tales. Two or more children of both sexes enter an
enchanted world via a door, or its equivalent — a picture that comes

34. Glover, *C. S. Lewis: The Art of Enchantment*, 56.

alive, or magic rings they must learn to manage.[35] In each tale, the children depend upon a nonhuman counselor, perhaps mythical, but always fullgrown: a beaver, raven, horse, or centaur. Sometimes they depend on an observer, but — whether eagle or hermit — not one they would meet at home. Notably, apart from Aslan, the animal companions change with the implied reader's age. In the first tale Mr. Tumnus the faun and Mr. and Mrs. Beaver are roughly the same size as the children, who can eat and converse in the Beavers' cozy home. In the *Horse and His Boy,* Bree and Whin require riders well into their teens; and the owl, eagle, or centaur who advise the protagonists of later books are clearly distanced by their size and/or mythological associations. In the first tales the children meet no parents, teachers, or other adult humans they can respect in the enchanted world, but only the witches, magicians, or sovereigns of fairy tales; in the later tales they begin to encounter good human adults, such as the Hermit and the large-hearted King of Archenland in *The Horse and His Boy* or Drinian and Lord Bern in the *Voyage of the "Dawn Treader."* In war, they use medieval weapons and tactics. They depend immediately on signs and omens but ultimately on Aslan the lion-god, a figure derived partly from Christ the Lion of Judah and perhaps partly from Richard the Lion-heart, but also from Lewis's dream of a lion. As in medieval romance, the stories always involve a quest, which takes them to an island, a castle, a subterranean prison, and ultimately a stable.

The enchanted world differs from their real one in its time-frame. During a school vacation, centuries of Narnian time can pass, a dynasty can rise and fall, children can function as adults[36] — kings or queens, generals or discoverers — yet never attain independence. In seeking self-sufficiency, Eustace finds loneliness and misery on Dragon Island, his precursor death. The enchanted world of Lewis offers escape, not only from childhood subservience to parents and teachers and from city life in an industrial country, but also from the whole notion of carving out one's own path in life. So in the author's view do myth, literary fantasy, and the Christian life. Yet the boy or girl character

35. On entrances, see Murrin, "The Multiple Worlds of the Narnia Stories."

36. Manlove points out that the child-heroes of MacDonald and Nesbit remain children (*C. S. Lewis: His Literary Achievement,* 122).

drawn into Narnia finally depends on Aslan, who with one exception[37] will interpret only his or her own life story.

In other ways the fantasy depends on reversal of normal distinctions between humans and animals, reality and imagination. Folklore becomes practical, and the folly or wickedness of practical people — Uncle Andrew, King Miraz, Nikabrik, the bureaucrat Gumpas, or the wily Tisroc — is sometimes cruelly exposed. The outdated education by Dr. Cornelius stands Prince Caspian in good stead, while Eustace has to unlearn his "progressive" education at Experiment House. The key elements of Narnian education are ethical and ecological: courage in battle, comradeship, cooperation with other species, and care of trees and plants threatened by commercial exploitation. The approaching end of Narnia is signaled by religious uncertainty or disbelief and a ruined environment.[38] Above all, the child characters play a crucial role in the enchanted world; instead of being marginal because of their inexperience and simplistic view of life, children affect the whole future of that world by making plans or decisions at places adults would consider marginal, historical, or imaginary: animal lairs; islands; castles; a subterranean, real, or remote wood.

The moral ground rules are those of the child reader's normal world, in that actions are always right or wrong, information true or untrue. At times, Lewis appears to share that simplicity. In this sense, his much-remarked immaturity enabled him to communicate with children. Consider, for example, Professor (Digory) Kirke's reasoning on Lucy's account of her first entry to Narnia:

> Either your sister is telling lies, or she is mad, or she is telling the truth. You know she does not tell lies and it is obvious that she is not mad. For the moment then and unless any other evidence turns up, we must assume that she is telling the truth. (*The Lion, the Witch and the Wardrobe,* 47)

37. The one exception Aslan makes to this rule is telling Digory what would have happened had he given his mother the forbidden apple (Myers, *C. S. Lewis in Context,* 168).

38. Myers, *C. S. Lewis in Context,* 132-33; Lindskoog, *The Lion of Judah in Never-Never Land,* 46.

Elsewhere Lewis used a similar argument to justify belief in the divinity of Christ. Further alternatives — daydream, wish-fulfillment, halluci-nation — would have taken him beyond the child reader's register and the context of the episode.

The increasingly subtle switching between viewpoint characters, as compared with the obtrusive switching in *That Hideous Strength,* may blind us to the fact that the viewpoint character is nearly always a juvenile extending his or her experience. The principal learner is Lucy, followed by Edmund, Eustace, and Jill. We enjoy the viewpoints of Narnian characters within single novels, *Prince Caspian,* the *Horse and His Boy,* or the *Last Battle.* Save for occasional passages in the viewpoint of Susan or Peter — or gap-filling by Trumpkin, the Hermit, or a nonhuman observer — the viewpoint character is of the child reader's presumed age. Thus, as Doris Myers remarks, the reader vicariously experiences life at different stages: young childhood with Lucy, middle or late adolescence with Shasta, the consciousness of age and impending death with King Tirian and Jewel.[39]

In one sense, the Narnian Chronicles are the medievalist's revenge upon the modernist; in another, as Kath Filmer notes,[40] they anticipate a civilization that still lies ahead. As in medieval stories, events and situations often conform to literary patterns or analogues. We have noticed the parallel between Caspian's urge to follow Reepicheep into Aslan's country and the Grail obsession. What is acceptable in a mouse or hermit would be neglect of duty in King Caspian. In his boyhood, Caspian, like Hamlet, disliked his usurping uncle, but without knowing why. Lewis departs from Shakespeare by making the Queen a wicked stepmother and the birth of her son the incentive for the now-redun-dant Prince to flee the court.

Near the end of *Prince Caspian,* Aslan, Bacchus, and the Maenads disrupt a dull history lesson. After transforming the girls' school into a "forest glade," its ceiling into tree branches, and the teacher's desk into a rose bush, they put to flight the teacher and all the pupils except for the inattentive Gwendolen, whom two Maenads whirl in a dance and help remove the "unnecessary and uncomfortable" parts of her

39. Myers, *C. S. Lewis in Context,* 125.
40. Kath Filmer, *The Fiction of C. S. Lewis: Mask and Mirror,* 73, 83-86.

school uniform (171). Lewis told Greeves of the joy and vitality he found in pagan mythology.[41] Though rightly condemning the ridicule of the woman teacher and schoolgirls, David Holbrook misses the point of the episode. Less convincingly than D. H. Lawrence, Lewis exposes the lifelessness of a culture bereft of the gods who infused pagan societies with energy and joy in life. To avoid the appearance of misogyny, in the following episode "pig-like" schoolboys are unconvincingly put to flight.

Lewis shows originality in blending derived with invented incidents. The baptismal bath of Eustace is preceded by the unpeeling of his dragon skin, and Lucy's magical restoration of the Dufflepuds to visibility takes place only after she eavesdrops on her schoolmates' conversation about herself. Mystery or enchantment attaches to figures and incidents drawn from literature or mythology, while invented elements are literal, even prosaic. Turkish Delight makes far more sense literally, as an inducement to betrayal at a time when candies were rationed in England, than in Holbrook's gloss of it as a disguised form of breast milk.[42] When Prince Rilian laments his ten-year subjection to the Witch as surrogate mother, surely any autobiographical reference is much more likely to involve Lewis's subjection to Mrs. Moore than the maternal inadequacy presumed by Holbrook.

Will the Chronicles continue to be relevant to the lives of children? A case can be made either way. Whether future generations of children will enjoy battles with swords and bows and arrows may be doubted, but they will unquestionably condemn clear-cut logging and slavery. The influence of Tolkien's readings to the Inklings from the *Lord of the Rings* is patent in episodes of *Prince Caspian* and the *Last Battle* that feature trees as combatants.[43] The popularity of Tolkien's trilogy at the dawn of the ecological movement was by no means coincidental. As yesterday's protest becomes tomorrow's orthodoxy, more and more stories are likely to involve preservation of the natural environment.

41. E.g., *They Stand Together*, 433 (Dec. 1931) Lewis writes of Morris: "his treatment of love is so undisguisedly physical and yet so perfectly sane and healthy — *real* paganism at its best, which is the next best thing to Christianity."
42. Holbrook, *The Skeleton in the Wardrobe*, 42.
43. Cf. Manlove, *C. S. Lewis: His Literary Achievement*, 142.

Whether instant and miraculous answers to prayers will endear the Chronicles to tomorrow's children is again doubtful. In alluding in *The Last Battle* to Aslan's nonappearance "nowadays" Lewis acknowledges the declining influence of religion. C. N. Manlove remarks that Lewis "was unusual among Christian writers in admitting the draught from outside [Christianity]."[44] In order of completion, the Chronicles show Aslan a central figure in the first two *(The Lion, the Witch and the Wardrobe; Prince Caspian)*, absent for long periods in the next three *(Voyage of the "Dawn Treader"; Silver Chair; Horse and His Boy)*, and returning to center stage in the conclusions of the final two *(Magician's Nephew; Last Battle)*. In their christological reference, they begin with the crucifixion and resurrection, continue with discipleship, the following of Aslan's path, the baptism and conversion of a modern spoiled child, and the renewed vision of eternal life, and end with the routing of secular magicians and gurus, Aslan's second coming, the ridicule of godless class-consciousness, and (skeptical Dwarfs excepted) the general entry into Aslan's country. There is no mention of Hell, for Calormenes killed in battle simply vanish. In the finale, the lost simply disappear into Aslan's shadow, while the saved from all seven books undergo no Last Judgment but a kind of evolution. Their eternal life perpetually unfolds, the root meaning of "evolve."[45] The metaphor of a book that improves chapter by chapter implies design by an Author warming to his subject matter. In this way Lewis marries an age-old Christian metaphor with a conception of divinely planned evolution common in his childhood[46] and extends to eternity the progressive revelation evident in the Old Testament.

As regards the moral "upshot" of the Chronicles, isolated incidents or phrases can be used to demonstrate antifeminism and a veneer of male toughness covering the unhealed wounds, but it is sounder to note the purport and emphasis of a whole story or major episode. The child reader cannot but condemn the willingness of Edmund to betray his brother and sisters to the Witch in *The Lion, the Witch and the Wardrobe*, still more

44. Manlove, *Christian Fantasy from 1200 to the Present*, 261.
45. A. Owen Barfield, *History in English Words*, 190.
46. The popularity of this concept of divinely planned evolution is attested to by a *Daily Telegraph* reader survey of 1904, cited in Hugh McLeod, *Class and Religion in the Late-Victorian City*, 155, 229-31.

his pretended disbelief in Narnia, from which he has just returned. The virtues of family loyalty and sincerity require no huddling together of schoolmates at Wynyard to explain them. Again, readers attuned to Lucy's love of Aslan will understand her pity at his humiliation and delight in his resurrection without recourse to Lewis's grief for his mother.

The upshot of *Prince Caspian* is less clear. Arguably, Caspian's love of old Narnian folklore and his happiness when with animals could promote an immature response to the troubles of adolescence. In a wider perspective, Dr. Cornelius saves Caspian's life both literally in urging him to flee the palace and metaphorically in nourishing his imagination with a cultural tradition that forearms him against the withering reductiveness of the commercially minded Telmarines, whose very name connotes both marring of earth *(tellus)* and skepticism ("tell it to the marines"). If the youngest readers see how the courtiers of the vain King Miraz manipulate him into accepting Peter's challenge, or even decipher the meaning of "Sopespian," the name "Glozelle" (liar) will surely escape any readers unfamiliar with medieval or Renaissance English. If death seems too harsh a judgment on Nikabrik for wishing to use the White Witch as an ally against Miraz, the author surely asserts principle against expediency. But nothing in the behavior or feelings of characters in *Prince Caspian* is so morally compelling as the treason of Edmund or the faith and love of Lucy.

In the *Voyage of the "Dawn Treader"* the reformation of a spoilt child and the assertion of common sense against excesses of chivalry and self-centered mysticism carry more conviction than any moral "upshot" in the *Silver Chair*. Instead, the latter story sheds light into the mind darkened by positivist conditioning against religion. In fact, later stories show a distinct shift in emphasis, for the practical sagacity commended in Puddleglum appears in Jill, Shasta, Aravis, and Lucy. What is rebuked is lack of empathy — by Aravis with the deceived slave girl, or by Jill when her posturing draws Eustace to the cliff edge. Yet Jill's devising of an escape from the castle of the giants *(Silver Chair)* and her shrewdly compassionate treatment of Puzzle *(Last Battle)* rebut Holbrook's charge of authorial misogyny based on passing references to tears spoiling bowstrings and blood wiped from swords.[47]

47. Holbrook, *The Skeleton in the Wardrobe*, 248.

The final issue between hostile and sympathetic readers of the Chronicles concerns the quality of the writing. In condemning a passage on the pleasure of eating freshly caught fish as being insensitive to children's feelings (*The Lion, the Witch and the Wardrobe*, 70), Holbrook puts his finger on the central difficulty of an Edwardian-reared adult writing for mid-twentieth-century children of any class.[48] The problem may be highlighted with his contrast between Lewis's "paternal respect" and "admiration of the children's energy and courage" when describing their regal appearance in fur coats and his "prep-school language"[49] when Peter calls the treasonous Edmund a "poisonous little" beast and Edmund thinks the others "stuck-up, self-satisfied prigs" (*The Lion, the Witch and the Wardrobe*, 55). Both use the Edwardian public-school argot perpetuated in magazine stories up to the Second World War. Reared in an era and class that wore fur coats and used such terms (as he sometimes did to Greeves), Lewis could not plausibly have employed the diction of children from any class in the 1940s. Instead, he kept author-to-reader address to a minimum by staying within viewpoints. For example, this description follows Peter's suggestion to the others that they spend the rainy morning exploring the house:

> Everyone agreed to this and that was how the adventures began. It was the sort of house that you never seem to come to the end of . . . full of unexpected places. The first few doors . . . led only into spare bed-rooms, as everyone had expected . . . but soon they came to a very long room filled with pictures and there they found a suit of armour; and after that there was a room all hung with green, with a harp in one corner; and then came three steps down and five steps up, and then a kind of little upstairs hall and a door that led out on to a balcony, and then a whole series of rooms that led into each other and were lined with books — most of them very old books and bigger than a Bible in a church. (*The Lion, the Witch and the Wardrobe*, 11)

This atomistic account of a house conceivably inspired by Little Lea sets the tone of medieval romance and ends with an illustration that all readers can picture.

48. Holbrook, *The Skeleton in the Wardrobe*, 39.
49. Holbrook, *The Skeleton in the Wardrobe*, 45-46.

A little later, as Lucy enters the wardrobe, advice is given from her viewpoint. She leaves the door ajar "because she knew that it is very foolish to shut oneself into any wardrobe" (12). When Edmund goes in, he closes the door, "forgetting what a very foolish thing this is to do" (30). Lewis uses advice probably drawn from experience with evacuees at The Kilns to suggest prudence in the girl with second sight and willfulness in the skeptical boy.

In the stories the narrator sometimes takes sides, with unfortunate results. In *Prince Caspian,* Lewis's forgivable hit at a modern materialist history lesson contributes nothing to the story; in addition, as Holbrook says, the partial stripping of Gwendolen may strike readers as indelicate, while the transformation of disorderly schoolboys into pigs (172-73) is pointlessly petulant. The same may be said of Polly's aspersions upon Susan:

> I wish she *would* grow up. She wasted all her school time wanting to be the age she is now, and she'll waste all the rest of her life trying to stay that age. Her whole idea is to race on to the silliest time of one's life as quick as she can and then stop there as long as she can. (*Last Battle,* 124)

A far more important aspect of Lewis's writing, one unremarked by Holbrook, is Lewis's use of a repertoire of styles to fit incidents and speakers. He shifts at will from plain speech for Peter to Morrisian medieval language for Reepicheep or Tirian ("Hast any skill with the bow, maiden?" [*Last Battle,* 55]) or *Arabian Nights* rhetoric for the Tisroc and Grand Vizier (*Horse and His Boy*). The array of styles is most dazzling in the *Voyage of the "Dawn Treader,"* which shifts within a page from hierarchic-feudal language to announce King Caspian "come to visit his trusty and well-beloved servant the governor of the Lone Islands" (51) to mumbled bureaucratese by the porter ("No interview without 'pointments 'cept 'tween nine 'n' ten p.m. second Saturday every month") to stage cockney ("'Ere? Wot's it all about?") at Bern's Shakesperian reproof "Uncover before Narnia, you dog" (51). In the next few pages (52-57), the bureaucratese of Gumpas ("Nothing about it in the correspondence. . . . Nothing in the minutes. . . . All irregular. Happy to consider any applications"), laced with economic jargon in support of the slave trade, alternates with plain but increasingly abrupt orders from Caspian. The slave auctioneer's sales-pitch swings sympathy away from the unseated governor, no longer "His Sufficiency."

Eustace's record of the resumed voyage, written in a plain style, betrays egotism in every "I" and self-righteousness in every account of a disregarded suggestion. When Caspian dismisses his idea of rowing back to Doorn on account of the water shortage, Eustace writes, "I tried to explain that perspiration really cools people down, so the men would need less water if they were working. He [Caspian] didn't take any notice of this, which is always his way when he can't think of an answer" (65-66).

Near the end of the *Voyage,* the style shifts to the plain but solemn phrases of the ancient star Ramandu, recalling those of the "Great Dance" episode in Perelandra:[50] "And when I have become as young as the child that was born yesterday, then I shall take my rising again . . . and once more tread the great dance" (177), punctuated by the chivalric speech of Reepicheep. As the ship nears the world's end, the style changes to the romantic, northern expressions of Lucy, exhilarated by the sea's "fresh, wild, lonely smell" (201).

How long children will continue to read the Chronicles of Narnia may depend on considerations unrelated to their artistic merits: reception of stories via electronic media rather than books; the religion or irreligion of parents and school librarians; social or educational changes rendering some episodes less comprehensible. Already schoolchildren must find the animus against coeducation difficult to understand. While at present Holbrook's view of the tales as unfit for children seems as perverse as Eliot's judgment of *Hamlet* ("an artistic failure"), many incidents or passages that Holbrook finds morally or stylistically objectionable do show a lack of restraint in the author. Lewis's achievement as a storyteller was limited by over-hasty production and unwillingness to take his fiction as seriously as his major critical works. As novelists, the perfectionist Tolkien and the boyishly eager Lewis represent opposed extremes.

While the images and values of the Chronicles had been in Lewis's mind for decades, the energy that enabled Lewis to complete the

50. The similarity was pointed out to me by Dr. Edwards.

Chronicles within seven years (1948-54) may well have been generated by personal stresses: Mrs. Moore's senility, his entanglement with Joy Davidman, the denial of promotion at Oxford, and the campaign to defeat his ill-judged candidacy for the Professorship of Poetry. Undoubtedly anxiety or anger from these stresses as well as his bereavement and exile in childhood affect a number of episodes. What I have tried to show is that, so far from distorting or blurring the impact of a story, such "speaking pictures" (to quote Sidney) and moral attitudes at times enhance it. Even Holbrook appears moved by Digory's anxiety to heal his mother and finds the *Silver Chair* a well-told tale of adventure. Yet of all the stories the latter is most susceptible to the now dated academic game of psychoanalytic reductionism: the Witch as Mrs. Lewis turned nasty, or Prince Lewis unable to mate because he never got over the Queen's death. As Freud maintained, most if not all works of art spring from some trauma — in Edmund Wilson's phrase, a creative "wound." The only issue that should concern a critic is the quality of craftsmanship evident in the resultant works. The late John Peter, himself a Leavisite critic and Pulitzer Prize–winning novelist, once told me that while he detested Lewis and "everything he stood for," when reading the stories with his children he discerned "quality." For all their imperfections, they constitute a body of fiction worthy of their immense and sustained readership.

CHAPTER 7

Failed Poet?

THE LATE POSITION of this chapter may surprise readers who think Lewis gave up writing verse after publishing *Spirits in Bondage* (1919) and *Dymer* (1926). In fact, as Hooper says, he continued to write poems for the rest of his life.[1] Most had Barfield as their first reader.[2] Lewis composed two further long narratives, *The Queen of Drum* (1927-36) and *The Nameless Isle* (ca. 1930), included sixteen lyrics in his *Pilgrim's Regress,* and published poems in magazines from 1934 to 1957, usually under his pseudonym "N.W." ("nat wilc," Old English for "anon."). But after *Dymer* failed to sell, he ceased to think of himself as officially a poet.[3] How far his verse, like his prose, bears his unmistakable impress will be considered later in this chapter.

Spirits in Bondage

Published as part of a series of works by dead or returned soldiers, this slim volume is divided into "The Prison House" (poems I-XXI), "Hesitation" (XXII-XXIV), and "Escape" (XXV-XL). Of the forty lyrics, fourteen came from a group of "Metrical Meditations" composed in

---

1. Walter Hooper, preface to Lewis, *Poems* (1964), vi.
2. See Barfield's comments in *Owen Barfield on C. S. Lewis,* 162.
3. *They Stand Together,* letter 149 (18 August 1930), esp. pp. 378-79.

1915-16 and lodged with Greeves during the author's war service.[4] As the book's title and subheadings indicate, it embodies a disillusioned young man's inversion of the opening books of *Paradise Lost,* representing a spiritual change from enslavement by a malign deity called Satan and blamed for the war to freedom, solitude, and joy. The rebellious persona of the poems reappears as John in the *Pilgrim's Regress,* but his God is a more complex figure than the Puritan deity called the Landlord. In "Satan Speaks" (XIII), the speaker proclaims himself responsible for matter, nature, and the human reversion to bestiality, dismissing prayer to the remoter God of "endless day" as a vain pursuit.

The volume could have been even slimmer, for, as George Sayer remarks, too many poems consist of a mythological mishmash, while too few evoke realities felt or observed.[5] In their vague romanticism typical of the 1890s rather than the postwar years, many show traces of classical, Norse, or Celtic myths or of poems by Keats, Tennyson, Arnold, MacDonald, Francis Thompson, or the early Yeats. The confusion of the various allusions can be illustrated from three poems: "Song of the Pilgrims" (XXV); "Victory" (IV); and "'Our Daily Bread'" (XXXII). In the first, the nameless "we" reproach those who dwell "at the back of the North Wind," for reasons that are unclear. "In the green Northern land to which we go" are red and white roses more "real" than those of earth, yet the paradise named after Mac-Donald's fantasy[6] is also a "Land of the Lotus" and "of the Lake," as in poems by Tennyson and Scott. Incompatible allusions cause even more confusion in the second poem, where the transience of fame and ideals is inferred from the passing of Roland, Cuchulain, Helen, Iseult, Arthur, the fairies, dryads, and Triton. In the third, the poet juxtaposes the supernatural with the natural by alluding to Thompson's "In No Strange Land" and Blake's visions of angels, then envisages making his pilgrimage through "alien woods and foam" as in Keats, before leaping into a "gulf of light" like the hero and heroine who climb up the rainbow at the end of MacDonald's story "The Golden Key."

4. *Collected Poems of C. S. Lewis,* x. The full title of this group of poems is "Metrical Meditations of a Cod" ("cod" is an Irish term for "oddball").

5. George Sayer, *Jack: C. S. Lewis and His Times,* 76-85.

6. George MacDonald, *At the Back of the North Wind.*

Confusion does not reign throughout, for "How He Saw Angus the God" (XXXIII) permissibly imbues mountain and woodland at dawn with Celtic mythology, while "Irish Nocturne" (V) conveys the sinister aspect of night via allusions to *Beowulf* and Celtic myths, before applying its images of sea-mist and cloud to the "dim and dreamy" people of Ireland, with their "many words and brooding and never a deed." Nevertheless a brief appearance by Lewis the Mentor, who replaces the Dreamer for "In Praise of Solid People" (XXIV), comes as a relief. Though here and there flat, the poem creates a coherent image of "folk" who "sit and sew and talk and smoke," envied by the speaker who vainly yearns and broods in his study.

The final and in several ways most seminal poem, "Death in Battle" (XL), voices a death-wish born of disgust at what war makes of young men:

Open the gates for me,
Open the gates of the peaceful castle, rosy in the West,
In the sweet dim Isle of Apples over the wide sea's breast,
Open the gates for me!

In the *Pilgrim's Regress* a western Island becomes the object of John's longing and the source of his mystical Joy. The paradisal and maternal images of "Apples" and "breast," together with that of the castle, recur in episodes of the Narnia stories and in *Perelandra*, where Ransom is "breast-fed" by the planet Venus. In the poem, the speaker, instantly relieved of heat and pain, finds himself where "All's cool and green," as in the Wood between the Worlds of the *Magician's Nephew*. He longs for solitude in vales and in the "garden of God" and relief from the "brutal, crowded faces," his own included, that warfare has transformed into those of demons. In the final stanza, the "Country of Dreams" with its "dim woods and streams" becomes identifiable as Ireland, and the emotion as homesickness. In his final letter to Greeves, in 1963, Lewis was to complain of having come out of a coma in which he had "glided so painlessly up to the Gate" only to see it close in his face.[7]

Even more remarkably, "World's Desire" (XXXIX) anticipates *Till*

7. *They Stand Together,* 566 (11 September 1963).

We Have Faces, published almost forty years later. Addressed to a name-less "Love," the poem features a castle on a rock between a forest and a mountainside. From across a "ravine" echoing the noise of a "mighty river," sunlight picks out the castle's white turrets, ivory gates, and copper roofs. Guarded by "watchful dragons" and so unvisited by man or god, it remains a prospective "resting-place" for the speaker and his beloved. A "faerie maiden" voicing "the world's regret" weeps in vain, "For her soulless loveliness to the castle winneth never." The name "Psyche" signifying "soul," can we miss the anticipation of Psyche banished from the Shadowbrute's palace? As Lewis claimed, he created his fantasies from images long in his mind.

In this first book by Lewis, the Dreamer gets out of hand, yet *Spirits in Bondage* remains of interest for its anticipatory phrases and images and for its early evidence of his interest in poetic meters and stanza forms. Of the forty poems, he cast eleven in couplets, fifteen in variously rhymed quatrains, and five in tercets, and though usually employing iambics or trochees, rang the changes on his line-lengths. Even so, had he not identified himself as its author, after using his pseudonym "Clive Hamil-ton" in the original edition, the book might never have been reprinted.

Narrative Poems

The great disappointment that led Lewis to seek fulfillment in prose was the poor sale of *Dymer,* the only narrative poem published in his lifetime. In 1916 he wrote a now lost prose version, in 1922 completed Cantos I-IV under the title "The Redemption of Ask," then added Cantos V-IX before publishing the whole poem in 1926.[8]

The poem depicts the adventures of the nineteen-year-old Dymer, whose name probably originated in "dyme," an obsolete form of "deem," meaning judge, criticize, or condemn.[9] Having first laughed

---

8. Hooper, preface to Lewis, *Narrative Poems,* vii-ix, xiv. Lewis explained "Ask" as derived from Old Norse "Ash" (*Narrative Poems,* ix), but it could also allude to Askins, Mrs. Moore's brother who went mad in 1923, as Lewis thought from dabbling in occultism.

9. *Oxford Dictionary.*

at, then struck dead an elderly professor, he flees exulting into untamed woodland, whence he follows haunting music into a vast palace where in a mirror he sees himself "naked" and "wild-eyed" (II, st. 5). Donning robes and consuming a banquet he finds before him, he condemns the realm he has fled, an amalgam of Plato's ideal republic with the self-complacent Ulster, Malvern, and Oxford of the author's youth. Somewhat unconvincingly, the author's preface to the 1950 edition extends the application of this utopia in which Dymer had been "vaccinated, numbered, washed and dressed/Proctored, inspected, whipt," and "examined" (I, 5-6) to the postwar British Labour regime.

Thus far the story seems the wish-fulfilling fantasy of a young aspirant to Academe who felt his path blocked by the "scarlet conclave of old men," as he complains in his diary for 1923. In his hero's subsequent euphoria the poet fantasizes himself casting off the discipline imposed by two demanding degree courses and the domestic responsibilities he had prematurely assumed. Significantly, he finished the poem in the year of his appointment as Fellow of Magdalen College.

To return to the poem, after passing through a curtained door into a dark place where he enjoys an "undivided sense of being," Dymer embraces foliage that turns into the "breast and thighs" of a girl, with whom he makes love and sleeps. Knowing neither her name nor her face, he seeks her next morning only to find his path blocked by an old woman of "matriarchal dreadfulness" (III, 24). Here the symbolism suggests sexual development arrested by fixation on the mother-figure who anticipates the maternal deity Ungit. At the end of Part I, as a thunderstorm echoes Dymer's frenzied despair, he hears from a dying refugee of the revolution and civil war that followed his killing of the professor. Its leader's prominent red hair suggests both the Russian Revolution and the Irish "troubles."

These effects, however, seem tangential in comparison with the love-making, in which the author's sexual frustration and preoccupation with his mother perhaps find unintended expression. It is possible, though highly unlikely, that the love-making and its sequel represent a brief sexual relationship with Mrs. Moore. If there was such an "affair," it is inconceivable that Lewis would publish a disguised account of it yet continue to live in the household of the woman he had so unfavorably represented. An unverifiable conjecture is that the episode represents a fantasy of sexual intercourse with Mrs. Moore's daughter, imagined as grownup, to be followed by confrontation with her mother.

The poem's second half, completed after heavy revision,[10] makes more of Dymer's effort to reproduce the (musical) experience of *Sehnsucht* that had led him to the palace and the girl, as it was to lead John in the *Pilgrim's Regress*. Recalled to reality by impending starvation and to hope by a singing lark, Dymer accepts the hospitality of a "Master" occultist modeled on Yeats, who intends to recruit him as apprentice. Alienated when the Master shoots the lark for interrupting his meditation, Dymer rejects his offer to conjure up the girl in a dream and is expelled. In the poem's most impressive dialogue (VIII, 1-19), he at last has the opportunity to reproach her for not answering his summons. She rejoins that he failed to ask her name. Though realizing his suffering, she must appear in what shape the bidder desires. This seems retrospectively to identify the old woman Dymer had addressed as "Good Mother" (III, 24). Regretting his vain quest for "the Spirit" and imploring the girl's "human love," Dymer is forbidden by the goddess, as the girl proves to be, to "ask of life and death" in the "withering breath/Of words," which will only cause "truth" to die away "among ancestral images" of "names" (VIII, 18). Ordered to stop brooding on death, he rests in a churchyard.

In a conclusion that owes something to *Paradise Lost,* to Malory's *Morte d'Arthur,* and to masonic ritual, Dymer passes through three "degrees" in which he is whirled upright by the wind, made aware of a musical lament, then of "sidereal loneliness." From a sentry, he learns that by mating with a goddess he has begotten a "Beast"; at daybreak, in a "ruinous land," he is slain by the "Beast" he has begotten. Concerning the fear of unchastity implicit in the begetting of the monster by a sexual rather than a revolutionary act, we should note Barfield's remark that Lewis passed from a child's indifference to an adult's desire without going through the phase of adolescent adoration.[11] Dymer's failure to ask his partner's name hints at this; he knows a body, not a person.

10. Lewis's chronology and record of revisions can be found in "The Lewis Family Papers," comp. W. H. Lewis, IX, 129-30; reprinted in Lewis, *Narrative Poems,* 176.

11. *Owen Barfield on C. S. Lewis,* 130.

The viewpoint shifts as the Sentry sees the "brute" transformed into an angel with shoulder-length and "foam-like hair" as in a Blake engraving and hears trumpets and bells proclaim the earth's renewal by Balder. As in *Spirits in Bondage,* there is some confusion of mythologies, for Balder ushers in "long-lost Saturnian years," yet the earth's renewed fertility recalls Malory's motifs of the sick king and Waste Land used by Eliot.

In this poem of 2,065 lines, Lewis makes varied and usually expert use of the Chaucerian "rhyme royal" stanza. After describing the hero's death, from the Sentry's viewpoint, in crisp images ("A leap — a cry — flurry of steel and claw,/Then silence" [IX, 30]), he depicts a vernal awakening that resembles the return of spring to Narnia in *The Lion, the Witch and the Wardrobe:*

> The wave of flowers came breaking round his feet,
> Crocus and bluebell, primrose, daffodil
> Shivering with moisture: and the air grew sweet
> Within his nostril, changing heart and will,
> Making him laugh. He looked, and Dymer still
> Lay dead among the flowers and pinned beneath
> The brute: but as he looked he held his breath

as the monster turned into an angel (IX, 33).

Whether an Ezra Pound could have compressed *Dymer* into a poem capable of catching on as did Eliot's *Waste Land* is more than doubtful. The disasters brought about by the solitary young man of *Dymer* pale beside the revolution and turmoil symbolically represented in Yeats's "Second Coming." To adapt a once-famous title, Lewis failed by poetry direct to make the impact Yeats and Eliot made by poetry oblique.[12] To observe how Lewis told where Eliot showed, one need only compare the taut, enigmatic speeches of the neurotic woman in the *Waste Land* (II, 115-34), with Dymer's appeal to his beloved:

> Where? Where? Dear, look once out. Give but one sign.
> It's I, I, Dymer. Are you chained and hidden?
> What have they done to her? Loose her! she is mine.
>
> (*Dymer,* III, 30)

12. E. M. W. Tillyard, *Poetry Direct and Oblique* (1945).

In the 1920s, the diminishing public for long poems preferred the compressed, contextless utterance and varied meters of the *Waste Land* to narrative in rhyme royal. Should that taste change, *Dymer* may yet find a public. One hesitates to predict this, however, for its anti-romantic and antirevolutionary theme, though of universal import, is subsidiary to a sexual frustration personal to Lewis. Though not without personal reference, the symbols of *The Waste Land* have retained their significance for readers of poetry in all English-speaking cultures.

The Queen of Drum: A Story in Five Cantos runs to about two-thirds the length of *Dymer*.[13] Yoked to a senile King, the young Queen seeks fulfillment in nocturnal wanderings, for which she is censured by the Council. When she rejects attempts to dissuade her by the Archbishop and General, the latter seizes power and orders her imprisoned. Escaping her youthful custodian, she flees the castle and realm, evades her hunters, rejects a call to repentance by an apparition of the now-martyred Archbishop, and escapes either to the land of Faerie or to Hell.

Hooper thinks this poem the author's best owing to its apt variety of metrical forms and its explicitness in comparison with *Dymer*.[14] When John Masefield read the manuscript in 1938, he advised Lewis to delete the King's dialogue with the Chancellor in Canto II, the Archbishop's effort in Canto III to reconvert the Queen from occultism to Christian orthodoxy (two hundred lines), and a hundred lines from Canto IV in which the General orders the Archbishop's death by torture after failing to win his support.

Had this advice been followed, the poem would have consisted of the decrepit King's reproach of the night wanderings; a Council meeting in which the Chancellor and a "raw-boned boy," representing politic age and impetuous youth, successively urge firmness upon the King while informing him of the Queen's rumored necromancy and of murmurings against the King; the General's bark "Have a wife and rule a wife" (I, 182) and the Queen's counter-plea; the youth's announcement of the military coup; and finally the Queen's flight. To delete the

13. First published in *Narrative Poems*. Hooper dates the poem 1933-34 (preface to *Narrative Poems*, xiii).

14. *Narrative Poems*, xii-xiii.

martyred Archbishop's warning that she should shun as a demon (V, 249-65) the "pale king," who in a parody of the Eucharist tempts her with honey and sweet bread while dismissing heaven and hell as a "fable" (V, 192-95, 211), would both remove spiritual tension from the final episode and rule out the ambivalent ending. Yet as Masefield evidently perceived, the General's attempt to suborn the Archbishop gave the poem a double focus: on the traditional plight of a woman trapped in a loveless marriage; and on the Church's duty, however inadequately performed, to resist the idolatry of dictators.

The full-length version has admirable characters, incidents, and dialogues: the placid Archbishop with silver beard and gown apparently modeled on the martyred Cranmer; the Queen's sudden entry to the Council chamber, described in juxtaposed animal and sculptural figures (I, 198ff.) of flashing eyes and hair, widened nose, bared teeth, and "Robe caught breastward in one hand" (I, 201); and her Browningesque dialogue with the Archbishop.[15]

Its fourth canto depicts a General who proclaims himself "Fuhrer" but resembles Mussolini, who was more in the limelight than Hitler at that time. Switching from couplets to quatrains to relate the coup from its perpetrator's viewpoint, Lewis alludes to Mussolini's notorious sexual predations as the General, tapping his whip on his jackboots, calls "Now for the girl" (IV, 82), assures the King and Archbishop they have nothing to fear provided he has his way, and instructs the Queen to spend her nights in his bed. Skillfully, she flatters the autocrat into letting her await his pleasure in her tower, and once in a youth's custody she escapes by using her wedding ring as a knuckle-duster.

While Chad Walsh rightly finds many passages to praise,[16] as the foregoing commentary should have demonstrated, the poem's chief weakness is an inconsistency of tone. This becomes painfully apparent in the youth's Marlovian tribute: "Oh brave to be a Duce! brave to drink/The melted pearls of Tessaropolis/And burn the towers of many a captive isle" (III, 242-44), and the General's sentence on the Archbishop: "You've played a dirty trick, and now you'll rue it! . . . Boys!

15. Compare III, 151-83 with Browning's poems "Bishop Blougram's Apology" and "A Death in the Desert."
16. Chad Walsh, *The Literary Legacy of C. S. Lewis,* 51-54.

put him through it" (IV, 249-50). Yet, in addition to the sustained excitement of the Queen's flight from her hunters, the descriptions of her and the Archbishop go far to justify Masefield's tribute to the "extraordinary beauty" of "its main theme — the escape of the Queen into Fairyland."[17] All told, however, *The Queen of Drum* is more of a patchwork than *Dymer,* hence a lesser achievement.

In the 300-line fragment concerning Lancelot and Guinevere (written around 1930), a hermit speaks of the Fisher King "Who now lies sick and languishing and near to death" (l. 161), and in the concluding lines the Queen of Castle Mortal declares her intent to place knights she has murdered "Between my breasts and worship them till I die" (ll. 295-96). The first motif reappears in *That Hideous Strength,* while the other exemplifies a personal preoccupation of Lewis.

The Nameless Isle, fair-copied in August 1930,[18] is an experiment with the Old English alliterative line. A semi-allegorical tale of a ship-wrecked captain rescuing an enchanted maiden, with analogues in the *Odyssey* and especially the *Magic Flute,* it expresses its author's lifelong concern with industrial spoliation of nature. The mariner lands amid trees being breast-fed by a woman personifying Nature, who redirects his advances into a quest for her daughter, now petrified by an Enchanter signifying Industry, in a ruined paradise of clearcut forest devoid of wildlife. The captain finds a golden flute playable only by a Dwarf, who uses it to turn the Enchanter into a boy and to reanimate the petrified maiden and ship's company. The motifs reapply an age-old theme, in that music serves Nature by undoing the Enchanter's Art. The poem exemplifies the author's innate distrust of technology, which he represents here and elsewhere as black magic rather than science.

Lewis believed that the Old English line could serve the modern narrative poet. Despite some artificial diction, it enabled him to render vividly the flute-playing:

> Long and liquid, — light was waning —
> The first note flowed. Then faster came,
> Reedily, ripple-like, running as a watercourse,

17. *Narrative Poems,* 177.
18. *Narrative Poems,* xii.

> Meddling of melodies, moulded in air,
> Pure and proportional. Pattering as the rain-drops
> Showers of it, scattering silverly, poured on us,
> Charmed the enchanter that he was changed and wept
> At the pure, plashing, piping of the melody,
> Coolly calling, clearer than a nightingale,
> Defter and more delicate. . . . (ll. 517-26)

Even more convincing is the rhythm of the final lines relating the departure of the rescuers:

> . . . No ripple at all
> Nor foam was found, save the furrow we made,
> The stir at our stern, and the strong cleaving
> Of the throbbing prow. (ll. 731-34)

Poems (1964); Collected Poems (1994)

To avoid confusion, the two collections of non-narrative poems will be identified by title rather than by date. The later volume contains the poems included in the earlier volume, plus *Spirits in Bondage* and a "Miscellany" of seventeen poems, including ten of the early "Metrical Meditations." The front matter includes a new editorial introduction by Walter Hooper and a sardonic "Introductory Letter" by Lewis dated 1963 and addressed to a supposedly typical modern literary journalist who supposedly needs instruction in what used to be the fundamentals of verse, such as rhyme. This letter was intended to form part of a collection to be entitled "Old King Cole and Other Pieces." The penultimate paragraph of the "Letter" expresses the hope that the occasional reviewer might "love and understand" the poet's endeavor and consider how far each poem attains it, rather than label him as a "person or type."[19] Certainly this sounds like Lewis in acerbic vein after the death of Joy, and the authenticity of the letter is confirmed by Barfield, in a supporting paragraph included in Hooper's introduction.[20]

19. *Collected Poems*, xxi.
20. *Collected Poems*, xvii.

As Charles Huttar observes in his excellent essay "A Lifelong Love Affair with Language,"[21] there is room for a book-length study of Lewis's poems, taking account of all available manuscripts and texts. A chapter permits us only to note some discrepancies between texts of poems published in magazines and in the posthumous collections, briefly to indicate themes and kinds, and to offer an opinion as to which poems are likely to survive. Though Huttar is surely right in thinking of Lewis as a minor poet, pieces by minor poets do survive in anthologies.

The problem of varying texts and titles is complex and frustrating. In *Poems* Hooper included 127 items under five headings of his own: "The Hidden Country," "The Backward Glance," "A Larger World," "Further Up and Further In," and "A Farewell to Shadowlands."[22] In *Collected Poems* he changed the fourth heading to "Noon's Intensity," the title of the section's second item. Otherwise the headings reflect both the editor's enthusiasm for the Narnia stories and the conversion story related in *Surprised by Joy.* Hooper supplied titles for thirty-five hitherto unpublished poems, and by his own admission changed the titles of several poems previously published in magazines. He is alleged also to have altered some of the texts.[23]

It seems beyond belief that a student briefly acquainted with a famous and dying author could within a few months secure control of manuscripts and issue an edition, let alone be at liberty to alter titles and texts. As this book's concluding bibliography will show, however, within months of Lewis's death Hooper dedicated himself to editing poems, essays, and unpublished books, thereby doing much to maintain interest in a writer who might otherwise have suffered postmortem

21. Charles A. Huttar, "A Lifelong Love Affair with Language: C. S. Lewis's Poetry," in Peter J. Schakel and Charles A. Huttar, *Word and Story in C. S. Lewis,* 86-108.

22. Thirty-one poems are grouped under the heading "The Hidden Country"; twenty-nine poems under "The Backward Glance"; twenty-five poems under "A Larger World"; twenty-one poems under "Further Up and Further In"; and seventeen epigrams and epitaphs under "A Farewell to Shadowlands." Note, however, that the heading "Further Up and Further In" is used only in the 1964 paperback edition.

23. Variants have been detailed in the journal *The Lewis Legacy,* edited by Kathryn Lindskoog, especially nos. 65 (Summer 1995): 367; 66 (Autumn 1995): 10-12; and 68 (Spring 1996): 16.

rejection, as commonly happens. Before passing judgment we need to be sure that the editor was in fact responsible for all the changes. Some of his new titles, moreover, were improvements on the old. One such was "A Confession" (*Poems*, 1), first published in *Punch* as *"Spartan Nactus."*[24] The average reader must surely find Hooper's title more informative.

This poem is a good-humored riposte to T. S. Eliot's "Love Song of J. Alfred Prufrock" and *Waste Land*, with a tilt also at I. A. Richards. Stating that he has tried and failed for twenty years to see "any evening" as "a patient etherized upon a table" or to compare traditional beauty with modern squalor, the speaker laments that "Waterfalls" do not "remind" him of "torn underclothes,/Nor glaciers of tin-cans."[25] With apologies for resembling the Wordsworthian character to whom "A primrose was a yellow primrose," Lewis ends with a charmingly ironic pastiche of Eliot's famous lines on the "Falling towers" of "Jerusalem Athens Alexandria/Vienna London."[26]

In the text published in *Punch*, lines 26-30 run:

Compelled to offer Stock Responses.
Making the poor best that I can
Of dull things . . . peacocks, honey, the Great Wall, Aldebaran
Silver streams, cowslip wine, wave on the beach, hard gem,
The shapes of trees or women, thunder, Troy, Jerusalem.

The ending in *Poems* shows the following variants: "to live on" for "to offer"; "weirs" and "new-cut grass" for "streams" and "cowslip wine"; "hard" for "bright" [gem]; "shapes of horse and woman" for ". . . trees or women"; and "Athens" for "thunder." It may be argued that "live on" better expresses limitation, that "weirs" is less commonplace than "streams," and that "Athens" is in Eliot's lines quoted above (though "thunder" reverberates elsewhere in the *Waste Land*). On the other hand, new-mown grass is a cliché, while "cowslip wine" is characteristically rural English, and "horse and woman" is irrelevantly suggestive.

24. Originally published in *Punch*, 1 December 1954.
25. Cf. T. S. Eliot, "Love Song of J. Alfred Prufrock," lines 2-3 (*Complete Poems and Plays*, 3); *Waste Land*, 221-27 (*Complete Poems and Plays*, 44).
26. Cf. T. S. Eliot, *Waste Land*, 374-76.

In line 11 *Poems* has "Red dawn behind a hedgerow in the East" for the more specific and visually credible "Red dawn splashed back from windows facing east."[27] On balance, notwithstanding the Latin title, the readers of *Punch* enjoyed a more piquant and precisely worded poem.

It has yet to be proved that Lewis himself did not alter this and other items he intended to publish under the title "Young King Cole," a title used in *Poems* for a single poem.[28] In *Collected Poems* Hooper states, citing Barfield as his authority, that as early as 1954 Lewis began to collect and "extensively" revise pieces for the intended collection, but failed to complete the task owing to preoccupation with Joy's illness (*Collected Poems,* xvi). We can hardly dismiss all the revisions as those of one exhausted by age, grief, and ill health if Lewis set about them in 1954, when at the height of his powers.

Whoever may have been responsible for the alterations, some were disastrous. To illustrate, "The World Is Round," originally published in 1940, was retitled "Poem for Psychoanalysts and/or Theologians" (*Poems,* 113). Explicitly it describes man's expulsion from Eden, and implicitly both the individual's separation from the womb and the author's journey though life after losing his mother. In line 3, "Spicey odour of unmoving trees" becomes "Odour of windless, spice-bearing trees," with resultant loss of rhythm. In line 5, the scent "Sweetened the sheltered air" becomes "Made dense the guarded air," thereby obscuring the sense. In line 12, "I do not really remember that garden" becomes "All this, indeed, I do not remember," which improves the rhythm but forfeits a phrase frequently used by Chaucer of the enclosed garden in the *Roman de la Rose.* But the most maladroit change comes after "I heard the golden gates behind me" (line 14), when "Shut fast upon it [the garden]. On a flinty road/With east-wind blowing over the black frost" becomes "Fall to, shut fast. On the flinty road,/Black-frosty, blown on with an eastern wind" (lines 15-16). A clear and concise statement is changed to one beginning with a coined hyphen-word and

27. The text is that published in *Punch;* several of my comments previously appeared in *Lewis Legacy* 68 (Spring 1996): 16.

28. The single poem now titled "Young King Cole" was originally titled "Dangerous Oversight" (see *Poems,* vii, 142).

completed by a jog-trot of unaccented syllables. The new and provocative title seems an improvement until the end, when the expelled wanderer discovers that his pilgrimage is endless, for "The world is round."[29]

As Hooper indicates in his preface to *Poems,* the many undated items forbade chronological arrangement, but his appendix to the volume enables us to group some seventy-five according to original publication dates, and so to make a rough chronology:

1933: sixteen poems published in *Pilgrim's Regress* (fifteen of them given titles by Hooper)
1934-39: seven poems published in Oxford or Cambridge magazines
1938-42: two poems published in *Spectator*
1942-54: six poems published in religious magazines, three in *Time and Tide,* three in *The Month*
1945-49: five poems published in *Spectator*
1947-53: twenty-four poems published in *Punch*
1952-55: three poems published in *Times Literary Supplement*
1956-97: three poems published in Oxford or Cambridge magazines
1940-59: seven poems published as single entries in miscellaneous publications

Poems that anticipate prose works mostly appeared in the resulting novel or in *Punch;* verse experiments and those on literary topics in Oxbridge magazines, the *Spectator,* or *Punch;* those on social or political issues in Oxbridge publications or the *Spectator;* and protests against the spoliation of nature in various journals. Poems on cosmic and religious themes Lewis published in the *Times Literary Supplement, Punch,* and, of course, the *Pilgrim's Regress,* but his most profound and revealing lyrics remained unpublished in his lifetime. These included self-criticisms, elegies for Charles Williams, and some moving sonnets on the impending death of Joy. The unpublished items or undated items are too numerous for an account of his poetic development to be feasible. Since Charles Huttar has fully explored the language of

29. Texts compared in *Lewis Legacy* 65 (Summer 1995): 3, where the date is given as 1940.

many of the poems, the following study will be limited to one or two poems on each theme listed above.

If it could have been done without disrupting the sequence of this chapter, the natural place to mention "Joy" (*Collected Poems*, 243) would have been in connection with *Dymer,* since it was published in 1924 under Lewis's pseudonym.[30] His most cogent description of the trancelike experience he called "Joy," this poem compares the presence of Joy to a "huge bird" brushing him awake with its feathers. Under its influence he looks at a Northern Irish dawn landscape with the fresh eye of a Wordsworth or Hopkins. In six Spenserian stanzas he records a Wordsworthian feeling of release and freedom in the presence of nature, as when the burden slips from the hero's back in the *Pilgrim's Progress.* This is followed by an awareness of Joy's transience, as in Wordsworth's "Intimations of Immortality." The most thought-provoking stanza, the fourth, opens with these lines:

> We do not know the language Beauty speaks,
> She has no answer to our questioning,
> And ease to pain and truth to one who seeks
> I know she never brought and cannot bring.

and continues:

> But, if she wakes a moment, we must fling
> Doubt at her feet, not answered, yet allayed.
> She beats down wisdom suddenly.

Finally, as "we cling" to Beauty's "flying skirts," she fades "Even at the kiss of welcome, into deepest shade." In these lines Lewis speaks not only with his usual intellectual honesty and penetration but with a fluency and *cantabile* quality unusual in his reflective verse.

Most of the untitled lyrics included in the *Pilgrim's Regress* were submitted for Barfield's scrutiny in 1930.[31] In the novel, they tend to reflect the mood of their contexts: John's sense of entrapment by God, his

---

30. "Joy" was first published in *Beacon* 3 (May 1924), edited by Barfield (*Collected Poems*, xvii).

31. *Collected Poems*, xv.

own Manichaeism or spiritual aridity. Although "The Dragon Speaks" (*Poems,* 92-93) has richer and more interesting imagery than "Wormwood" (87), it anticipates later writings only in the dragon's reluctance to part with his gold, which resembles certain episodes in the *Voyage of the "Dawn Treader";* otherwise the dragon more closely resembles Smaug in Tolkien's *The Hobbit.* Vertue's song (*Pilgrim's Regress,* book 10, chap. 1), entitled "Wormwood" in the collections, has a fascinating range of anticipations and allusions. The context is the beginning of John's return home. He and Vertue learn of a "cold" dragon to the north, who seeks to encircle and possess, and a "hot" one to the south, whose breath melts and corrupts all it touches. Vertue must use this demon's warmth to become less cold and rigid. Vertue addresses "Wormwood" as a "dark and burning island among spirits," second only to God and "sprung of His fire" but bound within the "lightless furnace" of himself to rage eternally. Eventually the song focuses on God, but for our purpose its essential references are to the Epistolist of the *Screwtape Letters* and to Steiner's technocratic demon Ahriman, by whose name Vertue also addresses Wormwood. Beyond these, the poem alludes to the author's own pent-up rage and sadomasochism, admitted only in letters to Greeves.

As regards metrical experimentation, we have quite a choice, for, as Huttar remarks, Lewis loved nothing more than playing games with words and meters. We will look here at the "Narnian Suite" (*Poems,* 6), not because of superior merit or interest to such poems as "The Birth of Language" (10) or "On the Atomic Bomb" (64), subtitled "Metrical Experiment," but because of my inability to improve on Huttar's discussion of the latter poems.[32]

The "Suite" has two movements, or marches, respectively for "Strings, Kettledrums, and Sixty-three Dwarfs" and for "Drum, Trumpet, and Twenty-one Giants." As may be expected, the rhythms of the first are light and pattering, those of the second heavy and insistent. The first abounds in trochaic nouns and adjectives, the second in iambic verbs and participles. To illustrate, the first begins:

> With plucking pizzicato and the prattle of the kettledrum
> We're trotting into battle mid a clatter of accoutrement;

32. See Huttar, "A Lifelong Love Affair with Language," 105-6, 87-88.

and the second:

> With stomping stride in pomp and pride
> We come to thump and floor ye.

In each movement, the characteristic patter or thump is maintained almost throughout. The endings of the two marches are quite different. After trouncing their human foes, the unnamed speakers of the first, who prove to be dwarfs, return "by crannies and by crevices" to their "forges and furnaces," the "caverns of the earth." The second chorus describes the impending panic of their enemies, then fades out in a "diminuendo" of drum-rolls:

> Your kings will mumble and look pale,
> Your horses stumble or turn tail,
> Your skimble-skamble counsels fail,
> So rumble drum belaboured —

then in the final line "rumble" is repeated five times.

Thus by contrasting patterns of sound and rhythm, together with onomatopoeic and alliterative phrasing, Lewis creates the verbal equivalent of a tone poem in two sections. To a greater extent than elsewhere he indulges in pure verbal and metrical play, with no suggestion of a "message" or personal emotion. His Narnia books and massive history of sixteenth-century literature recently completed, he indulges a moment in revelry before turning to his final mythopoeic novel. Unfortunately, he or his editor chose to mar some of his finest sound effects by changes of word order in the second part, as when wrecking the climax of verbs in the original version of line 9 by turning "We'll bend and break and grind and shake" into a diminuendo of verbs, ". . . grind and break and bind and take."[33]

On literary themes, apart from "A Confession" the choice lies between antimodernist and pro-Romantic poems. Of the former, "Odora Canum Vis" (*Poems,* 59), ironically subtitled "A defence of certain modern biographers and critics" and originally published in the

---

33. The texts appearing in *Punch,* 4 November 1953, and in *Poems,* 6-7, are compared in *Lewis Legacy* 66 (Autumn 1995): 10.

Jesuit journal *The Month,* is marred by scurrility. To refer to one's nameless critics as "smut-hounds" for the crime of being godless Freudians and to invite dogs to eat their corpses is to pass beyond the civil leer.

This narrows the choice to "A Cliché Came Out of Its Cage" (*Poems,* 3) and "To Roy Campbell" (66), which deal in quite different ways with complementary aspects of literary culture. In the former, Lewis looks at the cliché "The world is going back to Paganism" in a way that is anything but hackneyed. Beginning with a charming fancy of Leavis and Bertrand Russell bedecked with flowers and leading "white bulls" to a "Cathedral of the . . . Muses" to pay tribute for "their latest theorem," he examines the implications of the supposed return to paganism. Does it imply the gravity of classical ritual and willingness to do battle for one's city, a "Puritan Sophrosyne"? "Oh, inordinate liar, stop." Alternatively, does the saying refer to a Norse myth enacted, to the gods of Asgard making their last stand against the dragon and wolves? The tone suddenly becomes somber, for "the end of man is to partake of their defeat and die/His second, final death in good company." Here Lewis sounds with mournful resolution the bugle call he sounded briefly for King Tirian in the *Last Battle* and will sound again at the end of *Letters to Malcolm.* This poem, too, ends on a sour note, for if this be paganism, let the "dogs" who uttered the cliché "crouch" before their "betters."

In "To Roy Campbell," which addresses the Catholic poet who supported the Fascist cause in the Spanish Civil War and apparently disapproved of the Romantic movement, Lewis embodies a miniature literary history in verse paragraphs of couplets. He traces English Romanticism first to Scott, and from him back to the medieval chivalric ethos, and second to Coleridge, that "ruinous master" who, as Newman said, "restored our faculty for awe." In a third and final paragraph he claims that Wordsworth is "far more ours than theirs," meaning far more Christian than secularist. The appeal of the poem derives less from its argument than from its alternation of grave respect and outrageous frankness. Compare, for example, its tribute to Scott, who in old age would "Work without end and without joy, to save/His honour and go solvent to the grave," and its assertion that a single Scott novel has "characters and scenes" enough for ten modern ones, with the paragraph's conclusion: "The very play/Of mind, I think, is birth-controlled to-day."

Similarly, in the second paragraph the praise of Coleridge for having "pricked with needles of the eternal light" a land "half numbed to death" by the "wintry breath" of Paley, Bentham, and Malthus is followed by "For this the reigning Leftist cell may be/His enemies" yet "why should we?"

Lewis shows himself an uneven poet, for his incisive image "needles" is followed by an awkward string of possessive proper nouns, and at the end he goes overboard in imaging that any reputable critic would describe the well-read Wordsworth as a "rude, raw, unlicked, North Country boy."

The same unevenness mars another address to Campbell, "To the Author of *Flowering Rifle*" (*Poems*, 65). While all can applaud the poem's defense of humanitarianism against the sneers of tough-minded party zealots on either side in Spain, the phrase "Charlies on the Left" is too cheap and the assertion that Communists and Fascists are "two peas in a single pod" is too obvious for the context. The poem is somewhat redeemed by the final picture of a ruined church, "Sacred because, though now it's no-man's-land/There stood your father's house; there you should stand."

By contrast, "On the Atomic Bomb" (*Poems*, 64) is less ephemeral because more open-ended. Addressing readers at large, the poet counsels restraint, both in fear of the new weapon and in the hope some entertained of its putting an end to war. Finding the bomb "No huge advance in/The dance of Death," he names existing or previous causes, "cold, fire, suffocation, Ogpu, cancer," foreseeing no sudden end of history in a "bright flash," but rather its "tragic" continuance, a "Road" that "new generations" will "trudge." Others have already remarked the chiming consonants of "engine," "injury," "angels," and "plunges" in the opening stanza, but less attention has been paid to the verbs that metaphorically represent the instability resulting from fear of the new weapon, "The world plunges,/Shies, snorts, and curvets like a horse in danger." The final image remains intriguingly in mind, that of the soldier or civilian "who marches/Eyes front," oblivious to the "fields" and "happy orchards" on either side. The reader is left to tease out its implication — that wisdom consists in attending to life about us, rather than becoming obsessed by the prospect of nuclear war.

Lewis took far more interest in environmental issues than in party politics. His posthumously published "Lines During a General Election" (*Poems,* 62) leaves one with the impression that he was about to vote against whichever party favored holiday camps, development, and road building. Technology, the poet fears, could ultimately render the earth a "charabanc" (tour bus) destined to "stink and roll" through space, "subtopianized from pole to pole."

In consequence, the alterations in the text of Lewis's most cogent environmental poem, "The Condemned" (*Poems,* 63), are more than usually frustrating. In the first of its three quatrains, the speakers claim that "There is a wildness in England" which is "Easy to kill, not easy to tame" and not to be bred in zoos, for "It will not be planned." The original version published in the *Spectator* has the more appropriate phrasing "not easy to keep," reserving "tamed" for creatures bred in captivity. In the second stanza, "woodland folk" is altered to "hedgerow folk," diminishing the sense of wildness, and, more pardonably, the name of George Borrow is added to a list of conservationists that includes Johnson, Landor, Cobbett, and Blake. In the third stanza, the addition of extra syllables — such as "have understood" for "understand" — slackens the rhythm.[34] Needless alterations apart, the poem protests on behalf of wild creatures against the human attempt to organize nature. Within a few years of Lewis's writing that "animal wisdom" picked up a "message" of "guns, ferrets, traps" and officials "gassing the holes in which we dwell," rabbits by the million were suffering from officially induced myxomatosis. Nowadays species seem to disappear by the hour. In its cogency and prescience, "The Condemned" seems more durable than the earlier "Future of Forestry" (*Poems,* 61), a fantasy of a future England in which children will ask what a chestnut was.

A piece midway between naturalism and mythopoeia is "On a Picture by Chirico" (*Poems,* 69). Published by *Spectator* in 1949, it may well have been written as Orwell was publishing *Nineteen Eighty-Four.* Reflecting on the picture of two wild horses on a beach, the poet imagines them having survived an attempt to kill them for food by the

34. The texts of the poem published as "Under Sentence" in the *Spectator* (7 September 1945) and as "Condemned" in *Poems* are compared in *Lewis Legacy* 66 (Autumn 1995): 12-13.

few survivors of a thousand years' war that wiped out the rest of humanity. As they sniff the sea air on a cold spring morning, they seem unlike the tamed horses familiar to us, for "the old look/Of half-indignant melancholy and delicate alarm's gone." So might have appeared the paradisal pair of horses from whom the whole species was descended. Presumably the painter showed them lifting their heads while neighing, for the poet imagines responding to a call to "leave the places where Man died" in search of a Promised Land for "Houyhnhnms."

For his poetic animation of a still life, Lewis draws partly on the biblical and secular apocalyptic prophecies, but also, of course, on the narratives of the Fall and Exodus and on Part IV of *Gulliver's Travels*. Every word contributes to the meaning of the four-line stanzas, with rhyming middle lines, that mark stages in the animation. The poem's limitations are that its meaning is exhausted at a single reading and that its horses do not, as it were, neigh to us.

Nevertheless, a judgment of Chad Walsh that whatever Lewis said in verse he said at least as well in prose[35] is challenged by this poem, by "The Condemned," by some religious or introspective poems, and by several on the deaths of Charles Williams and Joy. To say this, however, is not to predict a future for all of them. For example, in the posthumously published "Apologist's Evening Prayer" (*Poems*, 129), the speaker's regret for "cleverness shot forth" in God's defense, which amused audiences yet made "angels weep," would undoubtedly interest readers of Lewis's apologetics and sermons, but the poem's long-term survival depends on its conclusion, calling for "fair Silence" to free him from unceasing thought and the "Lord of the narrow gate, and needle's eye" to remove his "trumpery lest" he "die." How far will the range of meanings implicit in "die" interest future readers?

From the introspective poems it is tempting to choose "Two Kinds of Memory" (*Poems*, 100), published in 1947, for its contrast between the "compassionate" memory personifed as Persephone and the "iron" memory called "Hades." Undoubtedly the experiences of self-forgiveness and self-torture are so widespread as to be understood by all readers of poetry, yet the final stanzas remain as obscure after many readings as after one.

35. Walsh, *The Literary Legacy of C. S. Lewis*, 55-56.

Though likewise based on Greek deities, the posthumously published sixteen-line "Reason" (*Poems,* 81) has the lucidity proper to a poem about Athene, and it rises to a memorable climax. Likening the soul to a city and reason to the statue of an armed "virgin" upon its "acropolis," the opening lines assert the unforgivable nature of intellectual dishonesty or irrationalism, for "No cleansing makes his garment white" who "sins against" reason. In contrast to the opening lines on Athene, the middle section describes Demeter, her mother, representing imagination. Here the poet falters, for no such clear image as that of Athene emerges from the commonplace periphrasis and adjectives used of Demeter: "Warm, dark, obscure and infinite, daughter of Night." Recovering his stride on introducing a Christian image, he asks "who will reconcile in me both maid and mother . . . depth [of Demeter] and height [of Athene]?" Needless to say, the depth image refers to the unconscious root of imagination. Could its "dim exploring touch/Ever report the same as intellectual sight," he could "Then wholly say, that I BELIEVE." Though not given to ambiguity, Lewis surely realized how the self-deceived are apt to mislead others.

Until the final couplet rhyme, the last word of each alternate line has rhymed with "light," with which in line 2 the virgin Athene, or reason, communes. It is natural to wonder why Lewis never managed to publish a poem of such artistry. At first sight, one may wonder whether he composed it after his holiday in Greece with Joy in April 1960 and felt it too personal to make public, but Hooper lists it among the poems on religious subjects sent to Barfield in 1930 (*Collected Poems,* xv).

Undoubtedly Lewis wrote his most poignant verse out of grief. Three months after his friend's sudden death, he published "On the Death of Charles Williams" (*Poems,* 105, as "To Charles Williams"). In the "new light" after that death's "strange bugle call," the world seems "larger," life's "contours" changed. Wincing in the "bleak air," he asks whether the chill signifies the onset of the world's "great winter" or its "spring." With whom could he speak of this, "unless it were you?" The concealed image is the sounding of the Last Post and Reveille at Remembrance Day or military funeral services to signify death and resurrection. The final question, therefore, implies no nonsensical assertion that by dying his friend had precipitated the end of the world, but that only with Williams could he freely discuss matters of faith, such as the Apocalypse. It is worth noting that the poem was published in the same year as *That Hideous Strength.*

Lacking a title, the enigmatic ten-line epitaph originally commemorating Williams (*Poems,* 137) can easily be missed.[36]

> Here lies the whole world after one
> Peculiar mode; a buried sun,
> Stars and immensities of sky
> And cities here discarded lie.
> The prince who owned them, having gone,
> Left them as things not needed on
> His journey; yet with hope that he,
> Purged by aeonian poverty
> In lenten lands, hereafter can
> Resume the robes he wore as man.

"Peculiar" signifying unique, we can read the lines that follow as referring to the fictive world, indeed universe, of the dead poet and novelist. The odd phrase "buried sun" alludes to Apollo's traditional role as inspirer of poets. The final lines could mean that on rising from Purgatory the "prince" will resume his singing robes or royal robes in Heaven, or that he will reappear on earth in his works, or both. In any case, it is difficult to see how his poverty can be "aeonian" — that is, eternal. Yet the rhythms of the first five lines and the phrase "lenten lands" (the title of Douglas Gresham's memorial to Lewis and Joy) echo in the mind like few in the entire volume.

After Joy's death Lewis adapted these lines into an eight-line "Epitaph for Helen Joy Davidman" (*Collected Poems,* 252), which was carved on her tombstone. He changed the opening lines to include features of the earth and heavens "Reflected in a single mind," "aeonian" to "holy," and the ending to "Resume them on her Easter Day." The pronoun refers to "cast-off clothes" (line 4), a simile denoting the "world" that she both left behind and represented to the poet. Of the two epitaphs, the first is moving because of its form and substance, the second because of its occasion.

36. Quoting the poem, Barfield says, "I think he had Charles Williams in mind" (*Owen Barfield on C. S. Lewis,* 16).

All of the seven stanzaic sonnets addressed to Joy on her deathbed are more or less intensely wrought, but if any deserves to survive, it is "As the Ruin Falls" (*Poems,* 109-10). The poem's originality is highlighted by the conventional diction of the previous sonnet, "Old Poets Remembered" (*Poems,* 109), in which "One happier look" on Joy's "kind, suffering face" can summon up "Eternal summer" in the poet, while one "droop of" her "dear mouth" plunges him into a quasi-industrial wasteland.

At first sight, the opening line of "As the Ruin Falls" — "All this is flashy rhetoric about loving you" — and the series of lines in the octave that begin with "I" may seem forced. In keeping with the word "rhetoric," however, the author uses anaphora, which medieval poets conventionally used for emphasis by repetition. In this case it conveys his perception that until he met Joy he had been "self-imprisoned" within the "proper skin" of an egoist, who "never had a selfless thought," and wants "God," Joy, and his friends "merely to serve" his own purposes. After the iambics of the opening stanza, the second stanza of the octave begins with a change of rhythm: "Peace, re-assurance, pleasure, are the goals I seek," followed by anaphora for two lines, the second beginning "I talk of love." But as "a scholar's parrot may talk Greek," so Lewis had felt himself trapped in a circle until (as the sestet begins) "taught" by Joy his "lack." She had shown him the "chasm" between himself and the state epitomized in the succeeding lines. She "was making" his "heart into a bridge," that he might return "From exile, and grow man." As she lies dying "the bridge is breaking." Here "bridge" connotes his breaking heart and the path or crossing between his previous state as a bachelor and his recent fulfillment in love. The concluding couplet is almost unbearably poignant:

> For this I bless you as the ruin falls. The pains
> You give me are more precious than all other gains.

The ruin apparently denotes her body, nearing death, for the agonies caused him by her suffering show the "bridge," his heart, by no means eaten away. Thus by hindsight we see the exaggeration in the octave as an index of extreme stress. In the formal structure of the sonnet and its rhetorical devices, he seeks to channel his feelings of heartbreak.

Walsh's judgment mentioned earlier, that whatever Lewis said in verse he said at least as well in prose, may well apply to a group of five sonnets (*Poems*, 125-27) written after Joy's death, which can be closely paralleled with phrases and episodes in *A Grief Observed*. The first sonnet treats anger as the mind's "anaesthetic," dissipating grief. In chapter 3 of the book, Lewis describes his image of the "Cosmic Sadist" as a projection of hatred and vengefulness (*A Grief Observed*, 46). And as in the poem rage must give place to acceptance and a wish for "unearthly comfort, angel's food," so the fourth chapter alludes to reception of the Blessed Sacrament (*A Grief Observed*, 71). Again, the second sonnet denounces "fixed despair" as a false "repose." The mourner must mount a "crazy" stairway, for "one bereavement makes us more bereft." This recalls "Cancer, and cancer, and cancer. My mother, my father, and my wife" (*A Grief Observed*, 12). In the sestet, he cites Dante's bereavement and comfort, after descending to the "frozen centre" and climbing the "Mountain of pain." The book ends with a memory of Joy expressing her "peace with God" to the chaplain and a line by Dante: *Poi si torno all' eterna fontana*. The third sonnet repeats the book's metaphor of unanswered prayer as a door slammed in the mourner's face (*A Grief Observed*, 4), but also harks back to H. Rider Haggard, for those who "knock/At heaven's door for earthly comfort" find "only smooth, endless rock" that echoes their cries. As the beloved's face fades in the memory, the fourth and fifth sonnets contend with the paradox that while human nature rejects Dante's path to consolation as meant for "saints and mystics," to follow natural instinct is to become like a bee trying vainly to reach flowers through a windowpane. Told that its quest is futile, the bee might consign incomprehensible talk of window glass to "queens and mystics and religious bees." If more organized than the book, which is a step-by-step record of grieving, the sonnets read like a reflective postscript, less immediate and at the end somewhat fanciful.

Undoubtedly some poems by Lewis — "A Confession," "The Condemned," "As the Ruin Falls," "Joy," and perhaps *Dymer*, "On a Picture by Chirico," and "The Birth of Language" — deserve to be read outside the circle of Inkling-lovers. One that might retain its appeal is the clumsily titled "Leaving for Ever the Home of One's Youth" (*Collected Poems*, 245), written, of course, on quitting Little Lea in

1930. Although it lacks the lucidity and flow of "Joy," readers may continue to appreciate its emotional honesty and fine balance between nostalgia for childhood surroundings and resolution to "drive ahead" to his new home, even though "every other place must be/Raw, new, colonial country till we die."

Although I cannot agree with Huttar in thinking Lewis primarily an epigrammatist and neoclassic poet, some of the epigrams may well survive, for example the Miltonic address to the made-up woman:

> Lady, a better sculptor far
> Chiselled those curves you smudge and mar,
> And God did more than lipstick can
> To justify your mouth to man. (*Poems,* 134)

Among the humorous poems an even better candidate for survival is "Awake, My Lute!" (*Collected Poems,* 246), dated 1943. Written in dactyls, with even-numbered lines rhyming, it records a dream of being lectured by a "terrible bore with a beard like a snore" on a miscellany of scientific and practical topics such as the behavior of flowers, small animals, and electrons or a fantastic cure for "croup." As the poem progresses, the listener's imagined responses become more and more irreverent, his imagined student essay topics more fatuous. Laughable as the poem is, the topical allusions may prove a stumbling block for future readers. An example is the "Beverage Plan," a clever pun on the Beveridge Report then in the news for recommending the future National Health Service.

For all their careful craftsmanship, many of the poems interest because of their substance or occasion rather than because of their words, images, or rhythms. All too few lines, let alone whole poems, reverberate in the mind. While all young poets imitate established ones that they admire, Humphrey Carpenter is surely right to find even the mature Lewis too fond of pastiche.[37] Though gifted as an occasional and argumentative poet, Lewis really found himself in prose. It is an episode from a novel or tale for children, a phrase or analogy from a critical or theological work that abides in the mind.

---

37. Humphrey Carpenter, *The Inklings,* 31.

CHAPTER 8

Essayist, Pleader, and Speaker

TO STUDY ALL Lewis's essays and articles, apologetic and devotional books, lectures and addresses would take a large volume. In a single chapter one can only hope, at some risk of incoherence, to show his habits and strategies in writing prose for various readerships and audiences. The substance of his critical and religious books has been considered elsewhere in this book.

Lewis's career fell into three phases: the up-and-coming teacher and scholar, the established academic and religious broadcaster, and the distinguished professor. In the 1930s, like most young dons, he completed his first academic book and articles, read papers to undergraduate societies, and engaged in scholarly controversies.[1] His spreading reputation enabled him to publish the papers as *Rehabilitations and Other Essays* (1939), give the British Academy's annual Shakespeare lecture ("*Hamlet:* The Prince or the Poem?" 1942), address the English Association on "Kipling's World" (1948), review Eugene Vinaver's ground-breaking *Works of Sir Thomas Malory* for the *Times Literary*

---

1. For example, an early article is "What Chaucer Really Did to *Il Filostrato*" (1932); participations in controversy include *Personal Heresy* and "Donne and Love Poetry in the Seventeeth Century," with Joan Bennett's response "The Love Poetry of John Donne: A Reply to Mr. Lewis." An example of an early talk is "Variation in Shakespeare and Others"; a lecture is "Shelley, Dryden and Mr. Eliot," given at Bedford College, London. For a full list of Lewis's published essays, talks, and lectures, see the bibliography in James Como, ed., *C. S. Lewis at the Breakfast Table.*

Supplement (1947), give the lectures at Durham (1943) later published as the *Abolition of Man,* and address students at Westfield College, London, on "Psycho-Analysis and Literary Criticism" (1942).[2] Also upon request, he wrote *The Problem of Pain* (1940) and gave the four sets of ten-minute religious broadcasts (1941-44) that made his name a household word.[3] In 1948 his role as apologist came to a sudden end with his defeat by the philosopher Elizabeth Anscombe in a Socratic Society debate on *Miracles* (1947). Though he revised the chapter on "The Self-Contradiction of the Naturalist,"[4] henceforth he confined himself to writing fiction, criticism, and expository or devotional books for fellow believers.

The final phase of his career, beginning with the publication of *English Literature in the Sixteenth Century* and his famous Cambridge inaugural lecture "De Descriptione Temporum" (1955), was to be cut short by his terminal illness following that of Joy. His address to the Walter Scott Club at Edinburgh and two lectures on the medieval world to scientists at Cambridge, all in 1956, were, so far as I know, his last.[5] Certainly after Joy's death in 1960 he declined speaking invitations save for a broadcast paper on Bunyan. Freed from the burden of tutoring, at Cambridge he published or completed *Studies in Words, An Experiment in Criticism, They Asked for a Paper,* and *The Discarded Image.* He also made tapes for broadcasts by an American Episcopal Church radio

---

2. "*Hamlet:* The Prince or the Poem?," "Kipling's World," and "Psycho-Analysis and Literary Criticism" are reprinted in *Selected Literary Essays,* 88-105, 232-50, and 286-300, respectively. The review of *The Works of Sir Thomas Malory,* ed. E. Vinaver, is reprinted in *Studies in Medieval and Renaissance Literature,* 103-10.

3. The first and second series of talks, "Right and Wrong: A Clue to the Meaning of the Universe" and "What Christians Believe," were published with alterations as *Broadcast Talks* (1943) and as *The Case for Christianity* (1943). The third series was published as *Christian Behaviour* (1943), and the fourth as *Beyond Personality* (1944). All of the talks were revised, amplified, and published together as *Mere Christianity* (1952).

4. *Miracles: A Preliminary Study* was originally published in 1947 and was republished, with revised chapter 3, in 1960.

5. Lewis's toast to "The Memory of Sir Walter Scott" (Edinburgh Sir Walter Scott Club, 1956) is reprinted in *They Asked for a Paper,* 93-104, and in *Selected Literary Essays,* 209-18. The lectures on "Imagination and Thought in the Middle Ages" are reprinted in *Studies in Medieval and Renaissance Literature,* 41-63.

station and published them as *The Four Loves,* published *Reflections on the Psalms,* and completed *Letters to Malcolm: Chiefly on Prayer.* Within a year of Joy's death he had pseudonymously published *A Grief Observed.*

This is the profile of a compulsive writer and a speaker willing when able. Whether his relish in presiding over Socratic (religious) Society debates manifested the lawyer's son or the bully,[6] both it and his crowded lecture rooms showed that he always thought of language as spoken. We should therefore give first consideration to how he wrote for an audience. In our largely chronological survey, we shall notice again and again how subtly and deliberately he would use first-person pronouns to align himself with listeners or readers presumed sympathetic, or to depict his own past or a collective identity; use second-person pronouns to instruct readers as neophytes, or respect them as experts or judges; and employ third-person pronouns to set the psychoanalyst, Broad Church author, or literary modernist outside the circle that includes himself and his audience.

Religious Broadcasts, 1942-43

We will begin with the broadcasts rather than with the *Rehabilitations* papers because their familiar subject matter of basic Christian beliefs enables us to focus on Lewis's approach and presentation. Though their provocative titles probably passed by the listeners, their arresting openings and continuity were all-important for winning and keeping attention. Almost every talk begins with a brief, matter-of-fact sentence, usually reiterating a previous conclusion, and ends with a simple, sometimes stark assertion. In the first, "Every one has heard people quarrelling" introduces listeners to a series of overheard remarks culminating in the judgment that each (male) speaker appeals to a "standard of behaviour which he expects the other man to know about."[7] The talk

6. Compare John Wain's "The Great Clerk" and Walter Hooper's "Oxford's Bonny Fighter" (both in James Como, ed., *C. S. Lewis at the Breakfast Table*) with A. L. Rowse, *The Poet Auden,* 13.

7. Lewis, *Mere Christianity,* 3.

ends: "These two facts [that humans know but break the moral law] are the foundation of all clear thinking about ourselves and the universe we live in" (*Mere Christianity*, 7). By implication our "universe" is social and moral, rather than physical. The second series concludes with the parallel previously drawn in the "Great War" between the Second Coming and a playwright coming on stage. Our chance to choose "the right side . . . will not last for ever. We must take it or leave it" (52).

Lewis begins his third series, "Christian Behaviour," by citing a schoolboy's view of God as a spoilsport. "In reality," he counters, "moral rules are directions for running the human machine" (*Mere Christianity*, 55). The image of society as a machine recurs as persistently in this series as that of warfare appears in the first two. For example, society may be compared to a car, with perfect behavior, like "perfect gear-changing," an unattainable but necessary ideal (56). Or the individual may be described as a ship that must be well maintained and kept in convoy (56). Although he alludes to the current war throughout the broadcasts, Lewis uses the war image most specifically in "The Invasion," in his second series. On first studying the New Testament seriously, he was surprised how much its writers "talked" of a "Dark Power" responsible for "death and disease, and sin." Unlike Dualism, "Christianity . . . thinks" of a "civil war" in the cosmos and earth as "a part . . . occupied by the rebel." In the next and final paragraph, he draws a parallel with the current war: "Enemy-occupied territory — that's what this world is. Christianity" tells us "how the rightful king has landed . . . and is calling us all to take part in a great campaign of sabotage." To attend church is to tune in "to the secret wireless [radio] from our friends" (37). The preference for Anglo-Saxon monosyllables exemplified in this passage betrays Lewis into wordiness when he defines prudence as considering "what you are doing and what is likely to come of it" (60) instead of "your behaviour and its consequences."

The broadcasts are renowned for analogies and illustrations drawn from common life. In one cluster (110), a man confides once more in a "pretty" but indiscreet girl because "his senses and emotions have destroyed his faith" in "what he knows to be true." A boy fully aware that "an unsupported human body will not . . . sink" nevertheless panics when his swimming instructor's hand is withdrawn. In the next paragraph, a convert's intellectual conviction may be undermined by ill news, the skepticism of his peers, sexual temptation, or greed, so that his emotions or desires will "carry out . . . a blitz on his belief."

While the first series, originally published as *Broadcast Talks,* is held together mainly by reminders and recurrent images, the second, first published as *Christian Behaviour,* is more typical of a scholar-teacher in its quasi-medieval subdivisions and assumption of authority. Like the "famous Christian long ago" (St. Augustine), a believer might pray for chastity but not yet, perhaps because he believes the "lie" in films and advertisements that indulgence is always "healthy and normal," or because he assumes that chastity is impossible, or else because he confuses suppression with repression. Chastity resembles a "compulsory question," in that anyone who attempts it is bound to earn some marks: "You must ask for God's help" (*Mere Christianity,* 79-81). Here the Mentor comes into plain view.

In these broadcasts Lewis can be criticized for oversimplifying (Christ was either divine or a lunatic) or for drawing false parallels (we take Scripture, like history, on authority) or for harboring old-fashioned views on marriage, but never for dullness or obscurity. In a speaker whose interests were so remote from those of typical English town dwellers, they were a remarkable achievement.

Addresses to Students, 1937-45

Of the papers for student groups published in *Rehabilitations,* "William Morris" (1937) is the least remarkable. Admittedly, swimming against the tide was the author's favorite exercise, but to praise Morris for not describing scenes in detail yet also to praise his evocative power was going too far. In making fun of anti-Romantic critics who could not forever "suppress an author . . . so obstinately pleasurable" (*Selected Literary Essays,* 219), Lewis claimed objective validity for a personal response. Yet Morris's perception that death is responsible for life's supreme joys and sorrows elicited that memorable Lewisian phrase the "dialectic of natural desire" (220).

"Variation in Shakespeare and Others" should remove any doubt as to Lewis's capacity for detailed analysis. Dissecting well-known passages in *Macbeth, Paradise Lost,* and less famous texts, he contrasts the usual procedure of a dramatist, who builds impressions by repetition with variations, with that of an epic poet, who constructs scenes from particulars mentioned only once.

In two papers not tied to particular authors or texts, Lewis took up positions he never abandoned. In "Christianity and Literature," intended for a student religious society, he argues against the modernist scorn of *imitatio* and demand for continual innovation, on the ground that in the New Testament "Originality is . . . a prerogative of God alone" (*Rehabilitations,* 191). Denying the Ricardian view of a literary work as an objet d'art sufficient in itself, he concludes that "the greatest poems were made" by authors valuing something beyond art, which bestowed its own "gravity and sublimity" (196) on their work. His statement that "Christians know" the saving of one "soul" matters more than "the production or preservation of all the epics and tragedies in the world" (196) indicates that he felt among friends. Witness also his free use of "I" at the outset and audience-inclusive "we" in disparaging the notion of "Christian art" exempt from critical scrutiny. Like Orwell in another context, he ascribes feeble language in hymns to feeble subject matter.[8] Yet the confidence of one among friends is responsible both for the touch of sublimity in his description of humans as potentially "clean mirrors filled with the image of a force that is not ours" (191) and for the throwaway ending, a comic passage from the *Paradiso* on Pope Gregory's laughter upon finding, once in heaven, that his theory of the angelic hierarchies is wrong.

He is equally self-revealing and, dare one say, original in "High and Low Brows,"[9] where he claims that the literary canon changes from age to age. After assessing H. Rider Haggard's novels with all the discrimination a Leavis could desire, he proposes replacing an unreal and snobbish distinction by judgment of any work against those of admitted excellence within its genre. His fear that applying the high-brow-lowbrow distinction in schools would make reading "good litera-

8. George Orwell, "Politics and the English Language." Cf. the comparison of Lewis and Orwell in Kath Filmer, *The Fiction of C. S. Lewis,* 68-72.

9. Lewis, "High and Low Brows," in *Rehabilitations and Other Essays,* 95-116; reprinted in *Selected Literary Essays,* 266-79. This paper was originally read to the Oxford University English Society.

ture" a duty rather than a pleasure has been fulfilled at least in North America, where only course requirements keep many literary classics in print. Speaking to students of literature, he adopts a more formal style, but he permits himself a good-humored dig at Richards, who also used to read "lowbrow" books when ill. Ironically, when firing a salvo at neoclassicism in his excellent essay on Addison,[10] Lewis adopts a distinctly highbrow tone, reproving those who seek relief from political meetings and literary movements by falling "plumb down to the cinema and the dance band" (*Selected Literary Essays*, 168).

The audience at Manchester University might well have found "Bluspels and Flalansferes: A Semantic Nightmare"[11] distinctly heavy going. The title words, coined from "blue spectacles" and "flatland spheres," were supposedly invented by a teacher and pupil.[12] Their origins being forgotten and some syllables compressed, they typify dead metaphors that limit thinking. By alerting his listeners to fossilized metaphors Lewis hoped to discourage "verbiage" (*Selected Literary Essays*, 263), to encourage creation of fresh metaphors, and above all to show that language for anything beyond sense-perceived objects is inevitably metaphorical. Whatever success he enjoyed can be attributed to his inventive diction and his pitch for imaginative writing as against the nonmetaphorical language urged on scientists by the founders of the Royal Society. Noticeably, his "I" refers to suppositious statement, while his "we" embraces fellow students of the humanities.

There is more life in "Shelley, Dryden and Mr. Eliot."[13] The bite in the initial description of Shelley's idealism as too generous for cynics and too loose for "our 'humanist' censors" (*Selected Literary Essays*, 187) must have engaged the audience at once. So must his audacious claims that Shelley was more "classical" than Dryden, that the Augustans failed whenever they used classical forms, and that *Prometheus Unbound* was

10. Lewis, "Addison" (first published 1945 in a festschrift for David Nichol Smith), reprinted in *Selected Literary Essays*, 154-68.

11. Lewis, "Bluspels and Flanasferes," in *Rehabilitations and Other Essays*, 133-58; reprinted in *Selected Literary Essays*, 251-65.

12. Lewis cites as source Edwin A. Abbott's *Flatland: A Romance of Many Dimensions* (1884); see *Selected Literary Essays*, 254n.

13. Lewis, "Shelley, Dryden and Mr. Eliot" (lecture at Bedford College, London), in *Rehabilitations*, 1-34; reprinted in *Selected Literary Essays*, 187-208.

the nineteenth century's greatest long poem. As though himself influenced by neoclassicism, Lewis uses the periodic sentence with unusual frequency, while his "we" has a magisterial ring: "I do not think we can doubt that Shelley is right [to condemn self-criticism]. If a man will not become a Christian, it is very undesirable that he should become aware of the reptilian inhabitants in his own mind" (198). This lecture again illustrates Lewis's enjoyment of swimming against the critical tide.

During the 1940s, as an established academic, he honored numerous requests or commissions, from the *Problem of Pain* and sessions with airmen on religion to the British Academy Shakespeare Lecture. But the best evidence of his expository and critical approach is to be found in addresses to university literary societies. "Dante's Similes"[14] has the usual surprise opening — a claim that some good Old English poems have no similes — followed by a division of similes by Dante into Homeric or Virgilian, traveler's illustrations, cross-boundary comparisons, and, most Dantean, similes revealing profound philosophical likeness or identity. After a digression on travel books, Lewis subdivides his traveler's illustrations into those depicting a region in which readers literally believe (cf. Jules Verne), those expressing current ideas, those conveying religious allegory, and those based on the poet's own life story. Codifying, as he called it in the *Discarded Image*,[15] was a medieval habit he picked up while writing the *Allegory of Love*. In a later paper to the Dante Society, it becomes so obtrusive as to distract one from the argument.[16]

In "Psycho-Analysis and Literary Criticism" (1942),[17] Lewis propounded the distinction between wish-fulfilling and literary fantasy that became a cornerstone of his *Experiment in Criticism* (1961). In its suave irony, the complex opening sentence epitomizes the difference

14. Lewis, "Dante's Similes" (address to the Dante Society, Oxford, 1940), in *Studies in Medieval and Renaissance Literature*, 64-77.

15. Lewis, *Discarded Image*, 10ff.

16. Lewis, "Imagery in the Last Eleven Cantos of Dante's 'Comedy'" (address to the Dante Society, Oxford, 1948) in *Studies in Medieval and Renaissance Literature*, 78-93.

17. Lewis, "Psycho-Analysis and Literary Criticism" (originally read to a literary society at Westfield College, London), reprinted in *Selected Literary Essays*, 286-300.

between his approach here to an academic audience and the approach he used to the general public in *Broadcast Talks,* published in the same year: "The purpose of this paper is by no means to attack psycho-analysis, but only to contribute to the solution of some frontier problems between psycho-analysis and literary criticism" (*Selected Literary Essays,* 286). Giving his earlier contrast between treatment of poems as artifacts and as documents[18] a humorous twist, he refers to psychological criticism as the poet's "pathology" (286) inferred from the poem. He uses English literary examples to undermine Freud's reductive account in *Introductory Lectures on Psycho-Analysis*[19] of the "latent content" of art and literature as fantasized wishes or fears. Distinguishing between self-centered daydreams and literary fantasies, Lewis notes that Trollope and the Brontës began with the first but discarded them or else shaped them into the second. Instancing his own (Boxen) fantasy of a "Snug Town" complete with river, bridge, shipping, and "anthropomorphised mice" in Dutch clothing (287-88), Lewis insists that the town was adorable in itself, and in no way involved him as participant.

Beyond the merit of his argument, Lewis uses two devices to win over his audience. The first is a use of pronouns setting Freud as "he" against "I" who will modify his theory of art and "most of us" who have distinguished between the two kinds of fantasy "ever since we can remember" (*Selected Literary Essays,* 287). The second device consists of illustration from extremes of poetic and mundane language. The hungry man dreams not of "honey-dew and elfin bread, but of steak and kidney puddings," the sex-starved one not of "Titania or Helen" but of "real, prosaic flesh-and-blood" (289). The penetrating wit of Lewis's ending would surely have drawn laughter and applause from any student body. After complimenting psychoanalysts on admitting depths in literature denied by materialists, Lewis instances Jung's attribution of excitement generated by "certain images" to the collective unconscious, and in a send-up of psychoanalytic pretensions concludes: "the mystery of primordial images is deeper, their origin more remote, their cave more hid, their fountain less accessible than those suspect

18. Lewis, "Donne and Love Poetry in the Seventeenth Century," in *Selected Literary Essays,* 108.
19. Freud, *Introductory Lectures on Psycho-Analysis* (1916-17).

who have yet dug deepest, sounded with the longest cord, or journeyed farthest in the wilderness — for why should I not be allowed to write in this vein as well as everyone else?" (300).

Public Lectures, 1942-52

The Academy lecture "*Hamlet:* The Prince or the Poem?," also delivered in 1942, begins with a disclaimer of pretensions to Shakespearean scholarship. Lewis found much of his material in eighteenth- and nineteenth-century critical works from which he had scribbled quotations in the end-papers of his Arden edition.[20] The handwriting and the date of the last book cited, 1922, suggest that he inscribed them before Granville-Barker's *Preface to "Hamlet"* (1934). His marginal notes within the text, however, mention Dover Wilson's New Cambridge edition (1934). A surprising omission from the end-paper notes is Bradley's *Shakesperean Tragedy.*

Nearly all the end-paper notes concern Hamlet's character. Lewis divides explanations of Hamlet's inaction into four: "pressure of grief," "Shakespeare bungling," "madness," and an "orthodox tradition" of personal weakness. His own view when inscribing these notes was that, while nothing could be known of Hamlet before the events began, the Prince's weakness was that of any thinking person disillusioned, haunted, rejected in love, and confronted by death. This amounts to a focus on the hero's character that Lewis deplores in the lecture. By 1942 he directed his attention to the play as a whole, as expressing the horror and fascination excited by death. He attributes his new approach to the influence of Barfield, whose essay on *Hamlet* was already in draft.[21] Though Lewis's marginal notes within the text were editorial or semantic, his view in the lecture is surprisingly relevant to theatrical production. Dismissing Eliot's view of *Hamlet* as "an artistic failure,"[22] on

20. These notes and quotations are detailed in my article "C. S. Lewis's Annotations to His Shakespeare Volumes."

21. A. Owen Barfield, "The Form of *Hamlet*," in *Romanticism Comes of Age*, 2nd ed. (1966), p. 8: "the first edition . . . appeared no less than twelve years after the latest of the essays it contained."

22. T. S. Eliot, "Hamlet" (1919).

account of its power to attract playgoers and readers alike, he ascribes its "quality of darkness and misgiving" to its representing in the hero our common self-consciousness and fear of *"being dead"* (*Selected Literary Essays,* 99).

The difference between experiencing *Hamlet* in the classroom and in a good modern production lies precisely in the producer's coordination of speech, lighting, and scenery to transport the audience into the "spiritual region" (*Selected Literary Essays,* 101) implicit in the text as a whole. The producer makes the effort of imagination that so sensitive a reader as Lewis could make for himself.

Two features in the lecture's style and approach repay attention. The first is a progression in the opening from a "critic" who, feeling like a "child" brought in to recite before adults, modulates into an "I" who decides that dwelling on some minor issue will not impress the audience, and therefore lays his "childishness" before them. Later, "I" implicitly includes the listeners, for they likewise need not "cross the room" to meet Hamlet, who is "always where I am" (*Selected Literary Essays,* 100).

The second device is a clever use of the child-image in the conclusion. After citing modern authorities, Lewis insists on the traditional character of his argument, his aim being to "recall attention from the things an intellectual adult notices" to external details (darkness, the castle, a man dressed in mourning) that any "child or a peasant notices" (*Selected Literary Essays,* 104). Enlarging on the child's fidelity to details, he claims that only adults who have preserved their "first childish response to poetry" (105) amid all subsequent "enrichments" have truly matured.

In 1952 Lewis gave a British Academy lecture on "Hero and Leander."[23] As compared with that on *Hamlet* ten years earlier, this shows less modesty — real or assumed — and less effort to lead the audience toward his own viewpoint, but the same device of an opening expanded in the conclusion. Initially recommending his audience to read as one the versions of the myth by Chapman and by Marlowe, he finally recommends them to do so as children, who "would not care whether two or twenty-two had written it" (*Selected Literary Essays,* 73).

23. Lewis, "Hero and Leander" (Warton Lecture on English Poetry) in *Proceedings of the British Academy* (1952); reprinted in *Selected Literary Essays,* 58-74.

The English Association lecture "Kipling's World" (1948) has both an opening designed to provoke curiosity and attention by picturing Kipling as "poet of work" rather than propagandist of imperialism and a balanced conclusion: though enslaved to an imaginary "Inner Ring" of power wielders,[24] Kipling was "a very great artist" in that he opened up the new territory of work as locus and proving ground for the human spirit.

As his review of Eugene Vinaver's edition of *The Works of Sir Thomas Malory* (the first edition so titled) shows, Lewis was incapable of discussing a topic without leaving his stamp on it. The edition is "a very great work," yet not all Vinaver's views, "of course," can be expected to "win the acceptance of scholars" (*Studies in Medieval and Renaissance Literature*, 103). As a bookman writing for bookmen, Lewis calls the *Morte d'Arthur* "a sacred and central possession of all who speak the English tongue" (104), instancing Milton, Tennyson, and Morris. Yet Malory is a "responsive, not creative" artist (107), reacting to whichever source text he is using; thus "We should approach" the *Morte,* he concludes in a nice analogy, as if approaching not Liverpool but Wells Cathedral (110).

Apologetic Books, 1940-47

Lewis wrote nothing more eloquent than his introductory chapter of *The Problem of Pain.* Its impressiveness is a matter of style and tactics, for much of its argument crumbles under analysis. No surviving verse or prose since two letters to Greeves in 1916 substantiates the opening clause "Not many years ago, when I was an atheist." Those letters express disbelief on three grounds: that prescientific man invented myths to account for natural processes; that the Christ-myth originated in legends about the historical Jesus; and that accepting death as final is preferable to believing in a deity who torments forever the vast majority unable to practice the Christian ethic. Only the last is detectable in *Spirits in Bondage,* and during his "Great War" with Barfield Lewis modulated from pantheism to monotheism.

24. Cf. Lewis, "The Inner Ring."

Preserving credibility by the conditional clause "if anyone had asked me," he gives as grounds for disbelief the age, size, and emptiness of the cosmos; competition between species; suffering, especially if foreseeable; human cruelty; and the transience of civilization, indeed of humankind. If God exists, he must be either amoral or evil. In a version of *certum est, quia impossibile,* Lewis contends that despite such realities, more evident to our ancestors than to ourselves, Christianity and other world religions arose because of numinous and moral experience, prophetic teachings, and the Incarnation. To show that the immensity of the cosmos was a fact long known, Lewis naively assumes that all our medieval forebears had access to Ptolemy's teaching on the subject. More soundly, he assumes them familiar with waste and suffering.

Having (fortunately for his readers) never quite outgrown his boyhood, he begins a list of numinous experiences in literature with Ratty's ecstasy at sunrise in the *Wind in the Willows.* Then follow more famous episodes in Wordsworth's *Prelude,* Malory's *Morte d'Arthur,* the book of Revelation, and pre-Christian texts from the *Aeneid* to Genesis. During the chapter, the grammatical subject shifts from "I," the former Lewis, to "he," modern and rebellious man, who by shutting his eyes to the numinous and dismissing the "moral law as an illusion" cuts himself off from humanity's "common ground . . . the great poets and prophets." Man so cut off will "remain a barbarian" worshiping sex, his ancestors, the "life-force or the future" (*Problem of Pain,* 13). Hitherto the author has addressed "you," a readership presumed open to reason. In the final paragraphs, "we" could not have dreamed up the Christian religion, which has the arbitrariness of modern physics (a false analogy slipped in), but if we pursue "the course on which humanity has been led" by adopting it, we "have the 'problem' of pain" (13). In the antireligious argumentation, simple or compound sentences make points that complex ones explain or justify. Much of the impact comes from final monosyllables, as in this passage: "And what is it [life] like while it lasts? It is so arranged that all the forms of it can live only by preying upon one another. In the lower forms this process entails only death, but in the higher there appears a new quality called consciousness which enables it to be attended with pain. The creatures cause pain by being born, and live by inflicting pain, and in pain they mostly die" (p. 2). The proportion of polysyllables increases as Lewis reaches his mature viewpoint. As unbeliever he uses the plain man's vocabulary, as believer that of a well-read one.

His argument in *Miracles* is that we must choose between Naturalism (belief limited to what the senses can perceive) and Supernaturalism, the source of reason and (unconditional) morality. To believe in a transcendent and personal God is to admit his occasional interference in natural processes, notably in Christ's incarnation, resurrection, and miracles. As in science, claims of miraculous events must be judged by one's "innate sense" of their "fitness" (*Miracles*, 126), that is, their compatibility with what is known of God and nature.

Before discussing the book's style and strategy, I should mention the chapter revised for the 1960 edition, in consequence of the debate with Elizabeth Anscombe. Forced to distinguish between the possibly nonrational *cause* and the valid or invalid *ground* for any belief, Lewis changed the title of chapter 3 from "The Self-Contradiction of the Naturalist" to "The Cardinal Difficulty of Naturalism" and expanded its argument thus. To attribute an illness to something eaten is to relate effect and cause. To say that a man must be ill because he remains in bed is to relate ground (staying in bed) and consequent (belief he is ill). The cause-and-effect of one step in thinking becomes the ground-and-consequent of the next. Thus eating (ground) and feeling ill (consequent) become feeling ill (cause) and deciding to stay in bed (effect). The inference from ground to consequent may be psychological (staying in bed and the presumed illness) or objective (others reported ill after eating the food concerned). Only the latter can claim to be real insights. To make this inference is to reason, to perceive order amid the chaos of events, and thereby to free oneself from nonrational causality.

As in *Broadcast Talks*, Lewis began the book with an attention-grabbing recollection, of a man who had seen a ghost yet still disbelieved in immortality. Likewise he ends the first two chapters with succinct, simple sentences. Thereafter, he either becomes absorbed in his arguments or else writes for the educated reader rather than the common listener. Hence his presumption that because the immensity of the cosmos was known to Ptolemy, Boethius, King Alfred, Dante, and Chaucer (*Miracles*, 58) it was known to all is more pardonable here than in the broadcasts.

As in them, he draws on the recent war for imagery. Reason can invade the natural realm to take captives and colonize (*Miracles*, 34). Miracles occur as steps in God's planned invasion (131), but as with sightings of enemy agents, most reports are just rumors (146). Since the Fall, the Spirit has survived on earth like a garrison in rebel-held territory.

Lewis used similar language outside the book as well. In D. S. Brewer's words, Lewis, being "deeply disturbed" at his defeat by Miss Anscombe, compared it to that of "infantry thrown back under heavy attack."[25] As A. N. Wilson notes, the defeat redirected Lewis from religious argument to embodiment of the Christian "myth" in stories for children,[26] with, I would add, comparable images of invasion and reconquest. Despite some unfortunate intrusions by the Mentor, in the Narnia stories the Dreamer comes into his own.

Miracles is enlivened by Lewisian asides and witticisms. "Modern Reader, how your spirits rise" on hearing of an emergent deity (39). No one equates the Resurrection accounts with pious chit-chat of "Mother Égarré" (French for "mislaid") finding her thimble with help from St. Antony (patron saint of mislayers) (129). Some analogies and illustrations are drawn from within, some from just outside the author's circumscribed experience. As radio only partially reproduces human speech, so a nation's ethos transmits only the part of divine wisdom its history and economic system permit. When thinking of London, he has a mental picture of Euston Station (where in his childhood he first arrived in the capital). As physicists have ceased representing atoms as tiny balls, so the Christian Fathers knew better than to conceive God pantheistically.

The book has eloquent passages and phrases. Just as only those familiar with another language sense the distinctive quality of their own, so only believers in the supernatural are aware of nature, "this astonishing

---

25. Brewer told Hooper of Lewis's "real horror" when describing the debate two days afterward: "His imagery was all of the fog of war, the retreat of infantry." In his diary, he records Lewis as "deeply disturbed" because "Miss Anscombe . . . had disproved some of the central theory of his philosophy about Christianity." See Walter Hooper, "Oxford's Bonny Fighter," 137-85, esp. 163, and D. S. Brewer, "The Tutor: A Portrait," 41-68, esp. 59, both in James Como, ed., *C. S. Lewis at the Breakfast Table*.

26. A. N. Wilson, *C. S. Lewis: A Biography,* 214-15.

cataract of bears, babies and bananas; this immoderate deluge of atoms, orchids, oranges, cancers, canaries, fleas, gases, tornadoes and toads." How could we have thought nature all there was? How could we think her just "a stage-set for the moral drama of men and women? She is herself. Offer her neither worship nor contempt. Meet her and know her." If she be mortal, we shall "miss . . . this ogress, this hoyden, this incorrigible fairy, this dumb witch." But if she be redeemable, her "character" will be reformed, though not "tamed," so we shall hereafter know "our old enemy, playfellow and foster-mother" as "not less, but more, herself. And that will be a merry meeting" (*Miracles,* 81). Amid all the concrete nouns, rhetorical questions, imperatives, and variously constructed sentences can be discerned not only the Venus encountered by Jane in *That Hideous Strength,*[27] but the child (and Dreamer) in Lewis who was to depict Narnia's ruin and redemption.

With or without Miss Anscombe's help, *Miracles* fell somewhat flat. The *Hibbert Journal* reviewer damned not only the "Naturalism Is Self-Refuting" chapter but also the attempt to refute Hume's case against miracles.[28] Subsequent editions consist of an abridgement and the revised edition, which suggests poor sales.[29] Reasons can be discerned both a priori and in the text. As Wilson says, the advent of logical positivism and neo-Thomism left someone who taught philosophy before 1922 vulnerable to attack by someone like Miss Anscombe, a Catholic pupil of Wittgenstein.[30] To illustrate the book's occasional descent into obscurity or persiflage, a long footnote describes myth as neither devilish or human deception nor historical error but "a real though unfocussed gleam of divine truth falling on human imagination" (*Miracles,* 161n). In the same chapter we are informed that though God is behind every human or animal conception, when he removed nature's "glove" to impregnate Mary with his bare hand, the "soiled

27. Dr. Edwards drew my attention to the similarity between Venus in *That Hideous Strength* and Nature.

28. An anonymous review in *Hibbert Journal* 45 (July 1947): 373-77.

29. See Lewis's preface to the abridged edition, dated 1958. No reprint of the book has been undertaken by Collins since its takeover of Bles.

30. A. N. Wilson, *C. S. Lewis: A Biography,* 211-14; George Sayer, *Jack: C. S. Lewis and His Times,* 186-87, who also cites Lewis's personal account of having been "proved wrong."

and weary universe quivered at this direct injection of essential life"
(168). A further reason for the book's poor sales is the author's ambivalent attitude toward the reader. From "centuries of logical analysis"
by Aristotle and the scholastics "we" have learned to view heaven more
subtly than New Testament narrators of the ascension (188), yet "you"
must learn to "eradicate from your mind the whole type of thought in
which you have been brought up" (198). The educated skeptic might
find a claimant's "innate sense of fitness" insufficient basis for judgment
of a supposed miracle. Earlier, the reader has been invited to view
entropy as reversible on the ground that the cosmos must once have
been "winding up," just as Humpty Dumpty, who must once have
been placed on the wall, will at the general resurrection be reinstated
there (181). Need one be a physicist to find this naive?

In short, the book falls between two targets: the general reader
and the graduate in philosophy. When a reader compared Lewis's works
to a cathedral, Lewis pictured *Miracles* as the cathedral school and the
Narnian tales as side chapels with altars.[31] If Lewis were still living, he
might wish to invert this priority.

Two years after the debate on *Miracles,* pessimism about the future
of Christianity is implicit in a striking comparison in the lecture "The
Literary Impact of the Authorised Version."[32] Downplaying the impact,
Lewis compares a discarded holy book to a dethroned monarch: one
may approve the deposition yet disavow personal antipathy by offering
sentimental praise. Save among a "believing minority" reading for
instruction, the Bible must either "return as a sacred book" or else
"follow the classics . . . into the ghost-life of the museum and the
specialist's study" (*Selected Literary Essays,* 145).

Cambridge: Lectures and Essays

Pessimism becomes explicit in the lecture *"De Descriptione Temporum,"*
which inaugurated the final phase of Lewis's career, as holder of a

31. Lewis, letter to W. L. Kinter, 28 March 1953.
32. Lewis, "The Literary Impact of the Authorised Version" (Ethel M. Wood
Lecture, March 1950). Reprinted in *Selected Literary Essays,* 126-45.

specially created chair at Cambridge. At a British university an "in-augural" was expected of any newly appointed professor. At the older universities especially the lecture would be well attended and subse-quently published. Lewis chose a Latin title to emphasize his bookish and clerkly cast of mind, as a medieval and Renaissance scholar oper-ating within an unbookish post-Christian culture. After discussing the claims of the fall of Rome, the Renaissance, and the Reformation, he concludes that the Industrial Revolution marked the "Great Divide" (*Selected Literary Essays,* 3) between ancient and modern civilization. This radical shift of boundaries was enough to make the lecture famous. What made it also notorious was the apparent egocentricity of using himself, even humorously, as paradigm of "Old Western Culture" (12). The recurrent "I" in the opening statements on the need for the first holder to "create the part" by "explaining . . . the way in which I approach my work, my interpretation of the commission you have given me" (1) creates an impression of self-importance dispelled only slowly, if at all, when he turns to the blurring of the old distinction between medieval and Renaissance culture and "I" gives place to "we." In his concluding passage Lewis supplies ammunition to both admirers and detractors. After his delightful picture of speaker and audience looking back out of curiosity while fleeing a laboratory invaded by a dinosaur, he draws a parallel between an Athenian's familiarity with Greek tragedies and his own familiarity with "Old Western literature," to acquire which his listeners must "unlearn" the "habits . . . acquired in reading modern literature" (13). Even while modestly proposing that where he fails "as a critic" he might be valuable "as a specimen," he urges students to make use of their "specimens" since "There are not going to be many more dinosaurs" (14). What amuses the admirer may incense the detractor.[33]

In his altogether less self-conscious address to the Sir Walter Scott Club of Edinburgh in 1956, Lewis paid one of the best tributes ever accorded that novelist.[34] Plunging straight in with "Here in Edinburgh, on 7 June 1826," Lewis proceeded to relate that when kept awake by

---

33. See John Wain, "C. S. Lewis," and Graham Hough, "Old Western Man," both reprinted in George Watson, ed., *Critical Thought I.*

34. For a contrary view of the paper see John Wain, "C. S. Lewis."

a dog's howls, the overworked and recently bereaved Scott commented in his journal, "Poor cur! I dare say he had his distresses, as I have mine" (*Selected Literary Essays,* 209). Lewis concluded his address by applying Scott's comment, minus the final clause, to "our juniors." One of these had sought to undercut Jeannie Dean's integrity by ascribing it to jealousy of her sister's beauty. Apart from the Lewisian stratagem of aligning his audience with himself in "our," the conclusion is remarkable for its foreboding of a "barbarism" that may be "humanity's last illness" (218). The "barbarism" consists partly of psychoanalytic reductionism and partly of the overseriousness about art that Lewis thinks responsible for the undervaluing of the "fine, careless, prodigal" Scott and the "exuberance" of Chaucer, Dickens, or Cervantes, in favor of the "self-probing literary conscience" of a Walter Pater or Henry James (215). Here Lewis for once loses his sense of proportion, but his disparagement of self-reflexive art and critical probing for self-contradiction in Scott's text anticipates the era of deconstruction. No contemporary literary theorist can honestly use "we" when addressing a book-loving but largely nonacademic audience, nor would many theorists engage in Lewis's balanced judgment, in setting Scott's civility, sanity, and historical sense against his polysyllabic diction, unevenness, and at times undue levity.

The two lectures on "Imagination and Thought in the Middle Ages," fashioned in the same year from his "Prolegomena" course for a group of Cambridge scientists, are remarkable for their witty and engaging images. Though as "crowded . . . as a railway station" at holiday time, the *Divine Comedy* is "patterned and schematized as a battalion on ceremonial parade" (*Studies in Medieval and Renaissance Literature,* 44). The medieval cosmos was "an answer, not a question" (48) and, though illusory, "perhaps the greatest work of art the Middle Ages produced" (62). It was bonded by love, or rather "appetite," God being the "quarry," "mistress," and "candle," the angelic "Intelligences" the "huntsmen" and "suitors," the "universe the moth" (51).

While Joy lived, the wit remained good-tempered. Cosmology in medieval art and literature resembled a village "Mothers' Union" performing a "play . . . done in London," "absurd" but "very good fun for all concerned" (*Studies in Medieval and Renaissance Literature,* 61). After her death, in his writings and solitary broadcast, Lewis's tone became graver, his wit more acidic, his belief less assured. The change can be illustrated from essays and books produced after the summer of 1960. "Four-Letter Words" (1961) ends with a delightful barb on a then celebrated legal case: though *Lady Chatterley's Lover* had survived "prosecution by the Crown," it had yet to face "more formidable judges. Nine of them, and all goddesses" (*Selected Literary Essays,* 174). This sentence concludes a demonstration that obscene words in medieval and classical literary texts were used, *pace* Lawrence, with primarily comic intent.

The tenor of the arguments in both "The Anthropological Approach" (1962),[35] an attack on books by R. S. Loomis and J. Speirs,[36] and the broadcast "The Vision of John Bunyan" (1962) shows a striking convergence with the Leavisian critical approach. Anthropological critics have imported into the medieval romance a "distorted version" in which the "forests" are not those of the imaginary world but "of anthropological theory" (*Selected Literary Essays,* 310). Though never discourteous, Lewis eventually compares Speirs's line of criticism to the allegorizing of Virgil, Homer, and the Song of Solomon: "The forest is after all enchanted: mares have built nests in every tree" (311). In the broadcast, though he admits being repelled by the doctrine in the *Pilgrim's Progress,* he praises the work for its "mimesis of ordinary conversation" (146). He also applauds the coalescence of folktale and the "contemporary life Bunyan knew" (147): giants and dungeons, yet also Mr. Worldly Wiseman, talkative neighbors, and a bullying magistrate. He attributes Bunyan's power as a writer neither to his sincerity nor to his familiarity with the Authorized Version of the Bible but to his "perfect natural ear" (150).

The weakening of certainty is less easily demonstrated. In 1954 Lewis finds "undeception" the key to all Jane Austen's novels save *Mansfield Park.*[37] *Undeceptions* is the English title of *God in the Dock,* a posthumous collection of his moral and theological essays. In the

35. Lewis, "The Anthropological Approach," originally published in a festschrift for J. R. R. Tolkien; reprinted in *Selected Literary Essays,* 301-11.

36. R. S. Loomis, "The Origin of the Grail Legends," in Loomis, ed., *Arthurian Literature in the Middle Ages* (1959); J. Speirs, *Medieval English Poetry: The Non-Chaucerian Tradition* (1957).

37. Lewis, "A Note on Jane Austen," reprinted in *Selected Literary Essays,* 175-86.

majority of these essays, he sought to undeceive readers of some modern illusion or false teaching. Significantly, only three were written after 1960. In the last of these, "We Have No Right to Happiness" (1963), which was destined to be his final essay, he denied our inherent right to the sexual and conjugal felicity that Jane Austen's lovers attain by being undeceived and that he had briefly known with Joy. It is doubtful whether the acidic phrase "four bare legs in a bed" (*God in the Dock,* 320) would have sprung to mind before her death, for *The Four Loves* evinces no disrespect for *eros.*

Later Devotional Books

The Four Loves originated when in 1957 Lewis was asked by an Episcopalian radio station in Atlanta, Georgia, to tape some broadcasts. After consulting Joy, he chose a subject then on his mind, finished the scripts by the following summer, and recorded them in August 1958. The talks had less impact than those of the forties, partly because he spoke too fast, but also partly because the American bishops judged the scripts too frank to be widely broadcast.[38] A third reason, I imagine, lay in the frequent (English) literary allusions. Most of the American listeners doubtless knew the story of King Lear, but not many would have a detailed knowledge of *Tristram Shandy* or recognize the MacDonald reference in "Anodos has got rid of his shadow" (*The Four Loves,* 120).[39]

Though little noticed by reviewers, *The Four Loves* has been well received by readers.[40] As Lewis acknowledged,[41] apart from its account

---

38. George Sayer, *Jack: C. S. Lewis and His Times,* 236-37.

39. The allusions, which are mainly in chapters 3 ("Affection") and 4 ("Friendship"), are to texts by Shakespeare (*Four Loves,* 17, 41-42, 55); Wordsworth (21-22); Sterne (34, 45); Samuel Butler (40); Cervantes, Dickens, Grahame (34); Milton (35, 103); Austen (50); Wagner (51, 92); Tennyson (55); Froissart (76); Dunbar (84); Orwell (87); Morris (107); Lovelace (114); and MacDonald (120). There are also references to *Beowulf* (59) and various mythical or literary friendships.

40. Mrs. Walmsley, then a director of Collins, reported sales by 1986 as 278,000 copies.

41. Lewis, letter to Miss Hodges, 14 December 1960: "the division of love into 4 was forced . . . by all ordinary experience."

of charity *(agape)* as an essential element in friendship and familial or erotic love at their fullest, it could be read as a secular text. (A psychologist's survey of patterns of loving among Americans discovered no reference to *agape,* a value not of this world.)[42] *The Four Loves* is devoid of the attention-grabbing openings, stark conclusions, and striking analogies of earlier religious broadcasts. Its humor is mainly evident in domestic or collegiate situations involving invented but typical characters: Mrs. Fidget the possessive housewife, or Dr. Quartz the reclusive don. Until the concluding chapter, Lewis classifies and subdivides the various forms of love as neatly as ever. There he gives a wordy and self-conscious explanation of his two reasons for not discussing charity earlier (*The Four Loves,* 108-10). It would be tempting to blame this on pressure or fatigue near the end of writing he found laborious,[43] but for the unstated presence of Joy's illness in his discussion of St. Augustine's case for loving God only. The force of Lewis's response that in such renunciation "I seem to be a thousand miles away from Christianity," the insistence that "To love at all is to be vulnerable. Love anything, and your heart will certainly be wrung and possibly be broken" (110-11), suggest that while writing the *Four Loves,* in Joy's last full year of health,[44] he was realizing the cost and peril of his commitment. Otherwise the book shows no sign of doubt or unease. The Christian beliefs, even the Garden of Eden (107-8), are taken for granted and applied to each form of love. Yet the gentle tone, deep understanding of love, and pervading good sense should endear this book even to the least religious.

No doubt is discernible in *Reflections on the Psalms,*[45] only humble awareness of being an Anglican layman helping others resolve difficulties the theologian no longer sees. From his own initial responses to the Prayer Book psalter Lewis infers the sorts of things that could trouble the unlearned user: the psalmists' gleeful anticipations of divine judgment, vindictiveness, self-righteousness, pleas to be spared death,

---

42. John Alan Lee, "The Styles of Loving."

43. George Sayer, *Jack: C. S. Lewis and His Times,* 236-37.

44. The recurrence of Joy's cancer was diagnosed October 1959 (A. N. Wilson, *C. S. Lewis: A Biography,* 278-81).

45. Lewis, *Reflections on the Psalms.* Page references are to the first edition (1958).

delight in the very Law from which St. Paul felt delivered by Christ, and constant exhortation to praise the Lord. Describing himself merely as a "teacher" by trade, he gives his readers no orders, and indeed carries modesty to the point of untruth when claiming "little" knowledge of Latin, Greek, and ancient history (27) and offering as "one man's opinion" (42) his readings of verses expressing unchristian sentiments. He only drops his pose of the fellow pupil when appreciating psalms as poems and giving Christian interpretations to some psalms prescribed for major festivals. One appreciates by hindsight the supple intelligence that sees the psalmists' longing for divine judgment as that of plaintiffs seeking redress rather than of criminals on trial, and that attributes their delight in the Mosaic law to love of order and symmetry. The cleverly placed word "legislation" (56) highlights the paradox of poets delighted to study the code spelt out in Leviticus, Numbers, and Deuteronomy.

The opening chapters concern what is disagreeable in the Psalms. Disagreeable aspects of Lewis appear in covert references to "half-believers" as "enlightened and progressive old gentlemen whom . . . no modesty" will "disarm" (9), to "bad" critics who have "continually narrowed the list of books we might be allowed to read" (94), and to Ministry of Education officials as "ignorant meddlers" hampering "real, practical teachers" (70). He makes this final aspersion when discussing modern forms of collaboration with the unrighteous in power, so frequently condemned in the Psalms.

Though attacked by John Wain for its "truculent" passages,[46] *Reflections on the Psalms* represents an admirable effort to take cobelievers from his own naive first impressions to a conviction that the Psalms were provided for our instruction. No book by Lewis is richer in analogies, of which a whole cluster illuminate an argument in favor of their Christian reinterpretations (*Reflections*, 100ff.). Apparent anticipations of Christ range from pure coincidence, illustrated by a Roman bath attendant's accidental prediction of a fire, to the religious insight evident in Plato's portrayal of the death of Socrates. In one series, Lewis envisages an unknown species seen by prophetic vision, invented by a fantasist, and hypothesized by a biologist. Finding the species on some

46. John Wain, "C. S. Lewis," esp. 33-34.

other planet would in the first and third cases be proof of visionary power or scientific insight, but in the second of nothing beyond chance. If attributing the death-and-resurrection theme of some pre-Christian myths to an intuition that to live fully man must die (106-7) might not convince a skeptic, *Reflections* represents Lewis at his happiest, a year or more before Joy's cancer returned. By significant coincidence, in a passage on temple festivities he draws a Barfieldian picture of a prelogical unity between sacred and social rejoicing, as when peasants celebrate Christmas or harvest (46-47).

Uncertainty returns, accompanied by dismay and bafflement, in *A Grief Observed.* Why does God not respond to the widower's plea for help? But the focus here is on his feelings. Doubt, or at least ambiguity, comes at the end of the broadcast on Bunyan. Having attributed the "energy" and "continual sense of momentousness" in the *Pilgrim's Progress* to its author's vision of hellfire, Lewis leaves disbelievers in life beyond the grave to imagine this ultimate urgency in their own ways. The majority, he says, have found that to live is to undergo "delights and miseries" beyond what "imagination could have anticipated," to realize how important were their choices at critical junctures, and to understand how "short cuts may lead to very nasty places" (*Selected Literary Essays,* 152-53). Worded so generally, this can be interpreted as a Christian or as a secular-existentialist maxim. In 1956, Lewis had advised a schoolgirl to ensure that each sentence she wrote was clear and unambiguous.[47] Breaking the rule he had always kept suggests a decline not in ability but in certainty.

This letter and a similar one three years later[48] yield a set of precepts very like those in Orwell's famous essay "Politics and the English Language." The writer must take trouble to ensure that her meaning is clear and cannot be mistaken through the omission of some detail she expected the reader to know. She should prefer brief, explicit words to polysyllables or abstractions ("deaths" to "fatalities"). She should listen to each sentence and change it if the sense and rhythm sound wrong. Since noise from a

47. Lewis, letter to Joan Lancaster, in W. H. Lewis, "C. S. Lewis: A Biography," 402; *Letters of C. S. Lewis,* 270-71.
48. Lewis, letter to "Thomasina," an American schoolgirl, in W. H. Lewis, "C. S. Lewis: A Biography," 434; *Letters,* 291.

typewriter will impair her sense of rhythm, she should write longhand. The most interesting reflection is that as in the *Prelude* Wordsworth often describes the circumstances but not the contemplated object, so any author is lucky to catch the object in an occasional sentence.[49] As Hopkins suggests in the first line of "The Windhover," perception is a grace, not an attribute of authorship.

Talk of declining certainty seems refuted by the uncompromising orthodoxy of the last book Lewis lived to complete, usually called *Letters to Malcolm*.[50] In some ways his strangest work, it differs from the *Screwtape Letters* in featuring Lewis the widower and semi-invalid as epistolist and in being addressed to a fictive friend "Malcolm," who might be an Inkling or at times even Warnie, who like Malcolm accompanied him to the Forest of Dean and to Edinburgh. Since in his final years Lewis could only scrawl brief notes or dictate letters for Warnie to type, the Epistolist's intention to write twenty-two four- or five-page letters, though fulfilled in the book, seems like a wish-fulfilling fantasy of better days. One catches this note of wistful retrospect in references to happier times "when I was a walker" and in arrangements for Malcolm's son to visit him for dinner in college and for the writer to visit Malcolm, who need no longer move a bed downstairs.

In a way Lewis pretends not to be writing a book. Public disparagement of self-analysis would incur the wrath of Freudians (letter 6). Much as a "good book on prayer" is needed, he will "never try to write it" (letter 12). What else, one may ask, is *Letters to Malcolm?* Though some commentators see in it a loss of grip, Lewis maintains the pretense by increasingly unstructured writing. The paragraphs of the first letter flow perfectly, whereas letters in the second half of the book are full of ad hoc rejoinders to criticisms by Malcolm or his wife. How far this is calculated is hard to determine, for when Malcolm's son is thought to have cancer the comparison with Lewis's own bereavement leads to a nadir of doubt at the book's midpoint (letter 11). In a sentence verbless

49. Lewis, letter to Joan Lancaster. In Wordsworth's *Prelude* (1850), books 1 and 2, compare the abundant detail regarding mundane "comforts" in book 1, lines 504-43, and book 2, lines 33-47 and 138-64, with the relative sparseness of detail regarding the mystical experiences described in book 1, lines 280-339, 357-400, 425-63, and book 2, lines 165-88.

50. *Prayer: Letters to Malcolm* (1964).

for emphasis, the writer struggles to "go on believing that there is a Listener at all." Two early letters (5 and 6) analyze the Lord's Prayer clause by clause, always with fresh insight; later, responses to objections by Malcolm or his wife are interspersed with reflections on a lengthening prayer list (letter 12), God as ground of our being (letter 13), belief in hell as required for a living faith in heaven (letter 14), "phantasmal" images of God and the writer (letter 15), inability to profit from Ignatian meditation (letter 16), the necessity of regular prayer (letter 21) and belief in purgatory (letter 20), the meaning of bodily "Resurrection," and the danger Christ's teachings represent to liberal theologians (letter 22). Several later epistles begin in mid-response to criticisms or suggestions and end with arrangements for visits in which the writer will assume his former role as host or guest. He recalls his prime and anticipates heaven, where deceased friends will greet him and he can walk with Malcolm through the fields of his boyhood, long built over.

The book indeed affirms the faith, but it also considers the risk of its being mistaken. In this life prayers can go unanswered, perhaps unheard. Modernizers win no converts from unbelief, yet see traditional apologists as selling the pass — that is, betraying the cause. In the end, using the Norse imagery beloved in his youth, Lewis seems to align himself with a God who is, after all, defunct. Suppose God should admit having misled his adherents: "I die, children. The story is ending." Though "Giants and Trolls" prevail, let Lewis and Malcolm "die on the right side, with Father Odin" (letter 22).

CHAPTER 9

Letter Writer

N EARLY THIRTY YEARS AGO, on first reading his letters to Arthur Greeves, I thought Lewis among the great letter writers in English, but I have since realized that no consensus exists as to who these may be, that only medieval literary theory considered letter writing an art form, and that the telephone and camera have rendered long letters almost obsolete. Lewis was, at any rate, the most assiduous of correspondents. Though he had an increasing proportion typed by his brother, while he was fit Lewis answered every incoming letter, even if that meant spending Christmas at his desk. The cost is apparent in the deterioration of his handwriting.

The cool reception of *They Stand Together* having apparently stalled the projected three-volume edition of his letters, one can only give an impression of his vast correspondence by considering specimen letters that convey his feelings or ideas; offer personal, religious, or literary counsel; interpret his own works; or attempt pastiche. (Business correspondence has already been illustrated in letters to his publisher.) Though invaluable as biographical information, his brother's selection *Letters of C. S. Lewis* consists largely of excerpts with no context.

Personal Expression

Walter Hooper's meticulous edition of letters to Greeves from Lewis's last term at school until two months before his death contains the fullest published record of his personal and literary development. Both in quality and in substance, the letters written in his youth are the best, despite an unexplained hiatus between 1923 and 1926. From about 1935, as his circle at Oxford grew, he told his boyhood friend less of his daily activities and concerns.

Changes in form and style become evident if we focus on letters written during three-year periods of Lewis's adolescence, young manhood, and old age. Between 1914 and 1917 he wrote almost weekly in term time. Though unparagraphed, undated, and somewhat formless, these letters from Great Bookham and Oxford have an engaging immediacy and frankness. More than any others they express that side of his personality I call the Dreamer, but from time to time the Mentor takes charge. After describing an autumnal landscape with a newcomer's enthusiasm, Lewis the Dreamer remarks on the truth of a tale by Wells in which the "SEEING ONE walks out into joy . . . unthinkable, where the dull, senseless eyes of the world see only destruction and death."[1]

The next several letters feature scenarios for a proposed music drama "Loki," but soon he is contrasting Malory's "genuine" *Morte d'Arthur* with its "delightful . . . reproduction" in a romance by Morris (64). Critical discrimination is thus in evidence from the beginning, but as yet without the power of exact expression. He praises several fantasies by Wells while deploring the presumably scientific or political "rubbish" Wells "puts in" (49).

At times he says outright what he might later imply. He finds the *Canterbury Tales* typical of the "Middle Ages" in "garrulity and coarseness," and he always warmed more to Chaucer's chivalric romances than to his fabliaux. *Troilus* and also *Gawain* (in modern English) he loved at first sight, as he did Sidney's *Arcadia* and the *Faerie Queene*.

---

1. Letter of September 1914, possibly the 26th, according to Hooper. *They Stand Together*, 49. Subsequent page references will be given parenthetically in the text.

He at first detested (197) but came to love *Tristram Shandy,* yet he remained remarkably consistent in his love of myths and also romances and fantasies written or inspired by MacDonald, Morris, or Malory. For months on end, he would address Greeves as "Dear [pure-hearted] Galahad."

Even the inconsistency of professing indifference to novels while enthusing about those of Charlotte Brontë and Scott reveals unwilling growth. When trying to complete his own chivalric romance the "Quest of Bleheris," he unfavorably compares its descriptive opening with the *in medias res* one of a story by Greeves (117), and later he remarks on Scott's "dry as dust" openings followed by "interesting" middles (130).

Yet even in the bookish enclave of Great Bookham, there was more to Lewis than the Dreamer. Responding to his friend's pique at being told only of books and music, he discloses his intention to stay till the Oxford entrance examination in December (1916) and thereafter (against his father's wishes) to enlist in the British Army (116-17).[2] This shows him coming to terms with the outside world, for two years earlier he had been bored by Mrs. Kirkpatrick's conversation about the war, as distinct from "really important" topics such as science, literature, and the arts (56). Having developed a vein of self-mocking humor, he fumes when unable to use his fellow pupil's exercise paper for the current letter by reason of its owner's presence in the common work-room (125).

Whether he was maturing as regards girls and women is more doubtful. At first entranced by Mrs. Kirkpatrick's playing of Chopin preludes and a Beethoven sonata, he later complains of her teatime chatter about the war and "everyone's servants" (84). In February 1915, he probably, as Dreamer, invented an unkept date with a Belgian refugee girl, for the following week he reports an apparently unresentful letter from her. In October of that year, again as Dreamer, he prefers vicarious experience via Catullus, Shakespeare, Jane Austen, or the Brontës to the folly of loving in person. It was to Greeves, however, that he confided his more realistic and growing interest in his cousin Cherry Robins.[3]

2. Being Irish, Lewis would be exempt from conscription (*They Stand Together,* 117n.).

3. *They Stand Together,* 187, 189, 192.

As Mentor, he rebukes Greeves for laziness, threatening in legalese to break off contact unless a promised story is received by a deadline (110-11). More obliquely, he deplores the complaints of Greeves at working in the family office, but in August 1918 he wields the lash in this memorable sentence: "How many men to-day, living in holes and mud-heaps, driven, hunted, terrified, verminous, starved for sleep, hopeless, would give their very souls to change places with you even for twenty four hours" (228). This letter from a camp in England shows a compassion never quite evident in his letters from the battle front.

By far the most enjoyable letters are those Lewis wrote between his father's death in September 1929 and his final conversion to Christianity two years later. Though overusing the word "delicious," they show an attachment to the English earth and rural characters that was intensified by relief from the "horror" of nursing his father in preparation for surgery, returning for the start of term, and being at once recalled to arrange his father's funeral. Delighted to awake with a "sense of peace and safety and home," he sings in his bath before taking his dog for an early morning "run." The least inspiring literary work may remind him how often he has been "kicked into conquering new countries" where he has become "at home" (310).

For the next two years, the theme of home and homeliness recurs like a leitmotif, as does "earth" or "earthy." Walking with Barfield, he is attracted by greenhouses, an old gardener potting, and celery trenches, calling "trench" a "delicious earthy word spoilt by" wartime use. The poems of MacDonald's *Diary of an Old Soul* have a "home-spun, earthy flavour" like those of Herbert (311). On another walk, vegetation in a ditch reminds him of herbalists and their "retired private wisdom" in seeking out plants ignored by most walkers. What "mysteries" intertwine beneath our feet, where "homeliness and magic embrace" (327). On worms, he reflects that "earth is such a lovely thing" as to reconcile him to its "contents" (315).

Another leitmotif is delight in winter. In October 1929, as the "mere nature and voluptuous life of the world is dying," another life is stirring (311). On Christmas Eve, his first in Oxford, he enjoys walking in "mellow sunlight slanting through the half-frosty mist" on elms as still as the air. That night at the College service the "glorious windy noise" of bells and the beauty of boys' voices infuse such a "blessed sense of charity" that his "worst enemies" seem merely "funny and odd." Next day he takes pleasure in trees "lashing" each other in a "bitter wind" against a steely sunset (320-21). Most of all, he loves the "rarified afternoon sunlight" that is "the peculiar glory of the English winter" (326). On Boxing Day, as he passes a manor house and church, an old horse and peal of bells evoke a sense of "homeliness, Englishness" and "Christendom" (322).

Homeliness applies also to religion. He cites Barfield's comment that MacDonald, Chesterton, and Lewis himself saw the "spiritual world as *home*," finding the newest experience a kind of homecoming (316). This was in November 1929, two years before his profession of faith and two months before he took Bunyan's "horrid" passage about the saved rejoicing at the judgment of sinners as echoing an utterance of Christ, whose benignity could be inferred only by "picking and choosing and slurring over" (330). While selling the family home and settling in his own, he experienced his slow conversion as a homecoming rather than simply a reversion to childhood faith, for he was moving toward one altogether more logical and credal. Heedless of liturgical or denominational differences, he saw Christianity as a matter of common principles and beliefs based on the Gospels and Epistles, the faith of his forebears, and the great Christian authors. In January 1930, he records reading MacDonald's *Diary of an Old Soul,* then adds that to make an "attempt" at religion is to take "the main road" and to compare notes with such former travelers as Chaucer, who counseled readers "Repeyreth home from worldly vanitee."[4] It is "emphatically coming home" (333-34).

Yet Lewis never lived more intensely in the present. On a walk with Barfield he notes species of birds and that winter records "almost cruelly poignant" birdsongs (338) with such delight in the winter landscape as to make him stop and spin around. Equally rapt, he notes odd characters he has met, such as an octogenarian[5] priest who can still drive, do carpentry, or mend radios, who adores Boswell, *Tristram Shandy,* and

4. *Troilus and Criseyde,* book 5, line 1837, misquoted as "Returneth home from worldly vanitee."

5. Lewis overestimated the age of Rev. Edward Foord-Kelcey, who was born in 1859 (*They Stand Together,* 573).

Pickwick Papers while caring for no poetry save Shakespeare's, and who abhors mysticism. The portrait is by no means a still life, for Lewis finds the old man in his workshop with shavings about his feet and one eye screwed up against a circular saw, yet ready to enthuse about (Laurence Sterne's) Uncle Toby. An eccentric don named Farquharson comes "gliding" toward Lewis, his egglike face surmounted by "sandy hair fringing a bald patch," wringing his hand and "cooing" appreciation of a purely academic visit, while his face signaled "what a pair of fools we are" (335). Lewis suggests uncharitably that Farquharson calls himself "Lieutenant Colonel" on a slender war record,[6] then in conclusion notes Farquharson's contrasting pose of seeking Lewis's opinion on an obscure point of Greek about which Farquharson knows "twenty times" as much and then telling a string of indecent stories. In his descriptions and portraits Lewis combines the fresh eye and senses of one half his age with the critical gaze of a mature scholar.

He responds just as intensely to new literary or musical experiences. In January 1930, he and Barfield sat through the night over Dante's *Paradiso*, which "opened a new world." The *Paradiso* strikes him as the most *"important"* poem he has read. As in scholastic theology, he finds "wheel within wheel . . . the One radiated through the Many" (326). He realizes that the poem is "too Catholic" for an Ulster Protestant like Greeves, who would, however, have appreciated the dawn cock-crow more than did Barfield.

Lewis had begun to share literary experiences not only with Greeves but also with the English friends later called the Inklings. In 1933, he supplied by request a detailed interpretation of MacDonald's *Lilith*, and in 1936 he urged Greeves to read Williams's *Place of the Lion*, a "deeply religious," "profoundly learned book" from which he has learned much about humility (479). More usually, he mentions his current reading without expecting his oldest friend to follow suit.

The preceding letter mentions their sustained argument about Sibelius, whose music Lewis compares to that of Wagner in being not "noble" like Beethoven's, but natural and *"Northern,"* redolent of "birch

---

6. Hooper says that Farquharson was twice mentioned in despatches and awarded a Commander of the Order of the British Empire (*All My Road Before Me,* 463-64).

forests and moss . . . , salt-marshes and cranes and gulls" (478). The nature of their shared interest, their old passion for things northern, is easily perceived.

By 1960 the letters had become brief and irregular. Those after March 1960, when Lewis revealed that Joy's cancer had returned, make sad reading. A letter of 8 August announces her death three weeks earlier. A comparison with accounts in biographies shows Lewis making light of his own trials — her screams and his struggle to get her a private room[7] — and selecting details to suit Greeves: two hours of agony that morning, removal to the hospital, her last words "You have made me happy" and "I am at peace with God." Of this, the first peaceful death he had witnessed, he remarked, "There's really nothing to it, is there?" (553). But of Warnie's consequent alcoholic binge and removal to the hospital he spared Greeves nothing. The fraternal role of sharing and support fell to Joy's seventeen-year-old son Douglas Gresham.

The following January Lewis invited Greeves to visit him for two days in June. Hearing in May of his friend's heart attack, he chartered a taxi from London. "The party," he added, was thinning out, and each would soon be "be leaving" (556). Excited about meeting his old friend, he adds in conclusion, "Heaven send that nothing goes wrong." Nothing did, for on 27 June, after mentioning his impending prostate surgery, he exclaimed, "How I did enjoy our two days together." A few days later he recalled that time as among his "happiest . . . for many a long day" (560).

The operation never took place, nor were the friends destined to meet again. By 22 March 1963, after Greeves had arranged for Lewis, escorted by Douglas, to join him at Port Ballintrae in July, Lewis congratulated him on assuring them of "some days together. We're both too old to let our remaining chances slip" (565). On 11 July Lewis had to cancel the holiday owing to his own heart trouble, and within a few days sank into a coma that lasted twenty-four hours. In his final letter to Greeves, on September 11, he described his consequent delusions as "quaint" rather than alarming but regretted having "glided painlessly up to the Gate" only to find it "shut" and still have to die. But chiefly he lamented that they would never meet again in this life. Despite his brother's absence on yet

---

7. See Roger Lancelyn Green and Walter Hooper, *C. S. Lewis: A Biography*, 278-79; and A. N. Wilson, *C. S. Lewis: A Biography*, 281.

another binge and failure to acknowledge appeals to return, Lewis was being well tended by his new housekeeper and coping with the "horrible burden" of correspondence usually handled by Warnie. Yet his last words to Greeves, "But oh Arthur, never to see you again" (565-66), were the most pathetic he ever wrote. They imply no loss of faith — while pitying Lazarus he has just concluded "God knows best" — but rather a welling up of childlike grief at separation. As under emotional strain "Warnie" flew to the bottle, so "Jack" turned to his oldest friend.

He told Greeves of books and authors during their first twenty years of correspondence, but in the final years almost the only literary comment was a scathing one on Robert Lee Wolff's *Golden Key*, a Freudian biocritical study of MacDonald that he had hoped in vain to review. Otherwise, he confined himself to commending Traherne's *Centuries of Meditation* or the *Theologica Germanica* as more suitable for Greeves than the *Imitation of Christ*.

Ideas and Opinions

As regards philosophy and religion, Lewis said most in the "Great War" with Barfield. On contemporary life he wrote mostly to several American pen pals. These included two women, Vera Gebbert (née Matthews) and Mary Shelburne, a surgeon named Warfield M. Firor, other men named Edward Allen and Dan Tucker, and a whole family of children, the Kilmers. In Britain he corresponded over many years with an Anglican nun, Sister Penelope, and the poet Ruth Pitter. For shorter periods he wrote to his former pupil Dom Bede Griffiths and the Anglican monk Brother Every, the poets Martyn Skinner and Kathleen Raine, and numerous other readers and academics. In so vast a correspondence one can only note permanence and change in tastes and opinions.

Some authors or texts he always relished. As early as 1920 he described Milton and Spenser as his "canonical poets."[8] He often

8. Letter to Leo Baker, April 1920. Lewis's unpublished letters are contained in the Bodleian Library, Oxford, and in the Marion E. Wade Center at Wheaton College, Wheaton, Illinois, each of which has a collection of Lewis manuscripts and copies of originals held by the other.

praised Sir Walter Scott, and, less often, Coventry Patmore.[9] Between Edward Gibbon — whose Romans were eighteenth-century figures — and Lord Macaulay, historians had gained a sense of period from reading the Waverley novels.[10] At each rereading he found Wordsworth's *Prelude* "a little better" than expected, and he continued to mention Matthew Arnold's *Sohrab and Rustum* and, of course, the fiction of Williams and MacDonald. In 1951 he proclaimed the nineteenth century "almost" his favorite period,[11] and three years later he rated the novels of Scott and Dickens far above those of Thackeray, singling out the prodigality of invention in *Bleak House*.[12]

Unmentioned and perhaps unvalued by Lewis was his talent for pastiche. Apart from several poems published in *Punch* under his pseudonym "N.W.," this found expression in correspondence in Maloryese with the novelist E. R. Eddison during the winter of 1942-43 and briefly in correspondence with Barfield in 1950. Following his necessary but frustrating practice, Lewis discarded Eddison's typed letters after replying. Eddison's drafts being rendered almost illegible by numerous insertions and erasures, the correspondence is difficult to report in detail. Lewis began it by praising Eddison's *Worm Ouroboros* (1922), comparing it to works by Homer and Morris, and venting his dislike of poems by Swinburne, Eliot, Pound, and Lawrence. As the exchange continued, Lewis saw Eddison's writing as a blend of Homeric, Morrisian, and Swinburnian. Their friendship culminated in a visit by Eddison and his wife to Magdalen College and an evening with Tolkien, Williams, and W. H. Lewis. Both observed medieval conventions and phraseology. Eddison's "ladye," for example, was to "lye" in the College's "guest-chambre." The last such letter came from Lewis in September 1943, but in April Eddison had used modern English when praising the "comfortable warmth" of Lewis's imagination in *Perelandra*. The

9. See, for example, a letter to Owen Barfield dated 10 June 1930, in *Letters of C. S. Lewis*, 141. In a letter to Sister Penelope of 19 November 1941 he described Scott as "perfect . . . in his own range." To Ruth Pitter on 20 August 1962 he spoke of Patmore as a "great poet" in a "narrow field."

10. Letter to Harry Blamires, 12 October 1945.

11. Letter to Ruth Pitter, 29 December 1951.

12. Letters to Alan Richard Griffiths, 23 and 30 January (*Letters of C. S. Lewis*, 254-55) and 5 November 1954.

correspondence ended in April 1944, after Lewis had dined with Eddison, who died the following August.[13]

In a foreword to Eddison's *Mezentian Gate,* Lewis says that rarely does an author open for a middle-aged reader that "door" so readily opened in childhood and adolescence. A new "literary species," Eddison's "heroic romances" were establishing a "new rhetoric" and "climate of the imagination." Their uniqueness lay in their blend of "hardness and luxury," "lawless speculation," and "sharply-realized detail," cynicism, and magnanimity. While these qualities can be detected in Lewis's own *That Hideous Strength* and unfinished "Dark Tower," an unpleasant sexual fantasy that has of late received undeserved attention,[14] the *Worm Ouroboros* has more of the nobility Lewis valued in the *Lord of the Rings.* In his own fiction for adults he attained this, if anywhere, in the Narnian tales and *Till We Have Faces.* To Greeves, Barfield, and the science-fiction writer Arthur Clarke he praised the fantasies of Wells.

His enjoyment of some books was transient. During the 1940s he fell in love with the fantasy novels of Eddison, in which he found a "startling greatness" save for a "horrid" strain of "Aphrodite mysticism."[15] Thereafter he scarcely mentioned them. In the late 1920s he somewhat oddly rated Edith Sitwell with Milton, Thomas Hood, and Robert Southey.[16] Later he praised Kafka's *Castle.* In 1930 he recommended to Greeves the *Precious Bane* of Mary Webb (*They Stand Together,* 362), which had attracted him by its rural flavor. In his next letter, he cites Tolkien's remark that what had been local "earth, air and corn really was *in*" people of the past, whereas moderns, on their cosmopolitan diet, were "artificial beings" compounded of no special place on earth (364).

13. Drafts of Eddison's letters can be found in the Leeds Public Library.

14. Lewis, *"The Dark Tower" and Other Stories,* ed. Walter Hooper. The authenticity of this story has been questioned by Kathryn Lindskoog in *The C. S. Lewis Hoax,* but the handwriting of the "Dark Tower" manuscript was pronounced genuine in a review of Lindskoog's book by Nicholas Barker in *Essays in Criticism* 40, no. 4 (October 1990): 358-67.

15. Letter to Ruth Pitter, 31 August 1948; in a letter to Mr. Miller, 29 April 1946, Lewis notes the thinness of contemporary prose other than Eddison's.

16. The letter, written to Owen Barfield, is dated 10 September; no year is specified, but it was probably before 9 September 1929, when he describes nursing his father.

Lewis came to admire the *Canterbury Tales* and *Tristram Shandy*, but otherwise his letters rarely indicate a change of taste. Novels by Thackeray, for example, remained out of favor as representing "the world," and soon after finishing the Narnia stories he condemned Lady Castlewood as a "grande dame" thinking herself in no need of rebirth.[17] Though T. S. Eliot had angered him in 1930 by taking six months to reject the originating essay of the *Personal Heresy*, he came to like Eliot while they worked on the *New English Bible;* but he never cared for Eliot's poems.

Lewis distinguished between a writer and his works when calling E. M. Forster the "silliest" of contemporary humanists even while enjoying Forster's novels.[18] He told Sister Penelope in 1943 that authors did not create *ex nihilo,* but merely rearranged "elements" provided by God.[19] Sixteen years later, regarding a recent reworking of a medieval romance, he told Eugene Vinaver that Middle English texts were usually adaptations of older ones and should be taken as they stood, not dissolved into "linguatients."[20] Here Lewis set his face not just against "originality" but also against what is now called "deconstruction." In a rare instance of shilly-shallying, Lewis immediately withdrew a sneer at Samuel Alexander's concept of an emergent godhead as whatever Nature seemed about to do.[21]

Like most of us, he wrote more frankly in letters than when bent on publication, dismissing T. H. White's *Sword in the Stone* as the product of a "sad, shabby little mind"[22] and calling the recently deceased Dylan Thomas a "drunken, illiterate Welsh foghorn."[23] Having testily declined Ruth Pitter's offer of a new anthology of modern verse on the ground that he did not feel obliged to read contemporary poems he disliked,[24] he can hardly have been intimately acquainted with those of Dylan Thomas. In 1962 he referred to the supercilious

17. Letter to Owen Barfield, 20 August 1945.
18. Letter to Ruth Pitter, 5 March 1955.
19. Letter to Sister Penelope, 20 February 1943, in *Letters of C. S. Lewis,* 203.
20. Letter to Eugene Vinaver, 19 May 1959. The term he uses is not in the *Oxford English Dictionary* but pertains to language or sound.
21. Letter to Ruth Pitter, 4 January 1947.
22. Letter to Brother Every, 11 December 1940.
23. Letter to Ruth Pitter, 22 April 1954.
24. Letter to Ruth Pitter, 6 January 1951, in *Letters of C. S. Lewis,* 225-26.

tone of Matthew Arnold's criticism and to the "yahoo howls" of Leavis, presumably against C. P. Snow's lecture "Two Cultures and the Scientific Revolution."[25] If his usually admiring comments on new poems by Ruth Pitter seem inconsistent with his antipathy to contemporary verse, the explanation probably lies in shared religious beliefs.

We cannot, alas, request a dead writer to explain a comment that was doubtless clear enough to his correspondent. Why, for example, did Lewis reject Keats's famous dictum that nothing can be known as true until it is "proved on our pulses"?[26] What did he have in mind when noting how much literally infernal literature was circulating in 1953?[27] Was he referring to some more recent works than Stapledon's *Star-Maker* (1937)? Eight years before a reviewer called the Leavisite premises of the concluding volume of the *Pelican Guide to English Literature* a "party line," the target of Lewis's remark that those in need of a lecture called "Return to Poetic Law" judged an idea's merit on whether it came from "one of the Party or an outsider"[28] is unspecified.

We are spared this frustration when Lewis comments on contemporary affairs or on religious issues, the reference being common knowledge. American correspondents heard much about the shortcomings of the postwar Labour government, yet some gentler and more balanced comments in 1958 and 1959 show him taking account of experience. Despite having called that regime the "Farewell State," on reading that Mary Shelburne could not afford medical treatment he retracted the "hard things" he had said about the National Health Service. Despite all the needless calls upon doctors, it was "better than leaving people to sink or swim."[29] He told the journalist Dan Tucker that as politicians

---

25. Letter to George Watson, 12 May 1962. Leavis's response to Snow was presented in the 1962 Richmond Lecture, Downing College, Cambridge; it was not intended for publication, but was published in the *Spectator,* 9 March 1962, 297-303. See William Walsh, *F. R. Leavis,* 36-37.

26. Letter to Brother Every, 11 December 1940.

27. Letter to W. L. Kinter, 15 September 1953.

28. Letter to Ruth Pitter, 2 January 1953. Philip Toynbee's review of the *Pelican Guide to English Literature,* vol. 7, appeared in the (Sunday) *Observer* upon its publication (1961).

29. Letter to Mary Willis Shelburne, 7 July 1959, in *Letters to an American Lady,* 81-82.

attain power by offering relief from the prevalent anxiety, the Labour Party had promised freedom from the fear of poverty, and that its Welfare State provided everyone with "a square meal" and "decent" housing.[30] Lewis never quite shared the nineteenth-century optimism about democracy as a panacea; in 1940 he pronounced himself a democrat because postlapsarian rulers could not be trusted with absolute power.[31] Yet now, he told Tucker, "real" issues were settled in secret, while the press entertained the public with spurious ones. Democracy had ruined the American educational system and was undermining the British one.

He was equally ambivalent about ambition. In 1949, he told Firor that in youth he had rightly preferred winning professional renown to merely wishing for it. Three months later he cast doubt on the modern view of ambition as a virtue. Until the eighteenth century, "gentry and labourers" coexisted with integrity "outside the rat-race." To spread the "good life" might be to destroy it.[32] This recalls the "purer epoch" he thought represented by the older fellows of Magdalen College in the late 1920s, as depicted in *That Hideous Strength*.[33]

When the science fiction writer Arthur Clarke criticized his portrayal of Weston in the first two space novels, Lewis described amoral technocracy as a potential "cancer."[34] In 1959, he foresaw scientists gaining power as a result of general anxiety about overpopulation.[35] Lewis was equally pessimistic about the future of Britain and Europe, but at the height of the "communist conspiracy" theory he reported to Edward Allen that a Western journalist had found the Russians just as fearful of an American attack on them.[36]

Naturally, more original ideas came through personal experience. In 1929, while nursing his terminally ill father, he candidly remarked to Barfield that intimacy with a woman need not imply familiarity, for which "*storge* or *eros*" was requisite. But having "talked to a man about his

30. Letter to Dan Tucker, 8 December 1959.
31. Letter to Brother Every, 11 December 1940.
32. Letters to Dr. Firor, 5 December 1949 and 12 March 1950.
33. Letter to Owen Barfield, probably sometime in 1928, discussing Weldon.
34. Letter to Arthur Clarke, 7 December (1953? before sequence dated 1954).
35. Letter to Dan Tucker, 8 December 1959.
36. Letter to Edward Allen, 20 December 1954.

soul" one could without embarrassment help him use a catheter. Though his father was not in pain, they had so little in common that Lewis found nursing him "almost unendurable."[37] Here is the seed of *The Four Loves,* published some thirty years later. His longing for his mother and troubled relationship with his father partially explains his preoccupation with *Sohrab and Rustum,* his puzzlement as to why he found that poem's simple sentences linked by "and" almost heartbreaking.[38] To his conflict with Barfield over anthroposophy he owed his perception of three "perennial" worldviews: materialism from Democritus to Marx, "high Paganism" from Iamblichus to Steiner, and Christianity.[39]

Though unable to read biographies for pleasure,[40] Lewis was unusually preoccupied with the phases of human life. In the same letter to Barfield, he referred to his "ignoble" adolescence.[41] In 1953, he told a recently bereaved widow of having felt a "cold blast" of insecurity "on the naked heath" when his mother died, so that there was still much of "mummy's little boy" about him.[42] In 1948, he speculated to Ruth Pitter that the "experiences of youth" seemed isolated and therefore suitably conveyed in lyrics, while those of age seemed "woven into wholes" and demanded the long poem, a *Winter's Tale* or *Samson Agonistes.*[43] In 1942, he noted the quick passage of time as a sign of aging,[44] and in 1948 he mentioned the inability to read new verse as another such sign.[45] In 1951, he felt more inclined to read prose than verse because of his age, yet he did not wish himself younger.[46] By 1962, osteoporosis had rendered him too "old" and "stiff" to form letters properly.[47] Premature old age in Lewis can be

---

37. Letter to Owen Barfield, 9 September 1929; the first two quotations are found in *Letters of C. S. Lewis,* 137.
38. Letter to Ruth Pitter, 6 December 1948.
39. Letter to Rev. W. Wylie, 28 March 1958.
40. Letter to Dr. Firor, 14 April 1950.
41. Letter to Owen Barfield, 9 September 1929, in *Letters of C. S. Lewis,* 138.
42. Letter to Mrs. Sandeman, 31 December 1953.
43. Letter to Ruth Pitter, 11 December 1948.
44. Letter to Sister Penelope, 22 December 1942.
45. Letter to Owen Barfield, 10 November 1948.
46. Letter to Ruth Pitter, 29 December 1951.
47. Letter to Mr. Green (not R. L. Green), 21 June 1962.

ascribed to overwork, worry, and bereavement, but also to a kind of self-conditioning.

Religious and Personal Counseling

On some occasions Lewis offered primarily religious advice, as when he pointed out to a woman feeling victimized by a supervisor that the New Testament dwells more on Christ's humiliation than on his other sufferings. On other occasions, as when he advised another woman against resigning her university position, his counsel was wholly personal and secular. In many letters, however, he found himself dispensing both religious and personal advice.

This was especially the case in his longest correspondence with anyone but a personal friend. *Letters to an American Lady*[48] gives abundant evidence of his kindness and tact. In 1950 Mary Willis Shelburne, widow and minor author, wrote from Georgia praising his books and confiding her troubles. Feeling bound to encourage a fellow Christian, Lewis responded by seeing evidence of divine help in her freedom from bitterness. Two years later, upon her conversion to Roman Catholicism, he remarked that "real" believers of any persuasion had more in common than "liberalizing" half-believers (11). Thereafter he took examples from Catholic devotional writers, pictured his move from the Oxford to the Cambridge college of St. Mary Magdalene as a journey under that saint's protection, and wrote as a fellow believer in Purgatory. Save when preoccupied with examinations, Christmas mail, or Joy's illness, he wrote monthly until 30 August 1963, by which time his illness permitted no more than "a wave of the hand" (121). Occasionally Warnie, Joy, or Walter Hooper wrote on his behalf.

Mrs. Shelburne told of difficulties with colleagues and supervisors, financial troubles resulting from spells of unemployment, her reluctance to accept aid from relatives, and her illnesses. In response he offered a diagnosis of "disagreeable" people as reassuring themselves of their

---

48. The manuscript can be found in the Wade Collection at Wheaton College. Page references given parenthetically in the text are from the edition published by Eerdmans.

status by arrogance; a recollection of being persecuted as a schoolboy, army trainee, and junior don; and advice on controlling anger. In 1953 a congratulatory letter on her finding work begins with charming immediacy, "Oh, I am glad, I am glad" (21). As Barfield remarks, to read his letters was to hear his voice.[49] Upon the abolition of currency regulations, he directed Barfield to send her a small sum at Christmas 1958; by March 1961 he had instructed his American publishers to pay her a monthly allowance. Her accounts of medical and dental expenses made him retract his aspersions on the Welfare State (113, 69, 81). When she balked at accepting support from her family, then at entering a retirement home, he pointed out how dependent on the labor of others was anyone of independent means. Yet he harbored no illusions, for when appealing on her behalf to her "nephew" Hugh Kilmer, he described her as "silly, tiresome and probably disagreeable" yet "old, poor, sick, lonely and miserable."[50]

To speak of epistolary strategies would represent Lewis as more deliberate than he was. The impetuous openings, "Oh, I do so sympathize" (on seeking work; 20), or "Oh, what bad luck!" (on dental bills while unemployed; 67), come from a busy man, but one able to feel for a woman he had never met as if she sat before him. Likewise a dismissive ending from 6 April 1962, "Sorry you've run into more trouble" (100), betrays both an invalid's fatigue and patience worn thin. More deliberate was the empathy in "You and I" being lovers of fairytales and therefore immune from nostalgia for childhood, or in the rhetorical questions (1961-62) "We must beware of the Past, mustn't we?" (96), on harboring grievances; "Nausea's horrible, isn't it?" (103); and "Like old automobiles, aren't they?" (sick bodies; 107).

If these sound somewhat patronizing, when Lewis remarked that to hear voices was not mere superstition (23), told Irish tales of fairies, described a leprechaun's shoe he had been shown (32), or fancied Purgatory as a vast disorganized kitchen (103), he was not pretending.

49. *Owen Barfield on C. S. Lewis,* 3.

50. Mrs. Shelburne was a friend and honorary "aunt" of the Kilmer family. Hugh Kilmer comments on Lewis's letter of 17 February 1961 that Lewis forgot that Mrs. Shelburne had encouraged the children to write to him about the Chronicles of Narnia.

From the kitchen image, he inferred that a female convalescent must learn "to sit still," and a male to spring into action. Such distinctions may have been based on his experience of Mrs. Moore and her many maidservants. Belief in action for action's sake, he said, was characteristic of Mrs. Shelburne's generation, country, and sex. Misplaced zeal at work might spring from self-importance. The letter ends wittily, "Just you give Mary a little chance, as well as Martha" (51). Within two months Mary was again looking for work — one hopes that she did not lose her job through following this advice.[51] Had he felt to blame, Lewis would surely have apologized, but earlier advice to lament misfortune with a "good honest howl" (25) appears sounder.

By 1962 he excused his brief replies on the ground that men hate letter writing while women love it (101). Certainly Lewis hated his self-imposed slavery. At Christmas or Easter he would complain of endless pen-pushing with a rheumatic hand and implore Mary to avoid writing then. One letter to her was his eighth that day, another the tenth. In one he complained that it was already 11:25 and "Not a stroke of my own work done" (45).

Out of compassion he encouraged and reassured a woman easily hurt. In a quarrel, he advised, she should seat everyone and try to slow their speech. As the atheist Bertrand Russell concluded his farewell appearance on television by advising viewers "Love is wise; hatred is foolish," so Lewis told his fellow Christian that her loving self was "good," her angry self "infernal" (90). He would dwell on praiseworthy features in the poems and stories she sent, while briefly mentioning defects. To offer such responses without forfeiting the goodwill of a writer reduced to poverty was no mean feat. He sought to cool apprehensions, whether material or spiritual, by assurances that God would strengthen her to bear actual and present ills, not those she foresaw (57). Since she could not change her circumstances, and only God could change herself, she should stop fretting about her condition (46). As her conception had resulted from a sexual act, rather than feelings of love, so God's presence did not depend on her awareness. She could not love animals or plants too much, only God

51. Advice given 19 March 1956. On 15 April, sympathy at a "shock" she received, along with the loss of her job, mentioned on 21 May.

too little. If her devotions seemed barren, she should listen to God rather than talk.

Lewis used the conception image the year before his civil marriage to Joy. Even before his ex-pupil Fr. Bide conducted a marriage service at her hospital bedside in March 1957, he applied Joy's prospect of death to himself and Mary in a way that drew uneasy protests. One day Mary's tribulation would be all over (62). The last-minute payment of her rent was a divine mercy, but "in a comparatively few years" they would "all be out of it" (63). Soon after a laying-on of hands by Fr. Bide, Joy began to recover while Lewis suffered pains akin to hers and heard a rumor of his own death (65).

Showing an increasing and self-referring concern, he asked why he should avoid mentioning death, which awaited them both. As Joy continued to recover, he consoled Mary for her worries by quoting "Sufficient unto the day . . ." and looking to their joint awakening from the "nightmare" of this existence (67). The following year, when told of Mary's dental treatment, he pictured the body as an old car to be replaced by a new model at the resurrection (75). In May 1959 he asked her to pray for Fr. Bide, whose wife had cancer, and in June asked why she should think it "morbid" to look forward to the divine summons. The modern and "healthy" attitude to death was more "uneasy and precarious" than either fear or desire (81). In October he reported that their "reprieve" from Joy's cancer was over (85); the next April he gave a brief, poignant account of Attica and Rhodes, comparing the tour to a "last breakfast" prior to execution (88).

In the end, the condemned man was Lewis, who never recovered from the death of Joy. Douglas Gresham, summoned from school, found his stepfather visibly aged and shrunk.[52] To Mary, Lewis described his bereft existence as sleepwalking, and he pictured grief as a journey with a new prospect round each bend. As in *A Grief Observed*, he recorded that his most urgent prayers received no answer, and that he felt nearest to Joy when not seeking her presence (89). In March 1961 he told Mary to set her mind on ceasing to exist as a person. In January 1962 he thought that by prolonging life modern medicine had made old age bleaker, and in November 1962 he again called

52. Douglas Gresham, *Lenten Lands*, 127.

their bodies "old rattletraps" (108) about which they sentimentalized as about old cars. By March 1963, he contemplated death without fear, asking what he and Mary had "to do but make" their exits (111). Next month he responded to her protest by asking what had distressed her about an "old man" telling an "old woman" this "obvious fact" (112). Two months later, he felt "overjoyed" at a "blessed change" in her feelings about death, wondered why doctors, or even God, tormented patients by keeping them alive and pitied her for recovering from an illness still "on the wrong side of the door" (115). In September he repeated the image to Greeves, after coming around from a coma (*They Stand Together,* 566). The act of marrying a woman who, like his mother, was intellectually gifted and stricken with cancer induced a death wish that resurfaced following her death, and which, with the kindest intention, he communicated to his American correspondent.

Literary Advising

Lewis conducted both two-way and one-way literary correspondence. With those outside academic life — Mary Shelburne or Sister Penelope — and the poet-academic Kathleen Raine, he exchanged and commented on drafts. His former students Harry Blamires and Martyn Skinner he simply advised. His earliest two-way relationship was, of course, with Owen Barfield, but his most sustained in middle life was with Ruth Pitter. Introduced in 1946 by the poet Herbert Palmer, they met only in company and took until 1953 to use first names. As a nongraduate poet and furniture painter, Miss Pitter might well stand in awe of the famous literary scholar whose broadcasts had converted her to Christianity, but as poet Lewis deferred to her, her poetic mentor being his fellow Inkling Lord David Cecil.[53]

On 29 July 1946 Lewis praised her volume *Trophy of Arms* (1936) for a classical coolness recalling the Lady in Milton's *Comus.* Several of his comments suggest a sensibility fixated in the past. Inverted rhythms in opening stanzas of "Help, Good Shepherd" (*Trophy of*

---

53. Arthur Russell, ed., *Ruth Pitter: Homage to a Poet,* 38.

Arms, 27) reverberate within as few verses since the Middle Ages. In "A Certain Philosophy" (59-60), though "raiment" is a poeticism, no other word will suffice, since no single author can heal the "wound in the language." With perhaps unintended ambiguity, he says that "cadaverous" in "Storm" (18-20) explores "regions" unvisited in verse for a century.

For the next seven years, Miss Pitter sent him copies or drafts of each book as she produced it. Lewis's remark on encountering "old friends" in *Urania* (1950) might refer either to her sending drafts or to her habit of republishing poems. The most revealing comments came early in the friendship. "Love and the Child" is the best poem to result from the work of that "woolly old wiseacre" Freud.[54] Despite how well "Cygnet"[55] deals with air-raids, large-scale destruction never works in literary texts: a million deaths are less tragic and ten ghosts less "disquieting" than one. On "Persephone in Hades," Lewis remarks how difficult it is to make a poem of a tale already poetic, hence the inferiority of Arnold's *Balder Dead* to his *Sohrab and Rustum.* Great myths survive best in allusions. Sometimes he cites parallels to phrases, such as "death's filthy garment," also in "Cygnet."

Some poems provoke him to justify deep-seated convictions. To "Funeral Wreaths"[56] he responds, "No, no, no, no. The moderns have got at you," going on to say that "sordid facts in sub-poetical rhythms" do not a poem make.[57] Illustrating the value of noun-metaphors from Donne and Shakespeare, he finds "perfection" attainable in various modes — language rough or smooth, metaphorical or literal, colloquial or rhetorical — and commends Barfield's *Poetic Diction.*[58] Stephen Spender's objection to "willed" as distinct from spontaneous poetry is plainly wrong, for both "ritual" and "frolic" have their places. Lewis attacks subjectivism, yet leaves room for reader response. Poets do not create but like mothers bear works fathered by the cosmos. Like grown-

54. Letter to Ruth Pitter, 29 July 1946. Ruth Pitter, "Love and the Child," in *Collected Poems,* 103 (originally published in 1939 under the title *The Spirit Watches*).
55. Ruth Pitter, "Cygnet," in *The Bridge,* 11-16; reprinted in Ruth Pitter, *Urania,* 121-28.
56. Pitter, "Funeral Wreaths," in *The Bridge,* 58f.; *Urania,* 171f.
57. Letter to Ruth Pitter, 29 July 1946.
58. Letter to Ruth Pitter, 10 August 1946.

up children, their poems will make their own "friends" after their "parents" have died.[59] How Miss Pitter valued his advice can be judged from her comment that as a critic Lewis was "not fallible in any way that self-discipline could remedy."[60]

On his own poems, his deference to her opinion was not absolute. When she used one as a "source," he responded that he understood how Lodge might have felt at being drawn on for *As You Like It*. But although she chose one of two drafts of Lewis's poem "Two Kinds of Memory," the published text includes lines from each.[61] In July 1946, he sent drafts on which he requested an opinion as to whether they were "real poems" or whether "content and form" remained "separable." In a memorandum dated two years later she mused on whether his learning inhibited his poetry. Did Lewis "catch some bit of emotional thistledown (like most of us)" and proceed from that, or did he "plan . . . like an architect"? He had "the makings of a poet": a "strong visual memory," childhood "recollections," "yearnings for a lost Paradise," a "primitive intuition of the diabolical," and a "child's sense of glory and nightmare." His "adult disciplines," however, "inhibited his poetry, which is, perhaps . . . most evident in his prose."[62] Miss Pitter seems to equate poetic talent with romanticism.

Most aspiring authors who sent manuscripts received the sound advice on writing noted earlier. Upon reading the script of a play for children by Sister Penelope, he suggested, in the vein of Eliot, that symbols could enter the mind of readers before being understood, that the "deepest truths" did so as "arbitrary marvels" rather than as "theorems."[63] Occasionally, as with her translation from Athanasius, he gave successful advice on publishers.[64]

---

59. Letter to Ruth Pitter, 10 August 1946.

60. The comment appears in a note appended to a letter from Lewis dated 12 February 1947 on her poem "Persephone."

61. Lewis, "Two Kinds of Memory," *Time and Tide* 28 (7 August 1947): 859; *Poems*, 100-101.

62. This memorandum from Ruth Pitter can be found in the Bodleian (File III, no. 63).

63. Letter to Sister Penelope, 25 March 1943.

64. Sister Penelope's translation of *De Incarnatione* was rejected by SPCK but submitted to Blès on Lewis's advice of 20 February 1943.

The issue in another case was less fortunate. Between 1945 and 1955 his former pupil Harry Blamires sought advice on various book manuscripts. The first, "Scott and His Predecessors," was conceived in two parts dealing with earlier novelists and with Scott. On hearing of the project, Lewis said Blamires had "struck gold," but he should make more of Scott as a historical novelist, for the Waverley novels had created a sense of period. He objected to Blamires's disparagement of Jane Austen, noting shrewdly that critics would pounce on this point to the neglect of any merits in the book.[65] Four years later, he declined to write a preface but agreed to read the typescript,[66] discussed his findings over dinner,[67] and in a brief commentary advised Blamires to avoid portraying Scott as more egalitarian than he was. He also objected to novel-by-novel treatment as being repetitious, suggesting as alternatives a chapter each on the greatest novels, chapters on the best in several groups, or treatment by topic. Blamires complied, with disastrous results, for he cut up and rearranged the typescript only to have his revised version rejected. Having kept no copy of the original, he felt unable to start again. In his view he received advice from a scholar able to "flit about," on a work intended for less learned readers.[68]

Evidently the two remained on good terms, for a year later Lewis advised Blamires not to rewrite a manuscript on "English in Education" but simply to correct and resubmit it to Geoffrey Bles, whose memory, *"entre nous,"* would not suffice to tell how far it had been changed. Though again asked for a preface, Lewis agreed only to supply a paragraph for the blurb, pleading preoccupation with another preface, the hostility of the educational world, and a crippling accumulation of "little jobs."[69] In 1952, he commented in detail on Blamires's manuscript "A Christian Philosophy of Education" but suggested the deletion of compliments to himself in its preface, as the association would "damn" Blamires "with certain reviewers."[70] In

65. Letter to Harry Blamires, 12 October 1945.
66. Letter to Harry Blamires, 14 November 1949.
67. Mentioned in a letter of 12 December 1949.
68. Comments by Blamires were prefixed to a group of letters from Lewis.
69. Letter to Harry Blamires, 18 October 1950.
70. Letter to Harry Blamires, 19 January 1952.

1954, praising the moral theology of Blamires's religious fantasy *The Devil's Hunting-Grounds,* he noted the "blessed paradox" that "our pupils" were devastated not by our snubs but by our "dealing dispassionately with the facts." Necessary as humiliation may be, the "*intention* to humiliate, being wicked, is always frustrated."[71] Later that year, he declined Blamires's offer to dedicate a new book to him, again because the more Blamires was associated with himself, the less original he would be considered by reviewers.[72] In 1955 he offered brief but discriminating comments on the manuscript of "The Cold War in Hell," and later that year (12 December) he commiserated on the cool reception of Blamires's trilogy. He recalled his own disappointment while first unpublished, then unnoticed, as a kind of bereavement. Blamires should lay his disappointment "before God," who would either treat it as real or reduce it to its proper proportion. As it turned out, the disappointment was less severe than Lewis supposed, since several of Blamires's books were taken up in the United States by the Episcopal Book Club.

Seven years into the relationship, Lewis invited Blamires to use his surname, but never first names as with some American correspondents; he seemed more comfortable with intimacy at a distance. Likewise he used surnames in occasional correspondence over twenty years with the poet Martyn Skinner, whose *Letters to Malaya* enjoyed a vogue in the 1940s. In 1941 Lewis defended the Popean couplets of Skinner's *Sir Elfadore and Mabyna* (1935) as "still" among "the best ways of getting things said."[73] The following year he defended the *Problem of Pain* as extending the Keatsian image of this world as "a vale of soul-making,"[74] and when Skinner praised *The Abolition of Man* he disclosed that "Gaius" and "Titus" taught in Australia.

After praising *Letters to Malaya,* Lewis suggested a poem on King Arthur's return to modern Britain as a vehicle for Skinner's satire and fantasy. He offered as plot a sequence of episodes culminating in the arising of the mysterious but hitherto disguised and ridiculed king to

71. Letter to Harry Blamires, 14 March 1954.
72. Letter to Harry Blamires, 8 October 1954.
73. Letter to a Mr. Saunders, 22 March 1941.
74. Letter to Martyn Skinner, 23 April 1942.

slay his enemies like Odysseus.[75] In June 1951 he praised *Merlin,* partly read in a borrowed copy, as Skinner's best work yet, far superior in wit and invention to "dreary modern-orthodox" poems he had tried in vain to enjoy. Though dismayed to think "how little chance of a fair hearing" long poems stood at that time, he advised Skinner to finish his "Tartarology" whatever critics might say.

Generally Lewis focused on words and phrases, but in 1959 he praised episodes in the first two parts of the *Return of Arthur* as blows for the "right side" in an action hitherto controlled by "the enemy," presumably secular humanism. But what demon, he asked, had led Skinner to make Arthur speak "like a leading article?"[76] The Christmas mail rush and return of Joy's cancer, mentioned in the letter, made him less tactful than usual. In particular, he regarded dialogue in the style of Byron's *Don Juan* as suited only to vulgar or depraved characters. He also told Skinner to stop assigning his best dialogue to Arthur's foes and to find a style suitable for "great and wise and almost numinous" speakers. Skinner recalls being so enraged that he thought he had destroyed the letter. When told that such elevated speech was outside Skinner's range, Lewis fired off a postcard beginning "Stuff and nonsense" and instructing him to make Arthur "grope" for words like a noble but "inarticulate peasant."[77]

Commenting on the letters, Skinner calls Lewis "prodigiously kind" and explains that only upon receiving the criticisms had he learned how much Lewis loathed the neoclassical and *Don Juan* styles and realized his critical "generosity." After Lewis's death, his brother complimented Skinner on the completed poem.[78]

Lewis's seven-year occasional correspondence with the poet and academic Kathleen Raine included some quintessential aphorisms. It began in April 1956 when she sent Lewis some poems. In his reply Lewis at once struck the right note for a poet of Scots and Northumbrian descent by comparing them to a Highland walk, "cold, bright,"

<hr>

75. Letters to Martyn Skinner, 5 November and 1 December 1947.
76. Letter to Martyn Skinner, 31 December 1959, on *The Return of Arthur,* book 2, canto 7.
77. Letter to Martyn Skinner, 6 January 1960.
78. Letter from W. H. Lewis to Martyn Skinner, 11 April 1960.

and with a "dark earth-taste."[79] Some months later her compliments on *Till We Have Faces* elicited an account of Orual that we will discuss in the next section.[80] During her brief marriage to the poet Charles Madge, he used her married name when apologizing for taking some time to read "One Foot in Eden," which enchanted him despite "intolerable metre" and "flat" diction.[81] By May 1958 he used the transitional "Kathleen Raine" when approving the argument of her "Blakiana" and pointing to the "unclassical nature" of classical verse.[82] Later that year, he predicted that her critical commentary on Blake would render previous ones obsolete. "A good commentator," he added, "is worth a wilderness of evaluative critics."[83]

By the following summer, he was using first names when advising her against a probably irreversible departure from Cambridge following a disappointment. Being able to write poems, she would do so wherever she lived, but the hope of renewing her muse where it first came might prove delusory.[84] Ms. Raine stayed and remained grateful for his good advice. Responding to her letter of condolence on Joy's death, Lewis called them fellow members of a "secret society," presumably of Christian academics, who should "beware" of esotericist "phenomena."[85] In a postcard soon after, he compared her illegible signature to "the peace of God" and wondered whether some undergraduate fan mail for his *Experiment in Criticism* indicated a turn of the tide at Cambridge.[86] A fortnight before his death, he praised her latest work on Blake in what proved to be his final words on literary scholarship: "Plenty of fact, reasoning as brief and clear as English sunshine, and no personal comment at all."[87]

79. Letter to Kathleen Raine, 11 April 1956.

80. Letter to Kathleen Raine, 5 October 1956.

81. Letter to Kathleen Raine, 7 November 1957.

82. Letter to Kathleen Raine, 12 May 1958.

83. Letter to Kathleen Raine, 5 December 1958. Raine's commentary on Blake was a work in progress, including, among other works, *Blake and Tradition* (1964).

84. Letter to Kathleen Raine, 19 June 1959, in *Letters of C. S. Lewis,* 288.

85. Letter to Kathleen Raine, 8 August 1960.

86. Letter to Kathleen Raine, 25 October, year omitted.

87. Letter to Kathleen Raine, 7 November 1963, on the Andrew Mellon Lecture "Blake and Tradition," delivered in 1962 and published in 1968.

Self-Interpretation

Kathleen Raine's compliments on *Till We Have Faces* must have given especial pleasure as coming from a fellow Platonist and lover of myth. In his response, Lewis explained that Orual differed from the archetypal amazon in being sexually unattractive. Forced into the roles of ruler and warrior, she suffered agonies both on being treated as male and on killing her first man. He added examples of the woman-combatant archetype and expounded Orual's concept of Psyche as bride and enemy.[88]

Many of his self-interpretive comments have been mentioned in preceding chapters. Those noted here result from reader response, from hindsight, or from writing in progress. He several times expressed pleasure at the understanding shown by "scores of children" of the Narnian stories, and especially of Aslan.[89] Answering one letter the day before his death, he claimed that children always but adults never understood that Aslan was the Christ of Narnia.[90] He was astonished how young were some who read the sombre *Silver Chair*.[91] While answering a girl's objection to Edmund's word "kids" in *Prince Caspian,* he inquired whether her younger brother had been scared by the Dark Island episode in *The Voyage of the "Dawn Treader,"* retained because no author could know for certain what would frighten children.[92] His surviving letters bear out his claim that children care only about the story, never about the author or his intentions.[93] Only adults required him to interpret archetypes and symbols such as the Witch and the Stone Table,[94] explain that eldila were not fairies but angels,[95] or categorize the Chronicles as romance, not allegory.[96]

Sometimes an idea from a text still to be written, or recently

88. Letter to Kathleen Raine, 5 October 1956.
89. Letter to Miss Carlson, 26 April 1962.
90. Letter to Phillip Thompson, 21 November 1963.
91. Letter to Harry Blamires, 14 March 1954.
92. Letter to Phyllida, 14 September 1953.
93. Letter to Ruth Pitter, 28 November 1950.
94. Letter to W. L. Kinter, 30 July 1954.
95. Letter to W. L. Kinter, 22 January 1957.
96. Letter to Miss Hook, 29 December 1958, in *Letters of C. S. Lewis,* 283-84.

published, will lie hidden in a letter. In 1956, three years after his *Silver Chair* but five before his *Experiment in Criticism,* he answered a query about masturbation by saying that imagination should deliver us from our "little dark prison" so as to attain virtue, success, or distinction not in egocentric fantasy but in real life.[97] His self-description as a compulsive writer would ring true at any time, but reflections on his own writing vary according to time and circumstance. When he argued cryptically that a novelist finds virtue more difficult to portray than vice, because to imagine conduct worse than his own he need only desist from acting, whereas to imagine better conduct he must act, he was addressing a nun interested in moral theology, while Britain was bracing for war.[98] In 1946, at the height of his popularity as a religious apologist, he expected to be remembered not for the *Allegory of Love* but for the *Problem of Pain* and *Screwtape Letters.*[99] In 1948 an American correspondent had only just heard of his renown as literary scholar.[100]

Most comments on his own career come from an author well established or nearing retirement. In 1943, sympathizing with Sister Penelope, he recalls the many manuscripts rejected in his youth.[101] In 1947, upon having a poem rejected, he notes having forgotten the flavor of the "little printed slip." In 1946, his preference for American reviewers because "they do read the book" was based on considerable experience.[102] Still more was the advice to a younger academic in 1962 to disregard critical reconstructions of a work's composition, which in his own case had "never once been right."[103] His account of composing stories from mental "pictures" of unknown origin[104] and his predilection for *Perelandra* and *Till We Have Faces*[105] are familiar enough, but his claim to have chiefly enjoyed writing fic-

97. Letter to Mr. Masson, 3 June 1956.
98. Letter to Sister Penelope, 5 August 1939.
99. Letter to Dr. T. Wilkinson Riddle, 16 July 1946.
100. Letter to Edward Allen, 20 April 1948.
101. Letter to Sister Penelope, 5 October 1943.
102. Letters to Ruth Pitter, 4 January 1947 and 24 September 1946.
103. Letter to George Watson, 12 May 1962.
104. Letter to Miss Salzberg, 5 February 1960.
105. Letter to Miss Lee, 6 December 1960.

tion[106] suggests either fond recollections of working with Joy or that his aversion to writing the *Screwtape Letters* applied only to works written to order. A sense, no doubt, of being driven from within rather than without led him to judge *Perelandra* as worth a score of "Screwtapes."[107]

When about to leave Oxford for Cambridge, Lewis offered a thoughtful and revealing self-description by invitation of the Milton Society of America. First and foremost an "imaginative man," he had vainly sought to become a poet, but for the same reason had responded to poems read by becoming a critic. As imaginative convert to Christianity, he had expressed his convictions in apologetics and mythopoeic or symbolic fiction. Most recently, he had chosen a variant of fairy-tale as best embodying what he "wanted to say." His omission of scholarly curiosity as his motive, and of two great works of literary history as its product, is the more remarkable in a document addressed to a learned society.[108]

106. Letter to Miss Lee, 6 December 1960.

107. In notes compiled for Fr. Peter Milward. No date is given, but the notes refer to the impending publication of *Surprised by Joy* (1955).

108. The paper was written for the "Milton Evening in Honor of Douglas Bush and C. S. Lewis," Conference of the Modern Language Association, 28 December 1954; it was published in *Letters of C. S. Lewis*, 260.

CHAPTER 10

Conclusion

A S CHAUCER WOULD SAY, it is time to make "of my longe tale
an ende." My "entente" has been to look at all sides of Lewis the
born and compulsive writer. Had his circumstances been other than
they were — had his mother or wife lived longer, had his father not
supported him in his postgraduate years, had he married while young,
had he not known Tolkien or Williams — he would have written
otherwise, but only an efficient secret police could have stemmed the
flow of ink from his steel-nibbed pen. I have tried to see how, rather
than why, he set about writing poems, critical books, novels, apologetics, devotional books, essays, and letters, and, while refraining from
religious controversy, to estimate his achievement in various modes of
writing. I have sought also to discover his standing as a critic and scholar
— for example, among students of Milton and Spenser. To write about
Lewis without taking sides in literary controversy seems impossible.

What, in the end, did all his writing amount to? As what kind of
writer is he likely to be remembered? Will he, like Johnson, be remembered as a personality rather than read, or like Coleridge be read by
scholars and students but attacked by those unsympathetic to his tastes
and beliefs? Will his reputation fade as the film *Shadowlands* leaves the
cinema and video store for the film archives, or will some of his books
outlive their critical or religious contexts? The question involves three
subsidiary questions.

If the foregoing chapters have demonstrated anything, it is that academic or literary fashions are repudiated as completely as they were once endorsed, but in time they become sources of new trends, as in the thesis, antithesis, and synthesis of Hegelian and Marxian dialectic. Historical criticism, once all the rage, was denounced by New Critics before being combined with materialist ideology into New Historicism. Microscopic examination by New Critics was disowned by structuralists, only to be intensified by deconstructionists. But critical work based on misstatement or misunderstanding will not survive. First, therefore, what influence are *The Allegory of Love, A Preface to "Paradise Lost," English Literature in the Sixteenth Century, An Experiment in Criticism, The Discarded Image, Spenser's Images of Life, Studies in Medieval and Renaissance Literature,* and *Selected Literary Essays* likely to retain? Second, will any of Lewis's fiction for adults and children survive the social and religious context in which it was written? And third, will he, after all, remain of interest as "moralist, novelist, and critic" in that order, as in the *Everyman's Encyclopaedia* article cited in chapter 1?

As we have seen, Lewis's critical books and essays fall roughly into four groups. The first consists of histories of periods between the twelfth and seventeenth centuries, focusing on prevalent ideas and ethics rather than on political, historical, or biographical considerations. The prime example is *English Literature in the Sixteenth Century, Excluding Drama.* The second group consists of interpretations of specified literary works produced during those centuries, notably *A Preface to "Paradise Lost."* The third includes accounts of more recent works and their authors, such as Addison or Scott. In the fourth group of books and essays, Lewis expounds a mode of literary theory, as in his *An Experiment in Criticism.* Some portions of *English Literature in the Sixteenth Century,* however, exemplify the second kind, while *The Allegory of Love* has elements of both the second and the fourth.

As literary historian Lewis has been challenged for making the influence of ideas and beliefs appear more universal than it was by projecting it from the highly literate to the subliterate classes, notably in *The Discarded Image.* Some critics fault him for allowing his own beliefs, responses, or prejudices to influence his judgment, as in the introduction to *English Literature in the Sixteenth Century* and comments in that book or elsewhere on Shakespeare's sonnets, the poems of Donne, and Bacon's essays and theory of inductive science. What continues to appeal is Lewis's fluency, incisiveness, wit, and power of apt and arresting illustration, not to mention the breadth and exactness of scholarship and historical imagination that make *English Literature in the Sixteenth Century* among the most readable of literary histories and *The Discarded Image* an unsurpassed introduction to medieval literature. More continues to be heard of his contention, in the Cambridge inaugural lecture, that the "great divide" in the history of Western civilization was not the Renaissance but the Enlightenment and Industrial Revolution.

As expository critic, he has been challenged for misunderstandings and wrong emphases in his work on *Paradise Lost* and even the *Faerie Queene* and for a "romantic" interpretation of *Troilus and Criseyde* based on a too-literal reading of clerical satire. The neo-Augustinian interpretation by D. W. Robertson and his disciples being itself under criticism nowadays, the jury is still out on Lewis's reading of *Troilus,* though the phrase "courtly love" sounds distinctly passé. Any critic who values the epics of Milton and Spenser, however, thinks that Lewis's expositions repay scrutiny. Regrettably, his brief studies of Addison, Jane Austen, and Scott are less widely known, but he was mainly responsible for the recent revival of interest in the fantasies of Mac-Donald. His advocacy of twentieth-century mythopoeic authors has either been superfluous, in the case of of Tolkien and Williams, or unavailing, as with E. R. Eddison or Mervyn Peake.

Yet his love of myth and fantasy enabled Lewis to make his most influential and probably most enduring contribution to the theory and practice of criticism. That enthusiasm is discernible not only in his own studies of texts from *Hamlet* to the tales of H. Rider Haggard but also in scores of novels inspired by myth, romance, or science in the middle and late twentieth century. It also underlies his essays on storytelling and on writing for children.

As regards the love-allegory he set out to expound, his theory, once in vogue all over the English-speaking world, has been questioned and even thought to have misled students. Outside schools of English literature, however, the term "courtly love" retains its meaning.

How far the *Experiment in Criticism* is or will remain influential is not easily determined. It was a needed corrective to a strain of evaluative criticism that, while encouraging students to form and justify honest opinions, encouraged arrogant, premature, or superficial judgments by those needing to read more widely and with more open minds. Yet Lewis's own division of readers into "literary" and "unliterary" poses a similar danger of encouraging elitism. The *Experiment* remains valuable, however, for its test of literary merit based on the ability to sustain rereading and for its advocacy of receiving rather than using texts. It is his only critical work that is applicable to other arts, primarily to music.

To some extent our second question, as to the fictional works likely to survive, is answering itself. Fifty years ago any general reader asked to name a book by C. S. Lewis would have responded, *"The Screwtape Letters."* Now the books everyone has heard of are probably the Chronicles of Narnia. *Out of the Silent Planet* was once included in the syllabus of a General Certificate of Education examining board, but like *That Hideous Strength* and even *Perelandra,* it is now read mainly by aficionados of Lewis. The current transition from print to electronic media renders all prediction unsafe, but the novels most deserving of survival are *Till We Have Faces* and *Perelandra,* to both of which Frye's aphorism that all literary texts depend on other literary works is more than usually applicable. Readers of the *Pilgrim's Regress, Great Divorce,* and short stories are now pretty certain to be practicing Christians or academics working on Lewis or his fellow Inklings. This still constitutes a sizeable minority of the reading public, but one unlikely to grow.

The question, then, may be simplified to this: Will the Narnian stories retain their appeal for children? The most probable readers are children of church-going but also of environmentally conscious parents. As Kath Filmer ably demonstrates, the tales show a concern for preservation of forests and of other species that should enhance their appeal to many parents. But the central issue in the Chronicles is the reality of God, the spiritual world, and the afterlife. Because of this, agnostic parents or those conditioned to disbelief by exposure to linguistic analysis, literary theory, or scientific positivism might discourage their children from reading them. It is their Christian worldview, rather than what David Holbrook sees as their violence and antifeminism, that may limit the number of children with access to the Chronicles at home or at school. What cannot be predicted is the effect of transposition to film or television and of discovery by independent-minded children, from whom parental censorship has never yet kept such enthralling tales.

While children who read any of them will probably wish to read the whole series, if only to find out what happens in the end, some tales and characters seem more likely to lose ground than others. That coeducation has become the norm rather than the exception bodes ill for portions of *The Silver Chair*. The continuing erosion of class distinctions could render some of the dialogue in *The Voyage of the "Dawn Treader"* and *The Last Battle* less comprehensible. Yet the love tinged with anxiety that Digory feels for his mother and the enjoyment of poking fun at pretentious adults are so universal among children as to endear *The Magician's Nephew* to even the most secularminded. Any tale can be analyzed in such psychosocial terms, with its obsolescent features set against the quality of its narration and characterization. Two predictions that appear safe are that the appeal of episodes dependent primarily on obedience to directions will diminish as children become less trusting of authority figures or of God, and that those revealing conscious authorial intrusion or religious conditioning will appeal less than those in which Lewis simply found words for images that came from his unconscious or heaven knows where.

The third question, whether Lewis will survive as moralist, has no clear-cut answer. While only an Islamic conquest of the Western world can restore women to what he saw as their role, his view of punishment as retributive, though out of favor among those professionally concerned, is becoming popular in the backlash against crimes of violence. Some of the essays collected in *God in the Dock, Christian Reflections,* and *Present Concerns,* however replete with good sense, however plainly expressed and memorably illustrated, run so counter to the main currents of twentieth-century society that nothing short of a fundamentalist coup seems likely to bring them into prominence. *The Four Loves* is mainly familiar, alas, to churchgoers.

More relevant to present concerns are two issues raised in the *Abolition of Man.* One is the modernist (and postmodernist) conditioning of students to disregard, rather than consciously reject, language pertaining to inward or spiritual states or responses, as being less real and meaningful than verifiable statements pertaining to the external world. A further concern, increasingly important in our heterogeneous society, is raised by the survey of moral injunctions in different religious traditions. Do all the major religions prescribe or condemn essentially the same kinds of behavior? If, as Lewis maintains, something not far removed from the Ten Commandments can be extrapolated from his citations of the *Encyclopaedia of Religion and Ethics* as acceptable to Jew, Christian, Muslim, Hindu, and Buddhist alike, a case could be made for filling the present vacuum in the teaching of ethics in secular schools without impinging on the rights of religious minorities.

The two issues become one insofar as the devaluation of nonreferential language threatens not only to impoverish the emotional and imaginative lives of students but to blunt their moral sensibilities. To cite an extreme instance, upon my saying that to knock down an old lady and steal her handbag was by any standard wrong, a young woman student replied that I had merely expressed my "point of view." Neither I nor her fellow students could convince her that moral statements could be anything but subjective. Conversely, widespread and systematic teaching by literary theorists that individuals are totally conditioned by their society and its language, that talk of the autonomous psyche, or soul, is meaningless metaphysics, can only exacerbate the danger so dramatically conveyed in Lewis's title. So long as deconstructionism, with its opposed but symbiotic extremes of unrestrained licence to reinterpret texts and incipient totalitarianism, continues to exert its remaining influence in university courses, so long will "The Poison of Subjectivism" and *The Abolition of Man* remain necessary counterweights. I wish I could believe what A. D. Nuttall has argued so brilliantly, that subjectivism "lies dead" at the hand of Lewis.[1]

The talk of the Inklings being mostly unrecorded, and the most ebullient of them long interred in Headington churchyard, the personality that speaks to us from some sixty-odd books and countless articles and papers has two faces. One is that of the Dreamer, an ever-curious child or adolescent who was as bent on discovering old poems and romances as on creating other worlds; as critic, he regarded literary texts and literary education as of supreme value in emancipating readers and students from bondage to their time and place. The other face is that of the Mentor, a lecturer who exposed confused thinking or concealed assumptions, a broadcaster who ridiculed unbelief, and a large-hearted counselor who gave all too much time and not a little

1. A. D. Nuttall, "Jack the Giant-Killer."

wealth to fellow Christians in trouble; later in his life the expositions become more patient and less inclined to overconfidence.

The faith in evolutionary progress that Lewis so memorably ridiculed having been exploded by two world wars and a host of smaller ones, it is a pity that he did not live to apply his logic and common sense to predictions concerning the information culture ushered in by the computer and "information superhighway." For he will be remembered, if at all, as one who imparted his love of reading and of making books to numbers of students and readers beyond all computation.

Bibliography

THROUGHOUT the bibliography, the place of publication is London unless otherwise stated.

Works by C. S. Lewis

The Abolition of Man, with Special Reference to the Teaching of English in the Upper Forms of Schools. Oxford University, 1943.

"Addison." In *Essays on the Eighteenth Century Presented to David Nichol Smith.* Oxford: Oxford University, 1945. Reprinted in *Selected Literary Essays,* 154-68.

All My Road Before Me: Diaries of C. S. Lewis, 1923-27. Edited by Walter Hooper. San Diego: Harcourt, Brace, Jovanovich, 1991.

The Allegory of Love: A Study in Medieval Tradition. Oxford University, 1937; revised 1938; reprinted 1948.

"The Anthropological Approach." In *English and Medieval Studies Presented to J. R. R. Tolkien on his Seventieth Birthday,* 219-30. Edited by N. Davis and C. L. Wrenn. Allen and Unwin, 1962. Reprinted in *Selected Literary Essays,* 301-11.

Beyond Personality: The Christian Idea of God. Bles, 1944.

"Bluspels and Flalansferes." Lecture given at Manchester University. In *Rehabilitations and Other Essays,* 133-58. Reprinted in *Selected Literary Essays,* 251-65.

Boxen: The Imaginary World of the Young C. S. Lewis. Edited by Walter Hooper. Collins, 1985. (Originally written by 1913.)

Broadcast Talks. Bles, 1943.

"Bulverism." *Socratic Digest* 2 (1944): 16-20. Reprinted in *God in the Dock*, 271-77. (Originally published in a shorter form in *Time and Tide*, 29 March 1941, 261.)

The Case for Christianity. Macmillan, 1943.

Christian Behaviour: A Further Series [of Broadcasts]. Bles, 1943.

Christian Reflections. Edited by Walter Hooper. Collins, Fount paperback, 1981; reprinted 1985. (Originally published by Bles, 1967.)

"Christianity and Literature." In *Rehabilitations and Other Essays*, 184-96. Reprinted in *Selected Literary Essays*, 177-79.

"Clivi Hamiltonis Summae Metaphysicae contra Anthroposophos Barfieldus." Unpublished manuscript (1928) in the Marion Wade Collection, Wheaton College.

Collected Poems of C. S. Lewis. Edited by Walter Hooper. HarperCollins, Fount, 1994.

"Dante's Similes." *Studies in Medieval and Renaissance Literature*, 64-77. (Originally an address given at the Oxford Dante Society, 1940.)

"The Dark Tower" and Other Stories. Edited by Walter Hooper. Collins, 1977.

"De Audiendis Poetis." In *Studies in Medieval and Renaissance Literature*, 1-17.

"De Bono et Malo." Unpublished manuscript (n.d.) in the Marion Wade Collection, Wheaton College.

"De Descriptione Temporum." Cambridge: Cambridge University, 1955. Reprinted in *Selected Literary Essays*, 1-14.

"Different Tastes in Literature." *Time and Tide*, 25 May and 1 June 1946. Reprinted in *Of This and Other Worlds*, 153-61.

The Discarded Image: An Introduction to Medieval and Renaissance Literature. Cambridge: Cambridge University, 1964; paperback edition, 1967; reprinted 1970.

"Donne and Love Poetry in the Seventeenth Century," in *Seventeenth Century Studies Presented to Sir Herbert Grierson*, 64-84. Oxford: Clarendon Press, 1938. Reprinted in *Selected Literary Essays*, 106-25.

"Douglas Bush['s] 'Paradise Lost' in Our Time: Some Comments." *Oxford Magazine*, 15 February 1947, 215-17.

Dymer. With a new preface by Lewis. Macmillan, 1950. (Originally published by Dent, 1926, under the pseudonym "Clive Hamilton.")

English Literature in the Sixteenth Century, Excluding Drama: The Completion of the Clark Lectures, Trinity College, Cambridge, 1944. (Oxford History of English Literature, vol. 3.) Oxford: Clarendon Press, 1954.

An Experiment in Criticism. Cambridge: Cambridge University, 1961; paperback edition, 1967; reprinted in 1969.

"Four-Letter Words." *Critical Quarterly* 3 (Summer 1961): 118-22. Reprinted in *Selected Literary Essays*, 169-74.

The Four Loves. Bles, 1960.

"The Funeral of a Great Myth." In *Christian Reflections,* 110-23.

George MacDonald: 365 Readings. Edited by Lewis. Macmillan, 1947.

"George Orwell." *Time and Tide,* 8 January 1955, 43-44. Reprinted in *Of This and Other Worlds,* 133-37.

God in the Dock: Essays on Theology and Ethics. Edited by Walter Hooper. Grand Rapids: Eerdmans, 1970. (Published by Bles, 1971, under the title *Undeceptions.*)

The Great Divorce. Macmillan, 1946.

A Grief Observed. New York: Bantam, with Seabury, 1964. (Originally published by Faber, 1960.)

"*Hamlet:* The Prince or the Poem?" *Proceedings of the British Academy,* volume 28. Oxford University, 1942. Reprinted in *Selected Literary Essays,* 88-105.

"Hero and Leander." Warton Lecture on English Poetry. *Proceedings of the British Academy,* 1952. Reprinted in *Selected Literary Essays,* 58-74.

"High and Low Brows." In *Rehabilitations and Other Essays,* 95-116. Reprinted in *Selected Literary Essays,* 266-79.

The Horse and His Boy. Bles (also Macmillan), 1954.

"Imagery in the Last Eleven Cantos of Dante's 'Comedy.'" In *Studies in Medieval and Renaissance Literature,* 78-93. (Originally an address presented to the Oxford Dante Society, 1948.)

"Imagination and Thought in the Middle Ages." In *Studies in Medieval and Renaissance Literature,* 41-63. (Originally two lectures, given in 1956.)

"The Inner Ring: An Oration" (presented in 1944). In *Transposition and Other Addresses.* Bles, 1949. Reprinted in *They Asked for a Paper,* 139-48.

"Kipling's World." In *Literature and Life: Addresses to the English Association,* 57-73. Harrap, 1948. Reprinted in *Selected Literary Essays,* 232-50.

The Last Battle: A Story for Children. Bodley Head (also Macmillan), 1956.

Letters of C. S. Lewis. Edited by W. H. Lewis. Bles, 1966.

Letters to an American Lady. Edited by Clyde Kilby. Grand Rapids: Eerdmans, 1967.

"Lilies That Fester." *Twentieth Century* 107 (1955): 330-41. Reprinted in *They Asked for a Paper,* 105-18.

The Lion, the Witch and the Wardrobe: A Story for Children. Bles (also Macmillan), 1950.

"The Literary Impact of the Authorised Version." Ethel M. Wood Lecture, March 1950. Athlone Press, 1950. Reprinted in *Selected Literary Essays,* 126-45.

The Magician's Nephew. Bodley Head (also Macmillan), 1955.

Mere Christianity. Bles (also Macmillan), 1952.

Miracles: A Preliminary Study. Bles, also Macmillan, 1947. Revised edition by Collins (Fontana). Abridged edition, with a new preface, New York: Association Press, 1958.

Narrative Poems. Edited by Walter Hooper. Bles, 1969.

"A Note on Jane Austen." *Essays in Criticism* 4 (October 1954): 359-71. Reprinted in *Selected Literary Essays,* 175-86.

Of Other Worlds: Essays and Stories. Edited by Walter Hooper. New York: Harcourt, Brace, Jovanovich, 1966; revised 1975.

Of This and Other Worlds. (Essays.) Edited by Walter Hooper. Collins, 1982.

"On Criticism." In *Of Other Worlds,* 43-58.

"On Reading 'The Faerie Queene.'" *Studies in Medieval and Renaissance Literature,* 146-48. (Originally published in *Fifteen Poets,* Oxford, 1941.)

"On the Reading of Old Books" (written in 1943). Published (1944) as introduction to *The Incarnation of the Word of God,* by R. P. Lawson. Bles, 1944. Reprinted in *God in the Dock,* 200-207.

"On Science Fiction" (written in 1955). *Of Other Worlds,* 59-73.

"On Three Ways of Writing for Children." Library Association Lecture, 1952. Reprinted in *Of Other Worlds,* 22-34.

Out of the Silent Planet. Pan, 1952; reprinted 1968. (Originally published by Bodley Head, 1938.)

"The Parthenon and the Optative." *Time and Tide,* November 1946. Reprinted in *Of This and Other Worlds,* 142-46.

Perelandra. Reprinted as *Voyage to Venus.* Pan, 1960. (Originally published by Lane, 1943.)

The Personal Heresy: A Controversy, with E. M. W. Tillyard. Oxford University Press, 1939.

The Pilgrim's Regress: An Allegorical Apology for Christianity, Reason and Romanticism. Collins, 1977. (Originally published by Dent, 1933.)

Poems. Edited by Walter Hooper. New York: Harcourt, Brace, Jovanovich, 1964.

"The Poison of Subjectivism." *Religion in Life* 12 (1943): 356-65. Reprinted in *Christian Reflections,* 98-109.

Prayer: Letters to Malcolm. Bles, 1964.

A Preface to "Paradise Lost." Oxford University, 1942.

Present Concerns. Edited by Walter Hooper. San Diego and New York: Harcourt, Brace, Jovanovich, 1986. (Originally published by Fount, 1986.)

Prince Caspian: The Return to Narnia. Bles (also Macmillan), 1951.

The Problem of Pain. Bles, 1940; reprinted 1943.

"Psycho-Analysis and Literary Criticism." *Essays and Studies of the English Association* 27 (1942): 7-21. Reprinted in *Selected Literary Essays,* 286-300.

Reflections on the Psalms. Bles, 1958.

Rehabilitations and Other Essays. Oxford University Press, 1939.

Review of *Arthurian Literature in the Middle Ages: A Collaborative Study,* edited by R. S. Loomis. *Cambridge Review,* 13 February 1960, 355, 357.

Review of *Life of Samuel Johnson,* by Sir John Hawkins, edited by B. H. Davis (1962). *Sunday Times,* 1 April 1962, 8.

Review of Logan Pearsall Smith, *Milton and His Modern Critics,* in *Cambridge Review,* 21 February 1941, 200.

Review of *Works of Sir Thomas Malory,* edited by E. Vinaver. *Times Literary Supplement,* 7 June 1947, 273-74. Reprinted in *Studies in Medieval and Renaissance Literature,* 103-10.

The Screwtape Letters: Letters from a Senior to a Junior Devil. Collins, Fount paperback, 1955; reprinted 1977. (Originally published by Bles, 1942.)

Selected Literary Essays. Edited by Walter Hooper. Cambridge: Cambridge University Press, 1969.

"Shelley, Dryden and Mr. Eliot." In *Rehabilitations and Other Essays,* 1-34. Reprinted in *Selected Literary Essays,* 187-208.

The Silver Chair. Bles (also Macmillan), 1952.

"Sometimes Fairy Stories Say What's Best to Be Said." *New York Times Book Reviews,* 18 November 1956, Children's Book Section, 3. Reprinted in *Of Other Worlds,* 35-38.

Spenser's Images of Life. Edited by Alastair Fowler. Cambridge: Cambridge University, 1967.

Spirits in Bondage: A Cycle of Lyrics. San Diego: Harcourt, Brace, Jovanovich, 1984. (Originally published by Heinemann, 1919; reprinted in *Collected Poems,* 1994.)

Studies in Medieval and Renaissance Literature. Edited by Walter Hooper. Cambridge: Cambridge University, 1966.

Studies in Words. Second edition, paperback, Cambridge: Cambridge University Press, 1967. (Originally published by Cambridge University Press in 1959.)

Surprised by Joy: The Shape of My Early Life. Fontana, 1959. (Originally published by Bles, 1955.)

"Tasso." In *Studies in Medieval and Renaissance Literature,* 111-17.

That Hideous Strength: A Modern Fairy-tale for Grown-ups. New York: Macmillan, 1965. (Originally published by Lane, 1945.)

They Asked for a Paper. Bles, 1962.

They Stand Together: The Letters of C. S. Lewis to Arthur Greeves (1914-63). Edited by Walter Hooper. Collins, 1979.

"Three Ways of Writing for Children." Reprinted in *Of Other Worlds,* 22-34.

Till We Have Faces: A Myth Retold. Grand Rapids: Eerdmans, 1966. (Originally published by Bles, 1956.)

[Toast to] "The Memory of Sir Walter Scott." Edinburgh: Edinburgh Sir Walter Scott Club, 49th Annual Report, 1956. Reprinted in *Selected Literary Essays,* 209-18.

"Variation in Shakespeare and Others." In *Rehabilitations and Other Essays,* 159-88. Reprinted in *Selected Literary Essays,* 74-87.

"The Vision of John Bunyan." Broadcast, *The Listener*, 13 December 1962. Reprinted in *Selected Literary Essays*, 153-62.

The Voyage of the "Dawn Treader." Bles (also Macmillan), 1952.

"We Have No Right to Happiness." *Saturday Evening Post*, 21 and 28 December 1963, 10, 12. Reprinted in *God in the Dock*, 317-22.

The Weight of Glory and Other Addresses. Macmillan, 1949.

"What Chaucer Really Did to *Il Filostrato*." *Essays and Studies by Members of the English Association* 17 (1932): 56-75; reprinted in *Selected Literary Essays*, 27-44.

"William Morris" (1937). In *Rehabilitations and Other Essays*, 35-56. Reprinted in *Selected Literary Essays*, 219-31.

Other Works

Adey, Lionel. "The Barfield-Lewis 'Great War.'" *CSL: Bulletin of the New York C. S. Lewis Society* 6, no. 10 (1975): 10-14.

————. "C. S. Lewis's Annotations to His Shakespeare Volumes." *CSL: Bulletin of the New York C. S. Lewis Society* 8, no. 7 (May 1977): 1-8.

————. *C. S. Lewis's "Great War" with Owen Barfield*. English Literary Studies Monographs, no. 14. Victoria: University of Victoria, 1978.

————. "'The Light of Holiness': Some Comments on Morris by C. S. Lewis." *Journal of the William Morris Society* 3, no. 1 (1973): 11-22.

————. "A Response to Dr. Thorson." *CSL: Bulletin of the New York C. S. Lewis Society* 15, no. 5 (1984): 6-10.

Alexander, Samuel. *Space, Time and Deity*. 2 vols. Macmillan, 1920.

Alpers, Paul. "The Rhetorical Mode of Spenser's Narrative." In *Spenser, "The Faerie Queene": A Casebook*. Edited by Peter Bayley. Macmillan, 1977.

Annan, Lord Noel. *Our Age: Portrait of a Generation*. Weidenfeld and Nicolson, 1990.

————. "The Study of Poetry." Introduction to *The English Poets*, edited by T. H. Ward (1880). Reprinted in Arnold, *Essays in Criticism*. Second series. Macmillan, 1888.

Bacon, Francis. "Of Death." In *Essays, Wisdom of the Ancients, and the New Atlantis*, 4-6. Odhams, n.d.

Barfield, A. Owen. "C. S. Lewis and Historicism." *CSL: Bulletin of the New York C. S. Lewis Society* 6, no. 10 (1975): 3-9.

————. "De Toto et Parte." Unpublished manuscript, in the Marion Wade Collection, Wheaton College.

————. "The Form of 'Hamlet.'" In *Romanticism Comes of Age*. Second edition,

85-103. Middletown: Wesleyan University, 1966. (Originally published by Anthroposophical Publishing Co., 1944.)

————. *History in English Words.* Methuen, 1926.

————. *Owen Barfield on C. S. Lewis.* Edited by G. B. Tennyson. Middletown: Wesleyan University, 1989.

————. *Poetic Diction.* Faber and Gwyer, 1928.

Barker, Nicholas. Review of *The C. S. Lewis Hoax,* by Kathryn Lindskoog. *Essays in Criticism* 40, no. 4 (October 1990): 358-67.

Bayley, Peter. "From Master to Colleague." In Como, ed., *C. S. Lewis at the Breakfast Table,* 77-91.

Berlin, Sir Isaiah. "Edmund Wilson at Oxford." *Yale Review* 76, no. 1 (1987): 139-51; excerpted in *New York Times Book Reviews,* 12 April 1987.

Beversluis, John. *C. S. Lewis and the Search for Rational Religion.* Grand Rapids: Eerdmans, 1985.

Biaggini, E. G. *The Reading and Writing of English.* N.p.: Hutchinson, 1936.

Bonnard, G. Review of *Allegory of Love* in *English Studies* 21 (1939): 78-82.

Boorstin, Daniel F. *The Discoverers: A History of Man's Search to Know the World and Himself.* Dent, 1984.

Brewer, D. S. "The Tutor: A Portrait." In Como, ed., *C. S. Lewis at the Breakfast Table,* 41-67.

Broadbent, J. B. *Some Graver Subject.* Chatto, 1960.

Brook, G. L. Review of *Allegory of Love* in *Modern Language Review* 32 (1936). Reprinted in Watson, ed., *Critical Thought I: Critical Essays on C. S. Lewis,* 94-95.

Brooke, N. S. "C. S. Lewis and Spenser: Nature, Art and the Bower of Bliss." *Cambridge Journal* 2 (1949): 420-34. Reprinted in Watson, ed., *Critical Thought I: Critical Essays on C. S. Lewis,* 105-19.

Brown, Carol Ann. "Who Is Ungit?" *CSL: Bulletin of the New York C. S. Lewis Society* 12, no. 6 (1982): 1-5.

Buning, Marius. "*Perelandra* Revisited in the Light of Modern Allegorical Theory." In Schakel and Huttar, eds., *Word and Story,* 277-98.

Burckhardt, Jakob. *The Civilization of the Renaissance in Italy.* Phaidon, 1945. (Originally published 1860.)

Burnett, Frances Hodgson. *The Secret Garden.* Heinemann, 1911.

Burrow, John. "The Model Universe." Review of *Discarded Image* in *Essays in Criticism* 15 (1965): 207-11. Reprinted in Watson, ed., *Critical Thought I: Critical Essays on C. S. Lewis,* 223-37.

Bush, Douglas. *The Renaissance and English Humanism.* Toronto: University of Toronto, 1939.

Carnell, Corbin Scott. *Bright Shadow of Reality: C. S. Lewis and the Feeling Intellect.* Grand Rapids: Eerdmans, 1974.

Carpenter, Humphrey. *The Inklings: C. S. Lewis, J. R. R. Tolkien, Charles Williams, and Their Friends.* Boston: Houghton Mifflin, 1979.

Chambers, R. W. *Thomas More.* Cape, 1939.

Chandler, Alice. *A Dream of Order: The Medieval Ideal in Nineteenth-Century English Life.* Lincoln: University of Nebraska Press, 1978.

Chaucer, Geoffrey. *Troilus and Criseyde.* In *Works of Geoffrey Chaucer.* Edited by F. N. Robinson. Second edition. Cambridge, MA: Houghton Mifflin, 1957.

Christopher, Joe. *C. S. Lewis.* Boston: Twayne, 1987.

Colbert, James G. "The Common Ground of Lewis and Barfield." *CSL: Bulletin of the New York C. S. Lewis Society* 6, no. 10 (1975): 15-18.

Como, James, editor. *C. S. Lewis at the Breakfast Table, and Other Reminiscences.* New York: Macmillan, 1979 (also Collins, 1979).

Cordell, Richard A. *Somerset Maugham: A Writer for All Seasons.* Bloomington: Indiana University, 1961.

Coveney, Peter. *The Image of Childhood.* New York: Peregrine, 1967. (Originally published under the title *Poor Monkey* by Rockliff, 1957.)

Cox, John D. "Epistemological Release in *The Silver Chair,*" in Schakel, ed., *Longing for a Form,* 159-70.

Damrosch, Leopold J. *God's Plot and Man's Stories: Studies in the Fictional Imagination from Milton to Fielding.* Chicago: University of Chicago, 1985.

Danielson, Dennis R. *Milton's Good God: A Study in Literary Theodicy.* New York: Cambridge University, 1982.

Davie, Donald. "Entering into the Sixteenth Century." *Essays in Criticism* 5 (1955): 159-64. Reprinted in Watson, ed., *Critical Thought I: Critical Essays on C. S. Lewis,* 206-11.

Donaldson, E. Talbot. *Speaking of Chaucer.* Athlone, 1970.

Donaldson, Mara E. *Holy Places Are Dark Places: C. S. Lewis and Paul Ricoeur on Narrative Transformation.* Lanham, MD: University Press of America, 1988.

Downing, David C. *Planets in Peril: A Critical Study of C. S. Lewis's Ransom Trilogy.* Amherst: University of Massachusetts Press, 1992.

Dronke, Peter. *Medieval Latin and the Rise of the European Love-Lyric.* Two volumes. Oxford: Oxford University Press, 1965. Excerpted in Watson, ed., *Critical Thought I: Critical Essays on C. S. Lewis,* 124-25.

Eddison, E. R. *The Mezentian Gate.* New York: Ballantine, 1969. (Originally published Plaistow: Curwen Press, 1958.)

Eliot, T. S. "Hamlet." In *Selected Prose,* 104-9. Harmondsworth: Penguin, 1953. (Originally published in 1919.)

————. "Milton I" (1936) and "Milton II" (Henrietta Hertz Lecture, British Academy, 1947). In Eliot, *On Poetry and Poets.* New York: Octagon Press, 1972.

————. "The Waste Land" (1922). In Eliot, *Complete Poems and Plays.* New York: Harcourt, Brace, Jovanovich, n.d. (copyright 1971).

Elton, Oliver. Review of *Allegory of Love* in *Medium Aevum* 6 (1936): 34-39. Reprinted in Watson, ed., *Critical Thought I: Critical Essays on C. S. Lewis,* 82-88.

Empson, William. "Love and the Middle Ages." Review of *Allegory of Love* in *Spectator,* 4 September 1936, 241-43. Reprinted in Watson, ed., *Critical Thought I: Critical Essays on C. S. Lewis,* 79-81.

————. *Milton's God.* Chatto, 1961.

————. *The Structure of Complex Words.* Chatto, 1951.

Encyclopedia Britannica. Ninth edition, 1875 (1886 printing); fourteenth edition, 1929 (1972 printing).

Everyman's Encyclopedia. Dent, 1967.

Filmer, Kath. *The Fiction of C. S. Lewis: Mask and Mirror.* Macmillan, 1993.

Fish, Stanley. *Surprised by Sin: The Reader in "Paradise Lost."* New York: Macmillan, 1967.

Fleming, John. *"The Roman de la Rose": A Study in Allegory and Iconography.* Princeton: Princeton University Press, 1969.

Flieger, Verlyn. "The Sound of Silence: Language and Experience in *Out of the Silent Planet.*" In Schakel and Huttar, eds., *Word and Story,* 42-57.

Ford, Paul F. *A Companion to Narnia.* San Francisco: Harper and Row, 1980.

Franceschelli, Amos. "The Teachings of Rudolf Steiner with Especial Reference to C. S. Lewis." *CSL: Bulletin of the New York C. S. Lewis Society* 4, no. 7 (1973).

Freeman, Rosemary. *"The Faerie Queene": A Companion for Readers.* Chatto, 1978.

Freud, Sigmund. *Art and Literature, Jensen's "Gradiva," Leonardo da Vinci and Other Works.* Edited by A. Dickson. Harmondsworth: Penguin, 1985.

————. *Introductory Lectures on Psycho-Analysis (1916-17).* Volume 15 in *Complete Psychological Works.* Translated by J. Strachey. Standard edition. Hogarth Press, 1963.

Frye, Northrop. *The Anatomy of Criticism.* Princeton: Princeton University Press, 1957.

Gibson, Evan K. *C. S. Lewis: Spinner of Tales.* Washington, DC: Christian University Press, 1980.

Gilson, Étienne. *La Philosophie au Moyen Age, des Origines Patristiques a la Fin du XIVe Siècle.* Paris: Payot, 1922.

Glover, Donald E. "Bent Language in *Perelandra:* The Storyteller's Temptation." In Schakel and Huttar, eds., *Word and Story,* 171-81.

————. *C. S. Lewis: The Art of Enchantment.* Athens: Ohio University Press, 1981.

Gordon, Ida. *The Double Sorrow of Troilus: A Study of Ambiguities in "Troilus and Criseyde."* Oxford: Clarendon, 1970.

Grant, Patrick. "The Quality of Thinking: Owen Barfield as Literary Man and Anthroposophist." *Seven* 3 (1982): 113-25.

————. *Six Authors and Problems of Belief.* Macmillan, 1979.

Green, Roger Lancelyn, and Walter Hooper. *C. S. Lewis: A Biography.* Collins, 1974.

Gresham, Douglas. *In Lenten Lands.* Collins (Fontana), 1990. (Originally published New York: Macmillan, 1988.)

Haggard, Sir Henry Rider. *Ayesha.* Ward Lock, 1905.

————. *She.* Longmans, 1887.

Hardie, Colin. "Dante and the Tradition of Courtly Love." In Lawlor, ed., *Patterns of Love and Courtesy,* 26-44.

Harding, Davis P. *The Club of Hercules: Studies in the Classical Background of "Paradise Lost."* Urbana: University of Illinois, 1962.

Hart, Dabney A. *Through the Open Door: A New Look at C. S. Lewis. . . .* University, AL: University of Alabama Press, 1984.

Henderson, Philip. *William Morris: His Life, Work and Friends.* New York: McGraw Hill, 1967.

Holbrook, David. *The Skeleton in the Wardrobe: C. S. Lewis's Fiction: A Phenomenological Study.* Lewisburg: Bucknell University; London: Associated University Press, 1991.

Holloway, John. "Grand Design." Review of *Discarded Image* in *Spectator,* 5 June 1964, 260. Reprinted in Watson, ed., *Critical Thought I: Critical Essays on C. S. Lewis,* 228-30.

Holmer, Paul. *C. S. Lewis: The Shape of His Faith and Thought.* New York: Harper and Row, 1976.

Hooper, Walter. "Oxford's Bonny Fighter." In Como, ed., *C. S. Lewis at the Breakfast Table,* 137-85.

————. *Past Watchful Dragons: The Narnian Chronicles of C. S. Lewis.* New York: Collier, 1979.

————, with R. L. Green. *C. S. Lewis: A Biography.* Collins, 1974.

Hough, Graham. "Old Western Man." *Twentieth Century,* February 1955, 102-10. Reprinted in Watson, ed., *Critical Thought I: Critical Essays on C. S. Lewis,* 235-45.

————. *A Preface to "The Faerie Queene."* Duckworth, 1962.

Hunter, G. K. *"Paradise Lost."* Allen and Unwin, 1980.

Huttar, Charles A. "C. S. Lewis's Narnia and the Grand Design." In Schakel, ed., *Longing for a Form,* 119-35.

————. "A Lifelong Love Affair with Language: C. S. Lewis's Poetry." In Schakel and Huttar, eds., *Word and Story,* 86-108.

Isidore of Seville. *Etymologiae, III.* Two volumes. Oxford: Clarendon, 1913, 1921.

Jones, Emrys. *The Origins of Shakespeare.* Oxford: Oxford University, 1977. Excerpted in Watson, ed., *Critical Thought I: Critical Essays on C. S. Lewis,* 219-22.

Kaminsky, Alice. *Chaucer's "Troilus and Criseyde" and the Critics.* Athens: Ohio State University, 1980.

Kerby-Fulton, Kathryn. "Standing on Lewis's Shoulders: Some Aspects of C. S. Lewis's Contribution to Medieval Literary Criticism." *Studies in Medievalism* 3 (1991): 257-78.

Kerrigan, William. *The Sacred Complex.* Cambridge, MA: Harvard University Press, 1983.

King, Alec, and Martin Ketley. *The Control of Language: A Critical Approach to Reading and Writing.* Third edition. Longmans, 1940.

Knights, L. C. "Milton Again." *Scrutiny* 11 (1942-43): 146-48.

———. "Mr. C. S. Lewis and the Status Quo." *Scrutiny* 8 (1939-40): 90-92.

Kocmanova, Jessie. *The Poetic Maturing of William Morris.* New York: Folcroft Library, 1970. (Originally published in Prague, 1964.)

Kouwenhoven, Jan Karel. *Apparent Narrative as Thematic Metaphor: The Organization of "The Faerie Queene."* Oxford: Clarendon, 1983.

Lawlor, John, ed. *Patterns of Love and Courtesy.* Arnold, 1966.

Lawson, R. P. (Sister Penelope). *The Incarnation of the Word of God.* . . . (Translation of St. Athanasius, *De Incarnatione Verbi Dei*). Bles, 1944. Introduction by Lewis ("On the Reading of Old Books.")

Leavis, F. R. "Education and the Universities: A Sketch for an English School." *Scrutiny* 19 (1951): 162-83.

———. *Revaluation.* Chatto, 1936; reprinted 1949.

———. " 'The Two Cultures' — The Significance of C. P. Snow" (Richmond Lecture, Downing College, Cambridge, 1962). *Spectator,* 9 March 1962, 297-303.

Lee, John Alan. "The Styles of Loving." *Psychology Today* 8, no. 6 (October 1974): 43-51.

Lewis, W[arren] H[amilton]. *Brothers and Friends: The Diaries of Major Warren Hamilton Lewis.* Edited by Clyde Kilby and Marjorie Lampe Mead. New York: Ballantine, 1988. (Originally published San Francisco: Harper and Row, 1982.)

———. "C. S. Lewis: A Biography." Unpublished manuscript in the Marion Wade Collection, Wheaton College.

———, comp. "The Lewis Family Papers." Unpublished manuscript in eleven volumes in the Marion Wade Collection, Wheaton College.

Lieb, Michael. *The Dialectics of Creation: Patterns of Birth and Regeneration in "Paradise Lost."* Amherst: University of Massachusetts, 1970.

Lindsay, David. *A Voyage to Arcturus.* Ballantine, 1972. (Originally published by Methuen, 1920.)

Lindskoog, Kathryn. *The C. S. Lewis Hoax.* Portland, OR: Multnomah Press, 1988.

————. *Finding the Landlord: A Guide to C. S. Lewis's "Pilgrim's Regress."* Chicago: Cornerstone Press, 1995.

————. *The Lion of Judah in Never-Never Land: The Theology of C. S. Lewis Expressed in His Fantasies for Children.* Grand Rapids: Eerdmans, 1973.

————, ed. *The Lewis Legacy,* nos. 65 (Summer); 66 (Autumn 1995); 68 (Spring 1996).

Lobdell, Jared C. "C. S. Lewis's Ransom Stories and Their Eighteenth Century Ancestry." In Schakel and Huttar, eds., *Word and Story,* 213-31.

MacDonald, George. *At the Back of the North Wind.* Strahan, 1871.

————. *George MacDonald: 365 Readings.* Edited by C. S. Lewis. Macmillan, 1947.

————. "The Golden Key." In *The Complete Fairy Tales of George MacDonald.* Edited by R. L. Green. New York: Schocken Books, 1977. (Originally published in *Dealings with the Fairies,* 1867.)

————. *Lilith* (1895), with introduction by C. S. Lewis. Grand Rapids: Eerdmans, 1981.

————. "On Imagination." In *A Dish of Orts,* 1-41. Dalton, 1900. (Originally published 1893.)

————. *Phantastes* (1858), with introduction by C. S. Lewis. Grand Rapids: Eerdmans, 1981.

Macdonald, Ronald B. *The Burial-Places of Memory: Epic Underworlds in Vergil, Dante and Milton.* Amherst: University of Massachusetts, 1987.

McLeod, Hugh. *Class and Religion in the Late-Victorian City.* Croom Helm, 1974.

Malory, Sir Thomas. *Works.* Edited by E. Vinaver. Oxford: Clarendon, 1948.

Manlove, C. N. *C. S. Lewis: His Literary Achievement.* New York: St. Martin's Press, 1987.

————. "'Caught Up into the Larger Pattern': Images and Narrative Structures in C. S. Lewis's Fiction." In Schakel and Huttar, eds., *Word and Story,* 256-76.

————. *Christian Fantasy from 1200 to the Present.* Notre Dame: University of Notre Dame Press, 1992.

————. *Modern Fantasy: Five Studies.* Cambridge: Cambridge University, 1975; paperback edition, 1978.

Martindale, Charles. *John Milton and the Transformation of Ancient Epic.* Croom Helm, 1986.

Mill, John Stuart. *Political Economy.* Two volumes. Parker, 1867.

————. *A System of Logic.* Three volumes. Parker, 1881. (Originally published in 1843.)

————. *"Utilitarianism," "[On] Liberty" and "Representative Government."* Dent, 1910; reprinted 1922.

Milton, John. *Paradise Lost* (1667).

————. *Prose Works.* Edited by J. A. St. John. Three volumes. Bohn, 1848.

Montrose, Louis A. "The Poetics and Politics of a Culture." In *The New Historicism,* 17 30. Edited by H. Aram Veeser. New York: Routledge, 1989.

Morris, William. *Love Is Enough.* In *Collected Works,* volume 9. Longmans, Green, 1910-15. (Originally published in 1872.)

————. *Water of the Wondrous Isles.* In *Collected Works,* volume 20. Longmans, Green, 1910-15. (Originally published in 1897.)

————. *The Well at the World's End.* In *Collected Works,* volume 18. Longmans, Green, 1910-15. (Originally published in 1896.)

————. *Wood Beyond the World.* In *Collected Works,* volume 17. (Originally published in 1894).

Murrin, Michael. "The Multiple Worlds of the Narnia Stories." In Schakel and Huttar, eds., *Word and Story,* 232-55.

Muscatine, Charles. *Chaucer and the French Tradition.* Berkeley and Los Angeles: University of California, 1969. (Originally published in 1957.)

Myers, Doris T. *C. S. Lewis in Context.* Kent, OH: Kent State University Press, 1994.

Nesbit, Edith. *The Story of the Amulet.* Harmondsworth: Puffin, 1965; reprinted 1983. (Originally published by Fisher Unwin, 1906.)

Nuttall, A. D. "Jack the Giant-Killer." *Seven* 5 (1984). Reprinted in Watson, ed., *Critical Thought I: Critical Essays on C. S. Lewis,* 269-84.

————. *Two Concepts of Allegory: A Study of "The Tempest" and the Logic of Allegorical Expression.* Routledge, 1967.

Ogden, C. K., and I. A. Richards. *The Meaning of Meaning: A Study of the Influence of Language.* Second edition. Kegan Paul, 1927. (Originally published by International Library of Psychology, Philosophy and Scientific Method, 1923.)

Orwell, George (Eric Blair). "Boys' Weeklies" (1940). In *Collected Essays, Journalism and Letters,* volume 1, 460-85. Edited by Sonia Orwell and Ian Angus. Four volumes. London: Secker and Warburg; New York: Harcourt Brace, 1968.

————. "Politics and the English Language" (1946). In *Collected Essays, Journalism and Letters,* volume 4, 127-40. Edited by Sonia Orwell and Ian Angus. Four volumes. London: Secker and Warburg; New York: Harcourt Brace, 1968.

Oxford Classical Dictionary. Second edition. Oxford: Clarendon, 1970.

Oxford Dictionary of Etymology. Edited by C. T. Onions. Oxford University Press, 1966.

Oxford English Dictionary. Compact edition. Two volumes. New York: Oxford University, 1971.

Peter, John. *A Critique of "Paradise Lost."* New York: Columbia University Press, 1960.

Piehler, Peter. "Myth or Allegory? Archetype and Transcendence in the Fiction of C. S. Lewis." In Schakel and Huttar, eds., *Word and Story,* 199-212.

Pietrusz, Jim. "Rites of Passage in the Chronicles of Narnia and the Seven Sacraments." *Mythlore* 54 (Summer 1988): 61-63.

Pitter, Ruth. *The Bridge.* Cresset, 1945.

———. *Collected Poems.* Petersfield: Enitharmon, 1990.

———. *A Trophy of Arms.* Cresset, 1935.

———. *Urania.* Cresset, 1950.

Purtill, Richard. *Lord of the Elves and Eldils: Fantasy and Philosophy in C. S. Lewis and J. R. R. Tolkien.* Grand Rapids: Zondervan, 1974.

Rabkin, Eric. *The Fantastic in Literature.* Princeton: Princeton University Press, 1976.

———, ed. *Fantastic Worlds: Myths, Tales and Stories.* New York: Oxford University Press, 1979.

Raine, Kathleen. *Blake and Tradition.* Princeton: Princeton University Press, 1968.

Reilly, R. J. *Romantic Religion.* Athens: University of Georgia Press, 1971.

Richards, I. A. *The Principles of Literary Criticism.* Kegan Paul, Trench, Trubner, 1924; reprinted 1934.

Ricks, Christopher. *Milton's Grand Style.* Oxford: Oxford University Press, 1963.

Riggs, William. *The Christian Poet in "Paradise Lost."* Los Angeles: University of California Press, 1972.

Robertson, D. W., Jr. "Chaucerian Tragedy." In Schoek and Taylor, eds., *Chaucer Criticism,* volume 2, 86-121.

———. *A Preface to Chaucer.* Princeton: Princeton University Press, 1962.

Robinson, Ian. *Chaucer and the English Tradition.* Cambridge: Cambridge University Press, 1972.

Robson, W. W. "C. S. Lewis." *Cambridge Quarterly* 1 (1966): 252-72.

Roston, Murray. *Milton and the Baroque.* Macmillan, 1980.

Rowse, A. L. *The Poet Auden: A Personal Memoir.* Methuen, 1987.

Rumrich, John Peter. *Matter of Glory: A New Preface to "Paradise Lost."* Pittsburgh: University of Pittsburgh Press, 1987.

Russell, Arthur, ed. *Ruth Pitter: Homage to a Poet.* Rapp and Whiting, 1969.

Salter, Elizabeth. " 'Troilus and Criseyde': A Reconsideration." In Lawlor, ed., *Patterns of Love and Courtesy,* 86-106.

Sasek, Lawrence A. "The Drama of 'Paradise Lost,' Books 11-12." In *Studies in English Renaissance Literature.* Edited by Waldo F. McNeir. Baton Rouge, 1962.

Sayer, George. *Jack: C. S. Lewis and His Times.* San Francisco: Harper and Row, 1988.

Schakel, Peter. *Reading with the Heart: The Way into Narnia.* Grand Rapids: Eerdmans, 1979.

————. *Reason and Imagination in C. S. Lewis: A Study of "Till We Have Faces."* Grand Rapids: Eerdmans, 1984.

————, ed. *The Longing for a Form: Essays on the Fiction of C. S. Lewis.* Kent: Ohio State University Press, 1977.

Schakel, Peter, and Charles A. Huttar, eds. *Word and Story in C. S. Lewis.* Columbia: University of Missouri Press, 1991.

Schneider, Armin, and Ascanio Mase. *Railway Accidents in Great Britain and Europe: Their Causes and Consequences.* Newton Abbott: David and Charles, 1970.

Schoek, Richard J., and J. Taylor, eds. *Chaucer Criticism.* Two volumes. Notre Dame: University of Notre Dame, 1961.

Shea, Victor. "New Historicism." In *Encyclopedia of Contemporary Literary Theory,* 124-30. Edited and compiled by Irena R. Makaryk. Toronto: University of Toronto, 1993.

Shepherd, A. P. *A Scientist of the Invisible: An Introduction to the Life and Work of Rudolf Steiner.* Hodder and Stoughton, 1954.

Shumaker, Wayne. *Feeling and Perception in "Paradise Lost."* Princeton: Princeton University Press, 1967.

Sidney, Sir Philip. *"Defence of Poesie," Political Discourses, Correspondence and Translations.* Edited by A. Feuillerat. Cambridge: Cambridge University Press, 1923.

Skinner, Martyn. *The Return of Arthur.* London: Chapman and Hall, 1966.

Speirs, John. *Medieval English Poetry: The Non-Chaucerian Tradition.* Faber, 1958.

Steadman, John M. *Epic and Tragic Structure in "Paradise Lost."* Chicago: University of Chicago Press, 1976.

Steiner, Rudolf. *Knowledge of Higher Worlds and Its Attainment.* Translated by G. Metaxa. New York: Anthroposophic Press, 1947. (Originally published as *The Way of Initiation,* 1919.)

————. *Philosophy of Freedom.* Translated by M. Wilson. New York: Anthroposophic Press, 1964. (Originally published as *Philosophy of Spiritual Activity,* 1894.)

Suleiman, Susan R., and Inge Crosman, eds. *The Reader in the Text: Essays on Audience and Interpretation.* Princeton: Princeton University Press, 1980.

Symonds, John Addington. Entry "Renaissance" in *Encyclopedia Britannica,* ninth edition, 1886.

Thompson, E. P. *William Morris: Romantic to Revolutionary.* Lawrence and Wishart, 1955.

Thorndike, Lynn. Entry on "Renaissance" in *Encyclopedia Britannica,* fourteenth edition, 1972.

Thorson, Stephen. "Knowing and Being in C. S. Lewis's 'Great War' with Owen Barfield." *CSL: Bulletin of the New York C. S. Lewis Society* 15, no. 1 (1983): 1-9.

———. "Reply" [to Adey]. *CSL: Bulletin of the New York C. S. Lewis Society* 15, no. 5 (1984): 10-11.

Tillotson, Kathleen. Review of *Allegory of Love* in *Review of English Studies* 13 (1936): 477. Reprinted in Watson, ed., *Critical Thought I: Critical Essays on C. S. Lewis,* 96-98.

Tillyard, E. M. W. *The Personal Heresy: A Controversy,* with C. S. Lewis. Oxford University Press, 1939.

———. *Poetry Direct and Oblique.* Chatto, 1945.

Todorov, Tzvetan. *The Fantastic: A Structural Approach to a Literary Genre.* Translated by Richard Howard. Cleveland: Press of Case Western Reserve University, 1973. (Originally published in Paris, 1970.)

Tolkien, J[ohn] R[onald] R[euel]. *Letters of J. R. R. Tolkien.* Edited by H. Carpenter. Boston: Houghton Mifflin, 1981. (Also Allen and Unwin, 1981.)

———. *Lord of the Rings.* Three volumes. Allen and Unwin, 1954.

———. "On Fairy Stories." In Lewis, ed., *Essays Presented to Charles Williams,* 38-89. Oxford University Press, 1947.

———. *The Silmarillion.* Edited by Christopher Tolkien. Boston: Allen and Unwin, 1977.

Veeser, H. Aram, ed. *The New Historicism.* New York: Routledge, 1989.

Wain, John. "C. S. Lewis." *Encounter* 22 (1964): 51-54. Reprinted in Watson, ed., *Critical Thought I: Critical Essays on C. S. Lewis,* 24-36.

———. "The Great Clerk." In Como, ed., *C. S. Lewis at the Breakfast Table,* 68-76.

———. "Pleasure, Controversy, Scholarship." Review of *English Literature in the Sixteenth Century* in *Spectator,* 1 October 1954, 403-5. Reprinted in Watson, ed., *Critical Thought I: Critical Essays on C. S. Lewis,* 201-5.

Waldock, A. J. A. *"Paradise Lost" and Its Critics.* Cambridge: Cambridge University Press, 1947; reprinted Gloucester, MA: Smith, 1959.

Wallace, David. *Chaucer and the Early Writings of Boccaccio.* Woodbridge: D. S. Brewer, 1985.

Walsh, Chad. *The Literary Legacy of C. S. Lewis.* New York and London: Harcourt, Brace, Jovanovich, 1979.

Walsh, William. *F. R. Leavis.* Bloomington and London: Indiana University Press, 1980.

Watson, George. *The Literary Critics: A Study of English Descriptive Criticism.* Revised edition. Hogarth, 1986. (Originally published Harmondsworth: Penguin, 1962.)

————, ed. *Critical Thought I: Critical Essays on C. S. Lewis.* Aldershot: Scolar Press; Brookfield, VT: Ashgate, 1992.

Watts, Isaac. *Works of the Reverend and Learned Isaac Watts, D.D.* Edited by George Burder. Six volumes. J. Barfield, 1810.

Weber, Burton Jasper. *The Construction of "Paradise Lost."* Carbondale: Southern Illinois University, 1971.

Wells, H. G. *The First Men in the Moon.* Newnes, 1901.

————. *The Time Machine.* Heinemann, 1895.

Williams, Charles. *The Place of the Lion.* Mundanus (Victor Gollancz), 1931.

Wilson, A. N. *C. S. Lewis: A Biography.* New York: Norton, 1990.

Wilson, Edmund. *The Wound and the Bow: Seven Studies in Literature.* Cambridge, MA: Houghton Mifflin, 1941.

Wingfield-Stratford, Esmé. *A Victorian Tragedy.* Routledge, 1931.

Winters, Yvor. Review of *English Literature in the Sixteenth Century* in *Hudson Review* 8 (1955): 281-87. Reprinted in Watson, ed., *Critical Thought I: Critical Essays on C. S. Lewis,* 212-18.

Wolfe, Gregory. "Language and Myth in the Ransom Trilogy." In Schakel and Huttar, eds., *Word and Story,* 256-76.

Wolff, Robert Lee. *The Golden Key: A Study of the Fiction of George MacDonald.* New Haven: Yale University Press, 1961.

Wood, Chauncey. *The Elements of Chaucer's "Troilus."* Durham, NC: Duke University Press, 1984.

Wrong, Charles. "Christianity and Progress." *CSL: Bulletin of the New York C. S. Lewis Society* 6, no. 10 (1975): 19-24.

Index